COLLECTIVE BEHAVIOR AND PUBLIC OPINION

Rapid Shifts in Opinion and Communication

The European Institute for the Media Series

⬤ THE EUROPEAN INSTITUTE FOR THE MEDIA

Kevin · Europe in the Media: A Comparison of Reporting, Representation and Rhetoric in National Media Systems in Europe

Noam/Groebel/Gerbarg · Internet Television

Lange/Ward · Media and Elections: A Handbook and Comparative Study

Van Ginneken · Collective Behavior and Public Opinion: Rapid Shifts in Opinion and Communication

COLLECTIVE BEHAVIOR AND PUBLIC OPINION

Rapid Shifts in Opinion and Communication

Jaap van Ginneken
University of Amsterdam

LEA LAWRENCE ERLBAUM ASSOCIATES, PUBLISHERS

2003 Mahwah, New Jersey London

MT

Lawrence Erlbaum Associates, Inc., Publishers
10 Industrial Avenue
Mahwah, New Jersey 07430

Cover design by Kathryn Houghtaling Lacey

[1]Translation from the Dutch *Brein-bevingen – Snelle omslagen in opinie en communicatie*,
published late 1999 by Boom, Amsterdam. Copyright rests with the author.

Library of Congress Cataloging-in-Publication Data

Ginneken, Jaap van, 1943–
   [Brein-bevingen. English]
   Collective behavior and public opinion : rapid shifts in opinion and communication /
Jaap van Ginneken.
      p.   cm.
   Translation of the author's: Brein-bevingen.
   Includes bibliographical references and indexes.
   ISBN 0-8058-4386-8 (hc : alk. paper)
   1. Public opinion. 2. Collective behavior. I. Title

HM1236 .G556 2002
303.3′8—dc21   2002019731
                                                                          CIP

Books published by Lawrence Erlbaum Associates are printed on acid-free paper,
and their bindings are chosen for strength and durability.

Printed in the United States of America
10 9 8 7 6 5 4 3 2 1

5/23/04

Contents

Preface

*I could honestly title this book "What I wish I had known forty years ago."
It is a book of ideas, observations and lessons learned, not a book of management techniques.*
—Richard Farson, American management consultant (Farson, p. 16)

*Of all the prizes that come from surviving more than 50 years, the best is
the freedom to be eccentric. What a joy to be able to explore the physical
and mental bounds of existence in safety and comfort, without bothering
whether I look or sound foolish.*
—James Lovelock, British environmentalist (Lovelock, 1979, p. 3)

The first ideas for this book occurred to me some 10 years ago. After a prolonged absence, I had returned to take up lecturing again at Amsterdam University's Baschwitz Institute for Collective Behavior Studies. Prodded on by its director, Professor Marten Brouwer, I had also (rather belatedly) completed my doctoral dissertation, on *Crowds, Psychology and Politics*. But I still felt ill at ease with the reductionist climate that prevailed in most relevant fields.

As a freelance writer and traveling reporter during the intermediary period, I had been confronted with strange distant cultures and with dramatic historical events, which seemed to challenge the standard research recipe: "To measure is to know, to know is to predict, to predict is to control." So I was very interested when I heard through the media about a major revolution that was apparently unfolding in the natural sciences, around such notions as "chaos and order," "complexity and simplicity," emerging patterns

tions as "chaos and order," "complexity and simplicity," emerging patterns and self-organization, and nonlinear qualitative change. I soon realized that such approaches could somehow be made useful within my own fields; that is to say, generally, the sciences of man and society; more specifically, of opinion and communication studies, as well as mass psychology and collective behavior sociology.

These were years in which I also did some "popular science" and science information projects. After having completed a small book on persuasion and "behavior management" in everyday life, I now embarked on a small book about the exact opposite: unpredictable behavior in markets. But this obviously was only a first stab at the problem of chaos and complexity, so I soon began to look for time and money to delve more deeply into this subject. My small, part-time contract at the university at the time, and prevailing rules at research foundations, however, seemed to hold out little hope. I was therefore thoroughly grateful when Professor Giep Franzen convinced the Foundation for Scientific Research of Commercial Communication (SWOCC) to participate for 3 months, and Professor Jan van Cuilenburg convinced the Social Science Faculty to participate for another 3 months. The other year or so which the project took, spread over several years, came from my personal budget. I also thank a number of private clients that asked for my advice about sudden shifts in opinion and communication during these same years.

When I first began the project, only very few people in The Netherlands were interested in such alternative approaches, such as Goos Geursen (1993, 1994), Loet Leydesdorff (1993, 1997), and Arno Goudsmit (1998). My thanks go to a number of present and former colleagues who were willing to read various drafts in whole or in part: Connie de Boer, Hans van der Brug, Mark Deuze, Eric Haas, Jeroen Jansz, Peter Neijens, and Pieter van Strien; as well as to successive classes of graduate students who were confronted with complete and incomplete, coherent and incoherent, earlier "workbook" versions. It goes without saying that the responsibility for the present text is mine and mine alone, including possible imperfections and controversial statements. Comments and suggestions remain welcome, even after the publication of the book.

—Jaap van Ginneken, Amsterdam

Introduction:
A New Vision

We must get away from the idea that serious work is restricted to "beating to death a well-defined problem in a narrow discipline, while broadly integrative thinking is relegated to cocktail parties."
—Murray Gell-Mann, physicist and Nobel prize winner
(Coveney & Highfield, 1994, p. 8)

Non-scientists tend to think that science works by deduction. But actually science works mainly by metaphor. And what's happening is that the kind of metaphors people have in mind are changing.
—Brian Arthur, economist (Waldrop, 1992, p. 327)

This book was published shortly after the dawn of the new millennium. The scare about a possible "millennium" problem occurred because many of the computerized systems on which we depend could not properly distinguish the year 2000 from the year 1900. It is a perfect illustration of the main claims made hereafter. Namely that minor details may cause dramatic shifts in many processes; from physical or technical to social or psychological. This observation does not square with prevalent thinking about the "controllability" (in principle) of almost anything. One of the fields in which "loss of control" has always been of prime importance is the twin one of "mass" psychology and "collective behavior" sociology. Yet this field has an uncertain status; so, in a way, this book is an attempt to revive the field. If someone is about to faint, one may shake him or her in order to bring about full consciousness. This is what I am going to try: to bring the field alive again by thoroughly stirring it, by trying to shift, broaden, and deepen it.

The shifting of the field entails the following: the studies of mass psychology and collective behavior sociology primarily concern crowds, and most of all, the derailment of crowds; for instance, in riots and panics. Second, and to a lesser degree, they include emerging social movements, and most of all, excesses of social movements; for instance, in splinter groups and sects. Third, and finally, other aspects of opinion currents and shifting public moods, such as fashion and fads are studied. This book reverses that order of priority. It is primarily about rapid, radical, and massive shifts in public opinion, and about the public perception of people and groups, products and issues.

The broadening of the twin fields in turn entails the following. Mass psychology and collective behavior sociology most of all tended to study all these phenomena within a social and political context. The last real revival of the twin disciplines took place in the 1970s, in reaction to the unrest of the 1960s. Yet throughout the 1980s and 1990s, other research themes came to the fore—such as economics and communication. Public relations people confidently proclaimed information and perception management, news and issues management. But it turned out that this management was not as easy as it seemed. This book will try to spell out why this is the case, and propose new approaches to rapid shifts.

The heart of the matter, therefore, lies in attempts to deepen our understanding of these phenomena. Theories in mass psychology and collective behavior sociology always had a kind of an ad hoc character. They meant to explain a mixed lot of anomalous events, which "ordinary" psychology and sociology were somehow unable to deal with properly. Similarly, the explanations were somewhat of a hodgepodge; they did shed some light on these curious occurrences, but often lacked an all-embracing view of broader organizing principles of reality and change. This is the main point this book tries to address, by suggesting a link-up with so-called "chaos and complexity" theory, a new development of the last 10 to 20 years.

Chaos and complexity theory originates from the natural sciences, but also hold a great potential for the sciences of man and society. Various scattered attempts at applying the new theoretical concepts to various problem areas have already been undertaken, but it remains a rather esoteric enterprise. Books have mostly been collections of conference papers, often written in highly abstract language for a rather small circle of initiated colleagues (see, e.g., Vallacher & Nowak, 1994; Robertson & Combs, 1995; Kiel & Elliot 1996; and Eve, Horsfall, & Lee, 1997). As far as I know, there are so far few books by one author that attempt to spell out in plain English and in an attractive format what the possible significance of these developments is for one appropriate, well-defined, and interesting field. Mass psychology and collective behavior sociology form such an appropriate field.

As a result of all these reflections, this book has achieved a somewhat hybrid format and addresses various audiences. First and foremost, it means to be up to academic standards, but without unnecessary jargon and abstractions. Students in the sciences of man and society, at university level and in higher education, should be able to use it with good results. Second, the book also speaks to professionals in the opinion and communication fields. It must provide them with a new and provocative understanding of what their trades can and cannot accomplish. Third, and finally, I have also tried throughout to keep the book accessible and interesting for a wider educated audience. My previous work in science journalism and science information has given me the ambition to explain complicated things in a simple way. Some high-minded thinkers may feel that I occasionally carry this too far; so be it.

The out-of-the-ordinary form and contents of this book result from a combination of all the aforementioned considerations. It has more or less evolved into three books in one, a trilogy. The first book provides "thick" descriptions of a number of recent, dramatic cases of shifts in public opinion and perception. These cases are easiest to read. The second book provides an overview of relevant explanations of such phenomena in terms of current psychology and sociology; in a way, this is the "backbone." But the third book tries to link this up with new metatheories about rapid shifts. This is slightly more abstract, although I have done my best to make it as concrete as possible. I could have placed these three books one after the other, but it would not have been very attractive or illuminating to read. I have therefore chosen to braid the three-level storylines into one. Every chapter begins with a case description, goes on to current analysis of the phenomena in question, and then a tentative link with new metatheories.

Let us briefly go over these three elements again. Every chapter begins with a section providing a case description. This is not unusual in management and marketing handbooks, and has even been done in some of the better known textbooks on collective behavior (such as the three editions of Turner & Killian; see Turner & Killian, 1987), but is somewhat unusual in other academic texts. I have allowed myself elaborate case descriptions, even longer than usual. Because this book is about complexity, the cases should not be reduced to a bare minimum, on the mere basis of elementary analytical profiles. That would have been too poor. These are often enigmatic phenomena, and it is good to develop a thorough "feel" for them, before moving on to the next layer.

There is also another reason, related to form. The latter part of the chapters often needs to veer off into somewhat abstract reasoning. It is good to have this preceded by some very concrete images. The case descriptions should function as a kind of "appetizer." These fascinating stories, with a slightly ironic touch, should make the reader curious about the underlying "why and how." In selecting the cases, I furthermore chose to ignore the collection of overly familiar examples in the existing literature, and to look for newer, lively examples of a more recent date, easily recognizable, for a younger international audience. (The case stories are partly based on my own extensive clipping archives from papers of record such as the overseas American *International Herald Tribune*, the French *Le Monde* and the Dutch *NRC Handelsblad*, as well as on a limited number of monographs.)

The second section of each chapter takes these cases as a departure point, but inserts them into a wider category of similar phenomena, about the why and how of which there already is a respectable literature. I have tried to provide an overview of some of the major approaches, but with a clear preference for the type of dynamic and open-ended explanations that are central to this book; that is to say, approaches that view these phenomena as relatively spontaneous and self-structuring. This does not mean that they do not possess a definite logic. Quite the contrary; there are many tendencies that recur time and again. But they are not as readily measurable, predictable, and controllable as one would be tempted to think. They are highly erratic phenomena, which can take all kinds of surprising twists and turns.

The most emphatic reason to choose the "braid structure" of the chapters, however, lies in the nature of the new overarching metatheories about chaos and complexity, with which I try to link up in the third sections. The problem is that many of these theories are originally of a highly abstract nature, and do not square with the scientific reflexes to which we are most accustomed. This led to two choices. After a general introduction, I had to introduce these theories in a series of ten or so smaller steps of increasing difficulty, which would be easier to grasp. I also had to try and demonstrate these metaprinciples with concrete and recognizable examples from other fields, in order to anchor them back into our everyday experience; to show that the most prevalent "common sense" often overlooks obvious aspects of our daily environment.

I hope that in the course of this book it will become increasingly clear that these alternative processes do indeed play a key role in mass psychology and collective behavior sociology, in rapid shifts of public opinion and public perception. Another question is, of course, to what extent they do also apply to ordinary psychology and sociology, economics, political science, history, and current affairs. I have taken the liberty to shuttle back and forth between many domains, particularly in these third sections. It is not so much the examples themselves that count, but their demonstration of certain universal principles of rapid change. I mean to stir up a further reflection in the reader, not to "wrap it up" with final proof and an unassailable "model."

Apart from that, I have organized these chapters three by three into four larger parts. Part I discusses the points of departure: the most relevant processes of opinion formation and communication; informal communication processes as they play a role in everyday conversation and hearsay, in gossip and rumor, in urban legends, and urban folklore; formal communication processes, too, as they play a role in media hypes. These three phenomena are then linked to the new notion of "complex adaptive systems," and to key processes therein, such as continuous mutation and feedback loops.

Part II is about phenomena on three different levels that have traditionally been studied within the twin fields of mass psychology and collective behavior sociology; that is to say, the levels of "visible" (physically assembled) masses, of "invisible" (or physically dispersed) masses, and of an intermediary category of masses that do occasionally and partially assemble—but need not necessarily; in other words, the levels of crowds, opinion currents, and social movements. What is typical about them is then linked to the metaprinciple of "emergence" on three different levels: synergy, pattern formation, and self-organization. In a sense, this is the heart of the book, both for the phenomena in question and for the metaprinciples invoked.

Part III is a further elaboration of all this. It focuses on the three prime forms of "emotional coloring" of opinion currents and public moods; namely, euphoric moods (as they prevail in fashion and fads), fearful moods (as they surround panic and scares), and hostile moods (as they dominate outrage and protest). These are then used to demonstrate some further relevant metaprinciples: those of evolving contexts, critical thresholds, and possible attractors. The latter notion refers to the fact that although these processes may be hard to measure, predict, and control, they may still somehow follow a kind of inherent global logic.

Part IV draws further conclusions. It begins with a discussion of a combination of some of the aforementioned phenomena: successive crazes and crashes in financial markets. In this context, the metaprinciple of "phase transitions" is introduced. Finally, we look at the question of why technological and economic, social and opinion forecasts do often fail so miserably. At the end of the book, this brings us to the metaprinciple of all metaprinciples: that of fundamental uncertainty. We spell out once again why many complex phenomena entail sudden surprises, and what this implies for science and management, including so-called information and perception management, news and issues management.

In sum, the central question of this theoretical investigation is the following. Do the new notions of chaos and complexity point to alternative ways of conceptualizing rapid, radical, and massive shifts in public opinion and perception? What can they contribute to the sciences of man and society in general, and to mass psychology and collective behavior sociology in particular?

Note. The reader who is extremely pressed for time may choose to skip the third part at first. As already indicated, it is a further elaboration and refinement of the major themes; the overall argument can well be followed on the basis of the other parts alone.

I

MIND QUAKES

Only fools, liars and charlatans predict earthquakes.
—Charles Richter, American seismologist (see Sherden, 1998, p. 259)

The preface has explained how this book came about, the introduction, how it is organized. We now come to Part I and the first three chapters, which acquaint the reader with some of the major starting points. We begin with a general outline of the approach, which will gradually be filled in. Not all questions can be answered right away, some will have to wait until the book and the argument have proceeded somewhat further. Because this approach is at variance with more familiar ones, it may take some time and patience before it "catches on" in the reader's mind, and before all the implications begin to unfold.

Like subsequent ones, the first three chapters all consist of three sections, which represent three levels of the argument: from concrete to abstract. The last and most abstract level is that of some relevant metaprinciple. In this part, they are the general metaprinciple of complex adaptive systems, and the more specific metaprinciples of continuous mutation and feedback loops. They have sometimes been identified in the past, but only sketchily. It now turns out that they play an essential role in almost any field: ranging from physics, chemistry, and biology to psychology, sociology, and economics. This volume tries to understand how they help put questions of accelerated change in different terms.

Thus the second and central sections of these three chapters look at some of the main subjects of this whole book: collective opinion formation, the shifting public perception of products and brands, institutions and is-

sues, and their "emotional coloring." This is followed by a closer look at
some of the communication processes involved (informal communication
processes, such as those involved in everyday conversation, in hearsay,
gossip, and rumor, in which messages change all the time; and formal communication processes, such as those involved in media hypes, in which
messages are boosted by "circular reaction"). These few basic elements
then enable us to proceed further.

1

Public Opinion as a Complex Adaptive System (CAS)

The certainties of one age are the problems of the next.
—R. H. Tawney, British historian (Gross, 1987, p. 321)

The true test of a brilliant theory [is that] what first is thought to be wrong is later shown to be obvious.
—Assar Lindbeck, Nobel Prize Committee
(Giacalone & Rosenfeld, 1991, p. 3)

The first section of this first chapter probes the case of Benetton, which acquired worldwide renown and notoriety, through the "3C" rock star strategy of continually courting controversy. By turning the Benetton brand into an issue, into a matter of recurrent reporting and conversation, it succeeded in boosting its visibility and recognizability from zero to close to 100%. In order to see how this works, we use the second section to delve somewhat deeper into the phenomenon of public opinion in general, which is often treated as if it were the mere sum of individual opinions of relative stability. Rather, it should be approached as a dynamic configuration in constant transformation. In the third section, this is further explored by taking a closer look at the newly discovered metaprinciples of complex adaptive systems. Within this framework, it becomes understandable how immeasurably small details may provoke dramatic turnarounds.

CASE NUMBER ONE: THE TRUE COLORS OF BENETTON

Let us take a look at a relatively recent controversy in public opinion, or rather a string of controversies, about a brand. It catapulted the brand into

3

the front ranks of world renown and notoriety, for better and for worse. It happened through a series of tremors. We later encounter other examples, where one mighty earthquake made public opinion shift from positive to negative, from sympathy to antipathy.

The story of the Benetton family is a classic "rags to riches" tale. The father was a simple bicycle repairman. After he died (around the end of World War II), the older children were forced to leave school early and try to make a living. The eldest, Luciano, became a ready-to-wear salesman; his sister, Giuliana, went to work in a ready-to-wear workshop. Ten years later, they set out on their own. Luciano made the rounds on his motorbike to sell what they produced. Giuliana used a knitting machine, on which she made colorful sweaters. Ten years later, they decided to change the label from the bland, French brand name, Très Jolie, into their own characteristic Italian family name, Benetton, and embarked on one of the major entrepreneurial success stories of our time. Gradually, the younger brothers Gilberto and Carlo joined the business as well (Moskowitz, 1987).

The success of the company was based on a unique configuration of factors. Style: They thrived on the long-term evolution from drab to vivid colors and patterns, natural fabrics, the emergence of casual youth, leisure, and sportswear. Production: They had a key part made on ultramodern machinery, and another part made by archaic subcontracting methods. This enabled them to maintain competitive prices, while at the same time circumventing employment rules and labor unions. Distribution: They developed a franchise formula, whereby shopkeepers put up the money, bought a fixed interior (and exterior) design, and a changing seasonal collection. Trends: The outlet PCs all came to be connected to a central computer system, which directed Benettons undyed sweaters to be instantaneously finished in the fashion color of the day for any region of the world, and to be airlifted there (van Niekerk, 1993).

By the late 1960s, they already had some 300 shops throughout Italy and opened their first shop in Paris. By the late 1970s, they already had almost 300 shops in France, hundreds elsewhere in Europe, and opened their first shop in New York. By the late 1980s, they had hundreds of shops in North America and some 5,000 worldwide. But they also ran into overexpansion problems. Whereas sales continued to rise, profits stagnated for the first time in 1988, and even fell in 1989. They launched minority shares, but this was not entirely successful. They tried to diversify, but had to make a U-turn back to their main business—fashion. Finally, Luciano Benetton and his family decided that they could restore profitability by having more of an "image."

For a few years, they worked with Oliviero Toscani. His father had been a long-time press photographer at the daily, *Corriere della Sera*. He himself had gone to art school in Zürich, Switzerland, and had in turn become a well-known fashion photographer, working for magazines such as *Donna, Moda,* and *Vogue.* He was very much a provocateur, in tune with the spirit of the times (Toscani, 1995).

After "Jesus Christ Superstar" had become a popular musical, a friend of his had launched a new brand of "Jesus" jeans, and Toscani had developed a promotion campaign of controversial images and texts. Predictably, they were attacked by the Vatican and their official newspaper, the *Osservatore Romano.* Later, when they criticized Toscani and his advertising agency of stamping the Benetton logo on all the misery of the world, and thereby exploiting it, he retorted without blushing by observing that this was exactly what Christ, his disciples, and the Church had done with the crucifix for almost 2,000 years. The Bible was an accumulation of unsettling stories and images, he said, no different from his own campaigns.

Later, Toscani had done the well-received "Real People" campaign for the new American fashion brand, Esprit. It portrayed ordinary people picked from the streets in their casual wear, rather than sterile super models. He also did a campaign for the new Italian fashion brand, Fiorucci, part of which was later bought by the Benetton family. That is how Toscani got to work for them as well. Until the late 1980s, Toscani's Benetton campaigns had been noteworthy, but not revolutionary. They portrayed lively youngsters—alone, in couples, or in groups—in vividly colored knitwear. From 1989 on, however, they developed a new focus.

On one hand, they had gradually shifted to a new name and logo in a green quadrangle, "United Colors of Benetton." This was vaguely reminiscent of the United States, the United Nations, and some kind of "global village," or melting pot. On the other hand, they had gradually shifted to matching new visual themes; bridging differences in national colors, skin colors, and so forth. It turned out this sparked recurrent controversies, which obviously served their purpose very well. The strategy was based on several elements: graphic and archetypical images, which could alternately be taken to confirm or disclaim stereotypes; toying with manifold possible interpretations by choosing never to "anchor" a simple meaning for the image in an explanatory by-line. There would be a contrasting reception of the images by different social groups due to cultural diversity, which would automatically stir up a debate.

There had been some minor controversy when they began by displaying the national flags of "opposite" countries. When Gorbachev visited Paris at the end of the Cold War, Benetton lined the entire Champs Elysées boulevard with posters featuring kissing Black twins clad in Soviet and American flags. Similar campaigns where based on the Greek and Turkish flags, the British and the Argentinian flags, the German and the Israeli flags. These depictions encountered fierce opposition; the first complaints: the media refused to print them, discussions were held at regulatory bodies, and there were problems with government restrictions imposed.

The campaign went into higher gear with a Black woman presenting a bare breast to a white baby. The ad was forbidden by the White minority in South Africa, and criticized by a Black minority in North America. The theme was further developed with a Black and a White hand tied by handcuffs, a Black adult hand and a White baby hand, Black and White toddlers with "devils horns" and an "angel curls" hairdo, Black and White toddlers kissing, on a potty, sticking their tongues out, and so on. In retrospect, it seems surprising that many of these apparently innocent posters stirred controversy and "free publicity" at all. But Toscani and Benetton had to continue to push the limits in order to keep the attention.

By the early 1990s, they chose a complete revolution in advertising strategy. On one hand, they would give up the visual theme of "united colors," and thereby all direct references to the product itself. On the other hand, they would simply focus on humanitarian subjects, with press photographs selected and acquired for that purpose. These were pictures about Mafia terror and Mafia victims in Italy, about civil and military violence, about refugees and poverty. Earlier, at the outbreak of the Gulf conflict, they had published pictures of a war cemetery. Later, when the Yugoslav conflict persisted, they published pictures of bloodstained clothes of a known soldier killed in the fighting. Although many protested against these pictures, a small Sarajevo agency asked Benetton to send thousands of free copies of such posters to line the streets of the Bosnian capital, and Benetton complied.

Most controversial of all were the "safe sex" and AIDS campaigns. Early forerunners were a poster with colored condoms, and another one featured test tubes with the first names of major political figures of the day: Yasser, Helmut, George, Mikhael, and Moammar. In 1992, Benetton gave worldwide exposure to a press picture of dying AIDS activist, David Kirby, surrounded and supported by his family. The latter condoned both the original publication of the pictures in *Life* magazine, and their later recirculation by Benetton. The chosen picture had earned its author several awards, and even a second prize at the World Press Photo competition. Yet its public exhibition as part of an advertising campaign stirred many protests, for instance, by the Catholic Church.

Toscani countered that it should be seen as the present-day equivalent of Michelangelo's famous Pietà sculpture. For once, it showed an AIDS victim supported by a caring family, rather than abandoned as a pestilent outcast. Philippe Ariès's famous study on *La mort et l'Occident* had already shown, he added, that death and its images had become a taboo subject throughout the West. Only on very few occasions had major Western media ever dared to show AIDS victims (or cancer victims, for that matter).

Others referred to the essays of Susan Sontag on "Illness as Metaphor" and "On Photography" to account for the strong reaction. The format of the picture, they said, reminded one of an intimate family snapshot, which was suddenly exposed to the impudent eyes of the public (van Niekerk, 1993, pp. 45–54). During a trip to the United States, Toscani saw a local television report about a row, when a student had come to the college gates, dressed in no more than a tattoo, "HIV Positive." This inspired another controversial picture and campaign.

Throughout the 1990s, the Benetton campaigns continued to divide people. No campaigns were more often denounced as immoral, or more often acclaimed as innovative. The critics repeated that advertising space should be filled with positive and uplifting images, that filling it with these negative and depressing images was confrontational, and amounted to a cynical exploitation of conflict, death, and sex for personal gain. The supporters repeated that the campaigns broke down artificial barriers, that most mass media were commercial anyway, and that there was no a priori reason why the huge budgets and space reserved for advertising could not be used to make people think about social problems. But they acknowledged that within 6 years, its strategy of thriving on controversy had propelled Benetton into one of the best-known brands in the world.

The Benetton case is particularly interesting and relevant, because it illustrates a number of complex processes that we elaborate on in the course of this book. Even though it was not so much an example of one singular, rapid, radical, and massive shift, but rather of a succession of smaller ones, which ultimately led to the creation of a new and compelling brand image. This thorough mutation was fed and sustained by ever-new debates. There were feedback loops and media hypes, there was synergy formation, and an emerging pattern. In a way it was a twin pattern, a split image, a dual public—of proponents and opponents—with few people remaining indifferent.

The campaigns were both clear-cut and ambivalent; they resonated with the deepest hopes and fears of each individual, and also with feelings of admiration and loathing. They had their social effect in a very specific set of circumstances. There have been many attempts to repeat the feat, but these attempts had much less impact. There was no guarantee at the outset that this approach would work, and there is no guarantee that it will continue to work. There is something profoundly immeasurable, unpredictable, and uncontrollable about public opinion. Rather than a stable aggregate, it should be seen as a dynamic configuration; or even a complex adaptive system. Let us take a closer look at what this implies.

THE PHENOMENON OF PUBLIC OPINION

Within a few years time, Benetton had succeeded in turning an unknown and bland fashion brand into one of the best-known and most forceful brands in the world. It succeeded, because photographer Oliviero Toscani intuitively exploited the laws of opinion formation. He provoked recurrent controversies and thereby created "issues" that stirred the media and the public over and over again to take sides. In order to understand this, we must take a closer look at the functioning of public opinion. Public opinion is not the static sum of individual opinions, but a dynamic process, which continually evolves new and shifting patterns. This section sketches some basic principles, which will be further refined in the course of the book.

Of course the first question must be what public opinion really is. By the time the notion had become broadly used, a handbook identified more than 50 different definitions (Childs, 1965). Let us therefore start from the words themselves. First of all, public opinion is about opinions, not about statements of fact. It is an opinion or value judgment about which people are divided.

Secondly, public opinion is "public." It does not refer to private opinions, which people may hold but keep to themselves. Public opinion is about opinions that people make public and express. Or, as Noelle-Neumann (1994) put it, it is "a social psychological process lending cohesion to human communities . . . a process in which agreement about the values of the community and the acts derived therefrom is continuously reestablished" (p. 98). According to this definition, public opinion is a key process in the formation, reformation (and dissolution) of groups. What is it that people want to identify with, belong to? And what is it that they do not?

Public Opinion and Opinion Polls

The notion of public opinion has a long and varied history. It was always related to some kind of public debate, in which a number of free citizens spoke out, to reach some kind of common understanding about public questions. During Greek and Roman antiquity, and in southern Europe, this was often related to outdoor meeting places such as markets and squares—the forum. During the Enlightenment, and in northern Europe, it was often related to new indoor meeting places such as the coffee houses in larger English cities, the salons in France, and the *Tischgesellschaften* in the German language area. Within these relatively open environments, new groups, new aspirations, and new ideas came to the fore; for instance, regarding further restrictions on the powers of the absolute monarch, and extensions of the powers of people's representatives in deliberative assemblies or parliaments, claiming to represent popular sovereignty and the general will (Lippmann, 1947).

Yet this public opinion of the late 18th and early 19th centuries remained an "elite opinion." Only a limited upper class was supposed to be well informed, capable of reasoned judgment, and therefore entitled to vote. A true "mass opinion" only came about toward the end of the 19th century. The rise of the popular press enrolled an ever larger share of the general public to participate in the ongoing debates. Workers and women claimed voting rights. It was only during these decades, then, that public opinion acquired its modern nature; that current opinions and public moods were discovered in their new form; in France, for instance, with the Dreyfus affair (see van Ginneken, 1992a).

It was also this wider context that triggered a sudden interest in the diagnosis and prognosis of public opinion (e.g., through the improved study of electoral geography), and in methods to continue to understand and improve on this geography beyond the elections themselves. Some early techniques evolved within the framework of social surveys. These were extensive investigations into the health and living conditions of the poor and the common man. They were usually initiated by politicians, in order to demonstrate the need for reform and to stave off the threat of unrest (for a historical overview, see Bulmer, Bales, & Sklar, 1991). Also within the framework of policy making, a periodic census of the entire population came into wider use.

Innovations in marketing and media research proved important, too. When national commercial radio networks emerged in the United States in the late 1920s, sampling techniques had to be further refined in order to be able to estimate audiences reached and establish advertiser rates. With the onset of the Depression, and the threat of political upheaval, electoral prognoses became more important than ever (for a historical overview, see Converse, 1987). On the eve of the 1936 elections, finally, George Gallup and others were first able to predict the outcome with confidence, after interviewing only limited samples (van Ginneken, 1986a, 1995, 1996/7, 2002/3, in press). This established the basic principles of the opinion poll. Just before, during and after World War II, the technique further spread to the rest of the Western world (van Ginneken, 1993a).

The opinion poll (and related techniques of media surveys, advertising surveys, market surveys, and personnel surveys) is first of all very practical. The point of departure is that one interviews people face to face, by telephone, in writing, or by computer. Although the problem is, of course, that people do not always know what they want, or say what they mean. The second principle is that one uses questionnaires with a certain structure and certain formulations; the problem is that with a slightly different structure or with slightly different formulations, interviewees may give completely different answers.

A third principle is the use of multiple-choice, "closed" answer categories, in ascending or descending order of intensity. A problem is, that this forces people into the mental framework of the interviewers, researchers, or sponsors—which is not necessarily their own mental framework. A fourth principle is the use of representative samples; a problem with this is that the sample provides, by definition, only an average, bland and "instant picture."

A fifth principle is that, with the help of statistical methods, the results are condensed into averages, percentages, scores, and other clearcut outcomes. The problem is that this creates simplicity, and kills complexity. In sum, it is a very useful technique to assemble certain basic data; but its routine use often ignores the limitations. Even the adding of other techniques (from in-depth interviews to group discussions, from expert interviews to consensus building) may fail to yield the underlying framework.

The main problem is twofold. On one hand, the technique leaves little room for configurations, in which the whole of public perception is more than the sum of its parts. On the other hand, it leaves little room for the potential of uneven change, in which accelerated shifts alternate with decelerated shifts. The American sociologist Charles Cooley already said that public opinion is "no mere aggregate of separate individual judgments, but an organization, a cooperative product of communication and reciprocal influence" (Fraser & Gaskell, 1990, p. 80). Alan Barton put it even more bluntly:

> Using random sampling of individuals, the survey is a sociological meat-grinder, tearing the individual from his social context and guaranteeing that nobody in the study interacts with anyone else in it. It is a little like a biologist putting his experimental animals through a hamburger machine and looking at every hundredth cell through a microscope; anatomy and physiology get lost; structure and function disappear, and one is left with cell biology. (in Rogers, 1995, p. 120)

Rather than interpreting someone's belief system as the sum total of his or her beliefs, and rather than interpreting public opinion as the sum total of the public's opinions, then, we should be looking for structure and function, for elements of unevenness, and for all the differences that make a difference. What is the reverse side of someone's expressed opinions, what is in the shadow and what is in the light? Do expressed opinions really correspond with deeper feelings and with behavior? How strongly is someone attached to his or her opinions? Under what circumstances could this pattern begin to shift? Can someone be easily persuaded, and by whom? Can he or she easily persuade others, and with what? What chances are there that group opinion may gradually drift in one direction, or in another? What factors play a role? How effective are interested parties in convincing others? What reactions may they provoke?

The relevance of such questions has been recognized by many researchers from early days (see Turner & Killian, 1987, pp. 189–192) until recently (see Fraser & Gaskell, 1990, pp. 84–87; Price, 1992, pp. 59–68). The problem is that such questions have only very partially been translated into new research methods embraced by a broad consensus of scholars, although there have been many attempts in that direction. Another reason is that many people feel research methods should be objective or "dumb" (the technique and the computer should provide the answers, the skills of the researcher should not play a role). But that is what research is all about; personal interpretation and strategic analysis by an experienced investigator is imperative in many stages of it.

This is of course the key paradox of all psychosocial science. It cannot limit itself to demonstrating lawful relations between clear-cut facts, because psychosocial science is not only about establishing clear-cut facts, but also about the attribution of meaning. Meaning is by definition complex, layered, and even contradictory. Furthermore, the interviewer, researcher, and sponsor are players in this game; they tend to accept certain interpretations over others. So psychosocial science is also about the understanding of meaningful relations. Whoever denies that interpretations are necessary and inevitable will be the first to fall victim to crude and obvious misinterpretations.

The Rise and Fall of Issues

One may also see culture or public opinion as a complex adaptive system, or a system of systems. Because a culture is a dynamic configuration of subcultures, and a public is a dynamic configuration of publics. Collective opinions, as well as individual opinions, may change every minute; every impression we undergo may slightly alter the pattern. Every event reported may do the same. Public opinion is not static, but dynamic. It is like a rivulet that seeks its way through the landscape; or rather like the duckweed or dust or oil on its surface, which is constantly forming newly evolving patterns.

The public is, in fact, an ensemble of "publics." Several authors have pointed this out. Turner and Killian's (1987) description, for instance, suits me well. They say, "a public is a dispersed group of people interested in and divided about an issue, engaged in a discussion of the issue, with a view to registering a collective opinion which is expected to affect the course of action of some group or individual" (p. 179). We may therefore best distinguish the public in relation to the issues involved. But what is an issue, then? An issue, according to Turner and Killian (1987), "consists of those points about which people agree to disagree" (p. 182). That is to say, it excludes the points about which people agree from the start. Those will not be problematized; they are perceived as mere background, taken for granted. But it also excludes those points about which people disagree so thoroughly that any meaningful discussion is excluded; those will not be problematized either—they cannot form a meaningful issue for debate. Issues are about the controversies that feed everyday debate and social interaction.

So controversies that lead to considerable polarization, for instance, about civil rights or abortion (or Benetton, for that matter), do not so much form one evolving pattern but two evolving patterns, closely interwoven; the discourse and network of the protagonists and the discourse and network of the antagonists, with only a small neutral zone in between. The patterns closely follow each other. It is like the moving divide between two fluids that do not mix; or like a tango—when one partner does a step forward, the other partner does a step backward. Yet they do not dance against one another, but with one another.

Turner and Killian (1987) were careful to add that there are hardly "isolated" issues, as such.

> Often it is an oversimplification to speak of the public as divided about an issue. Rather the public is frequently organized about a matrix of issues that are conceived by the public as belonging together. In some instances there is a clearly defined hierarchy of issues; in others people are uncertain what they are supposed to be deciding; and sometimes there are factional definitions of issues. (p. 192)

Think of the environment that has risen to great prominence in recent decades (and that returns throughout this book in many different guises). It could be seen as a super issue with many subissues, a matrix or hierarchy of issues.

So there is a multitude of spatiotemporal patterns in public opinion: patterns that emerge, spread, change, disappear, and reappear. The cycle usually begins with existing patterns becoming irrelevant, or loosing their grip. This is the trend toward loosing a temporary balance and advancing toward entropy, chaos, and a loss of structure. It is followed by other emerging patterns becoming more relevant, and fastening their grip. This is the trend toward establishing a new temporary balance and advancing toward *negentropy*, a new order and an increase in structure. In this context, Klapp (1978) most appropriately suggested that a kind of informational breathing takes place. That is to say an alternate "opening up for," and "closing off to," new information; a natural rhythm like ebb and flow.

Of course, all kinds of interested parties try to influence these processes. They try to get certain issues on the public agenda, and take other issues off the public agenda. They try to change the frames and grids through which public issues are defined—through key words, images, or events. An individual has an agenda, a meeting has an agenda, the media and the public have an agenda. An *agenda* identifies the subjects that need attention, and in what order of priority. In my previous book, *Understanding Global News* (1998, chap. 5), I demonstrated how the public agenda is largely framed by the media agenda, and the media agenda by the institutional elites. The battle for public opinion is not so much about what one wants the public to think, but about what one wants the public to think *about*. Whoever has a decisive influence over that has already half won the battle.

In her book *The Spiral of Silence*, Elisabeth Noelle-Neumann (1984) showed that self-reinforcing processes play a key role in the evolution of public opinion. Men are social animals, fearing exclusion and isolation. If they get the impression that their opinion is loosing ground, they will express themselves less and less forcefully on this score. If, by contrast, they get the impression that their opinion is gaining ground, they will express themselves more and more forcefully, until the former opinion almost disappears and the latter opinion seems to be accepted. One way to trace these processes is to ask people not only what they think, but also to ask them what they think most other people think. This will highlight attribution errors, which may be an indication of the "drift" taking place (see also Noelle-Neumann, 1994). We later return to a more elaborate discussion of such processes.

The coming and going of issues is a more-or-less spontaneous social process; some speak of an issue attention cycle in this context. Anthony Downs (1987) once identified five stages for the United States, which may just as well apply anywhere else. Firstly the "preproblem" stage; this prevails when some highly undesirable social condition exists but has not yet captured much public attention. (In fact, according to Downs, the situation was usually worse when it was still ignored than when it was finally recognized). Second, the stage of alarmed discovery and euphoric enthusiasm, which results in part from the claim that every problem can be solved. Third, realizing the cost of significant progress, which puts a damper on the initial eagerness. Fourth, there will be a gradual decline of intense public interest. Finally, there is the "postproblem" stage; a twilight realm of lesser attention or spasmodic recurrences.

In this latter context, the term, *issue fatigue*, has been proposed. Whenever a major new issue turns up in the mass media and in public opinion, and temporarily fills the entire screen, it is hard to imagine that it may just as easily fade away again, and be forgotten some day. Yet this is inevitably what happens if there is no periodic renewal, and often sooner than people think. Strictly speaking, this is not because people decide that the issue is no longer important. But it is because people suddenly feel that other, newer issues are important.

Living in the present, we all too often have the implicit idea that the future is (and will remain) blank, or a mere prolongation of what is already going on. This is an optical illusion (to which we return more extensively in the final full chapter). There will always be unforeseen and surprising new issues, phasing out existing ones and thereby completely restructuring the force field. Whenever there is a huge image crisis, therefore, public relations consultants often advise their clients to simply "lie low" for a while, because the storm will inevitably blow over. Unfortunately, the reverse is true as well; whenever somebody or something has once been controversial, only very little fuel is needed to revive the flames.

Emotional Coloring of Issues

The existing literature about public opinion places a heavy emphasis on rationality and lucid deliberation. This literature is a product of the Enlightenment, and is closely connected with the democratic ideal. The existing literature about rapid shifts in public opinion, by contrast, about mass psychology and collective behavior sociology, places a heavy emphasis on emotionality and "blind" processes. This literature is primarily about supposed threats to the liberal order (more in van Ginneken 1992a). Yet this strict opposition of "rationality" and "emotionality" is a typically modern Western illusion. There is hardly any rational behavior that is not colored by accompanying emotions, and there is hardly any emotional behavior that does not also have an underlying ratio. We later return to this subject, in Part III of this book, about shifting public moods.

But let us at this early stage delve somewhat into what emotions, emotional coloring, and moods really mean. Not all scholars agree, and handbooks distinguish a few major approaches. A handbook by Cornelius (1988) first distinguished the elder tradition of the British biologist Charles Darwin, who emphasized the role of emotions in adaptation and survival. Secondly, it identified the elder tradition of the American psychologist William James, who emphasized the nature of emotions as primarily physical reactions. Third, Cornelius (1988) identified the more recent tradition of *cognitivism*, which sees emotions as the "raw appraisal" of a situation. And fourth, he identified the more recent tradition of *social constructivism*, which claims that emotions are shaped by socialization and culture (see also Harré, 1986).

Yet all these approaches have a few points in common, for instance that emotions have a well-defined function. The handbook by Oatley and Jenkins (1996) stated that emotions are a way to deal quickly and efficiently with new and unexpected situations. Lower animals do not need emotions because their appraisal of the world is quite simple. God does not need emotions, because his appraisal of the world is perfect. Higher animals and humans need emotions, however, as a kind of heuristic; as a means to facilitate "approximately" adequate responses to new situations. They are partly innate, partly learned.

Fischer (1991) connected the psychophysiological notion of emotion to the sociocognitivist notion of "script." Fischer says that emotional scripts have three different functions. First of all they imply a raw appraisal of the situation. Second, they guide expression. And third, they imply expectations about the outcome of the behavior. Emotions thus provide a basic repertory of reaction patterns, which meaningfully connect various aspects of human functioning. In primary, secondary, or tertiary emotions, this need not always be aspects on the same levels. Sometimes the configuration includes physiological aspects (e.g., triggered by the autonomous nervous system), sometimes it includes neurological aspects (such as arousal), psychological aspects (tendencies to act), and so forth.

If we limit ourselves to cognitive functions alone, we see that emotions may activate and deactivate various functions, and lead to qualitatively different states of readiness. There is, for instance, selective exposure; fear may heighten alertness to marginal stimuli, which might otherwise be easily overlooked. There is selective perception; fear may automatically lead us to choose one interpretation of an ambiguous stimulus over another (i.e., to see it as a possible threat). There is selective retention; fear may activate or disactivate certain related memories. There is also selective reproduction, and so on (Oatley & Jenkins, 1996; also see Cornelius, 1996).

In Part III of this book, I propose to extend these arguments along two different lines. As some of the mentioned authors have already noted, not only flash emotions but prolonged moods also have similar aspects. They form qualitatively different basic configurations that facilitate our psychological functioning along certain lines. When we are joyful, we react differently to exactly the same situation as when we are depressed. As other authors noted, this does not only hold for individual behavior, but sometimes for collective behavior as well. We see in Part II (about collective behavior) how and why this is the case (also see Lofland, 1985).

We see that various moods do not only provide different frameworks for individual reactions, but also for social interactions (see Scheff's 1990, *Microsociology*, in this regard). The aforementioned Turner and Killian (1987) spoke about keynoting, symbolization, and coordination as three processes that give collective behavior its specific character. We see in Part III that this basic pattern is entirely different for collective joy or collective grief, collective fear or collective courage, collective outrage or collective resignation. What is more, minor details may help such moods slip from one mode into the other. But how should we conceive of such processes? Could chaos and complexity theory be of any help?

THE METAPRINCIPLE OF COMPLEX MUTATION

The Benetton controversy was an illustration of the functioning of public opinion. We have seen that traditional approaches see public opinion too much as a static aggregate rather then as a dynamic configuration. In the course of the next chapters, this book will gradually unfold an alternative view of rapid, radical, and massive shifts in public opinion, a view that also carries implications for many other psychological, sociological, economic, political, and most of all, communicative phenomena. For its outline, we take stock with a great paradigm shift that has been under way for some time in an entirely different field, that of the natural sciences.

This does not mean that I propose to reduce social and psychological phenomena to chemical and physical ones; quite the contrary. But it means that there already is an extended family of new approaches, throwing an entirely different light on the metaprinciples of accelerated and/or nonlinear change. This entails a so-called paradigm shift, which may ultimately affect all disciplines. *Paradigm* is Greek for a primitive word, an example, a model. In his influential book, *The Structure of Scientific Revolutions*, Thomas Kuhn (1962) introduced the term into the sociology of science. He noted that scientists, particularly those within one discipline and school, often were guided by a limited set of examples or models; not only explicit models, such as an elaborate theory and methodology, but also implicit models, such as metaphors and images.

Paradigms thus help shape "normal" science. But from time to time, anomalies turn up, which are at odds with what is expected. The initial reaction is often to ignore them as long as possible until they are confirmed, reconfirmed, and reconfirmed again, many times over. But if they persist in turning up, they may put existing presuppositions into question, or even force a crisis. A small minority of scholars will try to think of alternative explanations. After an often-protracted battle with vested interests in the field, the new view may ultimately come to prevail and establish a new consensus, until the process repeats itself. So new debates open, old debates close, and that is how science progresses.

Every generation, a new paradigm may turn up, which revolutionizes a discipline. Every few generations, a new metaparadigm may turn up, which revolutionizes various disciplines at once. During the first half of the 20th century, the theory of relativity and quantum theory began to shake our understanding of the physical world. During the second half of the 20th century, the theories of open systems and complex change played a similar role. They led to a revolution that affected the natural sciences one after the other, and is beginning to affect the sciences of man and society as well. The metaparadigm shift throws an entirely differently light on many seemingly capricious processes, which had always been hard to understand. But it also throws a different light on the nature of reality and change (Capra, 1975, 1997).

The history of this entire shift has been well described in various excellent books, such as *Chaos* by James Gleick (1987), *Complexity* by Mitchell Waldrop (1992), and *Complexity* by Roger Lewin (1992). Although occasionally they have a slightly ethnocentric drift, just like a more recent *tour d'horizon* of contemporary science by John Horgan (1996). That is to say, such Anglo-American overviews occasionally have a tendency to adopt the somewhat self-centered perspectives of their prime U.S. and U.K. sources, by overemphasizing northwestern contributions, and by disparaging southern (i.e., Latin) or eastern (e.g., Slavonic) contributions (not to mention Asian ones). Examples are the near absence of pioneers such as Maturana and Varela (1984) from this kind of literature, or the dismissive treatment of pioneers such as Prigogine and Stengers (1984). Of course a similar but reverse tendency can be noted in French or Russian histories of science.

All this does not change the profound significance of the entire metaparadigm shift. Reductionism and elementarism, determinism and even the ingrained notion of causality, have lost considerable ground. Contextualism and holism, uncertainty, and contingency have advanced on all fronts. Scores of scholars throughout the world have played a role. Often they met with strong resistance. When economist Brian Arthur (1988) showed his first major article to a colleague, she reacted, "They will crucify you." And they did. The pioneering piece was refused by all major, peer-reviewed journals, because it strongly went against the dominant tide. It was rewritten, refused again, for 6 years in a row. "That's when my hair turned grey," he said (Waldrop, 1992, p. 48). It was only later, that he was finally recognized as one of the most original thinkers of his generation.

Still, many scholars continue to disagree about key questions, and that is the way it should be (Horgan, 1995). At the same time, they have generated an entirely new framework of dozens upon dozens of interrelated notions, which provide us with a completely fresh look at reality and change; notions such as chaos and order, complexity and simplicity, emergence and self-organization, and many others. Sally Goerner (in Robertson & Combs, 1995) said that the scientific revolution is embedded in a much broader shift. "It is, in fact, part of a fundamental change in vision, a change from a controlled machine vision of the world to an evolving ecological vision of the world" (p. 17); or from a focus on systems with a very limited number of degrees of freedom (entities, variables, interactions) to a focus on systems with a very large number of degrees of freedom.

Newton's Apple and Lorenz's Butterfly

The modern Western sciences of man and society have been in existence for over 100 years, as has their general philosophy. This also holds for our thinking about opinion and communication. The metaparadigm of the sciences of man and society derived from the metaparadigm of natural science, which in turn derived from the "paradigmatic discipline" par excellence—mechanics—and Newton's 300-year-old founding text of the field. We all know the apocryphal story that Newton "discovered" gravity and the laws of nature when an apple fell on his head. Thus the traditional metaparadigm of both social and natural science could be described as that of "Newton's apple." But over the last 10 or 20 years, this apple has gradually been gnawed at and eaten away at by the contrasting new metaparadigm of "Lorenz's butterfly," to which we return.

Like so many other great pioneers, Newton himself was well aware of some limitations in his view, but his successors and followers ultimately evolved a simplified version and gave it wide circulation. According to this simplified version, the universe is nothing more than a collection of objects and a few forces of nature. Complex objects consist of a number of elementary components; the whole is little more than the sum of the parts. All these things are implicitly thought to have a definite substance and shape, quality, and quantity. Changes are linear; causes are proportional to consequences. Interaction is clear-cut; it can be measured, predicted, and controlled. It is the world of the cuckoo clock, of the machine, of the factory, of the primitive industrial age.

Next to mechanics, the early 19th century generated another paradigmatic discipline: *thermodynamics*, the science of heat and heat flows of energy. The first law of thermodynamics, the law of the conservation of energy, said that energy could change from one form into another (mechanical, chemical, thermic, electric), but could not be created or destroyed. One version of the second law of thermodynamics said that if such a transformation liberated energy, it would flow from high to low, from hot to cold, and so forth. Ultimately, therefore, energy would come to be spread more evenly. The result would be that *entropy*, chaos and loss of structure, would continually gain ground, whereas *negentropy*, order and structure, would lose ground. Thus the universe, the solar system, the earth, life, and mankind would ultimately fade away.

Next to physics other disciplines such as chemistry, biochemistry, and biology developed, including Darwin's theory of evolution. The curious thing is that they did in fact point in an opposite direction. Disciplines followed their own paradigms, and interacted less between themselves. Newton's mechanics and thermodynamics dealt with dead matter, Darwin's evolution theory and biology dealt with living beings. Yet evolution theory showed that decreasing order, loss of structure, and entropy did not prevail; but rather increased order, gain of structure, and negentropy. Or at least "islands" of increasing order, in the midst of an ocean of decreasing order. Somehow, change was not always what it seemed to be.

Only over the last 20 years has this key mystery of order and chaos gradually been cleared up, primarily in other disciplines such as meteorology and chemistry. In meteorology, this was related to the first attempts to improve weather forecasts, with the help of computers. American meteorologist, Edward Lorenz, developed a model to predict weather patterns in the northern hemisphere. He made a grid of points, postulated values for various parameters (temperature, humidity, sunshine, winds, etc.), in a number of decimals, and tried to simulate how weather patterns would evolve. He succeeded rather well until a minor incident occurred, something like a cup of coffee spilling over. Lorenz was forced to enter the same data all over again. But to his great surprise, the second prediction turned out radically different from the first.

Only then did he realize that, because of irritation and haste, he had reduced the figures by a few decimal points. These minute changes led to radically different prediction results. In a first scientific article, he compared this to the flap of a seagull's wings in one spot, which could ultimately help provoke a storm in another spot, far away. The image caught on. Even more, when in a later lecture, he added the intriguing question: Can the flap of a butterfly's wing over Brazil spark off a tornado in Texas? The answer was *yes*. Because it might help tip the entire system from one weather pattern and inherent logic to another. (We will return to these so-called attractors in chap. 9). Lorenz's latter lecture was held at the annual meeting of the American Association for the Advancement of Science, which always gets extensive media coverage. A colleague had meanwhile proposed the name "chaos theory," and that label stuck. The observation that such minor details could have dramatic consequences led to the discovery of universal principles, of a seemingly un-Newtonian nature.

Another breakthrough came from chemistry. At the end of the 1970s, the Russian Belgian Ilya Prigogine (Prigogine & Stengers, 1984) received a Nobel Prize for his work about dissipation. His book, *La Nouvelle Alliance* (written with Isabelle Stengers), was originally in French, translated into a dozen languages, but only came out in English in the mid-1980s, as *Order Out of Chaos*. It added two key observations to the standard interpretation of the aforementioned second law of thermodynamics, about the gradual increase of entropy, or chaos, and the gradual decrease of negentropy, or order. In this regard, Prigogine said, people first of all often lost the distinction between closed and open systems from sight. And secondly, they made no proper distinction between systems near equilibrium, and systems far from equilibrium.

In the latter case, two things happened. On one hand, the existing order in a system was completely dissipated. But on the other hand, these dissipation processes themselves tended to generate new dissipative structures. The reason was that they had a tendency of streamlining themselves, to make the process unfold more efficiently. Think of a bucket of water that you empty into a sink: a vortex may spontaneously appear. Others (such as R. Swenson, quoted by Goerner in Robertson & Combs, 1995, p. 18) later called this the MEP-principle: the principle of Maximum Entropy Production. So the paradox was, that the processes themselves that were driving toward chaos, triggered opposite processes, driving toward (a new) order. An important point was, it should be added, that there was no precise deterministic relation between the old and the new order, because infinitely small details governed the transition.

This was a major breakthrough, which had other major consequences; for instance, for the notion of time—to which we return in chapter 7. Futurologist Alvin Toffler, the inventor of the notion of a third wave of technical innovation, wrote an enthusiastic introduction to the revised English edition of the book (Prigogine & Stengers, 1984). He called it symptomatic for the shift from an industrial, mechanistic, control-oriented society to a post-industrial, information-oriented, evolving society. Prigogine and Stengers themselves added that anomalies in the old paradigm had long been obvious for anyone to see, but that scientists had ignored them in the cultural and ideological context of the day. As we will see, the new thinking had important consequences for key scientific claims of measurement, prediction and control.

Nowak and Lewenstein once again highlighted this point, in their contribution to Vallacher and Nowak's (1994) book, *Dynamical Systems in Social Psychology*.

> Sensitivity to initial conditions implies that the behavior of a chaotic system cannot be predicted in long time spans. In practice, it implies the breakdown of Laplacian determinism. Formally, the evolution of the system is deterministic in the sense that the behavior of the system is fully determined by differential or difference equations. In practice [however], the state of the system cannot be predicted over time. One reason is that we never know the initial data with infinite accuracy. Our knowledge always contains some rounding, errors, or uncertainty. All these inaccuracies are amplified by the dynamics. The second reason is that even the slightest and most momentary perturbation of the dynamics causes arbitrarily large effects after some time. (p. 31)

Think of the butterfly effect of the aforementioned meteorologist, Edward Lorenz, underlining that minute changes may cause major shifts, and of the fact that even with today's computer power, it is still impossible to make weather forecasts of even 1 week with a reasonable degree of certainty. We will later see that the same principle basically holds for the evolution of public opinion and public perception.

The Holy Faith in CAS

Prigogine's theory of dissipative structures forms an important bridge to another major theme: the evolution of complex adaptive systems (CAS) in nature and society. The worldwide scientific center and interdisciplinary meeting place for thinking about CAS is in Santa Fe, New Mexico. Mitchell Waldrop (1992) pointed to the interesting mix of elements surrounding this precise location.

The new Athens or the new Olympus of complexity theory used to be housed in a modest convent. *Santa Fe* is Spanish for "holy faith." The name had originally been given to the place by the order of Saint Francis: the patron saint of nature. The city is on the Rio Grande, which flows south, surrounded by arid land. Somewhat more to the west are the spectacular Rocky Mountains. The city lies in a breathtaking landscape of chaos and order. Culturally, furthermore, it is a real melting pot. New Mexico was one of the last states added to the United States, and has remained a bone of contention with the Southern neighbor. Just as in California to the west, and in Texas to the east, it is the meeting point of the Anglosaxon Protestant world with the Hispanic Catholic world, with old Indian tribes and "new age" groups thrown in for good measure.

The major research center close to Santa Fe is Los Alamos, where the first atom bomb was developed, and an advanced weapons lab survived. The first big interdisciplinary research project of the Santa Fe institute was sponsored by Citycorp of New York, one of the largest banks in the world. The oil crises of the 1970s had made banks imprudent in the 1980s; they essentially borrowed money from capital-rich developing countries to loan to capital-poor developing countries, but at increasingly "softer" conditions. This had created the risk that a string of third world countries might default, and that some $300,000,000,000 dollars might be lost. None of this had been foreseen by the world's financial experts.

So Citycorp was quite willing to spend a modest sum on two workshops at the Santa Fe institute to have physicists and economists discuss complex adaptive systems, and possible sudden shifts therein (Waldrop, 1992). Within a month after the second workshop, the stock market actually crashed. Around this "Black Monday" of October, 1987, the Dow Jones Industrial Index on Wall Street lost more points than during the notorious "Great Crash" of October, 1929. (I discuss both in my (van Ginneken, 1993b) book on crazes and crashes). Experts had claimed that this could never happen again in the same way because circumstances had profoundly changed. And even though the workshops in Santa Fe had not predicted the crash (as rumor would later have it), it certainly did underline the importance of a radically different approach to nonlinear processes.

So what was new about CAS and how did they differ? CAS usually involved large numbers of similar entities with similar behavior, interacting among themselves and with the environment, generating cohesive patterns that somehow adapted to changed circumstances. This purposely broad description covers an extremely wide range of phenomena—from dead matter (atoms and molecules, water drops and sand grains) to living material (genes and cells, plants and animals). Variation and selection seemed to make these CAS expand and evolve, sometimes reactively, and sometimes even seemingly proactively, whereby they would fill and exploit a new niche. We later see that the formation of human groups and communities, of public opinion and cultures, has similar aspects. But let us first continue our exploration of general CAS characteristics.

One of the prime reasons for the evolution of CAS lies in the nature of "manyness" or "multitude" itself. As the number of entities within a population grows, the number of possible mutual relations grows exponentially. Between two entities, there is only one mutual relation possible; between 20 entities, there are 190 mutual relationships possible. Between 200 entities, there are already 19,900 relationships possible. (According to the formula, n $x (n - 1)$: 2). This "explosion" of possible mutual relationships begs for further stream-lining, so to say.

A number of other observations should be added. First of all, however similar the entities and their behavior may be, they themselves, their position within the population, and with regard to the environment are seldom completely identical. Some are for instance at the periphery, whereas others are in the center. This promotes a division of labor, a differentiation between entities and relations. Some of these differentiations may create a lasting pattern, which stabilizes itself. But as the numbers and the population grow, it becomes increasingly difficult to consolidate these; only a hierarchization of entities and a stratification of relations may accomplish this. Primary systems with such forms of organization have a greater chance of survival and can better adapt to new circumstances.

These principles had already been identified in an essay with the provocative title, "More is Different," which the authoritative magazine *Science* had published in 1972. Its author was physicist Philip Anderson (quoted in Horgan, 1996) of Princeton University, who later received a Nobel Prize for his work on superconductivity. Reality consisted of levels, he said, each one semi-independent from the levels above and below. "At each stage, entirely new laws, concepts and generalizations are necessary, requiring inspiration and creativity to just as great a degree as the previous one. . . . Psychology is not applied biology, nor is biology applied chemistry" (p. 209). The claim of some scientists that everything could ultimately be reduced to nuclear physics was therefore patently wrong.

Shortly thereafter, Anderson received support from Herbert Simon (1973), in the first chapter of a book, *Hierarchy Theory—the Challenge of Complex Systems*:

> One can show on quite simple and general grounds that the time required for a complex system, containing k elementary components, say, to evolve by processes of natural selection from those components is very much shorter if the system is itself comprised of one or more layers of stable component subsystems than if its elementary parts are its only stable components. The mathematics of the matter is a straightforward exercise in probabilities . . . (p. 7)

So emerging patterns and systems evolved other patterns and systems on a higher level, which evolved still other patterns and systems on a still higher level, and so on. The relation between the levels was asymmetrical; the higher levels resulted from the lower levels, but could not be reduced to them. This type of system had a dual advantage. Because there was no one-on-one relationship between the levels, they were less vulnerable to errors and minor damage; they could cope and adapt. Also, they were able to evolve: They could deal with entirely new situations. But there also was a reverse side: Problematic patterns could be very persistent.

Computer scientist John Holland stated in a paper, and later in a book about *Hidden Order—How Adaptation Builds Complexity* (quoted in Horgan, 1996):

> Many of our most troubling long-range problems—trade imbalances, sustainability, AIDS, genetic defects, mental health, computer viruses—center on certain systems of extraordinary complexity. The systems that host these problems—economies, ecologies, immune systems, embryos, nervous systems, computer networks—appear to be as diverse as the problems. Despite appearances, however, the systems do share significant characteristics, so much that we group them under a single classification at the Santa Fe institute, calling them complex adaptive systems (CAS). This is more than terminology. It signals our intuition that there are general principles that govern all CAS behavior, principles that point to ways of solving the attendant problems. (pp. 195–196)

Regularity and Uncertainty

One of the most controversial points concerning CAS is the question of to what extent it makes sense at this point to develop mathematical formulas, statistical calculations, and computer models of their behavior. It certainly makes sense insofar as they help gain further insight in certain, well-defined, subprocesses. But it is sometimes premature, if they claim to recast chaos and complexity in a deterministic mold and to generate precise predictions for real life. Because one may surely identify a number of global regularities in many of these processes, but one can usually not eliminate the final uncertainties. This holds even stronger for the sciences of man and society.

Models of military interventions, or stock market crashes, or issues of management can not provide complete certainties, because it is fundamentally impossible to incorporate all the relevant factors into all of the relevant detail. Even more so, because the existence and even initial success of such models would subsequently change the behavior of the key players, for instance, by making them either more prudent or more self-confident. Human behavior is reflexive, and therefore different from other natural processes. Furthermore, social actions are nested in moving patterns of relevant contexts. That is to say, no two situations are entirely identical, and one should be careful in trusting "eternal laws." The fact that certain things have in the past always turned out in a certain way does not in itself guarantee that will hold in the future.

I have taken so much time to speak about CAS because I feel these same global principles do also apply to psychosocial science. The brain and the mind are CAS of staggering subtlety (see Eiser, 1994; Robertson & Combs, 1995; Vallacher & Nowak, 1994). Groups and networks are, too (see Kiel & Elliott, 1996; Leydesdorff, 1993, 1997; Luhmann, 1984/1995). Where social psychology and psychosociology meet, these systems interact. More than any other subdisciplines, mass psychology and collective behavior sociology have always made it their business to study the emergence of alternate patterns. But let us first take a closer look at some of the key communication processes involved.

2

The Continuous Mutation of Informal Messages

When two men communicate with each other by word of mouth, there is a twofold hazard in that communication.
—Senator Sam Ervin (Faber, 1980, p. 7)

Many ideas grow better when transplanted into another mind than in the one where they sprang up.
—Oliver Wendell Holmes, Jr. (Gross, 1987, p. 231)

This chapter is about informal communication, the everyday conversations during which we receive, transform, and pass on information. The first section describes a noteworthy example: a rumor that kidnappings of little children did periodically occur in the light, clean, and happy environment of Disneyland. The phenomena of "hearsay" are further analyzed in the second section, which discusses rumor and gossip. Some present-day versions are called "urban folklore" or "urban legends." The third section asks the question: What is so fundamental about these examples of informal communication (which are often intertwined with the more formal communication of the mass media)? One of the key aspects is that it inserts an element of "continuous mutation" into the vast ocean of mutual exchange. Stories we tell each other change all the time. Some variations do better, spread, and multiply, whereas others fade away.

CASE NUMBER TWO: THE HAPPY DISNEY FAMILY

Let us begin at the beginning. D'Isigny is a village on the Normandy coastline. One of the villagers joined the troops of William the Conqueror in the invasion of England, and founded the new village of Disney (near Coventry). Descendants later turned up in Ireland and in the United States. The best-known descendant was Walt Disney, founder of the largest company in the world that specialized in the development, illustration, retelling, and filming of children's stories.

Disney's genius was not so much that he made such good comic strips or cartoon movies, because other artists often contributed more literary and pictorial creativity to them. Disney's genius was that he was the first person in world history who knew how to organize the ongoing mass production of popular children's culture. It is true that he did develop some new characters himself, such as Mickey Mouse and Donald Duck. But neither did he hesitate to pillage all great classics of European children's literature, and paraphrase their characters. Alice of Carroll, Cinderella of Perrault, Bambi of Salten, the Beauty and the Beast of Madame Leprince de Beaumont, the Sleeping Beauty of Perrault, the Little Mermaid of Andersen, Mowgli of Kipling, Peter Pan of Barrie, Pinocchio of Collodi, Snow-White of the Grimm brothers, Winnie the Pooh of Milne. Anyone who had the guts to paraphrase his paraphrases thereafter, could count on a lawsuit for plagiarism. That is great business genius.

According to unauthorized biographies such as Marc Eliot's (1993) about *Hollywood's Dark Prince*, there was a curious resonance between the classical themes of children's literature and Walt Disney's own private tragedies. Disney was obsessed with "the happy little family." His father was abusive. Eliot claims that Walt Disney later wondered whether he had been adopted, and started a secret search for his true biological mother. His own relationship to his wife, daughters, and work was rather stereotypical. His youngest daughter was also adopted, but this was kept a secret from the outside world. Disney demanded unconditional devotion of his collaborators. After his first major animated cartoon success *Snow-White*, some of his most dramatic productions were about related archetypal themes: abandoned children, absent fathers and present stepmothers—in short, incomplete and unhappy families.

The most profitable part of the company, and the crown on his work, was the creation of a fantasy universe from which all nightmares had been banned and in which all dreams came true. At that time, he had already sold 1 billion movie tickets, and 130,000,000 comic books, so he had created a considerable audience for himself (Eliot, 1993). In 1955, he opened Disneyland, close to a major traffic junction in Anaheim, and not too far from Los Angeles. Its artery was "Mainstreet, USA," an idealized cardboard version of the little town in which he had grown up. Beyond it lay some fantasy lands, which embodied various stages in the history of civilization as he saw it. The virgin forests of Adventureland, the wild west of Frontierland, and later, a science fiction world in Tomorrowland.

Disneyland was surrounded by a kind of embankment, an earthen wall, which hid the ugly outside world from view. The inner environment was totally controlled. Clean-up teams collected all dirt; the few droppings of the horses were cleared right away. Personnel was obliged to adhere to an extremely strict appearance code. No long hair, beards, or moustaches for men. No wild hairdos, conspicuous make-up, or abundant jewels for women. A security service saw to it that antisocial elements were kept out, and that lost children would soon be returned. Pictures in promotional flyers were selected and retouched to show only clear blue skies and happy smiling faces.

Disney advertised his fantasy universe emphatically as "the happiest place on earth." Happy families should be able to spend a day (or more), mired in an enchanting world of juvenile innocence; because even adults carried this naiveté within them. "The worst of us is not without innocence, although buried deeply it might be," Disney said. "In my work, I try to reach and speak to that innocence." Disneyland thus became a kind of pharaonic monument, "dedicated to the happy childhood he never had" (Eliot, 1993, pp. VII, XXI).

But the consistent cultivation of this artificial image somehow provoked a dark reaction. It was, in the words of Freud, the inevitable return of the repressed; that is to say, of Disney's own nightmares of lost and lonely children, unhappy and incomplete families, vulnerable to Evil. A 1970's collection of urban legends noted that a strange rumor made the rounds throughout the western part of the United States (Brunvand, 1981). When parents had been distracted for a moment, a child was said to have been kidnapped in a major theme park. According to some versions, it was a White child kidnapped by Black adults or vice versa; according to other versions, it had to do with illegal adoption, organ transplants, or child pornography.

The story had first circulated among pious Mormon families in Utah, often blessed with many children, for whom an excursion to a worldly theme park was an exciting event. The rumor was not only about Disneyland in Anaheim, but also about other theme parks close by, such as Lagoon in Salt Lake City. Further inquiries at daily newspapers and broadcasting stations in the region turned up no reports of such incidents. But many people appeared to have heard the story and to consider it true. Every now and then, the story disappeared from sight, and then reappeared.

This did not keep Disneyland from continuing to be a great hit, even after Walt Disney himself had died. In 1971, a second, larger theme park, Disneyworld, was opened on the east coast, near Orlando, Florida. In 1982, it was further extended, adding the Epcot center; in 1989, with the Disney MGM studios; so that one could spend several days, a week, or even an entire holiday on the spot. But with all this, the limits of growth for the United States had more or less been reached. In 1983, therefore, a Tokyo Disneyland was opened in Japan. After that, possible sites were surveyed in Europe in England, Germany, Spain, and Italy.

In France, a popular front of socialists and communists had just come to power under President Mitterand, and Culture Minister Jack Lang called for a worldwide boycott of American cultural imperialism. French communication scientist Armand Mattelart had earlier published a resounding critique of the conservative or even reactionary slant of many Donald Duck stories, along with Chilean sociologist Ariel Dorfman who had worked for the popular front government of Salvador Allende, later evicted by a military coup, covertly aided and abetted by the American CIA (Dorfman & Mattelart, 1975).

But in the course of the 1980s the tide had turned. Disney had come to the conclusion that a location near Paris would be the best option after all, whereas the French socialists had meanwhile learned that it might not be such a bad idea to encourage foreign investment with attractive conditions. Yet social resistance to the project remained considerable, ranging from populist groups to the cultural elite. The famous theatrical and film director, Ariane Mnouchkine, called the opening of Eurodisneyland near Paris in 1992 a "cultural Chernobyl." The inauguration was preceded, accompanied, and followed by a string of conflicts with the trade unions over strict dress rules, over the alcohol ban in and near the park, over the official language of the park, and so forth. But a large part of the resistance remained underground.

Rumors about mysterious disappearances of adult tourists in Paris had already been making the rounds in mid-1992, according to a study by Véronique Campion-Vincent (1992). But within 2 weeks after the opening of the theme park, these rumors were suddenly about the kidnapping of children in Eurodisneyland. The newspaper *Salzburger Nachrichten* reported on July 25, that a children's trip had been cancelled because of the scare. Austrian researcher Wilhelm Brednich received a first letter indicating that a child had been lost in the park, and later found with a kidney removed. A newspaper in Sweden reported on August 8 that there had been several similar cases, which Disney was supposed to have tried to try and hush up. "But they would deny it anyway, even if it were true, wouldn't they?" people asked. And also, "Why would someone make such a weird story up, if it were not true?" (This type of reasoning often followed similar cases).

In 1993, the story turned up in Switzerland; mid-1994, the story was revived in The Netherlands. A provincial paper reported a disappearance from a family that had even won its trip to the park. A Belgian newspaper reported about the disappearance of a boy 13 years old; the Disney spokesperson was said to have reacted to inquiries in an irritated way. In a collection of urban legend stories, Dutch researcher Peter Burger (1995) reprinted a letter he had received about a couple that had lost their son right after arriving in the park. "At closing time they found him on a bench, deep asleep. After failing to wake him up, they brought him to a hospital. Which found that he was still under narcosis, from the surgical removal of a kidney" (Burger, 1995, p. 51). After this, the rumor faded again in The Netherlands. But 2 years later, it made a spectacular comeback.

On September 28, 1996, the morning paper *De Volkskrant* published a shocking full-page report with similar stories. The report quoted a German couple (identified by name and details), who said their daughter had been kidnapped in Eurodisneyland. She had only been found the next day, near an elevator; half-conscious, in an adult bathrobe, with make-up and a darkened skin, her hair cut, and in a different color. She had refused to talk, and had reportedly remained disturbed for many months. She only said her kidnapper had had a moustache. It was unclear what had happened, but the article suggested a link with sexual abuse. It also mentioned a Flemish girl, to whom something similar had happened. A Disney spokesman, identified by name, was reported to have confirmed that such incidents occurred once a month, on average.

As is often the case, reporters for other media tried to follow up on the story. The staff of a missing persons TV show went to look for the victims and the spokesman, but could not locate them. The original story had been written by a Flemish freelance journalist, who had built a reputation in recent years, with colorful reports for major papers. Gradually it turned out, that many of his characters and sources could not be traced and had most probably been based on hearsay. Certain specific details in the kidnapping story could be traced back to an archetypal version of the rumor found in the book *Het Volkslied* (The Anthem) by Christine Vetter, published in 1911! In spite of Disney denials, *De Volkskrant* initially stood by its man; only 8 weeks later did it correct the mistake and offer apologies.

In my view, there are many reasons why the age-old kidnapping rumor took on this form in these circumstances, and found a considerable following. The coupling of the story with the prime brand name Disney (rather than with some lesser known park) made it more interesting, and easier to pass on. It also resonated with the latent resistance against the global dominance of American cultural products. The contrast between the "innocent" world of Disney and child abuse, gave the story extra spice, just like the contrast between the "total control" of the theme park, and the farfetched nature of the event. Think of the fact that the only detail the German girl had remembered was that the kidnapper had a moustache (a clear indication of "loose character," according to the aforementioned Disney appearance code).

Other elements probably played a role, too. Paris (even more than Los Angeles) has the reputation of being a sinful city, particularly among lower class day tourists from provincial areas. But there was increasing public concern over sexual child abuse and pornography during these very same years. In the course of the same year, 1996, Belgium had been in the grips of a huge scandal about real-life child abductions by suspected pedophile rings. Belgium was also characterized by the ongoing conflict between its Germanic/Flanders region (home of both the freelance journalist and one of his supposed sources), and its Latin/Wallony region (home of the pedophile ring and major corruption scandals).

Further analysis may yield a number of other elements. But what interests us here is primarily that both the story and its context are "dynamic configurations," which resonate in various ways with each other. The result is a kind of "collective moulding" process, which transforms existing elements and existing story lines into some kind of best fit. Poor stories will spread poorly and may not even survive, whereas good stories will spread and survive successfully until they entirely dominate the field. Of course this is largely a blind process of variation and selection. An appropriate rumor may travel continents and survive decades, and even turn up as a media report every now and then. But what is a rumor really, and how does it spread?

THE PHENOMENON OF HEARSAY

First of all, the Disney rumor tells us something about communication. It is through communication that we submit propositions about what is true, real, and important to each other, negotiate these claims, and reach partial agreement or not. This holds for formal mass communication, whether news or fiction (van Ginneken, 1998). But it holds even more for informal individual communication, which precedes, accompanies, and follows it. Our daily interaction may be inconspicuous and taken for granted, yet the entire psychosocial process is rooted in it.

Peter Berger and Thomas Luckmann (1981) formulated it like this, in their important study about *The Social Construction of Reality*:

> The most important vehicle of reality-maintenance is conversation. One may view the individual's everyday life in terms of the working away of a conversational apparatus that ongoingly maintains, modifies and reconstructs his subjective reality . . . It is important to stress, however, that the greater part of reality-maintenance in conversation is implicit, not explicit. Most conversation does not in so many words define the nature of the world. Rather, it takes place against the background of a world that is silently taken for granted. (p. 172)

So we live in a world of listening and talking, of hearing and saying, in a world of hearsay. If someone says, "I have it from hearsay," we would suppose that the status of the information is not entirely certain; the information comes from others, who have it from others, who have it from still others. At first sight, the source is "just around the corner," a friend of a friend, an acquaintance of an acquaintance. But on closer inspection, the chain turns out to be much longer. The quest for the original source takes us into the haze at the horizon, and then beyond. It turns out the information may have been under way for years or decades. Yet much of our views of the world are based on such uncertain information.

In the course of time, the sciences of man and society have gradually focused on various forms of hearsay; on the one hand, phenomena such as gossip and rumor, which have been studied for 50 years or more. On the other hand, on phenomena such as urban folklore and urban legends, which have been studied in recent decades. In the former case, the emphasis of studies was often on the negative aspects and social dangers of gossip and rumor, because of the misinformation involved (e.g., in times of crisis and war). In the latter case of urban folklore and legends, the emphasis was more often on the positive aspects and stimulating nature because of the interaction involved. But in fact they are rather similar and closely related, and lie at the very basis of all social life. Although they usually deal with seemingly trivial matters, these forms of hearsay affect fundamental aspects of world view and group formation.

Gossip and Rumor

Forms of hearsay that have been identified since the dawn of history, and in the West, since antiquity, are gossip and rumor. When two people talk about an absent third one, they also redefine his or her social status. Gossip conversation today is fed by some kind of gossip media. The main subjects are social celebrities with whom we are made to feel familiar by the media. The events discussed are their success and failure in careers and personal lives. The media emphasizes that these celebrities are ordinary people just like us, for better and for worse.

The word "rumor" literally refers to "vague indefinable noises." Rumors can be seen as unverified and unauthorized information; unauthorized or non-authoritative for at least three reasons. First, the original author of a rumor is usually not known. Second, the author is usually not the appropriate authority to make official statements about the matter. And third, because the rumor is often explicitly at odds with authorized information. (On all three counts, there often is a suggestion of the opposite, but that is not essential). Rumors do often attempt to fill in the obvious holes in authorized information, point to the inconsistencies in it, and explore deeper layers of this information.

The first empirical social science research into rumors was linked to World War I, and even more, World War II, because rumors could play into the hands of the enemy, but also into the hands of allies or neutral parties; for instance, by boosting or sapping morale of civilians, the belief in the just cause, and in the inevitability of final triumph. Propaganda and counter propaganda, media manipulation and disinformation, so-called political and psychological warfare, were (and are) aimed at persuading relevant populations. Rumors can play a great role in this game: whether they arise spontaneously or are subtly encouraged (van Ginneken, 1998).

The first substantial American overview, *The Psychology of Rumor*, by Gordon Allport and Leo Postman (1947), was published just after the end of World War II. They observed that rumors filled a need for information and clarity. They also developed the basic formula $R \sim i \times a$. Or: the intensity of a rumor R is a function of the importance i (for the people conversing) and the ambiguity a (of the information available from other sources). They also claimed that the "passing on" of a rumor was subject to a process of "serial distortion" (to which we return), of repeated slanting.

Another study said that there were five conditions promoting the rapid spread of rumors. First of all, the rumor should be vivid enough to impress a person's memory. Second, it should evoke powerful emotions. Third, it should fit an established set of cultural expectations. Fourth, it should be plausible. And fifth, it cannot be forcefully refuted by an authoritative source (Hartmann, quoted in Perry & Pugh, 1978). All this obviously held for the aforementioned Disney rumor, in its many different guises.

Later studies further elaborated these same themes. In his book, *Improvised News*, sociologist Tamotsu Shibutani (1966) emphasized that people use rumors to develop alternative "collective definitions" of the situation. In their book, *Rumor and Gossip*, psychologists Ralph Rosnow and Gary Allen Fine (1976) emphasized that other parameters should be entered into the equation; for instance, the personality of the communicators and the nature of the context. It is obvious that these, too, affect the urge and the need to pass such stories on.

Rumor research did not limit itself to the United States; some interesting studies were done in other countries, such as France. Sociologist Edgar Morin (1969) wrote an elaborate case study of *La Rumeur d'Orléans*. It was a story about girls disappearing into trapdoors behind fitting rooms in fashion shops "run by foreigners." After which they would be entered into the Middle Eastern trade in "White [women] slaves." In spite of official denials, the rumor kept circulating. After it disappeared from one provincial town, the rumor turned up in another, and so on. Communication scientist Jean-Noël Kapferer (1990) later published the overview *Rumors*, which showed how certain themes generated an endless string of variations; for instance, the story that children in supermarkets had been bitten by large spiders or small snakes, hidden in banana boxes. The overall pattern of such rumors has several elements in common. There is a vulnerable group, in an anonymous environment, which is threatened by "alien" elements.

Older rumor research was primarily about the 3Cs: conflict, crisis and catastrophe. Newer rumor research, by contrast, is more about the 2Cs: commerce and celebrity; companies, shops, and products, and famous personalities. A well-known example of the latter was the notorious rumor that Beatle Paul McCartney had died in an accident, and had been replaced by a double because "the show must go on." A long list of clues and indications were brought to the public's attention. Older rumor research was often about essential political and social themes. Newer rumor research is often about seemingly trivial economic matters. But let us not forget that in both cases, major institutions may be involved with considerable interests at stake. They may sponsor ad hoc research projects, when their reputation is seriously put in jeopardy.

Rumors about brands, for instance, have become an increasingly noteworthy category. The financial value of brand names is today estimated at many billions of dollars, and a damaging rumor may cost millions. So there is a growing interest in these phenomena. An American overview of the field was *Rumor in the Marketplace*, by Fredrick Koenig (1985; also see Van Schravendijk, 1995). A chapter in my earlier smaller Dutch book about crazes and crashes (1993b) discussed rumors about such huge corporations as Procter & Gamble and McDonalds. My conclusion was that the existing literature and established consultants often tend to overlook one factor, which I labeled the "boomerang" effect.

Somehow, "reaction formation" is one of the key processes in chaos and complexity. Commercial rumors are often spontaneous reactions against elements that are somehow over, or underrepresented in official campaigns. Think of the Disney example. Specific elements of the rumor often resonate with marginal cues in the name or logo of the brand, the history or claims of the company, the nature and 'unnaturalness' of the product, the wider social and cultural environment, and so forth. For example, the three red surfaces on a package of Marlboro cigarettes can be read as KKK—an indication that the company is somehow linked to the Ku Klux Klan. Consider also the three curls in the original Procter & Gamble logo, which were interpreted as the number 666, and thus seen as a sign that the company was possibly owned by the devil himself! It often takes a rumor expert to decode these hidden hints, and to propose adaptations to established communication strategies.

Folklore and Legends

Another type of gossip and rumors, for which there has been a growing interest in recent decades, is in the field of folklore and legends. Many universities have departments for the study of folklore and legends, for instance, in their history and language departments. Originally, such departments were focused on the painfully detailed registration of the last surviving elements of old traditions and stories, whose origins could be traced to the countryside and outlying provinces. But gradually researchers realized that they tended to overlook another category of stories, that was both closer and more interesting; the Disney rumor is one such story.

The category was labeled *urban folklore* or *urban legends*, and has the following characteristics. First of all, they are stories situated in the here and now, or at least in the near environment and recent past. Second, the main characters are people just like you and me, and the implication is that these things could happen to any one of us. Third, what is related is usually an exceptional event that strikes the imagination. But there are other characteristics as well. Because fourth, they usually have a clear story line: a beginning, a middle, and an end. They have a plot or "point," often with a horror aspect. Fifth, in spite of their exceptional nature, they are still somehow plausible; one should be able to believe that it really happened. This impression is often reinforced by certain vivid details as in the aforementioned *Volkskrant* case of the girl supposedly kidnapped in Euro Disneyland. Sixth, the story is unverified but seems verifiable. Here, too, it is often said to originate with "a friend of friend." Seven, the story is mostly passed on through informal communication (conversation), although it may occasionally pop up in formal communication (the media) as well.

Finally, the story often has an implicit moral message. It warns against the invisible risks of modern life. Urban folklore and urban legends are a format that the public has evolved to express its hidden fears and taboo wishes, to submit them to others, and to consider and transform them. So they are the result of some kind of implicit, "collective deliberation" process. A classical example is the following. On a business trip, a male manager is seduced by an attractive lady. When he wakes up the next morning, he discovers a scar and a check. Apparently, a kidney had been surgically removed for the organ trade. There are all kinds of different versions of this story. The story "lives," so to say; it couples with other similar stories, it reproduces itself, and then produces offspring.

The best-known researcher in this new field of urban legends is Jan Harold Brunvand of the university of Utah. In 1981, he published his first collection of stories entitled, *The Vanishing Hitchhiker*. We have already mentioned the fact that it contained an earlier version of the Disney story, which turned up in Europe more than 10 years later. It was followed by other best-seller collections, and even by a comic strip book that illustrated the best-known stories. In The Netherlands, the writer Ethel Portnoy (1978) had earlier floated the label *monkey sandwich* stories for the phenomenon (also see Burger, 1992, 1996, 1997). Today, there even is an international society and a scientific journal for the study of the field of urban legends. A lot of knowledge has been accumulated.

So how do these stories evolve? Take the various versions of the "kidnapping" story. After the 1967–1968 race riots in Detroit, for instance, a story made the rounds that a mother had lost her young son in a supermarket, and later found him back in the toilets . . . castrated. In a version passed on by White people, the victim was White and the perpetrators were Black. In a version passed on by Black people, the opposite was true (Perry & Pugh, 1978). In his collection *The Mexican Pet*, Jan Brunvand (1986) related that at one point, a boy named Adam Walsh had really disappeared in a toy store. Major broadcasting network ABC ordered a "movie of the week" about this, which was broadcast in October, 1983. Since those days, such rumors have persistently turned up around the chain Toys R Us, and other supermarket chains. Meanwhile, the Chicago juvenile police department had picked up the story, and passed it on. According to this version, a girl had been found back in the toilet, in other clothes, with her hair cut and colored (just as in one of the later Eurodisney stories).

So urban legends about kidnapping vary along different dimensions. A first dimension is that of the victims: the small child, the beautiful young woman, or the businessman. A second dimension is that of the environment in which the evil deed takes place. Usually it is some kind of modern-day, large-scale, anonymous environment: a parking lot, a supermarket, a shopping mall, a theme park, or a hotel. It is an alien or strange environment, with strangers, often in another town or country. A third dimension is that of the implied purpose of the kidnapping: illegal adoption (for kids), the White slave trade (for young women), or organ theft (for adult businessmen and others).

During the late 1980s and early 1990s, for instance, there were recurrent rumors and media reports about kidnapping of children for illegal adoption or organ theft in Central and South America, with dates and places, names and details. There were even several television documentaries about these kidnappings. One French documentary received several prizes, and was shown worldwide. I later remembered seeing it myself at the time, without a shadow of doubt as to its authenticity. Meanwhile, several of these stories have been checked, for instance, by French expert Véronique Campion-Vincent (1997; see her well-researched 1997 French book, *Legends of Organ Theft*, and a related 1997 English article), and also by the Dutch expert Peter Burger (see his 1997 English article in *The Skeptic*). One "eye-witness" report after the other collapses, until little is left. This does not mean that nothing like this has ever happened, or may not still happen. But usually such "real events" are much more ambiguous than claimed.

Between the various categories of kidnapping stories, then, all kind of combinations and permutations are possible. One could make a kind of Rubik's cube, based on the three dimensions of three categories each, resulting in 27 possible combinations of key elements. An addition of three more would make the number rise to 81, and of still three more to 243. So there is a huge number of variations. New successful variations would probably resonate with the spirit of the times. The older variation of White women being abducted to be sold to some Middle Eastern harem, for instance, is rather 1950s and a bit outdated by now. But the newer variation of little children being abducted to be cast in pornographic movies, was much more 1990s.

Real-life events drew media and public attention to this possibility. Every parent considering even the faintest chance that his or her child could be abducted for such purposes would find it hard to put aside. It may easily become an obsessive thought, returning time and again. So apart from the few well-documented cases that have led to court cases, there are tens or hundreds of stories that might be true, but usually are not. They have enough concrete details, however, to be believable. Think of the recurring stories about "satanic sects" protected by people in high places. In a general environment of outrage over a hideous crime, such stories flourish. We briefly return to the subject of "moral panics," in the second section of chapter 9.

Worldview and Group Formation

Phenomena like gossip and rumor and urban folklore and legends are phenomena of continuous mutation. This process is not characterized as one message passed on from one person to the next; it is a whole series of such events, running parallel to each other, interfering with each other, alternately slowing down and speeding up each other. This is what makes informal communication a kind of "parallel distributed processing" within a CAS, with its eternal repetition of the Darwinian processes of variation and selection.

In principle, this type of reasoning about "why and how" stories spread can also be applied to the development of other beliefs and belief systems and of successive creeds and ideologies that have ruled the history of mankind. Just as with rumors and legends, one might surmise that specific aspects of great creeds somehow make them more effective reproducers. One might try to argue, for instance, which notions were easier to spread during earlier ages: those of a concrete personal God or of an abstract Divine principle, of many different Gods or one only, of heaven or hell. One might try to argue the paradoxical effects of celibacy; although the propagator of the faith does not propagate him- or herself, he or she may devote more energy to the propagation itself, and thereby be more successful (Dawkins, 1976).

A book by Aaron Lynch (1996) tried to argue why certain key elements in the three great Mediterranean religions were so successful, for example, Judaism, Christianity, and Islam; not only ideas about being chosen to convert others, but also about marriage and procreation, and about education and authority. And about how (within certain climate zones and protein production modes) the "do's and don'ts" of food and hygiene led to the survival and spreading of the believers. Or take the idea of martyrdom; the idea that whoever is willing to give his or her life for the good cause will be greatly honored and rewarded—if not in this life, then in an afterlife. This belief may not contribute to the survival of the individual, but it certainly contributes to the survival of the collective whole; and thereby to the survival of other beliefs linked to this particular one.

In his book about good and evil, *The Lucifer Principle*, Howard Bloom (1995) even went a step further. He tries to demonstrate that such key thoughts also welded together the secular ideologies of all great movements and empires. Along these lines, one may try to argue how specific notions contributed to the spread of new civilizations, and to the "total resource mobilization," which made the new civilizations triumph over older ones. One such notion is of course the idea of 'civilization' itself; some feeling of moral superiority, which also makes it necessary either to convert or to crush the "barbarians."

Of course such theorizing may take one in a more or less social-Darwinistic direction, but one could just as well give such trends a different meaning. Over recent decades, we have heard arguments about the biological survival value of genetic predispositions to egotism versus altruism. Similarly, one might argue about the survival value of cultural predispositions to "particularism" versus "universalism." Nationalist feelings remain surprisingly strong, for instance, but in the long run, some kind of internationalism or globalism seems to be gaining ground. Elitist feelings remain surprisingly strong, but in the long run, some kind of meritocracy or egalitarianism seems to be gaining ground. A very effective variation may be saying one thing and doing the next, although even this kind of dishonesty may eventually be counterproductive. In the long run, the autocrats have been losing ground, whereas the ideologies of "*liberté, égalité, fraternité*," of "one man, one vote" have ultimately been able to mobilize greater numbers and stronger alliances. But how do ideas and feelings spread? Do some of the newer theories provide alternative insights?

THE METAPRINCIPLE OF CONTINUOUS MUTATION

This chapter looks at information and the ways in which it is conveyed. In the case of the Disney rumor and other urban legends, information (or misinformation) spreads widely and rapidly, without the mass media necessarily playing a role. Which metaprinciples are involved here? Over the years it has gradually become apparent, that information may be even more fundamental to the organization and reorganization of the universe, than the matter and energy that holds and communicates the information. Information has been aptly described as "any difference which makes a difference" (Bateson, 1984). One may also describe information and the communication of information as a variation that "proposes" itself for selection (also see Luhmann, 1995). So entities within complex adaptive systems may react to each other, and to entities within other complex adaptive systems; that is to say, undergo minor changes that are reactions to other minor changes.

Within a public, audience, or group, these may for instance be thoughts, feelings, and behaviors. This section considers the various ways in which these thoughts and behaviors may affect each other, and how this has been conceptualized over the years. It is an exploration of older and newer views of this problem, and investigates whether complexity theory may provide other clues, other types of reasoning, which may lead to alternative insights. We once again do so by closely scrutinizing the various metaphors employed or implied.

One of the reproaches that might be made, of course, is that this book and author employ too many metaphors to make their points, because metaphors and analogies are not proof. They may just help to make something plausible or imaginable, which otherwise might not be. But this reproach tends to overlook the fact that the conventional wisdom of the sciences of man and society is itself interspersed with a myriad of metaphors hardly seen and understood as such. Certain words and images have become so common that we fail to notice their original meaning. A key example is the word "mechanism," which is widely used in contexts where the broader word, "process," might be much more appropriate—sometimes even in otherwise innovative books themselves (see, e.g., De Loof, 1996). The former word implies linearity and proportionality, whereas the latter word might also imply nonlinearity and turbulent change. Another example is the word "instrument" (e.g., in the context of "measurement"). In this way, such authors put themselves and their readers on the wrong foot from the start.

One series of processes that is often misconstrued by the uncritical use of such metaphors are those concerning the ways in which "messages" and "states" may be conveyed to each other by individuals within a group. It has often been noted within the field of mass psychology and collective behavior sociology that some people seem to be able to actually "infect" others with their feelings and moods. Sometimes the authors mean something like transmission or diffusion taking place, sometimes identification, imitation, suggestion, facilitation, or still other processes. Even closely related theories use the word "contagion" in a widely varying sense (compare, e.g., Turner & Killian, 1987; K. Lang & G. E. Lang, 1961; and Smelser, 1962, in this context). "Contagion" has become an unclassifiable term, whereas it originally carried a very specific meaning).

So it is useful to try and become more alert to such words, to track their etymology, the circumstances of their introduction into the sciences of man and society, and their respective strengths and weaknesses in helping us focus on (or get distracted from) key processes involved. In this section, therefore, we undertake a closer examination of four "families" of terms that are often used to denote ways in which people seem to convey thoughts, feelings, and actions to each other—for instance, in the case of the Disney rumor. We begin with the simplest, one-dimensional approach, and conclude with a more complicated multidimensional approach. So first we discuss the term, *transmission*, second, *diffusion*, third, *contagion*, and last, *mutation*. We use this latter term as a stepping stone to the newly proposed notion of "memes," which may help to throw some further light on the gossip and rumor and urban folklore and legends discussed in the previous sections.

Transmission

The first metaphor, or the first metaphorical model, which is widely used in this context, is the *transmission model*. It originates from technically oriented information theory. Within the sciences of man and society, it is particularly current within my current discipline—the science of communication. The model is highly one-dimensional, which may sometimes be an advantage, sometimes a disadvantage. An advantage because it chooses the simplest possible representation, to disassemble communication acts into their various parts and aspects. A disadvantage, because it is implicitly highly elementarist and reductionist, and abstracts from context. Although communication scientists usually feel they see that trap, they often end up falling into it anyway, somewhere down the line. Because they have themselves put on the wrong track by the transmission model's hidden assumptions.

Technically oriented information theory had already emerged around telegraphy and radiography during the pre-war period, but received a real boost during World War II. Claude Shannon and Warren Weaver worked at the research laboratory of the American Bell telephone company. After some earlier drafts, they published *The Mathematical Theory of Communication* in 1949. The basic model identified an "information source" with a "message," which a "sender" would transform into a "signal," which was conveyed through a "medium" (with "noise" interfering or not). This signal would then be picked up by a "receiver," which would bring it to its "destination."

Around that same time, political scientist Harold Lasswell used classical rhetoric to pose the key question of social communication: Who says What to Whom, using Which channel and with What effect? This rule of thumb identified five elements, one for each finger of the hand; namely, the source or sender, the signal or message, the medium or channel, the receiver or destination, and "the difference that made a difference" (in thoughts, feelings or actions). In line with this general approach, communication science tended to organize into five main domains: control, content and audience analysis, media, and effect analysis (O'Sullivan, Hartley, Saunders, & Fiske, 1989).

But gradually it became clear, that the model was too limited and needed further elaboration. First, R. Braddock proposed to add two more elements to the "Who–What" question, namely, "Under what circumstances?" and "For what purpose?" This brought the number from five to seven. Then George Gerbner extended the number of elements to 10. Finally, Melvin de Fleur doubled the process by introducing feedback. The problem was, of course, that the simple elegance of the original model was somehow spoiled by all these additions and conditions, and thus it lost its heuristic value (see the overview in McQuail & Windahl, 1993).

So the dilemma remained. On one hand, the model can well be used to analyze various stages and aspects of the communication process—as I have done in my previous book, *Understanding Global News* (van Ginneken, 1998). But at the same time one should always remain alert to the hidden implications of what I ironically call, "the PTT model;" namely, that information is a kind of unequivocal "thing," which is transported unidirectionally from point A to point B, where it must arrive undamaged. The Disney rumor and urban legends demonstrate that this is not always an appropriate approximation of what really happens.

Diffusion

The second metaphor, or the second metaphorical model, which is used widely in this context, is the *diffusion* (or *distribution*) *model*. It originates from our representations of fluid dynamics. The ways in which a solvent spreads in water, the ways in which a movement spreads in water, the ways in which water itself spreads in streams and circles; these are the images evoked. Within the sciences of man and society, the metaphor is widely used in the framework of the sociology and anthropology of innovation processes. It is not so much a one-dimensional but rather a two-dimensional model. Because it looks at how new ideas and practices "spread" on the surface of society.

A predecessor of this whole approach was the underestimated, late 19th century French criminologist, Gabriel Tarde. In his early and partially unpublished works, and in his later book on *Universal Contradiction*, he developed a cosmology of the ubiquity of difference, which foreshadowed many of the later theories on chaos and complexity discussed in this book. His best-known work on *The Laws of Imitation* sketched an image of how various currents of sameness and otherness criss-crossed through society, confronted and altered each other, and were channeled and dammed in by other forces; and how they were characterized by the threefold stages of invention, imitation and opposition (somewhat comparable to Hegel's well-known thesis, antithesis, and synthesis). The evolution of these opinion currents, he said, followed certain laws: they streamed from high to low, from inside to outside, and so forth. In his later studies, Tarde developed pioneer conceptualizations of mutual interaction, opinions, and attitudes, social and economic psychology—which had little direct influence in France, but much more indirect influence in the United States (see van Ginneken, 1992a).

Early 20th century diffusion studies primarily considered why certain primitive ideas, practices, and tools persisted within certain groups, and how more modern ideas, practices, and tools often came to be adopted only very gradually. That was a central question within ethnology and anthropology, but also within developmental and rural sociology. It was also a central question in the fields of popular education and popular health, government information, and product marketing. What factors played a role?

A rather complete overview of such studies can be found in Everett Roger's book *Diffusion of Innovations*, which has become (and remained) a classic. Its first edition appeared in 1962, a revised edition in 1971, a third revised edition in 1983, and a fourth revised edition in 1995. Rogers defined diffusion as "the process by which an innovation is communicated through certain channels over time among the members of a social system" (p. 5). These four elements were then thoroughly analyzed one after the other. He distinguished eight types of research focused respectively on earliness of knowing, rate of adoption of different innovations in a social system, innovativeness, opinion leadership, diffusion networks, rate of adoption in different social systems, communication channel use, and consequences of innovation. Even the diffusion of diffusion studies itself was not forgotten.

Rogers' (1995) study, and the earlier studies that were discussed therein, form a very rich source of observations on processes of diffusion. Yet they, and similar studies from the field of science dynamics, throw only limited light on the rapid, radical, and massive shifts in public opinion and perceptions that are our own main concern here; because they place disproportionate emphasis on material objects and practices with "objective" advantages, which were soon recognized by a "well-informed" group, and ultimately became almost universally adopted. By contrast, we are also interested in representations of ideas that are controversial, and may even be seen as complete delusions. In the former case, the process is greatly limited by concrete conditions; in the latter case, the number of degrees of freedom is significantly greater.

Let me illustrate this with a well-known example from the collective behavior literature, such as the "windshield pitting epidemic." At one point in time, American car drivers suddenly discovered many tiny pits or irregularities in their windshields. They drew the attention of other car drivers to this phenomenon, who then also discovered it in their own cars. A range of explanations was proposed, ranging from secret atomic tests to mysterious activities by enemies or even extraterrestrials. Within the somewhat paranoid framework of the Cold War, the tiny pits seemed to confirm the existence of some kind of strange threat. But it was only an illusion. The pits had always been there, they had just not been noted and "problematized" before.

Similar phenomena have been noted in boarding schools, factories, and university campuses. Someone would note a strange smell or taste, an insect, or another detail. The person suddenly feels unwell, and draws others' attention. They, too, are "infected" by the weird experience, and soon a large part of the group will be affected. But nurses, physicians and surgeons cannot find any cause (see Perry & Pugh, 1978). For such cases, the model of "the diffusion of innovations" only provides a partial explanation because it places too much emphasis on social effectiveness, and too little emphasis on psychological inclinations. So let us take a closer look at yet another approach.

Contagion

The third metaphor, or metaphorical model, which has been proposed in this particular context, is that of *contagion*. It originates from biology, from medical science, from epidemiology. Living beings may be "infected" by parasites or microorganisms, which somehow feed on their normal processes, and undermine their well-being. So they become dysfunctional, pathological, sick. This may be accompanied by a rise in temperature or fever, which helps mobilize and speed up the bodily processes that fight the threat. Whereas diffusion is a somewhat passive notion, contagion is a more active one. It involves an extra dimension. Parasites and microorganisms have a tendency to reproduce exponentially under the right conditions; things go from bad to worse, and ever more people are affected.

Within the sciences of man and society, these metaphors have traditionally been adopted in psychiatry, psychopathology, and criminology—as well as in social and mass psychology, particularly in trying to "explain" how strong emotions and moods spread rapidly between people, and lead them to deviant and norm-breaking behavior. Such transgressions were a central preoccupation of medical–legal (forensic) profession, which made early attempts to formulate a crowd psychology during the late 19th century, particularly in Italy and France.

In Italy, the anthropologist–psychologist Giuseppe Sergi wrote an essay on what he called "epidemic psychoses." After that, it was a pupil of the famous criminologist Cesare Lombroso, the young lawyer Scipio Sighele, who published the first monograph on *The Criminal Crowd*. In it, *contagion* was one of the central explanatory concepts (more in van Ginneken, 1992a). In France, the famous neurologist Jean-Marie Charcot noted in his studies about hysteria that emotional expressions seemed to have an extraordinary suggestive or even hypnotic power. In his classic book on the psychology of the crowd, the French physician Gustave Le Bon (1966) noted that some ideas, feelings, and moods seemed to have the contagious power of microbes. At the time, microbes had just been discovered by his compatriot, Louis Pasteur.

These observations were also linked to notions of psychological and social layeredness or stratification; higher layers in man and society were somehow thought to be less vulnerable to infection than lower and or deeper layers. Of course, the strong emphasis of these early crowd psychologists on the emotionality (and "therefore" irrationality) of popular movements and classes had strong ideological overtones; as White, adult, middle-class men, they tended to identify "mass feeling" with "primitive," childish, and feminine behavior. Yet there is more to it than that alone.

Research of recent years has confirmed that feelings and moods may indeed prove strong replicators. We often convey them unconsciously, particularly in face-to-face interactions between mutually dependent people. Emotional "coloring" may be a strong "attractor," which draws our individual behavior and interaction patterns into certain pathways. (We return more extensively to the notion of attractors in chap. 9). Penrose (1952) pointed out that both physical and psychological epidemics rest on a combination of three factors: virulence, transmission, and receptivity.

A few years ago, Elaine Hatfield, John Cacioppo and Richard Rapson (1994) published an overview of what is known about *Emotional Contagion*. Their book discussed findings from comparative (animal) psychology, developmental (child) psychology, clinical psychology, and also historical cases; for instance, findings concerning mimicry and synchrony (in facial and vocal expression) in involuntary movements, and the workings of the autonomic nervous system, in gestures and postures. They looked at individual differences in the capacity to "infect" others in those domains (and how this was linked to certain roles and professions); as well as in the capacity to be infected by others (and how this appeared linked to age and gender).

The study contains many recognizable, everyday examples. Certain strong emotions such as anger and fear do indeed seem to affect others quite easily. For instance, in hostile outbursts and panic (we return to those subjects in much greater detail). Certain semivoluntary, expressive behaviors may spread like wildfire in a group: yawning in a school class, coughing in a concert hall, laughter on the sound-track of a TV comedy. Mutually dependent relations are even more vulnerable to emotional contagion; for instance, those between mother and child, or between a pair of lovers. So there is ample evidence that feelings and moods can be highly contagious under certain circumstances. Yet this is still not the entire story.

Mutation

The fourth metaphor, or metaphorical model, which has received wide attention in recent years, is the transformation, transmutation or *step-wise change model*. This model underlies the heredity laws of Georg Mendel, and the chromosome theory of Francis Crick and James Watson. It has become the key notion in all of evolutionary biology and population genetics (and ultimately also in genetic algorythms and cellular automata). Growth, development and change in life (including "virtual" life) are driven by the Darwinian two-step of variation and selection, variation and selection, endlessly repeated. A minor mutation may start a positive feedback loop, and thereby result in a major shift within a biological (or computer) system.

There are various types of reproduction. Ordinary reproduction, in which special circumstances may provoke minor variations. Or sexual reproduction, which by its very nature leads to ever new combinations. In both cases, something "new" is periodically tried out. It may produce descendants who are better (or worse) equipped to survive in the struggle with congeners, with other species, with physical conditions, for the filling of an "environmental niche." It is the law of the "survival of the fittest," or rather the "survival of the fitting" because it does not necessarily represent the "ultimate optimum," but rather a solution that "will do" for the time being until it is superseded by something else.

In recent decades, great strides have been made in simulating and analyzing these processes. One may postulate various entities in a computer, which behave and interact in preprogrammed ways; furthermore, that they re-program and adapt themselves, that they learn and learn to learn. In this way, virtual aquariums have been created in the media lab of the Massachusetts Institute of Technology. Even outsiders may introduce their own preprogrammed life forms, which will then have to deal with other virtual life forms and the environment already there. They may spread or whither away; so the entire ecosystem evolves continually.

In the real world, genes do not correspond to bodily traits in simple one-to-one relations; it is rather their complex interaction among themselves (and with the environment) that determines the final result. Under certain, well-defined physical, chemical, electromagnetic (etc.) conditions, one gene "switches" another gene on or off, which then switches still another gene on or off, and so forth. So the number of possibilities is infinite. Man shares almost all of his genes with higher apes. Only a tiny fraction of human genes

accounts for "typically human" activities such as abstract and logical thinking, language, and culture.

What is noteworthy about human language and culture is that they have
opened up a completely new universe, in which information contributing to
the adaptive and survival skills of the individual and the group can be
passed on in nongenetic (or supragenetic) ways. The first few hundred
thousand years, this limited itself to gesture and talk. Only in the last few
thousand years have symbols and writing emerged, and a whole range of
techniques to store and access information at will—even much later, by
complete strangers, tens of thousands of miles away. Some cultural representations have survived, others have become almost extinct. How should
we understand these processes?

A New Notion: Memes

After the transmission, diffusion, and contagion metaphors, a new mutation
metaphor has come to the fore, to look at ways in which ideas, feelings and
actions spread within a population. The first impetus to this new approach
originated in the mid-1970s. In his monumental study *Sociobiology*, Edward
Wilson (1975) proposed to take a closer look at the evolutionary origins of
the human behavioral repertory. It looked as if this plea had conservative
implications, and liberal theorists were quick to mount an assault (overviews of the debate can be found in the books edited by Caplan, 1978, and
Ruse, 1979). Biologists such as Robert Trivers demonstrated that "altruistic
traits" might be just as effective in promoting survival of a group as "egotis-
tic" traits (see Caplan, 1978, pp. 213–226). This then led to the question,
what held such groups together and how.

One possible answer was proposed by the British evolutionary biologist,
Richard Dawkins (1976), in a kind of epilogue to his noted book *The Selfish
Gene*. He said previous attempts to explain the spread of certain ideas
within populations in terms of genes were unsatisfactory. Genes were simple replicators. But "I think that a new kind of replicator has recently
emerged on this very planet. It is staring us in the face. It is still in its in-
fancy, still drifting clumsily about in its primeval soup, but already it is
achieving evolutionary change at a rate which leaves the old gene panting
far behind" (p. 206). He proposed to call these replicators of thought patterns "memes" (from "imitation"). "The old gene-selected evolution, by
making brains, provided the 'soup' in which the first memes arose. Once
the self-copying memes had arisen, their own, much faster, kind of evolution took off" (Dawkins, 1976, p. 207). His colleague, N. K. Humphrey, concurred: "When you plant a fertile meme in my mind you literally parasitise
my brain, turning it into a vehicle for the meme's propagation in just the
way that a virus may parasitise the genetic mechanism of a host cell" (p.

208). At first, Dawkins's concept was received with a shrug, as just another metaphor. But with a changing spirit of the times (including the arrival of computer viruses and Internet rumors), a number of people began to realize that this alternate approach might indeed lead to new insights. Because it refocused attention on the "reproductive capacity" of ideas themselves, their form and content, irrespective of individual inclinations or intentions.

Dawkins had already noted that the "survival value" of replicators depended on three qualities: First, longevity, not so much of one meme itself, but rather of all copies taken together. Second, fecundity, which was probably more important. Some memes reproduce quickly and briefly, others slowly and lastingly. Finally, copying fidelity, which contained a paradox. On one hand memes should be able to produce ever new identical copies. On the other, they should also be able to change and adapt themselves to new circumstances because that was how they survived.

It has taken two decades for the meme notion itself to really catch on, and only over the last few years has a spate of studies been published further exploring the various implications of this new approach. One attempt to apply it to a range of subjects was Aaron Lynch's (1996) book *Thought Contagion: How Belief Spreads Through Society*. He surveyed a wide array of disciplines for possible memes: psychology, anthropology, sociology, politics, economics, history, and also related approaches such as game theory. The various chapters looked for widespread thought patterns in various domains such as health, sexuality, family formation, and so on. He identified "modalities" of thought contagion in opinion currents around social issues, as well as social movements around particular ideologies; namely, how they contributed to the number of offspring, the education of children, the conversion of others, keeping the faith, undermining rival ideas, and finally motivational and cognitive advantages.

In spite of the current revival, "memology" is only just taking off; there is no well-formulated and elegant model, even though there is obvious potential. In my opinion, many of the current observations remain tied too closely to the biological reproduction of the "carriers"; more observations should be derived from psychological and sociological processes. Think back, for instance, of the five conditions for widespread rumors, which we previously quoted. Le Bon's (1966) classical work, too, contains some useful observations in this respect. So the Disney rumor and urban legends could be seen as forceful memes and good replicators for precisely the reasons we have discussed.

But journalists and media also play an important intermediary role. Some stories are never picked up, others will always find "play." In the next chapter, we once again dissect one noteworthy case, as a stepping stone to a wider reflection on media hypes.

3

Circular Reaction in Media Hypes

News expands to fill the time and space allocated to its coverage.
—William Safire, American columnist (Faber, 1981, p. 81)

Once a newspaper touches a story, the facts are lost forever, even to the protagonists.
—Norman Mailer, American author (Gross, 1987, p. 288)

Next to informal communication through conversation, formal communication through media also plays a role in conveying ideas, feelings, and behaviors. Sometimes, the media willingly ignore a story for several years, then suddenly "discover" it and makes a fuss about it. The first section of this chapter describes a noteworthy case: The initial silence on the mid-1980's Ethiopian famine, suddenly turning into emphatic coverage. In the second section, we are brought to the phenomenon of media hypes in general, in which all media suddenly devote huge amounts and space to an ongoing event. How should we understand this? The metaprinciples underlying these processes turn out to be those of positive feedback, the self-reinforcing loop, and circular reaction, discussed in the third and final section. Certain filters built into the process become less active; certain amplifiers become more active; the process boosts itself.

CASE NUMBER THREE: THE HUNGER FOR NEWS

This case describes a noteworthy period of media silence, followed by a spectacular period of media attention, regarding a major famine. During the former period, the media did not report it because they felt it was not newsworthy enough, and other media did not report it either. During the latter period, the media extensively reported on it because they suddenly felt it was indeed newsworthy, and other media reported on it as well. So one vicious circle had suddenly been replaced by the next. The whole process was later carefully reconstructed by some of the journalists involved, and retold in a revealing two-part documentary made for the American PBS and the Dutch IKON broadcasting systems by Freke Vuijst and Ilan Ziv (also see: Benthall, 1993, Denselow, 1989, Fair, 1992, Philo, 1993).

The history leading up to this disaster was as follows: The African country of Ethiopia has two rainy seasons, *belg* (from February to May), and *meher* (from June to September). As early as May, 1981, the Ethiopian relief and rehabilitation commission (RRC) warned the United Nations that failing rains had caused a serious drought, resulting in harvest failures. In 1982, this pattern repeated itself and the RRC's urgent call for food was joined by private Western relief organizations. In November of 1983, the Ethiopian relief commission said, "The present drought is the country's worst in 10 years. If the international community is to avert mass starvation and death, it has to act today and now, for tomorrow might be too late" (Vuijst & Ziv, 1987, Part 1, p. 1). But there was no adequate reaction at all. In their most revealing book, *News Out of Africa*, Harrison and Palmer (1986) mentioned the following figures. By February 1983, 1.3 million people were already in relief camps; by early 1984, this figure had risen to 4.5 million. By August 1984, 6 million people were affected. In late 1984, the total had risen to 8 million. Two million refugees had already fled to neighboring countries. It was only at this point that a global effort began; 2 years after the problem had first been signaled.

Commissioner Dawit Wolde Giorgis of the RRC reported: "What my agency did was beg, literally beg . . . [in] particular the reporters and journalists to come and see the disaster and transmit it to the international community" (Vuijst & Ziv, 1987, Part I, p. 13). But there was no interest. David Kline is a free lance TV and newspaper journalist from San Francisco. He said, "I approached [the major American television network] CBS in the late summer of 1983 . . . The footage that I brought back to CBS, they felt that the images were not strong enough, or that the famine itself was not documented well enough" (Vuijst & Ziv, 1987, p. 5). He then offered it to their rivals NBC and PBS, but was turned down again. Their reaction was, he said: "You're offering a story about kids starving in Africa? Please, that's not a story—it's like saying the sun rises in the East" (p. 5).

At this point, international relief agencies stepped in to try and mobilize their media contacts. They organized guided tours for two groups of about 25 journalists each in the spring of 1984. In his subsequent book, *Africa in Crisis*, Lloyd Timberlake said, "So at that time there were about 50 journalists and they were all writing horror stories" (Harrison & Palmer, 1986, p.

100). But still there was little reaction. In June, 1984, Irish priest Mike Doheny and independent filmmaker Paul Harrison shot dramatic pictures of the famine. Harrison went to London to transfer the film to video.

"Shortly after we started two or three other guys joined us . . . would I be prepared to sell it as news?", Harrison reported (p. 1), and he eagerly agreed. Visnews (the major film news agency later taken over by Reuters) was interested. The news coverage manager made a call. The BBC was interested. Then he returned. They weren't interested anymore. Their own people were to go within 48 hours. The next day, Harrison went to show the tape to John Toker, of the commercial rival, Independent Television News (ITN). "There's a story there," Toker reportedly said. But he'd have to get approval from his boss. The boss had a different opinion: "Sorry, Africa isn't really an easy story to tell, the public is too far from them and a famine isn't really a nice news item." It was suggested that Harrison try Channel 4 News, which reaches a smaller audience. He met the foreign news editor but she was not interested. Two days later, the phone rang. She was interested after all. Because she had meanwhile heard, that ITV and its rival, BBC, were both going to give the Ethiopian famine major exposure. A week later, therefore, 4 minutes of Harrison's material was shown on Channel 4 News, and an even shorter version on ITN's News at Ten.

Meanwhile, Charles Stewart had been preparing a documentary on another subject in Ethiopia for Central Independent Television. They also stumbled across the famine, alerted the relief community, and triggered a race to be first. There was a short campaign for aid funds, but interest did not catch on or spread. Peter Cutler of the International Disaster Institute reported: "I remember coming back in September, 1984, and literally giving up. We were just banging our heads against a brick wall" (Harrison & Palmer, 1986, pp. 99, 109).

But in October, Visnews' Nairobi cameraman, Mohammed Amin, and BBC's South African correspondent, Michael Buerk, were finally able to travel to Korem in the North, and film a harrowing report. In retrospect, people have often wondered what made this item so exceptional. Why did these few minutes make an unprecedented impact, after 2 years of sustained indifference? There were several elements. Amin's images, their lighting and color, captured the massiveness of the exodus, as well as the individuality of the victims. There also was the familiar form of their faces: the western public could identify with them. Buerk's commentary, his choice of words and phrasing, further hinted at familiar archetypal scenes from the Old Testament: the Seven Plagues, the Flight from Egypt, and so forth. They revived vivid memories and fantasies derived from textbook images, and from the Hollywood pictures of Cecil B. DeMille, for example. They reached out to hit the collective unconscious and moral convictions of Europeans and Americans alike.

Upon Amin and Buerk's return, the film was shown as the first item on the midday news, and then again as an exceptional 6-minute piece on the Six O' Clock news. There had been limited coverage of the issue by the quality papers, but now there was extensive coverage by the popular papers as well. When the BBC had first offered stills from the film to the *Sun* (the largest daily newspaper in Britain) on Tuesday, their response had reportedly once again been short and clear: "We're actually not interested in famine" (quoted in Harrison & Palmer, 1986, p. 101). After seeing the impact of the subject, however, they changed their line.

A journalism review reported that the mass-circulation tabloids soon made frenzied use of Ethiopia in their long-running circulation war. Rupert Murdoch's *Sun* ran a "Sun to the Rescue" campaign and declared in an enormous page 1 headline on October 29, "Sun Sends 100.000 Pounds to Famine Kids" ... Murdoch's archrival, proprietor Robert Maxwell of the *Daily Mirror*, was not to be outdone. He organized a reader-funded jet "rescue" flight to Addis Abeba. The cargo included not only food and medicine but Maxwell himself, and the press baron's heroic doings were publicized day after day under the logo "Mirror Mercy Flight" (Boot, 1985, p. 48).

Yet it took some time before other countries woke up to the story as well. Kevin Hamilton reported:

> The European networks were offered the pictures by Visnews on the day that they landed in London, on the 23rd of October. We spoke to the [Eurovision] news co-ordinator, the person who makes the decision on behalf of all the European stations and told him that these were some of the most dramatic and telling images that we, Visnews, had ever handled in our entire history. He said: "I have no interest, thank you very much." He, like others, had heard about this famine in Africa, but frankly wasn't particularly interested in it. (Vuijst & Ziv, Part I, p. 19)

This only changed after the BBC item had made a major impact in England and the United States.

Kevin Hamilton of Visnews stated:

> NBC had been offered those pictures by the NBC London bureau, but the NBC Nightly News show producer had reacted: "I have no interest in them at all. It is just another famine." When the London bureau chief of NBC, Frieda Morris, and the European news manager at the time, Joe Angotti, saw the pictures on the BBC lunchtime news, they like everybody who saw them, were shaken to the core. And they phoned New York, to my knowledge several times, saying you must run these pictures, you must run them, must run them. NBC News New York said: "Thank you, the show is full, we don't have any room for them, why don't you send them over on an airplane, we'll take a look at them for next week." (Vuijst & Ziv, Part I, p. 20)

Morris and Angotti kept insisting that the images and commentary be beamed to New York by satellite at once, and that the news show producers at least look at these few minutes. But they balked at it. She [Morris] told them: "I will send this to you and you will run it, I guarantee it". She was right. According to Harrison and Palmer (1986): "when the film arrived, the whole of the NBC newsroom sat in silence watching it, totally stunned. Tom Brokaw, the presenter, said: 'Right, clear the decks, we're going to run this' " (p. 124).

Although the NBC staff was aware that it was a very forceful report, they were still surprised that it made a long-lasting impression. According to BBC correspondent, Michael Buerk: "I remember talking to NBC, who also ran the piece and had this amazing reaction. They told me: 'It'll only last a week: the American public will soon get bored with that kind of stuff' " (pp. 124, 130). But when NBC saw the impact it made, they decided to capitalize on its "scoop," and ran full-page ads in *The New York Times* and *The Washington Post*. They carried a picture of a starving black child clinging to its father. The text, starting with huge headlines, read: "The Ordeal of Ethiopia—The Compassion of America. NBC News will continue its special reports on Ethiopia . . ." (Boot, 1985, p. 48).

Suddenly, the competition was interested as well. ABC's senior foreign correspondent in London, Bill Redeker, who had also been trying for months to convince his superiors, reported: "Suddenly, we couldn't live without this story" (Hertsgaard, 1985, p. 38). CBS's coverage was to culminate in a special five part series on the famine. According to Kevin Hamilton: "All of a sudden, babies dying in Ethiopia became the flavor of the month. I am sorry to put it in a blunt negative term" (Vuijst & Ziv, 1987, Part I, p. 1).

Among the viewers awestruck by the broadcast of the Amin/Buerk TV report was Irish pop singer Bob Geldof, of the group Boomtown Rats. "That night, I could not sleep," he said. He contacted his friend Midge Ure, of the group Ultravox, to "do something" (Geldof, pp. 270–273). They sat down to write a song for the upcoming December season: "Feed the World—Do They Know it's Christmas?" They also invited colleagues to join their "Band Aid" initiative, as well as a hastily arranged recording session including Phil Collins, Duran Duran, Boy George, Paul Young and members of groups like Bananarama, Kool and the Gang, Spandau Ballet, Status Quo, U2 and others. The song was an immediate hit; during the first week after its release, it sold 600,000 copies at home, and another 600,000 abroad—far beyond anything they had hoped for.

During the first 2 weeks, it sold no less than 1.5 million copies in the United States. Singer Harry Belafonte said that he felt ashamed and embarrassed at seeing a bunch of White English kids doing what Black Americans ought to have been doing. Then Michael Jackson and Lionel Ritchie sat down to write another song, "We are the world." They also invited colleagues to join the "USA for Africa" initiative, as well as a hastily arranged recording session with Ray Charles, Bob Dylan, Diana Ross, Paul Simon, Bruce Springsteen, Tina Turner, Dionne Warwick, Stevie Wonder, and many others. The single was released by late March, 1985, and sold no less than 7.3 million copies over the next 2 months. An LP record (including previously unreleased recording tracks of the stars) sold 4.4 million copies over that same period. Together with books, posters, T-shirts, stickers, and buttons, some $45 million dollars, at this stage, was brought in.

Other groups and countries reacted as well. Julio Iglesias, José Feliciano, and a number of Latino stars in turn formed the *Hermanos* (Brothers) and also recorded the specially composed song, "*Cantare, Cantaras.*" Geldof noted that 25 such initiatives around the world were taking place, and everybody felt great about it. The recordings were often followed by benefit concerts, and soon the idea came up to stage a global super concert the next summer.

The senior vice president of finance and planning at the Los Angeles Olympics of the previous year, now with "World Wide Sports and Entertainment," got into the act. He helped find four major corporations willing to come up with $3 million dollars in "seed money," in exchange for positive free publicity: AT&T, Chevrolet, Kodak, and Pepsi. A Malaysian oil baron threw in a considerable sum as well. Thus, the organization lined up 13 satellites (as opposed to only three for the previous Olympics) and 22 transponders, so as to be able to provide a "live" radio and television feed throughout the world. The "Live Aid" concert was to take place simultaneously on both sides of the Atlantic, with one venue in England and another in the United States.

London's Wembley Stadium filled with 70,000 spectators, Philadelphia's JFK Stadium with 90,000. They saw a unique line-up of performers; many who had been involved in the Anglo-American pop recordings, and several who had been unable to make it at the time, including David Bowie, Mick Jagger, Elton John, Paul McCartney, and many others—a true "who's who" of the music industry. The events were broadcast live by the BBC in England, ABC in the United States, and by the MTV music channel all around; as well as in close to 100 other countries, where they were seen by some 1.5 billion viewers. The broadcast was interrupted by spots. The public relations manager of one sponsor later said that showing the pictures of starving Africans or drought areas in Africa in our commercial, they thought was a very good move because it didn't show AT&T's products and services, but left in the mind of the viewer the fact that AT&T cared.

The producer of the global telecast said that they also meant to use it as an information piece to tell the people of our planet that we could eradicate hunger within 10 years. Nothing of the kind happened, of course, and the writer of the educational segments later admitted: "Basically, we did not address some of the causes of hunger, because there are so many different causes of hunger. And you get into a philosophical debate with people" (Larry Hartstein, from Vuijst & Ziv, pp. 7–8). Communication professor Cees Hamelink explained: "These enormous events, whether it is Live Aid or [others] . . . by definition have to be apolitical. If that [political] reality were presented, we wouldn't have gotten that much money" (Vuijst & Ziv, 1987, Part II, pp. 7–11).

And money they got. During the last few hours of the concert, some 22,000 pledge calls were attempted every 5 minutes. Gifts ranged from wedding rings reluctantly ceded by old ladies, to 1 million pounds thrown in by a Dubai sheik. Immediate revenues were estimated to top $40 million dollars. Cynics remarked that this was an average of only a few cents per viewer (and that participating pop singers had boosted the sales of their other records with at least that same amount). But it is true that "Band Aid" and "Live Aid" had produced a unique series of "firsts": best-selling records, the largest pop concert and TV event ever, and a "global village" in true style.

Other branches followed suit: with "Opera Aid," "Fashion Aid," "Sport Aid," and the "Race Against Time"—from Africa to America, to New York and the United Nations headquarters, to convey a sense of urgency. The latter event took place in the spring of 1986, involved 20 million people, running in almost 80 different countries, and bringing in another $35 million dollars. All events taken together, therefore, brought in well over $100 million dollars. Costs were kept to a minimum, and almost all of the money was disbursed again, through well over a 100 different aid projects. By the time the first aid had arrived, however, the famine had already killed an estimated 1 million people. An estimated 3 million people, by contrast, survived due to this outside help.

Looking back on the events 15 to 20 years later, one cannot help but have mixed feelings. It is surprising that the world media chose to ignore the reports of such a huge disaster for a full year, or even two. It is also surprising that a TV report of only a few minutes, and an initiative taken by one singer, would in the end trigger an avalanche of sympathy. Yet, publicity about the famine itself was soon outdone by publicity about the celebrities involved. Today, malnourishment persists on a scandalous scale. The total number of chronically underfed was somewhat reduced from slightly over 1 billion to slightly under 1 billion, but then rose again after the Asian financial crisis, whereas development aid diminished (we return to this subject in chap. 10).

Looking back on this rapid, radical, and massive shift in public opinion, one may identify psychological as well as sociological catalysts. Everyone in the Western world felt vaguely guilty about the persistence of chronic malnutrition in large parts of the Third World, and the persistence of the civil wars and natural disasters that then triggered acute famines. Christians felt vaguely guilty about their lack in charity, and the biblical reports of Amin and Buerk obviously touched a nerve. What had long remained hidden suddenly leapt into view and forced itself on people. This contributed to the first psychological shift.

The political situation around Ethiopia had been totally blocked. Only an initiative from outside the political world, outside the diplomatic world, outside the relief community could unlock it. Only the initiative of a second-tier pop singer could mobilize first-tier pop singers. Their combined "news value" got the media hype under way. They became the "opinion leaders" who stirred the public to get involved. They did so with music; it made wealthy people feel good to help poor people. The "do good" tunes etched themselves into people's minds, and came to radiate a warm glow. It took hold during the dark days around Christmas, the season that annually inspires the media and the public in the Western world into becoming more sensitive to other's plights. This contributed to the second, sociological shift.

It triggered an avalanche of similar initiatives. We later see how processes running parallel, emerging patterns, self-organization, critical thresholds, and the like play a role in such cases. But let us first take a closer look at the phenomenon of media hypes in general.

THE PHENOMENON OF MEDIA HYPES

We noted in the previous chapter about hearsay that informal communication through conversation and formal communication through media do constantly alternate and are closely intertwined. Gossip and rumor, urban legends, and urban folklore do periodically pop up in the media, as true or untrue. Media material, in turn, may form the raw material for everyday conversations. This is particularly true for media material which suddenly turns up everywhere—continuously, and insistently.

Sometimes, as in the case of the African famine, all this attention is fully justified. But sometimes, it seems disproportionate, as in the case of the Band Aid initiative taken by Anglo-American show-biz stars. Under other comparable circumstances, such an initiative by others would not have received even 1% of the media exposure. On some occasions, the media hype even seems to be about next to nothing; it is like hot air, first filling a balloon, and then escaping from it again. A *media hype*, then, is something that is somehow inflated.

In his book, *Inflation of Symbols*, Orrin Klapp (1991) mentioned a whole series of words employed over time to identify cases of much ado about nothing: glitz, ballyhoo, flimflam, schmaltz, puffery, boosterism, hot air, hulla-balloo, hoopla. They often refer to the kind of intentional overpromotion that used to be a characteristic of fairground showmen and circus direc-tors, before advertisers and spin doctors took over. But sometimes, it is a more-or-less spontaneous phenomenon in the media world, whereby pa-pers and broadcasters suddenly give exposure to something because it al-ready has exposure, and whereby they persist in a certain angle because it already has that angle. It is a case of "circular reaction."

We see in Part III of this book that media hypes may be related to any do-main: fashion and fads, risks and panic, outrage and protests, crazes and crashes, and a range of other subjects. But at this point, it is useful to al-ready consider media hypes as a specific type of communication process. Seemingly capricious, because these hypes appear and disappear in a whim. Hard to predict, because relatively minor incidents may trigger a na-tionwide avalanche.

But let us first take a closer look at the relation between media coverage and true reality. Many journalists and most audiences tend to assume that the media are nothing more than a mere "window" on the world, or a "mir-ror" of the world, and that it is usually rather obvious which events are ob-jectively important and which are not, or even which events the public feels are subjectively important and which not. This is not the case. News is, just like other forms of knowledge, a social product, as has been demonstrated in famous communication studies by Altheide, Gans, Schlesinger, Schulz, Tuchman, and others (see van Ginneken, 1998). News turns out to be the re-sult of a complicated social process, in which scores of people interact.

The Creation of the World in the News

My book *Understanding Global News* (van Ginneken, 1998) was entirely de-voted to this question. The original Dutch version was even titled, *The Cre-ation of the World in the News*. It proclaimed the "Burda model" of knowl-edge production and knowledge exchange. *Burda* is a fashion magazine of German origin, which today has editions in many different countries and languages. It has a large centerfold page, with tens (at one time maybe over a hundred) clipping patterns for the skirts, trousers, and blouses in various sizes displayed in that issue, printed all through and over each other. Some in red, others in blue; some in dashed lines, others in dotted lines, and so on and so forth. At first sight, it is an utter chaos of lines and patterns, from which it is impossible to make any sense. You really have to take a felt-tipped pen and mark the lines for one chosen panel to be able to identify its form.

My point here is that this is exactly what happens in knowledge produc-tion in the real world. The physical and psychosocial reality that surrounds us at first makes a completely chaotic impression. It is only our socialization within a particular subculture that enables us to make sense of it; particularly our education, but also science and the media. They are like the felt-tipped pen, which makes some patterns stand out, while ignoring others. So making sense is done through what I have chosen to call "selective articulation." The book on global news shows in great detail how Western media selectively articulate certain views of other cultures—mostly unwittingly. For every famine that receives attention, for instance, there are a number of others that are overlooked; this holds even more for chronic malnutrition. It often happens even against the express desire of the journalists involved. But journalists are woven into psychosocial and economic–political processes, from which they cannot easily extricate themselves.

The news book starts from an adapted version of the "who says what to whom" model of transmission, which we discussed in the previous chapter. It demonstrates how certain views of what is true, real and important are being selectively articulated by the global media "machine." We may use the same approach for an analysis of media hypes. All kinds of filters and boosters intervene to produce a "circular reaction" on some occasions, and not on others.

The first question is: What is news? An even better question is: What is considered "nothing new?" They are related to the philosophy or epistemology of what is considered noteworthy and what is taken for granted. The contrast is of course highly questionable and arbitrary. The doings of individual celebrities in London and New York are considered highly newsworthy, for instance, whereas the fate of millions of paupers in Africa or elsewhere is not. Well-known products, brands, or companies can easily become newsworthy, whenever something out of the ordinary occurs. Think of the Disney case. Decades ago, Galtung and Ruge identified a dozen criteria that seem to make an event internationally newsworthy. These same criteria are still intuitively used by journalists today, often without them being aware of it. Even if the journalists are highly opinionated, there is near unanimity on the application of these criteria.

The second question is: What are the most influential media? Within the total media spectrum, there are only a small number that can "make or break" international news stories (e.g., the big Anglo-American broadcasters and newspapers, such as the BBC and NBC in the Ethiopia case). The top stories on the news programs of the major broadcasters, the lead stories of the major dailies, and the cover stories of the major magazines are followed closely by all editors, particularly those lower in the media "pecking order." If there has just been a release of a blockbuster movie by a major Hollywood studio on dinosaurs, meteors, tornadoes, or epidemics, this will lower the level for news on subjects—however vaguely related. The time when media closely identified themselves with one political or ideological current in society is fading. Furthermore, today media are mostly exploited by commercial companies obeying exactly the same rules and prodding each other onward along the same path. As the German sociologist Niklas Luhmann once put it: "The mass media represent a self-referential system which under certain conditions loses contact with the outside world and reacts mainly to its own activities" (quoted in Vasterman, 1997).

A third question is: Who become journalists, and how do they work? This is about professional sociology, with its do's and don'ts. The vast majority of influential journalists are being recruited from a very small segment of society—like the rest of the global elite. Their age and gender, their ethnic group and social class, do not correspond to a "representative sample" of the world's population. Also, they often have a similar education and career, and acquire similar views about the nature of their trade. In everyday practice, journalists covering the same domains cling together, visit the same events and hangouts, and form each other's prime reference group; whether it is "the boys on the bus" covering presidential campaigns, or the "parachute pack" covering crises abroad. They often disagree. But they also tend to close ranks whenever there is outside criticism.

A fourth question is: Who are speaking in and through the news, and who are the major sources? This is about the politics of loud and whispering voices. Content analyses of the front pages of the major newspapers have revealed time and again that institutional spokesmen form the prime sources of daily news. They often dictate the public agenda, propose the major issues for consideration, and try to put their own spin on them. These angles are not automatically taken for granted, but often not thoroughly questioned either—particularly in the international domain. One example is that relevant numbers are often quoted quite selectively and in suggestive ways (see the book by Paulos, 1993, on this score). Rather than saying that "this or that is the case," finally, media increasingly limit themselves to reporting that "this or that person claims that this or that is the case." This transfers responsibility for the correctness of the claim onto another party.

The fifth question is: When does something becomes news? This is related to the implicit construction of historical continuities and rupture points. Because of advancing electronic media, there is a growing emphasis on "live" reporting. This makes it very difficult to thoroughly check a certain presentation of "the facts" in breaking news. Journalists are afraid of missing deadlines. There is little time and money for truly investigative journalism, nor does it make many friends in high places. Drifting with the tide of the day is much easier. So the implied "historical frames" of most media hypes are very specific. Often there are claims that there is a dramatic increase of this, or a dramatic decrease of that; but only after some time does it turn out that this is, in large part, an optical illusion resulting from the labeling and categorization process.

The sixth question is: Where does the news come from? This is about the social geography of news flows. There is an implicit hierarchy of culturally influential and less influential continents, countries, regions, and cities in the world. North America and western Europe are keynoting continents. The United States, England, and other G7 countries are keynoting nations. New York, Washington, London, and Paris are keynoting metropolises. This is clearly visible in the "news soaps," which succeed each other ever more rapidly. Whenever something is going on with Anglo-American celebrities, the rest of the world follows suit—even if those names and issues are not truly recognizable. O. J. Simpson, for one, was originally a complete unknown abroad.

The seventh question is: How is reality described to us? This is about the linguistics of words and lines, and of reading between the lines. Media hypes are often phrased in superlatives; by the addition of suffixes like hyper, super, mega, or giga. A clever label is thought up, for instance, a neologism or a new word combination. Highly evocative metaphors are imported from other domains. Headline makers look for catchy alliterations, rhyme, and puns. In psychology, this is related to the salience of information; the result is that those terms get more impact. They are more readily noted, perceived, retained, and retrieved. So formal communication does more easily find an extension in informal communication, in highly activated chains of talk and hearsay.

The eighth question is: How is the world shown to us? This is about the iconology of what comes "into view" or is left out. It is noteworthy that many media hypes are triggered or accompanied by "archimages," which are highly graphic, forceful, and dramatic. They may be video and film sequences, stills pictures, or even artist's impressions and situation sketches. They seem to embody and summarize the moral message of the media hype, and may be endlessly repeated. The case studies in this book give several examples: Greenpeace activists nearly suffocating in tear gas thrown into their ships cabin by French riot police near Moruroa; baby seals clubbed to death in Canada; Bovine Spongiform Encephalopathy (BSE) cows scrambling on their hind legs, and so forth. Those images become icons, etched in our visual memory.

The ninth question is: What are the effects of such media reports? This is about the psychology of what is thought "typical." It implies a categorization into what is "the rule," for instance, and what obviously is "the exception." The events do not speak for themselves, but are made to say certain things through the ways in which they are embedded in the wider context. Sometimes the message is that things go from bad to worse. Sometimes the message is that progress cannot be halted. But in both cases "making sense" implies the integration into an existing framework, for instance on "us and them."

To sum up, the news gathering and news distribution process usually contains a number of filters and boosters. In media hypes, the filters of critical evaluation become less effective, for instance concerning eyewitnesses, spokespeople, other media reports, etc. At the same time, the boosters of dramatic amplification become more effective, for instance, concerning the use of highly evocative numbers, words, images, narratives, a moral, and so forth. Information streams begin to run parallel, normal resistance breaks down, and self-reinforcing processes take over. It is a special case of the metaprinciple of circular reaction, which we will take a closer look at in the final section of this chapter.

The Evolution of Media Hypes

In my view, then, media hypes are often characterized by principles of "serial distortion," similar to those which Allport and Postman (1947) identified in relation to rumors, and that we already discussed in the previous chapter. The principles of leveling, sharpening, and assimilation make a story "fit"; they promote the survival and spread of typical, stereotypical, and/or archetypical story lines that resonate with our deepest fears and hopes; story lines built around forceful memes, powerful replicators that temporarily overgrow all other elements, marginalize all dissent.

My colleague Peter Vasterman (1995, 1997) has been researching media hypes for many years, and is preparing a PhD thesis on the subject. He favors a scheme identifying successive stages in a media hype, similar to that proposed in the literature on deviance, stigmatization, and moral panics. The first stage is usually that of an arch event, an incident that is construed as a signal. It may be a minor news item; something that is normally covered with five lines in column four of the third page in the second section of a newspaper. One or more people have died, been wounded, or abused. This may be the result of a crime, an accident, some neglect. This has been recorded, reported, researched. Every single day, there are thousands of such reports. But for some reason, this particular one stands out. It has something strange or noteworthy, which makes it stand out and "jump" to the front page.

The next stage is that it gets tentatively connected to a wider problem or issue. The original incident is "read" as a strong signal for a deeper trend; an either desirable or undesirable state of affairs. A larger group of persons, authorities, or institutions is made responsible for the persistence of this state of affairs. So now it is no longer an isolated incident, about which one can shrug one's shoulders. It has become a structural affair, the repetition of which must be actively prevented or promoted. This demands the express intervention of relevant parties. The media and the public begin to ask that they "do something."

This feeds into the "widening and deepening" stage. *Widening* because the media and the public do suddenly begin to look for other similar incidents to substantiate the trend. The recent past and the wider environment are scanned for related signals. Things that have happened or are happening, and which could well be seen as fundamentally different, are suddenly placed into the same category. So the phenomenon seems to be on the increase. This is, of course, a self-fulfilling prophecy; if one expects to find similar cases, it can usually be done. But apart from this widening, there is also a deepening, an intensification, an emotionalization taking place. The whole set of incidents is put in a dramatic light. So opinion leaders and policy makers can no longer evade the issue.

Now the media hype reaches its height, with a "broad social debate" going on. Relevant authorities are asked for their reactions. These reactions elicit other reactions. Ministries defend their policies, parliamentary groups ask questions, political parties include it in their electoral programs, churches demand that an ethical stand be taken. Employer organizations and companies, trade unions, and consumer groups, lobbies, and associations all speak out. The best known course of action is that an investigative committee is formed to check the facts. Only very much later does it produce reports and recommendations, which are usually somewhat half-hearted. Sometimes this will revive the media hype, but often it has long subsided. People hardly remember what all the fuss was about.

Because, meanwhile, the ultimate stage has begun; that of "debunking" and/or extinction. In some cases, critical evaluation has finally taken off, however hesitating and marginal. Some cynic has taken a closer look at the "facts" of the story, at the "cold numbers." Gradually others, too, begin to realize that the media attention and public excitement were somewhat one-sided or disproportional. The advocates of the media hype become less vocal, and their involvement subsides. Issue fatigue takes over; everything has been said, the problem and the solution are not as clear-cut as we thought at first.

But more importantly, entirely different hypes have meanwhile manifested themselves, absorbed time and space in the media, and absorbed the attention of journalists and the public. This is hard to imagine whenever the media hype is still in full swing, and occupies center stage. But it will inevitably happen. Because it is the characteristic feature of news that it must deal with something perceived as new, not as "nothing new."

Media Hypes and the Status Quo

We have said that media hypes imply a disproportional attention for things that would otherwise receive much less coverage. In the case with which we opened this chapter, there was initially very little interest in the plight of millions of African paupers, but ultimately very great interest in the aid initiatives of a few dozen Anglo-American pop stars. The word "hype" refers to something that is somehow exaggerated. This observation usually leads to a dual value judgment; on one hand that media hypes are mostly about trivial events and marginal phenomena; and on the other hand, that they distract from truly important and fundamental things. The net result is thought to be that they somehow derail social reflection, and lead it onto a dead track. Yet that is only part of the story.

Daniel Boorstin, Marshall McLuhan, Joshua Meyrowitz, and others have gradually developed another approach to the role of media in society. They emphasized that media reporting has become completely intertwined with the social and political process itself. Douglas Rushkoff (1996) elaborated this argument. In his book *Media Virus*, he follows a reasoning that squares rather well with the meme theories that we discussed in the previous chapter.

He notes that media hypes do not only thrive on exceptionally forceful replicators, but also that these "viruses" take over and sap and change conventional views. Of course Madison Avenue (the street of advertising agencies in New York), and Pennsylvania Avenue (the street of image makers in Washington), try to steer our perceptions, he said, but that is often rather obvious and even counterproductive. Media hypes and news soaps cut through and disorganize these "official" economic, political, and moral discourses. Because all these manifest stories get infested with latent messages that often have different or even opposite implications. They may stir critical feelings and carry a "hidden agenda."

Take the long series of American news soaps around Clarence Thomas and Anita Hill, Nancy Kerrigan and Tonya Harding, Woody Allen and Mia Farrow, O. J. Simpson and Nicole Brown, Bill Clinton and Monica Lewinsky. Or the British news soap around Prince Charles and Lady Di, or other (ex-) members of the royal family. Did the extensive coverage of these affairs not contribute more to a reflection on the role of race and gender in public life, in the political and judicial system, but also in media and sports, than dozens of pages of heavy-handed op–ed pages?

Or take the few seconds of amateur video on Rodney King, who is Black, being beaten up by White cops in Los Angeles. According to Rushkoff (1996), such images are the "Trojan horses" that sneak into the citadel of established views, sap and change them. They force the power holders to bow to the media and the public. They force everybody to talk and reflect about the unspeakable and the unthinkable; as in the case of the pop stars and Ethiopia. So we may conclude that media hypes may have both negative or positive implications, neither or both. But the key question remains: What are the metaprinciples of feedback loops that are seen at work here?

THE METAPRINCIPLE OF CIRCULAR REACTION

Previous chapters have looked at how thoughts, feelings and behaviors can be communicated from one person to the next. The implied reference is to a straight line. In transmission, it is a straight line between sender and receiver. In diffusion, it is straight lines in all directions. In contagion, it is straight lines with some kind of acceleration factor. But, to reiterate, the implied reference is always to straight lines.

Many models in science somehow imply or use straight lines, whether in natural science or in the sciences of man and society. Books and overhead sheets are full of models made with the same "building blocks" of quadrangles with labels. These are postulated entities or factors. They are usually connected through lines or arrows. These are the claimed relations or influences. We assume as obvious that causes and consequences can easily be sorted out. But large parts of reality are not "built" that way.

Within a mechanical world view, the routine is first to disassemble entities and relations into their constituent parts, and then to reassemble them again. One is supposed to be able to understand the whole when one is able to understand the parts and the partial relations between them. Within an ecological/ environmental/ evolutionary model, by contrast, things are not so obvious. Sometimes that approach works relatively well; sometimes it does not. Because often the whole is much more than the sum of the parts. There may be a complex interaction between various components, creating alternative levels of coherence. Sudden changes and nonlinear shifts may occur within them.

Maybe it would be good to always remain alert to this possibility. To ask ourselves, every time we see such a simple model, whether this is really how things work; or whether the straight line and arrow should really be replaced by a circle or a fan of lines or some other representation. Many changes affect their own causes. Quite a few complex processes feed back upon themselves. For instance, media hypes. The consequences of change may be small and extremely varied, working in many different directions.

This section looks at a range of concepts to clarify this point. Not all of these concepts are entirely new. Like the transmission model in information theory, for instance, the feedback model in cybernetics theory dates back to the pre-war years. But at the same time, the ubiquity of these processes was not yet fully understood. Only in recent years has complex interaction become the focus of attention. This is once again related to the spread of both supercomputers and PC networks. Because one could do ever more elaborate calculations, the "limits of calculability" gradually came into view.

Self-Reinforcing Processes

Let us once again take a closer look at the metaphors with which we are well acquainted, and that tend to invade and steer our every reflection. If one tends to represent abstract entities as concrete things, and concrete things as quadrangles, this easily leads us to certain assumptions that may prove dubious after all. It suggests, for example, that abstract processes can easily be sorted out and separated, that the factors involved are somehow compact, that they are finite and measurable, and so forth. If one tends to represent hypothetical relations as straight lines, this in turn suggests that influences can easily be isolated, are simple, unequivocal, unidirectional, that there is no mutual interference, and so forth. In the end, our whole thinking about the problem is contaminated.

This is easiest to see in all kinds of "rakish" representations we tend to use for making category systems, but also in communication and organization models. Horizontal rakes of boxes and lines for communication processes; from one sender to many receivers; vertical rakes of boxes and lines for organization structures, with one chief and many divisions; there are many things wrong with this ingrained approach (see Morgan, 1986). In the latter model, for instance, information and energy seem to leak out at the bottom, because feedback has little or no place. Clients and citizens, furthermore, seem to be absent, although they are claimed to be the key reference group. The inadequacies of this whole type of thinking become immediately apparent whenever we discuss "mutualist" concepts such as employee morale, work atmosphere, or organizational culture.

We must learn to recognize that much is interwoven here. This should lead us to entirely different approaches, in terms of dynamical systems. After the natural sciences, this type of analysis now begins to reach the sciences of man and society. Vallacher and Nowak (1994) noted, for instance:

> Cause and effect acquire a new meaning from the dynamical systems perspective. In particular, the notion that theories should consist of causal laws specifying that an independent variable at time t1 leads to change in the dependent variable at time t2 needs to be reconsidered.
>
> The division into independent and dependent variables assumes an asymmetric one-directional relation. Quite often in psychology, however, we deal with symmetric relations in which each variable both influences and is influenced by the other ... Indeed, bi-directionality may turn out to be a fundamental feature of social psychological phenomena that have been explored primarily in terms of asymmetric causal relations ... Also because such change may reflect the system's internal dynamics. (p. 281)

In my opinion, all this is particularly true for CAS of collective subjectivity such as work atmosphere or public opinion or national culture. Sperber (1996) wrote in this context:

> Typically, public productions have mental representations among their causes and among their effects. Mental representations caused by public productions can in turn cause further public productions, and so forth. There are thus complex causal chains where mental representations and public productions alternate. (p. 99)

This leads to a situation where public productions can influence public productions—even of the same sort. One may imagine the processes involved as single or double loops, or flat "figure eights" lying on their sides, in which a representation is alternately externalized and internalized, undergoing minute transformations in the left or the right part of the flat figure eight. (The flat figure eight is also a symbol for infinity, which is quite appropriate.) Whenever one puts the emphasis on a combination of a circular movement and linear progress, by contrast, one may well imagine the processes involved as spirals or double spirals. (The double helix is a ground form of life, which is once again quite appropriate.)

So it may often look as if a public production may be both its own cause and effect; and as if a mental representation may be both its own cause and effect. To a certain extent, this is exactly the case with media hypes. But let us also look at some other psychosocial phenomena, which have the intertwining of cause and effect as one of their prime characteristics. For instance a category that has become known under the collective label of *self-fulfilling prophecies*.

Self-Fulfilling Prophecies

It is not only in natural processes that loops and near-vicious circles may help amplify small differences to fundamental changes. In the realm of psychology and sociology, too, such shifts may occur. The detail in question may be immaterial, and merely steer information-processing into an entirely different direction. The final result may well be a thorough restructuring of relevant phenomena. As in the fable of the Baron of Münchhausen, who succeeded in extracting himself from a morass by pulling himself up by his own hair.

The reason why these psychosocial processes are effective is that people are led by their anticipation of the future. We develop expectations, continually adjust them, and adapt our behavior. Only much later will it become clear whether these expectations were justified or not. But an interesting variation occurs when we adjust our expectations, adjust our behavior, and thereby contribute to making the future different from what it would otherwise have been. It makes no fundamental difference whether these expectations were completely subjective or had an objective basis. Because, as the American sociologist William Thomas once observed, "If men define situations as real, they are real in their consequences" (Sahakian, 1982, p. 98). Researchers in many disciplines came across variations of this phenomenon, which often messed up their data. It is insufficiently acknowledged, that this human consciousness and self-awareness is a key aspect of human functioning.

In medical and pharmacological science, the phenomenon has for instance been identified as the "placebo" (replacement) effect. The French playwright Molière already noted in *The Imaginary Invalid* (1673) that whoever feels bad may develop real symptoms, and whoever feels better may get rid of real symptoms. Conversely, it often means that if we can provide patients with impressive treatments with impressive names, this may decisively affect their well-being, even if those treatments or substances do not really involve (otherwise) effective ingredients. This increasingly became a problem when new elixirs and pills and new powders and ointments were tested. Because they often produced positive results, even if they were completely neutral. Today, therefore, we know that we should compare an experimental group with a control group receiving something that produces a similar impression; only then can we isolate the "real effectiveness" of the treatment. But there is more.

In psychology, the *experimenter effect* was discovered. Researcher R. Rosenthal (1976) demonstrated that experimenters who held a higher opinion about some test animals or human subjects than others (e.g., feeling that they were smarter), would unconsciously treat them better. The result was that they performed the test under better conditions, and scored better results—for no good reason. This tended to confirm the earlier prejudice. So today we know that a good experiment should follow "double blind" procedures. That is to say that the experimenters should not be able to form an opinion of the subjects, and/or not be able to affect the test results—however indirectly.

In pedagogy and education, furthermore, the so-called "Pygmalion effect" has been discovered, which involves similar processes. Rosenthal and L. Jacobsen (1968) had shown that teachers and trainers are often influenced in similar ways by the expectations they have of students and pupils. There were situations, for instance, where White kids with a middle-class background received better treatment in school than non-White kids with a lower class background—something that further reinforced existing disparities. Yet the teachers were absolutely unaware of this; moreover, they absolutely denied that this was the case.

Pygmalion is, of course, a figure dating back to antiquity. In Greek mythology, he was the King of Cyprus who fell in love with a statue of the goddess Aphrodite. Roman author Ovid made Pygmalion a sculptor who fell in love with his own statue of the ideal woman (who was then brought to life by the goddess Venus). In the modern play by the British author George Bernard Shaw, he became the linguist Professor Higgins, who fell in love with a flower girl to whom he gave speech lessons. Ultimately, the story was turned into a successful musical and a successful movie. But the moral remained the same: Whenever people feel you are nice and cute, this gives you an advantage in life.

Of course we all know how important it is to be judged positively. But recent empirical research has shown that people judged "likeable and beautiful" get better education and better jobs, with more prestige and higher salaries. Shortcomings, missteps, and even misdemeanors are more easily forgiven. Other researchers have subsequently identified a "Galatea" effect, named after the subject of Pygmalion's love. They noted that people who receive extra positive attention in this way, may internalize such judgments, and behave accordingly. Finally, there has been talk of an opposite "Golem" effect (after the Hebrew word for "dumbbell"), meaning that people who get little or negative attention from educators and teachers may also internalize such judgments, and behave accordingly.

Over the last 20 years, therefore, new forms of psychotherapy and attitude training have all emphasized that it is important to develop a positive self-image and a certain self-confidence. People with a negative self-image tend to neglect their nutrition, condition, appearance, and more in general, their whole self-presentation. The result is that they provoke negative reactions, which in turn undermines their self-esteem, and leads to further negative feelings, depressive moods, and so on. Psychotherapy and attitude training have stressed that it is important to be realistically optimistic about one's capabilities and possibilities, by contrast, and to label them positively. In the popular technique of neurolinguistic programming (NLP), this re-labeling, and the anchoring thereof in everyday attitudes, plays a central role.

These same metaprinciples do not only manifest themselves internally in the medical, psychological, and pedagogic realm. They also manifest themselves externally in the sociological, economic, and political realm. Microsociologist Erving Goffman (1956) has written a series of fascinating studies about subjects such as *The Presentation of Self in Everyday Life*, and *Behavior in Public Places*; also about *Stigma* and *Asylums*. They show that our identity is subject to an ongoing negotiation between ourselves and our social environment. On some occasions, we may be able to impose our own definitions on others; on other occasions, we get caught in the definitions that others impose on us.

Someone who is put in an asylum or a prison, for instance, sees all his former relations with others change. Many suddenly withdraw from contact, or build up many reservations. Even when he or she returns to "ordinary" society outside, the stigma remains. It hinders their chances to resume normal life, as if nothing had happened, and promotes the chances of a relapse. So the reaction promotes the very state that they seem to fear. This is a profound paradox.

Such processes cannot only be found at the margins of society, but also in its very heart. Elton Mayo (1933) did an early study, of how labor conditions, employee motivation, and productivity were linked at the Hawthorne electrical works in the United States. When labor conditions in an experimental department were slightly altered, motivation and productivity went up. But when they were changed in the opposite direction, motivation and productivity went up as well. It turned out that the employees did not so much react to the nature of the physical changes themselves, but rather to the fact that there suddenly was an interest in their well-being—something that had never occurred before. This was later called the *Hawthorne effect*.

Politics, too, are affected by such phenomena. Whenever a candidate, on the eve of an election, succeeds in projecting the image of a "winner," this may trigger an extra bonus from floating voters. This is called the "Bandwagon" effect (after the festive truck with the music band that people tend to follow). After the results become known, this even leads more people to claim that they had voted for the winner than had actually done so. The reverse happens as well. It is called the "Underdog" effect. Through it, a sympathetic candidate heading for heavy losses may get a last-minute boost. It is rather rare, though, that both effects occur at the same time and cancel each other out.

So we have seen that such subjective "loops" and circular reactions have been unearthed in all disciplines over the years, not only in medicine, psychology and education, but also in sociology, economics, and politics. Some time ago, the sociologist Robert Merton (1948) proposed a generic term to cover all these phenomena—*self-fulfilling prophecies*, or SFPs. It boils down to the fact that people have a certain expectation about the future, and begin to think, feel and act accordingly. This change in attitude itself, and that of like-minded others, may then contribute to the expectation coming true.

Yet the opposite may happen as well. In a *self-defeating prophecy*, the expectation change and the attitude change may contribute to the expectation not coming true. If in elections, for instance, an unsympathetic candidate seems on the verge of winning, this may provoke a mobilization of his foes, and a shift in their behavior. So it is important to try and identify the exact conditions in which one or the other possibility may gain the upper hand. This may once again depend on tiny details and last-minute incidents. So things may still go either way.

In recent years, some authors such as Robert Giacalone and Paul Rosenfeld (1991) proposed to try and use these processes in more systematic ways. Their book, *Applied Impression Management*, demonstrated how work relations are influenced by these processes in myriad ways. So one should try and turn negative spirals into positive ones. Some readers have decried this as an attempt at Machiavellian manipulation. But this overlooks to what extent we are already spontaneously doing these things anyway; and how self-fulfilling prophecies may indeed play a key role in maintaining motivation or morale, or effectiveness and achievement within an organization at either high or low levels.

Cybernetics and Feedback

Now let us take a closer look at loops and feedback from a systems perspective. Such phenomena were first identified in ancient Greece, under the name of cybernetics or helmsmanship, for instance, with sailboats. The helmsman should be well acquainted with the currents in the water, the winds in the air, and the capabilities of the ship in order to steer it from point A to point B, with a minimum of efforts and risks. After Norbert Wiener had published his *Cybernetics* in 1947, the term got its current meaning as the art and science of the steering, control, and management of systems, particularly of mechanical and organic systems (Wiener, 1986).

One of its key notions had earlier been elaborated by neurophysiologist Walter Cannon. It is the notion of *homeostasis*, or the conservation of (more or less) the same state in dead and living systems. That is to say that minor variations in that state can be absorbed and corrected by the system itself. Whenever the sailboat heels over too much, the skipper may ease the sail. Whenever our stomach is empty, we feel hungry, then procure and eat food. As our stomach fills, we lose our appetite, and stop eating. The same for thirst, and other bodily sensations. So these are homeostatic processes, which guard the approximate equilibria in our body. Similar things hold for our minds. In order to be able to do this, the body and mind need feedback loops. That is to say, the systems have certain margins within which they try to remain; so there needs to be processes that monitor changes in parameters, and initiate possible corrections (Cannon, 1933).

There are two kinds of feedback loops, negative feedback and positive feedback. We speak of *negative feedback* whenever a significant variation in one direction leads to reactive compensation in the other direction. The best known example is a thermostat. When a room gets too cold, the thermostat will note this, and turn on the heating system. When the room gets too hot, the thermostat will once again note this, turn it off again and maybe even turn on the air conditioning. So negative feedback is a stabilization process; it helps homeostasis or keeping the same condition.

The opposite of negative feedback is positive feedback. This is a key process in media hypes. We speak of *positive feedback* whenever a significant variation in one direction leads to still more variation in that same direction. Whenever several people in a group begin to display deviant behavior, for instance, this may lead to facilitation ("easing" or lowering of thresholds) of similar acts by others, and undermine conformity. Whereas negative feedback is a stabilization process, positive feedback is a destabilization process. It throws a system off the initial course. So it may help to throw further light on the rapid, radical, and massive shifts in public opinion and perception that concern us here. In the literature from the immediate post-World War II period, and from the 1950s and early 1960s, there was a hidden tendency to approach negative feedback and stabilization as something positive, to approach positive feedback and destabilization as something negative. There was a kind of conservative bias.

Only in recent decades, and with the emergence of successive strands of complexity theory, has this one-sidedness subsided somewhat. Because we have begun to realize that systems that are destabilized, lose equilibrium, and become turbulent (or even slide into chaos) are a necessary fact of life. If all systems always remained stable, then there would be absolutely no room for innovation and renewal. But life cannot do without death. For the positive continuation of vital processes, it is essential that some systems whither away. Only because old structures lose their grip, and entropy takes over, new structures can flourish. So positive feedback does not only imply destruction, but also creation. This also holds for media hypes—for instance, in the Band Aid case.

Amplification and Circular Reaction

Positive feedback often takes the form of amplification, a kind of self-reinforcement that drowns out existing signals and gives emerging signals the upper hand. We are all familiar with such phenomena in the realm of audiovisual appliances. Whenever you have a sound amplifier on, and inadvertently put the microphone in front of the loudspeaker instead of behind it, the signal will "blow up" to an extremely loud and very nasty beep sound. Whenever you have a video camera on, and aim it at the monitor rather than at something else, this may produce an image containing an infinite series of increasingly smaller versions of itself. In some cases, the interference may even generate moving geometric patterns. The manifestation of such metaprinciples is not limited to physical processes, but can be noted in psychosocial processes as well.

The aforementioned, microsociologist Erving Goffman (1964) showed in his book *Stigma*, for instance, that stigmatization may be subject to such amplification as well. Erich Goode and Nachman Ben-Yehuda (1994) showed in their book, *Moral Panics*, that moral outrages may amplify small perceived deviations to large perceived forms of social deviation. We return to this subject in chapter 9. But basically, all collective mood shifts that are discussed in Part III of this book involve similar kinds of amplification spirals. In their full-fledged form, such amplification spirals may lead to something called *circular reaction*.

Sociologist Herbert Blumer (1969) identified circular reaction as a key process in typical collective behavior. In cases of circular reaction, people imitate and adopt the thoughts, feelings, and behavior of others in relatively unmediated form; whereas under other conditions, such people would first critically evaluate them in the light of accepted norms and conventions. The result is that "alternate" patterns may spread rapidly throughout a group, in accelerated form. Therefore circular reaction is an important concept in the explanation of transgressive behavior of crowds, to which we return in the next chapter. But in a wider sense, it can also be applied to emerging social movements, to dramatic opinion shifts, and to noteworthy mass phenomena in general (and also to such media hypes as the one that surrounded Band Aid).

Whereas permanent mutation (e.g., in hypothetical "memes") constantly transforms minor details, circular reactions make some of these spread rapidly and in relatively unmediated form. Of course, this happens only exceptionally and under precise, well-defined circumstances; for instance, when there is some kind of correspondence and resonance with the wider context, or whenever a critical threshold has been reached. We later return to these other metaprinciples. For the time being, it is enough to establish that amplification and circular reaction may help a system break out of its previous parameters.

The phenomenon does not only manifest itself within psychological and sociological systems, but also within geographic and economic ones. Prigogine and Stengers (1984) noted that this is how an uneven distribution of populations and activities over a territory comes about. An initial settlement may occur in one location for reasons that may be irrelevant to later situations. A village may grow around an abbey, for instance, next to a chapel where a miracle is said to have taken place. The village may then develop into a town or a city, simply because it is there. It becomes a bigger center, because it already is a small center. The development may become "relatively autonomous."

The economist Brian Arthur (1990) also reviewed some of the fundamental laws of economics and competition in this regard. Within traditional industry, which transforms raw materials into manufactured products, there was said to be a "law of decreasing profits" at work. Within modern industry, which uses information to trade more efficiently, however, there seems to be a "law of increasing profits" at work. An information, or software, or media giant (such as Microsoft), or a country particularly strong in these fields (such as the United States), can easily translate small advantages into complete market domination. This has been labeled the "Matthew effect"; whoever (already) has shall be given (more). We will return to this phenomenon in our final discussion on the trouble with forecasts (chap. 11).

So the long, underestimated process of positive feedback is of great importance for the understanding of many psychosocial phenomena because it plays a key role in systems loosing equilibrium and heading for radical change. As the "futurologist" Alvin Toffler wrote in his Foreword to Prigogine and Stengers' (1984) chaos book:

> ... In far-from-equilibrium conditions we find that very small perturbations or fluctuations can become amplified into gigantic, structure-breaking waves ... A whole new approach is opened that makes it possible to relate the so-called hard sciences to the softer sciences of life—and perhaps even to social processes as well.
>
> Such findings have at least analogical significance for social, economic or political realities. Words like "revolution", "economic crash", "technological upheaval", and "paradigm shift" all take on new shades of meaning when we begin thinking of them in terms of fluctuations, feedback amplification, dissipative structures, bifurcations, and the rest of the Prigoginian conceptual vocabulary. (p. XVII)

These and other aspects of that whole framework reappear throughout this present book. But we have not yet explicitly identified a psychosocial domain to which they seem to apply specifically. In my opinion, the twin disciplines of mass psychology and collective behavior sociology are such a domain. So throughout Part II we take a closer look at both.

II

EMERGING COLLECTIVE BEHAVIOR

*God has put a secret art into the forces of nature so as to enable it to fash-
ion itself out of chaos into a perfect world system.*
—Immanuel Kant, German philosopher (Casti, 1994, p. 212)

After preparatory discussions on opinion and communication, we now come
to the heart of the matter; both concerning the metaprinciples involved and
the phenomena considered. After discussing the dual metaprinciples of continuous mutation and feedback loops, we now get to the threefold metaprinciples of synergy formation, pattern emergence and self-organization.
This involves processes beginning to run parallel, to link up with each
other, and clusters separating themselves. They are at the heart of complex
adaptive systems. Even if we get to other aspects as well, such as evolving
contexts and critical thresholds, and even more enigmatic notions such as
strange attractors and phase transitions. But we first have to complete our
general framework before delving into further complexities.

The phenomena identified in this part, too, form the heart of this present
book. We plan to take a closer look at newer discussions on mass psychology and collective behavior sociology before we move on to public mood
shifts in a more general sense. Typical collective behavior usually involves:
(a) relatively large numbers of people, (b) getting involved in a heightened
interaction process, and (c) the accelerated emergence of alternative patterns of thought, feeling, and action. This process involves relatively large
numbers because one characteristic is that people do not so much react to
each other as identifiable individuals, but rather to each other as a diffuse
group. There is also a heightened interaction process because it is some

kind of psychosocial, rapid occurrence. There are alternative patterns because it is a way to surmount conventional patterns, which are somehow experienced as inadequate or unsatisfactory. We further elaborate these themes.

The typical interaction pattern may manifest itself on three different levels; first, on the level of psychological crowds, relatively large groups of people, physically assembled in one time and place, and involved in mutual exchanges. They are groups within which there is direct contact through the senses; seeing and hearing, smelling and feeling. Second, there is the level of what I call "opinion currents"; relatively large groups of people, physically dispersed through time and space, but yet also involved in mutual exchanges, most of all through the communication processes we have previously discussed. And finally, there is the third and intermediary level of social movements; relatively large groups, parts assemble intermittently, but are also involved in indirect exchanges. The emergence of lasting coordination patterns is an important aspect.

Beyond these three themes, there is often a fourth that runs through the literature. That is the theme of a mass society, a mass media society, a media society, in which peoples are said to be more susceptible to such forms of mass and collective behavior. The underlying idea is that people in a premodern, traditional, agrarian society were held together by permanent bonds between families, villages, and regions; between trades, classes, and institutions. Whereas in a modern industrial society, people are said to form more amorphous masses of isolated individuals, with a higher degree of mobility and a higher capability for reorientation. Similar themes recur in discussions on postmodernism and the postindustrial society, on the information and multimedia society.

Sometimes this theme is given an optimistic tenor; people are supposedly increasingly free, are offered more choices, can develop new identities—with the help of new technologies such as the Internet and virtual reality. Sometimes, by contrast, this same theme is given a pessimistic tenor; people are supposedly uprooted, open to outside influence, or easily manipulated by higher powers. Something can be said for both types of reasoning. But we should not fall into the trap of all too easily judging the future with criteria derived from the past, or with norms and values derived from the past.

We should try to understand in what ways the future of man and society will become qualitatively different, without necessarily being either better or worse. That also holds for the various types of collective behavior, which may or may not be increasingly prominent.

4

The Formation of Synergy in Crowds

Everyone has observed how much more dogs are animated when they hunt in a pack, than when they pursue their game apart. We might, perhaps, be at a loss to explain this phenomenon, if we had not experience of a similar in ourselves.
—David Hume, British philosopher (Gross, 1987, p. 113)

We open this chapter with the case of a protracted global campaign, accompanied by hundreds or even thousands of mass meetings and demonstrations. Crowds have often been associated with pent-up emotions, excessive behavior, and violence. Yet here, too, these were the exception rather than the rule. How should we understand these occasional transgressions? Psychologists have proposed the so-called "deindividuation" theory; sociologists have proposed the so-called "convergence" theory. But what are the metaprinciples that underlie both? They are the principles of processes beginning to run parallel; the principles of synergy and rhythm, of synchronization and resonance. Resistance fades, and boosting emerges.

CASE NUMBER FOUR: THE MORUROA EXPLOSION

The next case study is a perfect illustration of the fact that crowd meetings proceed peacefully most of the time, and only "derail" every now and then. It describes the global protests against the French resumption of nuclear testing during the second half of 1995. They mobilized both the older anti-militarist movement and the newer environmental movement. This mobilization was a process that gradually reinforced itself, while all kinds of sounds and images came to resonate with each other. Hearsay (about possible radioactive fallout) and media hypes (about ongoing maritime confrontations) played a role.

Nuclear testing, nuclear weapons, and nuclear protests ("ban the bomb") had been recurring even during the Cold War between East and West. The five permanent members of the U.N. Security Council always co-founded their claim to "big power" status on the exclusive possession of 40,000 nuclear weapons of mass destruction. Under the guise of "nonproliferation"; furthermore, the big powers had discouraged emerging powers from trying to catch up with them. But developing and updating such nuclear weapons of course also implied testing them. The United States held some 1,000 nuclear tests over the years, the Soviet Union, 700, France, 200, Great Britain and China, some 40 each.

During the first 20 years, all experts seriously underestimated the radiation risks involved. Tests were held above ground and sometimes in the unprotected presence of humans. Land, oceans, and atmosphere were polluted. Even after the big five had shifted to underground testing, there continued to be occasional pollution by radio-active material. After the Cold War ended in 1991, however, Soviet president, Mikhail Gorbachev, proclaimed a unilateral moratorium on all nuclear testing. Gradually, the three Western nuclear powers adhered to it; only late-comer China pursued its own course.

The French nuclear program had originated with Charles de Gaulle. The famed general had been appointed president with extraordinary powers during the late 1950s to sort out the decolonization crisis, and to stem the country's decline as a big power. Although France also always maintained that there were no risks involved, it wisely chose not to hold its tests in its own Massif Central, but rather in its colonies; first in the Sahara Desert, and after Algerian independence, in the South Pacific Ocean. The island of choice formed half a ring of coral reefs on top of a volcano that had sunk below sea level; the French called it *Mururoa*. They shunned spelling it *Moruroa* ("language of secrets"), as natives and critics did, because it was vaguely reminiscent of the French word, *mort*, or meaning "dead."

Throughout 25 years, an atomic test was held on the atoll on average every other month or so. French engineers drilled well over 100 shafts relatively close together. Each one was between 600 and a 1,000 meters deep, and several meters wide. A device would be sunk in to explode. Although the shafts were later filled in again, part of the island was said to resemble Swiss cheese, full of holes. This came to worry more than one expert. One of the reasons the Americans had given up testing on the Pacific islands of Bikini, Eniwetok, and Kiritimati, they said, was the discovery of "tired mountain syndrome"—which gradually made the underground more fragile.

The explosions resulted in cracks and crevices. There was a risk of land-slides that might open up a leak somewhere in the vast complex of test shafts, and might have some nuclear material leak into the water or the air. There had reportedly been one particular incident in 1979, when a French device got stuck halfway down a shaft, but was exploded anyway, because it coincided with an official visit of the president himself. It was said to have caused a landslide and an ocean wave, felt as far as 1,000 miles away. When controversies over the tests continued to escalate, the authorities allowed brief inspections at selected locations by outside experts, but some relevant data remained incomplete and censored. The famed ocean researcher Jacques Cousteau, for one, became a noted critic of the program.

As we discuss elsewhere, the environmental organization Greenpeace owed some of its original *raison d'être* to its early opposition to American nuclear testing in Alaska. Its pioneer, David McTaggart, had led successive fleets of ships protesting the French tests (Brown & May, 1991). In 1985, there was a major incident when French saboteurs blew up the Greenpeace ship, Rainbow Warrior, in New Zealand. A Dutch–Portugese photographer was killed. The French government at first denied all involvement (Luccioni, 1986; Ten Berge, 1989).

Two of the secret agents were tracked, arrested, and sentenced to 10 years for manslaughter. But the very next year, New Zealand was pressured into agreeing to the transfer of the prisoners to a French military base. One year later, they were released without further ado; and on the tenth anniversary of the events, their one-time boss even got an official decoration. By that time, it turned out that the same secret service had been on the verge of infecting the crew of a Greenpeace replacement ship (on its way via the Dutch Antilles) with disease. It only canceled the plan after it had been able to get information on the ships communication frequencies, which were then systematically interfered with (according to the Dutch quality daily, *NRC Handelsblad*, in 1995).

Between 1981 and 1995, the French presidency had been held by Social Democrat François Mitterand. Almost half of all French nuclear tests took place under his reign, but in the end he had joined the moratorium on nuclear testing. His succession by Jacques Chirac, a former Gaullist prime minister, changed all that. Confronted with internal problems, which would be hard to solve, Chirac was eager to boost France's prestige overseas. On the eve of an official visit to the United States and of the summit of the G7 strongest industrial nations, Chirac announced that he would "irrevocably" resume testing.

The dramatic gesture had the dual effect of reminding everybody that France still had its nuclear *force de frappe*, and it still had its *miettes de l'empire* (crumbs of the empire) in and around various seas and oceans. It was later reported that none of his advisers had realized that the moment was particularly ill chosen. It was the eve of the tenth anniversary of the Rainbow Warrior bombing, and, even more important, the eve of the 50th anniversary of the Hiroshima and Nagasaki bombings with its hundreds of thousands of victims. Such coincidences often play an unforeseen role.

Greenpeace had already planned to commemorate the 10th anniversary of the bombing of the original Rainbow Warrior with a voyage by its successor ship, the Rainbow Warrior II. When it entered the territorial waters of Moruroa on that specific date, squads of riot police immediately boarded it. When the activists barricaded themselves inside the steering room, the police broke the windows and threw tear gas inside. There was a brief moment of panic, and a woman was heard to scream. What the French failed to realize, however, was that a television camera with an immediate satellite link-up registered the brutal scene live. Within hours, therefore, CNN, the BBC, and all other major newscasters in the world picked up the dramatic sounds and images. The impact of these few minutes of audiovisual material cannot be overestimated.

Meanwhile, Greenpeace had also decided to launch a major protest campaign with global crowd meetings against the new tests, and allegedly set aside no less than 10 million pounds for the ongoing test of wills. Paris never understood that a new social movement of this type could wield such budgets and power, and its prime minister, Alain Juppé, hinted that it was simply an instrument of a dark Anglo-American (and Australian) plot to extend their combined sphere of interest and to replace the French. French authorities even told visiting journalists that in Moruroa, there was less radioactivity in the air than in Paris, and that the water of the surrounding Pacific was cleaner than the North Sea.

The national holiday in France on July 14th commemorates an earlier crowd gathering (and even riot): the storming of the Bastille prison during the French Revolution, the proclamation of human rights, and the noble principles of *Liberté, Égalité, Fraternité*. It is usually celebrated with a huge military parade on Paris's *Champs Elysées* boulevard, and with diplomatic receptions in all overseas embassies and cultural centers. This time, many foreign dignitaries stayed away; however, uninvited protesters showed up, and demonstrators blocked the entrance to the gates. They had death masks on, and white T shirts with English texts such as "Hit the road Jacques," "Chirac doesn't care atoll," and "Napoleon Blownapart." Sixtyish "Ban the bomb" parties broke into lyrics such as, "Chirac, get back, don't be a maniac" (to the tune of the familiar Beatles song).

Crowd protests were even more vociferous all around the Pacific Ocean itself. The Hiroshima commemorations in Japan produced the "Hiro-Chirac" epithet. Australian prime minister Paul Keating did not hesitate to call the French president and used words like "arrogant," "stupid," and "ridiculous" on successive occasions. Various national and regional authorities said they would do no business with French companies anymore; transport and communication workers at one point denied their services to them.

New Zealand premier Jim Bolger called the French attitude "neo-colonial." According to opinion polls, more than 80% of the electorate felt that their government had not done enough to protest the French plans. More than 60% felt New Zealand should send a military frigate to Moruroa, but a smaller civil research vessel was sent instead. Smaller Pacific island nations recalled their ambassadors, and one even broke off diplomatic relations entirely. All these coast dwellers had a primal fear that their ocean paradise might somehow become polluted at some point in the distant future, possibly even long after the French would have left the region.

In August, a protest fleet gathered in Auckland, New Zealand, to set sail to Papeete on the famous island of Tahiti (the capital of French Polynesia), and then onward to Moruroa. There were to be several dozen smaller ships, including the yacht Vega owned by Greenpeace veteran, David McTaggart. There were several taller ships as well; the Rainbow Warrior II, which had been released and repaired; the MV (motor vessel) Greenpeace, which was especially equipped with a helicopter deck and with advanced communication equipment to host journalists and television crews; and a cruise ship, which had been chartered by and for MPs, and also hosted opinion leaders from various countries.

As soon as the ships arrived in the area, they began their cat-and-mouse game of small provocations, incursions, and diversions—under the watchful eye of the cameras. When the Rainbow Warrior II intruded into the territorial waters, it was boarded and impounded again, as had been foreseen. When its helicopter and rubber boats repeatedly infringed upon the territorial limits, however, the French felt they had a legal right to board and impound their mother ship, Greenpeace, as well—which had not been foreseen. On its playful "naval battle" map on the Internet, therefore, Greenpeace had to mark down its second major ship as "lost."

Because the latter ship had been the major remaining support for logistical operations, this was a severe blow indeed. Campaign leaders at headquarters later claimed that campaign leaders on the spot had disobeyed express orders not to take such risks, and had succumbed to pressure from journalists eager for ever more spectacular action and camera shots. They had themselves succumbed to the media hype, and thus fallen into their own trap. The internal dispute was indicative of a recurrent rift within the organization, between the proponents of "direct action" and of "solid organization" (Knappe, 1994). Whatever the case, the effectiveness of the protest campaign and its media coverage were vastly reduced for the remainder of the campaign. Greenpeace had overplayed its hand.

It was now early September, and everyone in Europe and France had returned from the summer holidays. Greenpeace planned to have its smaller ships steam up the SeIne river but they were blocked by the police. It planned another crowd demonstration to form a human chain straight through Paris, but this was prevented as well. Greenpeace tried to have representatives present 7 million protest signatures to the president, but he refused to see them. Most Frenchmen, opinion leaders, and media had somewhat contradictory feelings about the entire affair. On one hand, they felt that the resumption of tests at this point in time had not really been such a good idea. On the other hand, they also felt it was none of the business of all these foreign "do-gooders." So local protests remained relatively timid.

Emotions spilled over in an entirely different spot, however. In Papeete, the capital of Tahiti and the whole of French Polynesia, at 12 hundred kilometers from the testing grounds, an unprecedented group of 200 international journalists had gathered, representatives of the most influential media throughout the world. The local independence movement, which had only received 15% of the vote during previous elections, grabbed the occasion to vent its discontent with the blatant inequalities, the neocolonial situation, and the risks of radio-active pollution. It involved the *Tavini Huiraatira* party, headed by Oscar Temaru, and the *A Tia i Mua* trade union, headed by Hiro Tefaarere. Protest marches departed from various points on the island, and 2,000 to 3,000 militants converged on the capital.

The first test was held on Tuesday, September 5. There was a shocked reaction by foreign dignitaries present in Tahiti. Among them was the Japanese minister of finance, who labeled it "madness" and attributed "diabolical instincts" to the French president. A protest strike had been called for the next day. Already at 7 a.m., dozens of militants converged on the airport. In the course of the morning, their number swelled to hundreds. The only direct connection to France, the Paris flight, was about to depart. A rumor made the rounds that nuclear engineers were on board, and/or the Gaullist politician, Gaston Flosse—the major power broker on the island. Demonstrators tried to get into the aircraft; when they failed to board, they blocked the runway with tree trunks, canoes, and later with trucks.

The radio station of the independence movement called for calm, but instead drove more people to the airport. Riot police were mobilized, but their numbers were insufficient and they soon ran out of tear gas. Locals now barricaded access roads, reportedly armed not only with sticks, stones, and Molotov cocktails, but also with beer bottles and *pacalolo* (the local equivalent of marijuana). Cars in the parking lot were set afire. Violence spread to the main building. Windows were broken and luxury shops were plundered. Two people were seriously wounded, about a dozen less seriously, and some 50 people were arrested during the course of the day.

At 7 p.m., several hundred paratroopers and legionairs were hurriedly flown in from Moruroa to take over the defense of the airport, while new contingents of riot police departed from France. Meanwhile, unrest had spread to the town, where policemen soon lost control. Eight hundred demonstrators gathered in the town center, next to the office of the High Commissioner (the governor) and the building of the regional assembly. More windows were broken and more luxury shops were plundered or set afire.

One journalist reported how he had seen local women quietly filling their shopping bags at a perfume store, retreat as soon as police forces arrived, but return as soon as the police left again. Another journalist reported that he had seen looters walk away with sporting articles, fashionable clothes, fancy jewelry or even complete hi-fi sets. The incidents continued until Thursday, when sufficient reinforcements finally arrived. Total damage was later estimated at more than 2 hundred million Francs, or more than $30 million dollars.

Independence leader Temaru later claimed that the situation had gone out of control, and that the entire people had rebelled out of a sense of humiliation, frustration, and anger. But the French minister of overseas territories retorted that Temaru had been like the "sorcerer's apprentice" who had lit the fuse and made arsonists, wreckers, and looters commit their hideous acts. According to the local strongman, Gaston Flosse (quoted in French papers such as *Le Monde* and *Le Figaro*), it had been Greenpeace, the international delegations, and the foreign media who had stirred the trouble. Yet order was soon restored again, and protesters abroad looked for other targets.

Calls for a boycott of characteristically French goods resounded all over the world. The early *Primeur* of light Beaujolais wine was particularly vulnerable. Over previous years, its annual "release" by mid-November had been surrounded with ever more marketing hype. It had greatly benefited from this ostentatious "Frenchie" ritual, but now it was to pay the price for that close identification. Export losses for the *Primeur* were estimated at some 25%, for all Beaujolais at 12.5%. Other wines lost some ground as well. The president of an exporters association later estimated the overall sales loss (or missed growth) for all French wines over the entire year at three-quarter billion Francs (well over a $100 million dollars). Some market shares may even have been lost forever. To other *Primeur* wines from Spain and Italy (like the *Novello*), to good substitutes for ordinary Bourgogne and Bordeaux from the newly opened markets in Southeastern Europe, to new wine countries in the America's (the United States, Chile) and ironically also in the Pacific itself (Australia and New Zealand).

Meanwhile, France had announced that it would reduce the test explosions from eight to six. By late January, 1996, the last test was held, and France announced that it would join the ban again. The president of one of the most powerful nuclear nations in the world had capitulated to world public opinion.

Now what was remarkable about this entire global campaign, which resulted in a thousand peaceful demonstrations and in one violent explosion? It had taken the old powers several decades to reach an agreement on a suspension of nuclear tests, and the moratorium had held several years, before the French swept it aside again. But within the newly emerging post Cold War order, the Anglo-American media began to reign supreme, and did not hesitate to show their disdain for French pretensions. And other countries, even on the European continent itself, had also long held profoundly ambivalent feelings about that country and people.

The moment of the announcement had been particularly ill chosen, because it resonated with the Hiroshima commemorations. Arch images and key words play a huge role in the condensation and crystallization of unease and unrest, as we will see again in several later chapters. But other circumstances played a role, too. Seen from western Europe, the Pacific Ocean (with its dateline) is "the end" of the world, but also "the beginning" of the world; paradise itself; it is an idyll of purity. The local inhabitants want it to survive, even after the rest of the world has been destroyed by pollution. So, once again, a unique configuration of representations is decisive.

On September 6, a sudden resonance and link-up occurred between separate configurations, a global environmental campaign and a local anticolonial protest. It resulted in violence, when militants reinforced each other in transgressive behavior. There was a lowering of thresholds and an expression of rage, which would normally have been restrained. How does this come about? Why do crowds get out of control every now and then? Why do high-minded ideals cede to low impulses? What are the social and psychological processes involved? Can we explain what happens? Can we conceptualize and understand it? Let us take a closer look at crowd psychology.

THE PHENOMENON OF PSYCHOLOGICAL CROWDS

Crowds involve large numbers of people, present at the same time and in the same place. But we are not so much interested in purely physical crowds here; large numbers of people merely present at the same time and in the same place, as in a shopping street or train station. We are rather interested in psychological crowds, large numbers of people that are somehow psychologically connected to each other or to the same events because their attention is drawn by a performance or an incident. That will make them react to or with one another, become part of the same interaction pattern, and form a temporary group. So in this chapter we limit ourselves to this latter type of crowds. If (and to what extent) other types of masses display similar characteristics will be discussed elsewhere.

We look at the major approaches to psychological crowds in three steps. First a few words about the origins of the domain of mass psychology, which was long identified as such, but gradually came to be largely absorbed into the wider field of social psychology. After this historical introduction, I present two subsections on more recent approaches to psychological crowds (which may help explain why demonstrators in Papeete committed such excesses).

One of these more recent approaches concerns the so-called deindividuation theory—mostly adhered to by psychologists. The other of these more recent approaches concerns the so-called convergence theory—mostly adhered to by sociologists. But both are in a way about some kind of circular reaction and synchronization of thought, feelings, and actions—their causes and consequences. In my view, they complement each other rather well, and make some important observations. We later return more extensively to the sociology of collective behavior, which partially overlaps with mass and crowd psychology.

The Psychology of Crowds and Masses

The backgrounds of early crowd psychology have been closely reexamined over recent decades; for instance, in studies by Nye (1975), Giner (1976), Barrows (1981), Mucchi-Faina (1983), Boef (1984), Moscovici (1985), and Graumann and Moscovici (1986). My own doctoral dissertation of 1989 (published in 1992) was devoted to a thorough analysis of the social and intellectual backgrounds, the work and ideas of the five main early Latin authors: Taine, Sighele, Fournial, Le Bon, and Tarde (in that order). Since then, other overviews have been published by McClelland (1989), McPhail (1991), and others. The drift of all these studies is that early crowd psychology with its heavy emphasis on irrationality was ideologically biased in many respects. Basically these adult, male, White, middle-class authors dismissed the actions of rebellious crowds as infantile, primitive, feminine, and lower class.

One of the central questions of this early crowd psychology was how the minds of hundreds or thousands of unorganized individuals seemed to merge into a psychological crowd, how their thoughts, feelings and acts developed some kind of "mental unity" (Reiwald, 1946). One part of the question was what specific aspects of the individual psyche were mobilized here. It was widely assumed that powerful, deeper, and more primitive layers of personality were somehow involved, judging from the excesses that often occurred. Another part of the question was how these specific aspects of the individual psyche interacted and were somehow welded together.

The French physician Gustave Le Bon (1966) wrote by far the most influential early book about *La psychologie des foules*, translated as *The crowd*. He also claimed to be the inventor of the field, but derived most of his ideas from his immediate predecessors—usually without acknowledging this (van Ginneken, 1992a, pp. 119–26). He said masses somehow formed a single being, and were characterized by some kind of mental unity that arose because people quickly adopted each other's feelings; for instance through contagion, or the hypnotic suggestion exerted by powerful leaders using forceful imagery. After World War I, the British psychologist William McDougall (1920) in turn published a book, *The Group Mind*, which stirred debates as to what extent one could and should speak of some supraindividual entity emerging in this context. Similar discussions characterized early social psychology, and survive to this day (see Sandelands & St. Clair, 1993).

In my opinion, these recurrent discussions derive from an incomplete understanding of the phenomena of nonlinear emergence, which are the key concern of this present book, because the thoughts, feelings, and actions of people may be linked in profoundly different ways. They may be linked in a tight, direct, and relatively unmediated way. This results in the kind of alternative social behavior usually identified as *typical collective* or *mass behavior*. But they may also be linked in a loose, indirect, and highly mediated way. That results in the kind of *conventional social behavior* we are used to in most of ordinary life.

Between these two extremes there is a sliding scale. At some point on this scale, a gradual or quantitative difference turns into an essential or qualitative difference; or maybe even at a combination of points, because it is really a combination of such scales that related to various aspects of interaction. We return to this problem in chapter 10, about the metaprinciple of phase transitions. But let us not jump ahead, and first take time to consider various approaches to this enigmatic phenomenon of mass formation.

Deindividuation Theory

Great thinkers such as Schopenhauer and Nietzsche emphasized that man is the result and expression of some deeper life force. Psychologists and pedagogues have in turn discovered that individual consciousness is not "a given" from the start, but something gradually built. Such views transpire in many psychoanalytical and psychodynamic theories originating from the Germanic world.

Sigmund Freud claimed, for instance, that at the outset, the fetus and child experience themselves as symbiotically united with the mother. Through the succession of birth, the interruption of breast feeding, beginning to walk, toilet training, and so on, a gradual separation takes place—from the mother, the parents, the caretakers. At the same time, there is the growing awareness of an outside world. Carl Jung even claimed that we have a "collective unconsciousness" in common, and that growth and education imply some kind of individuation. Such authors also noted that upon complete submersion into a collective, the individual experiences a kind of "oceanic feeling": the pleasurable elimination of the painful separation from one's closest environment.

When the Nazi regime rose to power, many German, Austrian, and other psychologists and sociologists fled to the United States, and contributed to the further rise of an empirical social psychology. This led to studies on the effects of authority, conformity, and anonymity on group dynamics. Think of the classical experiments by Kurt Lewin and Solomon Asch, and later by Stanley Milgram and others (for an overview, see Cartwright & Zander (1959), Lindzey & Aronson (1954), Sahakian (1982)). It was in this context that Leon Festinger (1957) (along with Pepitone & Newcomb) proposed the term *deindividuation*, to indicate the complete merger of an individual with a group or crowd or mass, which led to a loss of restraint. Others contributed to the further elaboration of this notion.

One of the most elaborate and most influential discussions of this notion was the essay, "The Human Choice—'Individuation, Reason and Order Versus Deindividuation, Impulse and Chaos," which social psychologist, Philip Zimbardo (1969), presented to the *Nebraska Symposium on Motivation*. It referred back to the contrast between chaos and order, which had already been noted by the ancient Greeks, characterized by Dionysus and Apollo. It also referred to the large-scale manifestations of social unrest of the 1960s, ranging from students revolts, civil disobedience, and race riots, to death squads and other excesses. It proposed a better understanding of certain excesses by a further elaboration of the notion of deindividuation; or rather the conceptual scheme of deindividuation. Zimbardo undertook to link a whole range of psychological factors, which had earlier been identified in laboratory experiments and field research about individuals and groups. I sum them up here in some detail to give the reader an impression of the possible strengths and weaknesses of this conceptual scheme.

In order to understand what was going on in crowds, Zimbardo said that one had to spell out what was specific about them in three successive steps: the input, the psychological processing, and the output in those situations. As specific input variables, he mentioned anonymity, shared responsibility, group size and activity, altered temporal perspectives, arousal, sensory overload, physical involvement, reliance on noncognitive interactions and feedback, novel or unstructured situations, and possible altered states of consciousness (through lack of sleep, use of alcohol or drugs, etc.).

According to his analysis, all this might lead people to experience typical crowd situations differently from everyday social situations. The inferred subjective changes might take effect through a minimization of self-evaluation and concern for social evaluation. This would lead to a weakening of controls based upon guilt, shame, fear, and previous commitments; which would in turn result in a lowering of thresholds for expressing normally inhibited behaviors. So this is what could have played a role in the derailment of demonstrations in Papeete.

These mental changes might ultimately result in a range of alternative output behaviors. The behavior emitted could be emotional, impulsive, irrational, regressive, and with high intensity. It might not be under the controlling influence of the usual, external, discriminative stimuli; it would be self-reinforcing and difficult to terminate. Memory impairments and perceptual distortions even might result. There would be hyperresponsiveness to the behavior of proximal, active others and unresponsiveness to distant reference groups. The "released" behavior might lead to greater liking for the group or situation. At extreme levels, the group could dissolve, as its members became "autistic" in their impulse gratification. All this might contribute to the temporary elimination of traditional forms and structures.

Zimbardo's conceptual scheme seems to provide a satisfactory explanation of why crowd situations do sometimes lead to extreme excesses. In this type of analysis, deindividuation was related to the links between the thoughts, feelings, and behaviors of people in a crowd becoming shorter, tighter, less mediated and self-reinforcing. It would contribute to making processes run parallel. This synergy would help break down resistance and boost the power of the processes involved. It would provide a better explanation for the apparent "mental unity" and "group mind" that Le Bon (1895/1966) and McDougall (1920) had claimed. Over subsequent years, the deindividuation concept was further researched and discussed by other authors, such as Ed Diener (1976, 1979, 1980), Robert Dipboye (1977), Steven Prentice-Dunn and Ronald Rogers (1980, 1982) and others.

Yet the model was also criticized, by several authors we will consider later. It would still have the same shortcomings as the classical theories, described before; that is to say, the observations and analyses did almost exclusively apply to very exceptional situations (for instance riots and panic in their most extreme stages). But they were implicitly generalized to many, much milder forms of transgressive collective behavior, or even mass behavior that remained entirely within acceptable limits; for example, in ordinary protest demonstrations, such as those that dominated the rest of Greenpeace's campaign. On closer inspection, critics say, it is extremely rare that crowds derail, and most of the time they have good reasons to be outraged, as in the Moruroa case. Decision makers and riot police derail just as well, and maybe just as often. Small groups and isolated individuals are known to "freak out" on occasion. So why should this be attributed to the specific nature of crowds?

One group of critics of deindividuation theory in Great Britain even counters that the supposed mental unity of crowds may be largely an optical illusion. According to Henri Tajfel's "social identification" hypothesis, people continually define and redefine themselves and others in accordance with a scheme of social categorizations (Tajfel, 1978). Stephen Reicher (1984) noted that it is primarily people outside (or opposite) the crowd who tend to place the people inside the crowd into one social category, to ascribe a mental unity to them, including irrationality, and so forth. The people inside the crowd themselves do rather perceive diversity and rational reactions. He investigated the so-called St. Paul's riot in Bristol in 1980 in order to clarify these points (see Reicher in Tajfel, 1982; Reicher, 1984). To a certain extent, such observations might apply to the Papeete riot as well.

The Convergence Approach

The late 1960s and the early 1970s were an unruly period, during which the postwar generation contested the norms and values of the prewar generation. All around the world, this resulted in student protests and mass movements, in confrontations and riots. The impact of these events on the fields of mass psychology and collective behavior sociology was twofold. A new generation of liberal theorists rejected the old notion that crowds were merely irrational. At the same time, there were many opportunities to observe mass events empirically. This led to some other approaches, for instance in the United States, which was further becoming the leading power in everything, including the sciences of man and society.

In the fateful year of 1968, Carl Couch (see Evans, 1969) published an influential article in the *Social Problems* journal of the famous Society for the Study of Social Problems. It was titled, "Collective Behavior—An Examination of Some Stereotypes." It became a kind of manifesto. In it, he identified ten widespread stereotypes about collective behavior: spontaneity, lower class participation, suggestibility, emotionality, irrationality, mental disturbance, lack of self-control, antisocial behavior, destructiveness—but on occasion, also creativity. He proceeded to show that the arguments for this were weak, contradictory, and not well established. Couch and others therefore called upon experts to finally let go of the "armchair theories," and to do more empirical research on the everyday realities of collective behavior.

This further contributed to a wave of dozens of empirical studies, published over the next 20 years, and to the emergence of a family of theories that has been brought together under the label of the *convergence approach* and/or the *social behavioral and interactionist* (SBI) approach. The most important theoretical and practical work was done throughout the 1970s and 1980s by Clark McPhail (1991), along with colleagues such as David Miller (1985). First of all, they decided not to focus exclusively on (psychological) crowds, because the existing terminology was tainted, vague, and abstract. Rather, they chose to focus on *gatherings*, which formed a more neutral, well-defined, and concrete category. Often these were simple meetings or parades. Supposedly, "typical" collective behavior might emerge, but did not need to.

In such meetings, a number of people (two or more) would gather at a specific time, in a specific place. These events had a life cycle of their own, consisting of three phases: coming together, being together, and leaving. A number of typical situations were identified for each phase. Leaving, for instance, could be a routine affair or an emergency evacuation. The latter could be a reaction to a threat (an attack or a disaster, for instance), or to uniformed intervention (e.g., military or police), and so on. Each of these situations had their own inherent logic.

Collective behavior, furthermore, could take the form of "acting in concert" or "acting in common." Others made a similar distinction between "collective" and "collected" behavior (Lofland, 1985). In the former case, there was some kind of implicit coordination, in the latter just parallel reactions. McPhail identified six basic forms of acting in concert, and seven basic forms of acting in common. The latter basic forms could further be subdivided according to four to seven modalities each, he said: resulting in forty different categories that investigators could score on their forms. Namely, *collective orientation* (as in clusters or rings), *vocalization* (from "aah" and "ooh" to "boo"), *verbalization* (prayer and singing), *gesticulation* (the raised fist, the V-sign), *vertical movement* (from sitting to standing and jumping), *horizontal movement* (walking to running), and *manipulation* (involving hand movements from clapping to throwing). What one could observe was the constant emergence and dissolution of new patterns (also see Scheff, 1990).

After a large number of such studies in a range of different situations, McPhail concluded that mass and collective behavior was much more diverse and varied than had always been assumed, and usually formed some kind of "quilt" made up from pieces in many different colors and textures. He noted five misconceptions. The first misconception was that when collective behavior occurred, every member of the gathering was involved. The second was that only one sequence of collective behavior occurred in a gathering; the third that this would continue indefinitely. The fourth was that the collective behavior would be simple if not simplistic; and the fifth that it frequently involved competition if not conflict. Violence was the exception rather than the rule, he said (McPhail, 1991).

Meanwhile a number of other authors, too, had taken a closer look at the forms that collective behavior could take. Sam Wright (1978), for one, asked himself, "How do crowd members create and use group forms in nonverbal interaction as a mechanism for coordinating and carrying out collective activities?" (pp. 12–13). Did physical forms and arrangements somehow facilitate specific psychological and social arrangements? As we have seen, for instance, people could form clusters or rings or streams. Within a crowd, many different such physical arrangements could be distinguished, which somehow facilitated certain types of sensory perception or motor interaction.

Milgram and Toch had earlier (in the second edition of Lindzey & Aronson, 1969) mentioned the following everyday experiment. Go to a crowded beach on a nice summer day. Drag a large, noteworthy object ashore, such as an old sea chest, and begin to force it open. At close distance, a small group of curious people will form. They will probably form an imperfect circle; everyone wants to see, but does not want to stand in front of others unnecessarily. Now raise the trunk onto your shoulders, and begin to carry it inland. A procession will probably form; at least children and youngsters will tend to follow. After some distance, some will try to figure out what is going on to see whether it is worthwhile to follow you any farther. The arrangement of people thus facilitates certain sensorimotor interactions.

In another paper, the aforementioned Carl Couch spoke of "three dimensions of association" in this regard; namely monitoring, alignment, and acknowledgment. They lead people from independent individual behavior to interdependent collective behavior. Their perceptions and actions become intertwined (Wright, 1978). In still another paper, written with others, he identified five elements playing a role in this context: *mutual availability* (being able to see, hear, feel each other), *mutual attention, mutual responsiveness, mutual futures* (perspectives) and *mutual focus* (on an object of action; McPhail, 1991).

Richard Berk and others had meanwhile attempted to demonstrate that collective action was usually far from irrational, and could well be explained in terms of decision and game theory (also see Olson, 1965; Marwell & Oliver, 1993, in this context). According to such theories, people usually do six things in such situations: They try to collect information, list the possible courses of events, see whether they can influence them, decide which outcome has their preference, what chance there is that it will come about, and last but not least, what implies the smallest costs and the greatest benefits. The latter is usually labeled the "mini–max" strategy. He noted, for instance, how a barricade was erected at a student demonstration on a university campus. This radically changed the pattern of costs and benefits of possible types of behaviors; it restructured the situation. Much of collective behavior, including norm breaking, he said, could well be analyzed in such terms (see Genevie, 1978).

The empirical studies of the 1970s and 1980s have led to many practical observations and many theoretical innovations. We return to some. John Lofland (1985) noted that this led to a major shift in the study of collective behavior by putting more emphasis on the many things it had in common with "ordinary" conventional behavior. Participants are no longer seen as unorganized but as organizing themselves, no longer seen as being "norm-less" but as obeying emergent norms, no longer seen as without purpose but as purposeful, no longer seen as irrational but as just following a different ratio (McPhail, 1991). Yet one may agree with Goode (1992) that there is a certain tendency to "throw away the child with the bath-water" (p. 11).

One may well reproach the psychologically oriented deindividuation theory, that it is overly focused on the most extreme excesses of crowds, while implicitly generalizing crowd behavior to much milder forms of transgression, and even completely unproblematic forms of mass behavior. But one may in turn reproach the sociologically oriented SBI or convergence theory, that it dilutes the notion of psychological crowds to mere gatherings in order to observe that in most of these, nothing extraordinary is going on; or only in exceptional cases, which are then hardly a problem.

The operational definition of *a gathering* as "two or more persons," chooses to overlook a key psychological contrast. As there is a progressive rise in the number of active participants in a gathering, and therefore an exponential rise in the number of possible interactions, there will be a point at which the gradual and quantitative change will translate into a fundamental and qualitative change; in individual input, processing, and output. As Philip Anderson (quoted in Horgan, 1996) noted, "More is different." Under that threshold, individuals and their actions can all be separately and critically evaluated; but above that threshold, they blur into the perception of a diffuse group. The participants themselves also get the feeling that they are no longer evaluated as separate individuals, but as members of a diffuse group. So anonymity, a dilution of responsibility, and "risky shifts" can indeed be key aspects of the situation.

They facilitate unconventional types of expression, as well as the "circular reaction" of alternative thoughts, feelings, and actions. This is most obvious in extreme cases of crowd behavior. But maybe it is also true that it holds for social movements and opinion currents as well, albeit to a much lesser extent. But let us first look at how similar metaprinciples manifest themselves in nature and other domains in order to understand better what their further implications are.

THE METAPRINCIPLE OF SYNERGY FORMATION

At the beginning of this book, we tentatively identified public opinion, and comparable collective entities (such as crowds), as CAS. They consist of a multitude of individual units behaving in similar but not completely identical ways, interacting and forming dynamic configurations. They may get organized on various levels, and adapt to different situations. In the preceding and following chapters, we take a closer look at the many ways in which this may come about. One way is that entities may somehow convey their "alternate" states to others through transmission, diffusion, contagion, or even mutation. Another way is that "loops" form, which lead to positive feedback, amplification, and circular reaction.

We now come to yet another metaprinciple of how these entities may adapt to each other, a shift into a different mode. This metaprinciple concerns the various ways in which evolving processes may come to run parallel. In nature, this may take on various forms. First, movements and behaviors beginning to run parallel may reinforce each other; their movements begin to run in similar directions, their fluctuations may begin to synchronize, their rhythms may begin to resonate. Second, the net effect is that resistance diminishes and energy efficiency increases. Third, this contributes to boosting the whole process, to make it grow stronger. Fourth, this may help nature break out of its previous mold, and therefore trigger a nonlinear shift.

It may once again seem at first that these are gratuitous comparisons, analogies, and metaphors. But I hope to show that these are indeed relevant metaprinciples that can be found in nature and life, but also in man and society. We consider various aspects: movement and convergence of movement, fluctuation and synchronization of fluctuations, rhythms and resonance of rhythms, and finally, the overarching element of synergy and boosting.

Movement and Convergence

We already noted before that most things and forms are in fact collections of smaller entities, temporarily (never eternally) organized into larger configurations. They may seem hard and rock solid, but in the face of eternity, they are fluid or volatile. So the substance and the movement of these things are in part optical illusions; they are produced by the level on which the observation is made. This is particularly interesting whenever it concerns a powerful whole, consisting of seemingly insignificant parts.

A small movement of air may seem insignificant, but a strong draft may slam a door; the wind may bend huge trees, but a storm may make them snap like matches; a hurricane may flatten entire woods. Water may drip from a source, a stream may grind a bed; but a flood may pound the banks, collapse dams and dikes. A flake is feather light, a layer of snow may press a roof; but an avalanche may crush a house. One grain is insignificant, a pile may collapse something; but a sandstorm in the desert or a mudslide in the mountains may swallow entire villages.

All these examples of dead matter seem rather obvious, but the principle becomes more interesting when we move up the ladder of life, and take a closer look at plants and animals. The most fascinating examples are schools of fish, swarms of insects or birds, and herds or hordes of mammals. Under normal circumstances, such individual animals follow their own inclinations. But this changes when they embark on a major transmigration, usually once or twice a year, in order to reach alternative feeding or breeding grounds. This is a highly risky and dangerous undertaking; even under ideal conditions, a large percentage of the animals are lost, and die. With the right season and changing weather, then, such animals get restless, aroused, receptive, and spontaneously begin to form clusters and larger groups. These masses have little noteworthy hierarchy, except that some tend to operate in the front and others in the back, some on the periphery and others in the center of the group.

Now what is the phenomenology, the inherent logic, and the effect of this convergence of movements, this formation of "crowds'? First of all, movement and orientation are facilitated by the collective; there is no one single animal with a perfect sense of orientation and direction, a perfect representation of the goal and destination. But there are hundreds, thousands, tens of thousands of animals with an imperfect sense of orientation. This is another example where parallel distributed processing may lead to better results. At the same time the individuals are in a sense "dragged along" by the movement. Secondly, risks are minimized or distributed. Possible opponents and predators are sometimes intimidated by the seeming strength and power of the collective. Even if this is not the case, the chance of being targeted individually at any one point is diluted and becomes much smaller.

Similar principles are at work in human mass movements, ranging from the mass migrations of wandering nations to crowd phenomena. In that case, however, convergence is not limited to the physical level of mass formation and movement. It also has a psychosocial level. Because such movements do suddenly draw and recruit comparable groups, the composition is not merely a representative sample of the entire population, but a more homogenous selection. This holds for demographic factors such as age, gender, ethnicity, education, trade, class, and so forth. But it also holds for mental predispositions and states; this may concern personality, mentality, and arousal.

So even in their preliminary stages, mass mobilizations are always characterized by a heightened level of convergence, synergy, and boosting (of certain, thoughts, feelings and behaviors). This finds further expression during the actual "take off" stage. Think of protest demonstrations or the Papeete riots. Usually people know beforehand what types of behavior may be expected; expressive or active, supportive or hostile—and what objects or people they might target. Usually, too, they receive further cues at the outset and as events begin to unfold. Some of these messages may be implicit, some more explicit. People also have elaborate scripts and scenarios as to what will or might happen. For instance when some demonstrators break away from the "authorized gathering" and embark on an alternative path.

There are other aspects in this convergence. Such a crowd is more compacted than an average everyday situation; people are brought close together, their personal space and privacy shrink. Certain external signals of likemindedness are prominently displayed (also hairdo, clothing, symbols); signs of othermindedness (associated with the "other" party) are dissimulated. So movements, expressions, and feelings are being facilitated in one direction. By contrast, it becomes increasingly difficult to exert one's free will in the opposite direction. There are other conditions specifically associated with compact crowd situations. Whenever people are packed together, this may give rise to extra heat and humidity. There is sensory overload and noise. All this may contribute to intensify stress and arousal.

Some early crowd psychologists even suggested that under such circumstances, the electromagnetic fields around bodies could merge, and certain biorhythms (such as respiration and heartbeat) might tend to synchronize, so that in many ways, some kind of superorganism would form (see van Ginneken, 1992a). This may be stretching the argument a bit, but it is true that the "running parallel" of physical, psychological, and social processes in a compact mass situation is quite special. They may begin to link up and reinforce each other.

Fluctuation and Synchronization

Up to this point, we have primarily discussed the phenomenology of the convergence of movement. We now go one step further, and consider how variations and fluctuations of movement may link up with the variations and fluctuations of other movements, and how they may synchronize. Isolated fluctuations and periodic fluctuations may also interact in fascinating ways. This can well be seen in epidemics. The introduction of conscription, the mobilization of soldiers, the disorganization of World War I, followed by the sudden demobilization, contributed to the global spread of a flu—which claimed more victims than the entire war (and the subsequent wave of revolutions) taken together. The introduction of compulsory education in turn contributed to a spread of children diseases, which was only partly compensated by improved medical control by physicians. In many regions, the annual explosion and implosion of measles, mumps, and chicken pox closely followed the alternation of school periods and holidays because the microorganisms would be massively introduced into new environments, where resistance had not yet built, so that they developed freely.

Similar principles of fluctuation and synchronization can be seen at work in our psychosocial behavior. Our everyday behavior is based on an intricate grid of macro- and microfluctuations, which permits others to synchronize their own behavior with it. Hatfield, Cacioppo, and Rapson (1994) quoted Capella and Flagg in this regard, who had noted:

> In adult interactions, reciprocal mutual influence has been observed among various speech behaviors including accents, speech rate, pauses, latency to respond, vocal intensity, fundamental voice frequency, and turn durations. A range of kinesic behaviors exhibit mutual influence as well including postural and gestural behaviors, illustrators, movement synchrony, gaze, head nods and facial affect, facial displays of emotion, smiles and laughter, and more generalized hostile affect. (p. 200)

Recent research on meetings, conversations, and telephone behavior has shown that they are not only regulated by extreme subtle rules of turn-taking and/or interruption (better respected by women, but better infringed on by men). They also show how we obey emerging microrhythms. Expressions, gestures, and behavior of people involved and one and the same interaction turn out to be precisely segmented. Darren Newston reports, in his chapter on the "Coupling of Behavior Waves" (in Vallacher & Nowak, 1994): "the behavior stream has a clear-cut, underlying 'spike' structure. That is, it consists of periods of relatively smooth, low-magnitude position change, punctuated by spikes of high-magnitude position change" (p. 149). In a family having dinner together, according to some research, even the sounds of the cutlery turn out to obey hidden microrhythms.

In crowds, such forms of fluctuation and synchronization may emerge unconsciously, be adopted knowingly, or be staged explicitly for the purpose of the mass ritual. Think of Leni Riefenstahl's notorious documentary, "Triumph of the Will," which shows how Nazi party rallies in Nuremberg were staged. Ever since the idea of popular sovereignty evolved, both totalitarian and autocratic regimes have built huge palaces with high balconies on large squares, so that massive demonstrations of popular allegiance to the leadership could be staged. Electoral conventions in democratic societies, too, are designed and managed to highlight the uniqueness of the candidate, the enthusiasm of the supporters, and the inevitability of final victory.

Rhythm and Resonance

The principle of irregular fluctuation and synchronization is important, but regular rhythms and resonance may be even more important in the generation of synergy. The identification of regular rhythms makes it easier for processes to become intertwined and linked up, so that more coherence emerges. In man and society, all kinds of rhythms facilitate the anticipation of the thoughts, feelings, and reactions of others, and thereby the emergence of synchronization, which may produce synergy. In this way, some processes may reach more depth and height than they would otherwise reach, and thereby break out of their previous mold.

We tend to forget it, but the whole universe is of course an intricate melody of zillions of rhythms, and therefore of intertwined processes. This holds true for the macroprocesses of astronomy; planets circling stars, planets and stars turning around on their own axis, and so forth. On earth, such physical and chemical rhythms do of course translate into biological rhythms, and into the principles of life itself. The dance of moon with the sun and the earth translates into the rhythms of dark and light nights, for instance, in the ebb and flow of the seas, but also of ground water levels. The dance of the sun and the earth translate into the cycle of day and night, intertwined with the rhythm of the seasons. These two dances together determine the growth cycles of plants, the hormone cycles of animals, and even some behavioral cycles of humans. They regulate husbandry and agriculture, sowing and reaping, working and feasting. So it is not surprising that astronomy was one of the first scientific disciplines to develop in all cultures, and that astrology is so persistent.

In recent years, it has become gradually more apparent that functioning man and society, too, are primarily based on rhythms. At first we had only noted the rhythms of the lungs and heart, the rhythms of the stomach and kidneys. But ever more key rhythms have been discovered. Brain waves are today thought to be at the center of all thinking and consciousness. To this day, thousands of different biorhythms have been identified, and the number continues to grow. The interaction between these rhythms weaves complex melodies. There turn out to be "most appropriate" times for almost anything, as sports trainers, performance analysts, and prescribing doctors have come to realize. There are daily, weekly, monthly, annual and even pluri-annual rhythms that have fixed themselves in our bodies, our minds, and our lives.

Our thoughts, feelings and activities—both as individuals and as group members—tend to adapt to these cycles; daily, by eating, working, watching TV, and sleeping; weekly, by going out, going to church, visiting the sports club; monthly, by having a period or being fertile, but also receiving our wages and paying the bills; annually, there are a whole range of macrorhythms that punctuate our lives, such as seasonal activities and holidays. It is important to recognize that all of these rhythms make us periodically open ourselves up to or shut ourselves off from, certain thoughts, feelings, and behavioral repertoires; but also, certain forms of communication and interaction, certain groups, and mass phenomena. The beginning of the aforementioned Band Aid campaign, to give one example, "resonated" with the Christmas season; the Live Aid concert with the outdoor season (in the Northern hemisphere).

Our ideological and political calendars follow a similar rhythm: Labor Day and Armistice Day, the Opening of Parliament or the State of the Union.

The 4-year cycles of American presidential elections co-punctuate the economic and even military life around the globe because they imply more or less appropriate times for certain types of interventions. The Olympic games, in turn, favor waves of nationalist euphoria around the globe. Psychohistorian Lloyd DeMause (1982) has even suggested that such rhythms translate into identifiable waves, for instance, in recurrent media moods. That is an interesting thought, although it needs more corroboration.

Synergy and Boosting

The simplest and most familiar form of a regular rhythm is that of a clock with a pendulum that ticks away the seconds, minutes and hours of the day. In this regard, the early Dutch natural scientist, Christian Huygens, noted a curious phenomenon. When he hung two similar clocks on the same wooden wall, their pendulums would synchronize. The vibrations of the clocks themselves and of the wall had somehow become intertwined. This is called *entrainment*, and occurs whenever some oscillator "locks onto" a signal, and begins to react in synchrony (Davies, 1989, p. 149).

An interesting example of rhythm and resonance is the following: Long ago, man discovered that rhythm is a good device to coordinate the behavior of groups. Work songs help coordinate the execution of labor; marching songs help coordinate advancing battalions. Military leaders discovered, to their dismay, that it was not so easy to move compact groups over long periods and distances. Sooner or later they would become tired or distracted, would stumble and fall all over each other, and lose precious time and energy. Furthermore, marching songs conveyed a sense of cohesion, unity, and power. There is just one situation, they learned, when it is advisable to have soldiers march out of step. That is when they have to cross a shaky bridge. Otherwise it may begin to shake and shudder, vibrate and resonate, and may even collapse entirely.

So rhythm and resonance may in many ways contribute to synergy and boosting, which may help a process break out of its usual mold. This holds for the physical and chemical realm, but also for the biological and medical realm. Only recently has it been discovered, for instance, that some heart attacks do not result from an overly irregular heartbeat, but from an overly regular heartbeat. The heartbeat should show minuscule variations, in order not to provoke unwanted resonance. Similar things hold for the psychological and sociological domains, as we have already seen. Mass movements and convergence, fluctuation and synchronization, rhythm and resonance; they may on occasion break routines and provoke the exceptional.

It is sometimes because they follow a regular rhythm that such events may indeed grow in scope and intensity. This need not even be events that have been planned and announced long before. The public may understand intuitively—on the basis of precedents or conventions—what dates and times are appropriate for events to manifest themselves. In certain countries (such as China in recent decades), this may the anniversary of certain historic events, or the passing away of a popular politician. In other countries, it may even be the repeated commemoration of fallen martyrs. Within the Islamic world, for instance, there is a 40-day mourning cycle, which may be repeated several times. This played a decisive role in the chasing of the pro-Western Shah of Persia, and the subsequent return of the exiled spiritual leader, Ayatollah Khomeini, as described in a doctoral dissertation by van Dooren (1994).

> In November 1977, the mourning ceremonies following the death of Khomeini's son had been impressive, but relatively peaceful. The frontal newspaper attack on the Ayatollah in January 1978 however, incited the pent-up emotions and hostility of the clergy in Qom, where an unknown number of people were killed in confrontations between a clergy-led crowd and the police. This event set in motion a cycle of street demonstrations taking place at a 40-day interval, in commemoration of the martyrs who died in the previous clash between police and opposition. . . . On February 10 and 11, 1979, the downfall of the Pahlavi dynasty was sealed, when deserters from the army and the air force joined the revolutionaries. (pp. 199–200)

This series of events is a perfect illustration of the fact that such regular rhythms may not only contribute to a better synchronization of mass events, but also to growing synergy and boosting, until the cycle gains such strength that it shatters its previous limits and destroys the system. This is the deeper sense of the processes of both deindividuation and convergence in crowds. They make processes run parallel, accelerate, and break through barriers. This may serve good or evil purposes, or a mixture of both; that is not the point here. The point is that it is an another set of metaprinciples that collective behavior has in common with other natural processes.

5

The Emergence of Patterns in Opinion Currents

When things get together, there then arises something which was not there before, and that character is something that cannot be stated in terms of the elements which go to make up the combination.
—George Herbert Mead, American sociologist
(Eve, Horsfall, & Lee, 1997, p. 30)

He looked into the water and saw that it was made up of a thousand thousand thousand and one different currents, each one a different color, weaving in and out of one another like a liquid tapestry of breathtaking complexity.
—Salman Rushdie, British author of Indian descent
(Rushdie, 1990, p. 72)

Emergence is the key; it is the union between synergy on one hand and self-organization on the other. It is all about dynamic pattern formation in which the whole is more than the sum of the parts, and in which decelerated and accelerated change alternate. This is a general process underlying the rise and fall of opinion patterns, and of collective behavior in general. This chapter takes a closer look at the key phenomena.

CASE NUMBER FIVE: HUNTING THE HUNTERS

The next case is about the fading of an old pattern, and the emergence of a new one, within Western public opinion. Whereas the wearing of fur—particularly by certain social classes and during certain seasons—had long been a completely accepted phenomenon, it suddenly turned controversial. Strictly speaking, there was no rapid, radical, and massive shift in public opinion and perception, because it took several decades to take hold; yet it was no silent, gradual, shift either. It was brought about by a succession of tremors, and they did not primarily concern the most common types of fur, but rather the most exceptional ones (also see: Parmentier, 1996, and Schoonman, 1991).

Higher animals have long been killed for their meat and fat, but also for their bones and skins. The furriest animals do of course tend to live in the coldest regions. As western Europeans penetrated North America, the fur trade gained in importance. The production of native Americans and of Inuit aboriginals found its way to international markets. Hunting and trapping made poor country folk in Newfoundland and other Arctic areas earn extra income for the long winter months. Gradually, Canada came to supply and equip larger ships for the annual hunt of marine mammals. But Scandinavian ship owners and traders, with a longer tradition in these fields, took a big share of the profits.

Let us take a closer look at baby seals, and their twofold popularity; first as a source for fur coats, then as martyr animals. New techniques made it possible to penetrate deeper, longer, and more effectively into polar lands and waters, with powerful steamships and steel-hulled icebreakers, equipped with refrigeration units and radar scanners, accompanied by reconnaissance planes and helicopters. Increasingly, the most profitable hunt was for the skins of harped and hooded baby seals, with blue and white coats—the most innocent, yet fine-looking, of them all.

The baby seals had a protective camouflage of warm white fur during the first 10 days or so after birth, when they could neither swim nor "run," and would find themselves almost completely helpless on the isolated shores of snow and ice of the "nurseries," entirely dependent on their mothers. In order to spare the fur, their heads would be bashed in with a sharp point on a stick, a hakapik, after which they were skinned. According to one opponent, therefore, "it was not, after all, a hunt that was taking place—more like men walking through a field of ripe berries, squashing them with motorcycle boots" (Hunter, 1979, p. 277).

Under pressure to "harvest" a maximum number of skins in a minimum amount of time, hunters often worked in a hasty and sloppy manner, and caused unnecessary suffering in the animals. Because this slaughter took place in the remotest of places, in the absence of any outside witnesses or cameras, few objections had been raised before. Somewhere around the mid-1950s, however, doctors Joseph Cunningham and Harry Lillie were first able to film the bloody scenes of the hunt. Cunningham declared sealing to be "utterly degrading and cruel" and Lillie published a book that mobilized animal lovers.

Canadian radio journalist Alan Hersovici (1985) reported:

> The climax came in 1964. One hundred-fifty planes and helicopters took part in the hunt that year, in a "gold-rush" atmosphere that saw the arrival of many inexperienced hunters. There was great waste—more seals were killed than could be carried away . . . It was estimated that by 1964, the herd numbered about 1.5 million, down by 200,000 from 1950, and from perhaps 3 million in the mid-nineteenth century. (pp. 73–74)

Therefore, the Audubon Society of animal lovers appealed to the Canadian Minister of Fisheries to ask for tighter regulations and inspections.

There was a major row when another film highlighted the cruel nature of the hunt. In Montreal, the capital of Francophone Quebec, the government had commissioned a film company to produce a series of documentaries about fishing and hunting around the province. When it rejected some appalling footage of the seal hunt, Arktek films included it in a documentary of its own, which was then broadcast on a French-language television network and provoked an immediate outrage. The government countered with an investigation claiming that the most brutal scenes (such as those of a seal skinned alive) had been staged by the film crew and/or people hired by them. A foreign biologist and zoological society then had British pathologists examine a large number of seal carcasses. They concluded that more than 50% had still been alive while being skinned.

The ensuing campaign against sealing was fought in two waves. Between the mid-1960s and the mid-1970s, it centered on North America; between the mid-1970s and the mid-1980s, the focus shifted to western Europe. Spearheading the campaign was Brian Davies, a British-born Canadian immigrant. After the controversy over the Arktek film had erupted, he decided to go on an inspection tour, as field secretary for the Society for the Protection of Cruelty to Animals (SPCA) of New Brunswick. He concluded that the charges against the sealers were correct, and began to organize radical protests. In 1969, he even broke with the SPCA and founded his own International Fund for Animal Welfare (IFAW), which grew into a global organization with 800,000 donors and $6 million dollar annual budget, to save the seals. He soon mobilized foreign allies as well, like Alice Herrington and her Friends of Animals (FOA), based in New Jersey. Critics did not fail to point out that the combined budgets of such organizations soon exceeded the annual turnover of the entire seal hunt in Canada.

The actions of the alliance provoked a steady stream of press articles. The protest campaign collected 1 million signatures, and U.S. Representatives began to feel the heat. In 1972, therefore, Congress passed the Marine Mammal Protection Act, banning the import of products from nursing animals younger than 8-months old. Prices plummeted. The very next year, the

Convention on International Trade in Endangered Species (CITES) was signed in Washington. This provoked a prolonged debate as to whether or not harped and hooded seals were also endangered species.

During the 1974 Canadian elections, Brian Davies and IFAW mounted a major offensive with emotional "Stop the Seal Hunt" ads prepared by a professional agency, and billboards with the statement, "90,000 baby seals will be clubbed to death again this year." A Gallup poll found that more than one in two Canadians opposed the hunt at this point, and more than one in ten opposed candidates who did not (Hersovici, 1985). So the tide was turning. A few years earlier, the government had already felt forced to tighten the rules. A few years later, it even adopted a Seals Protection Act. But some claimed it was rather a "Sealers Protection Act" because it effectively forbade outsiders to approach the hunt or to interfere with it.

By the mid-1970s, another organization joined in the fray: Greenpeace, which had spread its wings from Vancouver to other major cities in Canada and the United States. Its first expedition in 1976 was welcomed by an angry mob of sealers in St. Anthony, the northeastern port of Newfoundland. They were forced to hand over the cannisters of green dye, with which they planned to spray the baby seals to make their skins worthless.

But they went on to throw themselves between the young animals and the hunters, and to place themselves in the way of an icebreaker. Environmental peaceful protester or "Eco dove" Robert Hunter (1979) wrote: "All of us entered a new psychological realm at this point . . . it had impacted against an iron wall . . . the captain had made her stop because *we* had made him do it" (p. 291). Of course the Greenpeace activists knew that this only postponed the killing for an hour or so. But the dramatic scenes were extensively captured on photo and film, they fed the ever-hungry media, and the news went all around the world to form another "mind bomb" in the heads of the public.

The second expedition in 1977 went to Blanc Sablon, on the Labrador border (whereas Brian Davies and his IFAW focused on St. Anthony this time). Greenpeace "eco hawk," Paul Watson, handcuffed himself to a loading cable, got smashed against the ship, and got dumped repeatedly into the ice-cold water. Unfortunately, cameras had not registered the scene, radio messages got garbled, and one foreign newspaper even reported that Watson had been killed. A foreign film crew, which had been unable to get onto the ice, by contrast, allegedly "borrowed a stuffed toy seal and hired a local man to pose on the ice, as though getting ready to strike it" (Hunter, 1979, pp. 369, 375). So confusion reigned supreme, but the battle went on.

The third expedition in 1978 brought along two American Congressmen who had played a role in having the House of Representatives pass a unanimous resolution to condemn the hunt. They were appalled at what they saw. Jim Jeffords, the Republican from Vermont related: "We saw three seal pups clubbed, and in each case the mother defended them as best as she could" (Hunter, 1979, p. 435). Leo Ryan, the Democrat from California said: "I'm in a state of shock. I just want to say enough . . . enough! Stop!" (Hunter, 1979, p. 435). Such campaigns resulted in a drop in the price of seal skins to less than 10% of their previous value (Hersovici, 1985), and of treated skins to one third of their previous value.

By this time, the second wave of protests had reached western Europe as well. Canada, the SPCA, and Brian Davies were all of "British stock," and stirred considerable media interest there. His book *Savage Luxury* had circulated widely. As early as the late 1960s, the *Daily Mirror* had published his stories and pictures, and carried a full frontpage picture by Kent Gavin, which earned him the title Photographer of the Year.

Peter Lust's articles for the German language weekly *Nachrichten*, in Montreal, were first reprinted by the *Morgenpost* in Hamburg, then by 300 other papers all around western Europe, and turned into a best-selling book entitled *The Last Seal Pup*. Sales in Germany, which had been the major sealskin market in Europe, reportedly dropped to half their former level. Bernhard Grzimek showed the controversial Arktek film on his television nature show, provoking a wave of 15,000 letters of protest to the Canadian prime minister. He had subsequently initiated the aforementioned research on the live skinning of seals, and reported the results in his influential multivolume encyclopaedia, *Animal Life* (1984).

Franz Weber (from the Swiss town of Basel) stirred much of the media hype around the second Greenpeace expedition; among other things, by coming up with the proposal of collecting several hundred thousands of dollars to set up a synthetic fur factory in Newfoundland for making seal pup dolls, and thus providing alternative jobs for unemployed sealers. Pressure mounted. Many fur shops reportedly moved their sealskins to the basement, and half of all major chains in Germany even decided to prohibit their sale altogether. The issue was forced onto the political agenda as well. Banner headlines in the tabloid, *Bild*, implored chancellor Helmut Kohl to "quickly help the little seals." Right wing Christian-Democrat leader (and hunter) Franz-Joseph Strauss was sarcastic about centrist FDP leader, Helmut Genscher, when the latter spoke out against the seal hunt in an interview with the Sunday edition of *Bild*. And even the more serious weekly, *Der Spiegel*, wondered in a cover story on the slaughter whether the FDP had done more for the seals, or the other way around (Wiedemann, 1983).

The French area had also been mobilized by the gruesome scenes in the early Arktek film in Quebec, and photo reports that Brian Davies helped arrange for the major weekly *Paris Match*, including the cover of a white coat with the banner, "Save the baby seal!" This resulted in letters of support from royalty such as Princess Grace (Kelly) of Monaco and Princess (now Queen) Paola of Belgium. Queen Margarethe of Denmark later took to wearing seal skin (though not baby seal skin) from Greenland, by contrast, in order to demonstrate her support for the Inuit hunters and their families. A campaign got under way to stop the massacre, spearheaded by fashion models and movie stars. It culminated in a sizable ad in the very serious daily *Le Monde*, reminding president Mitterrand that he had promised socialism "with a human face," and imploring him to intervene.

By this time, around the early 1980s, the European Community (EC) was affected as well. A multimillion letter campaign got underway; Greenpeace once again stepped up its campaign to "save the seals" and the IFAW even called for an international boycott of Canadian fish exports (a $1.6 billion dollar industry). In the spring of 1982, the European parliament in Strasbourg called for a continent-wide import ban on seal products. Canada protested that this would favor Greenland and Denmark. In the autumn of 1983, therefore, the Council of Ministers proclaimed a temporary ban on baby seal products, which was then implicitly made permanent. Immediately, the bottom fell out of the market. According to official figures, the 1984 Canadian "harvest" was reduced to less than 10% of its previous volume; all caught by landsmen and longliners, none from larger ships.

Over the next few years, however, it slowly rose again. Fishermen in the North Atlantic claimed that seal populations now grew too rapidly, thereby depleting fish stocks. Protesters retorted that this was really putting the onus on them. They also claimed that (a) white coats were still being smuggled into the EC, although temporarily dyed and labeled as sheep skin; (b) seal pups were still being killed, only a few days or weeks later, so that formally they were no longer considered babies; (c) the hunt for adult seals had gradually resumed, although presumably just by landsmen and longliners; (d) the authorities of the northern nations did much to conceal the present nature of the hunt; and (e) regulations and inspections were still insufficient.

This latter claim received a major boost when Odd Lindberg accompanied Norwegian seal hunting expeditions in 1987 and 1988 and wrote a highly critical report which was once again accompanied by gruesome photographs and video footage (Lindberg, 1988). When authorities claimed he had abused his position as an inspector and forbade their publication, he smuggled the photos and footage out of the country. Yet another inspector confirmed that the abuses were still taking place.

In 1989, the material turned up in the TV documentary "Seal Mourning," which caused another international stir. In Britain, 4,000 viewers jammed the Channel Four switchboard. *BBC Wildlife* magazine (Jan. 1990) named Lindberg the "Rushdie of the North" when threats forced him into hiding (also see: Lavigne, 1990). In 1992, there was another row over images, when the Norwegian TV documentary "Survival in the High North," by Magnus Gudmundsson, accused Greenpeace of staged atrocity scenes (Parmentier, 1996).

All people involved were keenly aware of the key importance of images. For decades, the hunt had taken place in distant territories, without outsiders being aware of it or even able to imagine what was going on. The few really strong photo and film reports that had been circulated and recirculated over the years had boosted the protests. The shift occurred when a clear majority of North Americans and western Europeans took notice, and began to take a firm stand.

Around 1970, all kinds of highly publicized events had still been marked by the conspicuous ubiquity of fur coats—including the soft white ones made from baby seals. Around 1990, by contrast, women hardly dared show themselves in public in fur, particularly in the metropolitan areas. They risked being insulted, or even sprayed with paint. In the meantime, fur and fur coats had suddenly become "an issue." Causing animal suffering for medicine or food was one thing, activists said, but doing so for luxurious or superfluous ornaments was quite another. Remaining traders felt forced to demonstrate that the animals were bred and killed in "humane" ways, and to shift attention to less sensitive markets (e.g., in eastern Europe and east Asia).

The interesting things about this whole question are the shifting psychological and sociological configurations that made the theme "catch on" with certain groups, or not. The emergence of such an issue is never simple; it is always complex; it is always surrounded by Gestalts and Gestalt "switches," and by ad hoc communication and mobilization networks.

Let us therefore take more time for this particular case study and take a closer look at the processes that accompanied, embedded, and proved conducive to these opinion "currents." Let us take a closer look at five psychosocial dimensions, which can readily be identified: The dimensions of age and gender, but also the dimensions of urbanization, class, and culture. These dimensions, taken together, played a major role in shaping the course of events and framing the issue. It underlines the roles of contingency, context, and complexity in change, of nonlinearity and even of "strange attractors" (see chap. 9).

The first important dimension was that of age. Baby seals are not only perceived as wet-eyed babies, but as "arch" babies, because even adult seals have some typical baby features. German clinical psychologist Harold Traue reminded us that

> there is a common law in human beings, and in animal beings too, that is called in German, *Kindkin* [*Kindchen*] schema. That's a scientific term: "child form." This is a term in the biology of animal behavior and it means that when animals, and humans too, are very young, they have a little body and a very large head with large eyes, and all the forms are rounded. And if you see such a form, an animal or a human being, you feel very good towards it. You feel like a mother. And that's biological law. (Hersovici, 1985, p. 93)

When it began its campaign, Greenpeace was well aware of "the depths of emotion that the killing of 'babies' generated in the breasts of millions of urban people, who, otherwise, with their cars and swimming pools and electric gadgets, were the worst environmental destroyers of all" (Hunter, 1979, p. 249). And so were fisheries experts:

> seals give birth to a helpless pup which is quite unprotected by a nest, burrow, vegetation or even camouflage. To add to this helplessness its mother is badly equipped to protect it. Also, it is covered in soft fur to keep it warm in a horrible climate, and our western culture loves all things young, furry and helpless. (Lister-Kaye, 1979, p. 13)

The second major dimension was that of gender. Hunting is a very "macho" activity, particularly in the extreme conditions of the far north. Furs are a very special gift and a very feminine garment, particularly the dense and soft furs of baby seals. Once again, early protesters were very well aware of this psychological dimension.

When Eileen Chivers, the companion of Greenpeace vice president Patrick Moore, turned up during the first Greenpeace campaign, Greenpeace president Robert Hunter said:

> She was the first of her sex to come to this place where, for centuries, Newfoundland males had entered their manhood by steeling themselves to kill the most beautiful infant creature they had ever seen ... the next seal hunter found himself blocked by a furious young woman, breathing harshly and gasping at him: "No! No! No!" ... A dozen times Eileen fell or was brushed aside, and a dozen times pups died almost within her reach.

But the photographer was there as well, to capture the moment

> when a woman of the twentieth century would rise between a man with primitive killing tools and an animal that died in its infancy to service equally primitive female vanity, a new age in collision with darkest antiquity. (Hunter, 1979, pp. 288–289)

During the second campaign, Greenpeace's Patrick Moore welcomed Brigitte Bardot to the ice (whereas IFAW's Brian Davics made do with the lesser star, Yvette Mimieux). This caused some vivid debates; Robert Hunter acknowledged that

> there could scarcely be a better way—at the level at any rate of sheer volume of coverage—than to bring the world's most famous "sex kitten" into action on the side of the milky-furred pups. Whatever clout Greenpeace might have earned in previous years, it was a drop in the bucket compared with the publicity tidal wave that was automatically displaced by her mere presence.

> Until her arrival, the seal-hunt "story" was all blood and death, but now it
> was blood and death and *sex*. No more potent combination could be put to
> gether. (Hunter, 1979, p. 377)

Alan Hersovici (1985) claimed that "the photograph of Bardot hugging a seal pup that appeared in Europe after that visit had perhaps more impact than any single action to rally Europeans for the import ban on white-coat hunting in 1983," that is to say half a dozen years later (p. 82). Movie stars and fashion models remained a standard "prop" over subsequent years, even as the campaigns widened to other furs.

The third major dimension was that of urbanization. Whereas the baby/adult and the masculine/feminine divides did largely have psychological overtones, other aspects decidedly had sociological overtones. From another point of view, for instance, the issue could also very well be construed as the people from the metropolitan areas of the world coming to tell those in the backwaters of the far north how to lead their lives and how to earn their living. Whereas the former were well attuned to the major media organizations in the world, the latter remained completely "alien" to them.

It has indeed been argued that environmental awareness and animal loving in their present forms are typically urban phenomena: the farther away people are from nature, the more they come to appreciate and idealize it. People raised and living in the countryside or on a farm may be closer to nature, but also feel they have to tame and manage it on an everyday basis. This may include cutting down trees and killing animals, which is never a nice thing to do.

The aforementioned German clinical psychologist, Harald Traue, surmised that in societies such as this, people have become completely alienated from such practices, because they no longer see life begin or end at all.

> Old people are hidden away in special homes, the handicapped in others.
> Only certain parts of the life cycle are acceptable and, therefore, made visible.
> As a result, when death (or birth, for that matter) is shown on television, it is
> shocking to people brought up in a sterilized, homogenized, climate-con-
> trolled environment. (Hersovici, 1985, pp. 94–95)

He even suggested that the younger urban generation may somehow unconsciously feel jealous of the older rural generation "possessed, as it were, by some archetypical rage at [their] own exclusion from the Garden of Paradise" (Hersovici, 1985, pp. 94–95).

The fourth dimension was that of social stratification, because, of course, the urban/rural dimension was intertwined with a class dimension. By the time the first wave of protest campaigns began, a large part of the fur trade was controlled by foreigners. An academic book on the history of sealing in North America reported that

> a pelt for which in the mid-60s a sealer might be paid $2–$3, was worth $50–$60 to a furrier, and $100–$125 to the consumer in the form of a coat—and only a very small share of that money ever found its way back to Canada. (Cooper-Busch, 1985, p. 247)

Radio journalist Alan Hersovici reported that

> Sealing was worth $13 million to Atlantic Canada in 1981. About $7 million went to the more than three thousand fishermen and two thousand Arctic Inuit who hunted the seal. After the EC ban, the value of sealing was slashed to less than $3 million; income to sealers fell to $1.3 million. In more personal terms, fishermen who earned an average of $2,000—often one-third of their annual cash income—for 4 to 6 weeks saw that slip to less than $400. Inuit average income from sealskins (usually from Ring seals) fell from $450 to $100 . . . (Hersovici, 1985, p. 70)

These were just the small annual cash injections, he said, which many needed to buy or update or repair their boats or gear. And he quoted a Canadian anthropologist who had observed that the groups in question were "about as low as you can go on the socio-economic scale in Canada, groups who have virtually no power to resist this type of international movement" (Hersovici, 1985, p. 102).

The fifth dimension was that of ethnicity and culture. Robert Hunter, a founding member of Greenpeace in Vancouver, recognized that the sealers in Newfoundland were really

> at the bottom rung of the working class [and that they had] virtually their own language, their own traditions and culture, and swiling lay at the heart of their sense of identity, for it had always been their central myth that it was on the ice, in darkness and cold, that manhood itself was earned. (Hunter, 1979, pp. 249–250)

Whereas the environmental movement in general and Greenpeace in particular had always cherished the myth of the "noble native," they now found themselves at loggerheads with these people. It was a "new kind of imperialism," some Inuits claimed:

> Over previous centuries "big city people" and other outsiders had imposed the fur trade on them, now they had changed their minds, and wanted them to get out again. It was like a new kind of genocide, some natives even claimed: "what is the difference in the annihilation of a people's social, eco-

nomic and cultural base, as opposed to doing it physically?" (Hersovici, 1985, pp. 105, 107)

Although IFAW stuck to its guns, Greenpeace decided to back down somewhat. Although it continued to oppose excesses in the seal hunt, it stopped opposing the seal hunt itself, as long as it remained a small-scale and local affair. But the "genie was already out of the bottle." The original campaigns had been aimed against the killing of baby seals, and the inhumane killing of seals in general. Many protest groups, as well as the media and the public, however, now opposed all hunting of seals and all selling of their skins.

A psychological "halo effect" occurred when the opposition further spread to all trapping of other furry animals on land, the hunting of other furry animals on land, and the keeping of other furry animals in factory farms. Between the late 1980s and the mid-1990s, for instance, both world fox and world mink supplies dropped by some 50%. In North America and western Europe, wearing any kind of fur in public was "out" and might provoke hostile remarks. By contrast, synthetic fur and prints, which had long been considered "tacky," were suddenly considered "in."

The dozen or so baby seals that had been killed in the presence of a well-connected photo or film camera thus proved the Nemesis of an entire worldwide industry by transforming themselves into "mind bombs" that exploded in the brains of billions of people. But how do we conceptualize the halting and intermittent emergence of such a new opinion current and perception pattern? Let us take a closer look.

THE PHENOMENON OF OPINION CURRENTS

We have seen that the scholarly reflection on crowds and masses had gradually been extended from large groups that were physically assembled to large groups that were physically dispersed. But this also demanded a new type of explanation. One could try to understand crowd behavior in terms of face-to-face contacts, based on personality characteristics. But in order to understand social movements and opinion currents, one needs a much broader interpretation of interaction and communication patterns between normal people—as in the baby seal case. Some types of argument could be maintained, whereas other arguments need reformulation. The principle of synergy formation is therefore supplemented with that of pattern emergence.

So let us follow that line somewhat further; the line that led from crowd or mass psychology to the sociology of collective behavior, and particularly the so-called "natural history" approach, identifying successive stages of pattern emergence. It is remarkable that some sociologists, specifically interested in this particular field, noted that this type of argument blended in rather well with the "general systems theory," which was gradually formulated during these same years. This was specifically true for the American sociologist Orrin Klapp (1972, 1973), who undertook early attempts to describe collective behavior processes in terms of the opposite universal metaprinciples of entropy production and negentropy production, of emerging chaos and an emerging alternative order.

The Sociology of Collective Behavior

The earliest European authors already began to often call crowd psychology "collective psychology" instead, paving the way for an extension of its "laws" to other mass phenomena—including social movements and opinion currents. The American sociologist, Robert Park, discussed the implications in his (German) dissertation, relabeled the field "collective behavior" studies, and abducted it to sociology by first identifying it as such in his famous, *Introduction to the Science of Sociology* (Park & Burgess, 1922/1970). Yet, here again, there was a noteworthy tendency to define collective behavior as an exception to the key criterion of the discipline. Psychologists had maintained that it was irrational; sociologists now noted that it was noninstitutional. But whereas psychologists had suggested that it was usually "regressive," sociologists claimed that it might also be progressive—that is to say, it might contribute to necessary social change.

This approach was further formulated by Herbert Blumer—known as the founder of the so-called "symbolic interactionist" school. For instance in his elaborate chapter on collective behavior in the subsequent reference work, *Principles of Sociology* (Lee, 1969). "While most of the collective behavior of human beings [that is to say social behavior in the widest sense] exists in the form of regulated group activity," he said, "collective behavior [in the narrower sense of typical mass behavior] arises spontaneously and is not due to preestablished understandings or traditions." The subfield should therefore concern itself with "the way in which the elementary and spontaneous forms develop into organized forms" and "the way in which a social order arises" (Lee, 1969, pp. 68–69).

A more detailed elaboration of this whole new perspective, however, was only undertaken by a next generation, the authors of three major handbooks pertaining to the field: Turner and Killian (1957/1972); Lang and Lang (1961); and Smelser (1962). Turner and Killian's (1972) central notion was the "emergent norm," because

A common understanding as to what sort of behavior is expected in the situation, seems to provide an explanation of a pattern of differential expression.

Such a shared understanding encourages behavior consistent with the norm, inhibits behavior contrary to it, and justifies restraining action against individuals of dissent. (1972, p. 22)

Remember how this worked out in the fur case.

Whereas Turner and Killian's handbook was rather fragmented, the second handbook on *Collective Dynamics* (K. Lang & G. E. Lang, 1961) was much more elegantly reasoned and written. Instead of the emergent norm, they chose "collective redefinition" as their central notion, as well as the "natural history" of stages therein. We return to this type of reasoning in later chapters. But the most ambitious attempt to develop a very detailed model was undertaken by Smelser (1962) in his *Theory of Collective Behavior*. It derived in part from the very influential general theory of social action formulated by Talcott Parsons. In it, Smelser defined collective behavior as "mobilization on the basis of a belief which redefines social action." Or, more precisely, as: "an uninstitutionalized mobilization for action in order to modify one or more kinds of strain on the basis of a generalized reconstitution of a component of action" (Smelser, 1962, pp. 8, 71).

This approach was elaborated with the help of a detailed grid with two dimensions. The four columns from left to right covered Parsons' four components of social action—from general to specific: values (which identified the goals of social action); norms (which regulated the means of social action); the mobilization of motivation (of participants); and finally, the situational facilities (and possibilities). The seven rows below were related to levels of specificity: from general to precise. The combination of columns and rows produced a table of $4 \times 7 = 28$ cells, ranging from *very general* in the upper left hand corner to *very specific* in the lower right hand corner.

The idea was, that if social action was somehow blocked (or hindered) by a specific component on a specific level, a new and alternative point of departure would be sought in a more general component on a more general level. People would try to circumvent inadequate or unsatisfactory elements by looking for more adequate or satisfactory ones. In his view, furthermore, six determinants of collective behavior played a role: (1) Structural conduciveness (it must be possible to express the behavior in question); (2) structural strain or tension (the behavior must have a motor, or driving force); (3) growth and spread of a generalized belief; (4) precipitating factors; (5) mobilization for action (of participants); and (6) social control.

He called it the "value added model." Because each condition should be fulfilled, before the other could take effect. They did not necessarily need to develop in chronological order though (Smelser, 1962, p. 382). The model did not only apply to psychological crowds, but also to social movements and what I tend to identify here as opinion currents.

The "Natural History" of Opinion Currents

The various publications of the authors in this section so far employ a slightly different terminology but hold a largely similar view. They all approach collective behavior as a new and alternative psychosocial pattern, which rises and spreads relatively rapidly within a group whenever an old and conventional pattern is experienced as inadequate or unsatisfactory. Within this process, one may try to identify various logical aspects and stages, even if they often coincide within a really dramatic shift. To begin with, Smelser's two initial conditions—structural conduciveness and structural strain—must be fulfilled. Some authors (such as Penrose, 1952) spoke of a "zero" or latency stage in this regard.

Subsequently, collective behavior and an opinion current become notable through the manifestation of some kind of unease with the available conventional repertory of thoughts, feelings, and behaviors in this regard (also see: Berk, 1974; Rose, 1982; Marx & McAdam, 1994). They may translate into mild forms of mental confusion and social unrest. All sorts of related terms have been proposed throughout the sociological literature, ranging from *anomie* or *loss of norms* to *alienation* or *estrangement*, and so on. One may also think of *disaffection* and *disorientation*. The essence is that established patterns loose their forceful grip so that there is more room for possible alternatives to take hold. People open themselves up for them or even go looking for them. Such moods of "softening up" and heightened receptivity for reorientation proposals may spread rapidly.

There often is some kind of "arch event" (or even several arch events). They demonstrate the inadequacy of conventional approaches to everybody concerned in a lively way. We have seen that in the context of scientific revolutions, Thomas Kuhn (1962) spoke of "paradigmatic events" that would stir a reconsideration of things taken for granted; they are the catalysts of change. They often have a concrete character, are translated through the senses (e.g., in salient images or slogans), and make a dramatic impression. Think of the shocking pictures of baby seals, skinned half alive after their heads had been bashed in. In the context of the opposition to the American intervention in Vietnam, for instance, there also were arch pictures of victims that seemed to sum up the hopelessness of the entire enterprise.

This leads to a broader collective redefinition of the situation that spreads rapidly through a relevant part of the population; or more correctly, a range of alternatives that arise more or less simultaneously, and one of which is experienced as more adequate than others. Salience is important; remember our discussion of memes and replication. This new nuclear definition of the situation also affects other aspects of our representational universe; of what is important or not, of what is legitimate or not, and so forth. It forms the basis for Smelser's (1962) spread of generalized beliefs.

This helps create new images of "us and them," of friends and foes. That is to say it creates rapport or understanding, or even solidarity and involvement, with people on one side of the issue; and disavowal or repudiation of those on the other side of the issue. The former camp is perceived as legitimate and rapidly growing, the latter camp as illegitimate and rapidly shrinking. In the case of the baby seals, these were the camps of the animal lovers and conservationists versus that of the hunters and fur tradesmen. It is important to note that this sense of a 'reversal of fortunes' is experienced as exciting or depressing; an existing equilibrium is progressively upset. It is very hard to make a correct appraisal of how it is all going to end. Optical illusions disturb the picture; those concerned easily over- or underestimate the rate of change.

As the opinion current persists, some psychosocial differentiation and division of labor become obvious. People identify with certain roles, such as that of the hero or victim. People adopt certain tasks, such as those of agitation and propaganda. People begin to differ in status; some are seen as more, some as less important.

> ... the process by which alienation from the social order finds expression in an elementary form of organization. Fluid forms of interaction become routinized, and fugitive patterns of behavior are transformed—we say they "crystallize"—into cohesive units with a sense of solidarity and with a more or less definite structure. (K. Lang & G. E. Lang, 1961, p. 179)

Finally, the ultimate dilemma of all collective behavior comes in sight— "volatilization" or institutionalization. Think of Bob Geldof's initiatives with regard to Ethiopia, to which he chose not to give a permanent structure. If an opinion current translates into a social movement, by contrast, and if the social movement translates into a lasting organization—then this does create a permanent structure; action and pressure groups, foundations and associations, with offices and fund-raising. We return to that subject in the next chapter.

Such new organizations may well oppose existing institutions, but they will inevitably become part and parcel of the total network of social structures, and thereby loose their original character. There is no middle way; emergent behavior and social patterns are by definition temporary. They either disappear again, or reintegrate the conventional framework. But they cannot indefinitely remain "emergent."

Early Systems Theory

The question remains, however, whether we can place emergent phenomena, such as the opinion current in relation to the fur trade, in a wider context. Because meanwhile there has been a widening interest in the metaprinciples of nonlinear change, and how they might not only apply in the natural sciences but in those of man and society as well. In chapter 2, on the conceptualization of "spreading," we briefly touched upon the information and communication theories of Shannon and Weaver. In chapter 3, on the conceptualization of feedback, furthermore, we briefly touched upon the homeostasis and cybernetics theories of Cannon and Wiener. Gradually, all such notions were integrated into a wider framework, which claimed to be relevant to all scientific disciplines.

The Austrian biologist Ludwig Von Bertalanffy had outlined the meta-principles of a general systems theory in German before the war, but he only translated them into English during his post-war American stay, and only spelled them out in detail in his 1968 work, *General System Theory*. He noted that apart from information theory and cybernetics, other disciplines had provided worthwhile contributions: classical mathematics, computer simulation, "compartment, set, graph and net theory," game and decision theory, and finally, theories about cellular automata and queuing. Von Bertalanffy said that one should not only be looking for analogies or superficial similarities, but for homologies or fundamental similarities; and distinguish between systems that only evolved through "fitness," and those that evolved through various forms of "directiveness."

At first, interest for general systems theory was largely limited to the natural sciences. But gradually, the sciences of man and society, too, awoke to the new insights. (See for the early history of this type of approach, the introductions to the books of Von Bertalanffy (1968) and Luhmann (1984/ 1995); as well as chap. 3 in Buckley (1967); chap. 23 in Kelley (1997); chap. 5 and chap. 8 in van Vught (1979); and many others). Walter Buckley, for one, had already published a 1967 book on *Sociology and Modern Systems Theory*, which tried to spell out to what extent groups, institutions, and societies could also be regarded as systems in formation (or re-formation). All this led to more attention for the dynamic aspects of social processes, where attention for static aspects had long prevailed.

Some notions from this whole framework had meanwhile spilled over to the collective behavior literature as well. Isolated concepts turned up in approaches of the symbolic interactionist school, which represented a minority within American sociology, but a majority in the collective behavior field (Turner & Killian, 1987; K. Lang & G. E. Lang, 1961). The broader framework of general systems theory was more apparent in approaches of the structuralist–functionalist school, by contrast, which represented a majority in American sociology, but only a minority within the collective behavior field (Smelser, 1962).

One of the first who tried to integrate the broader framework of general systems theory with the symbolic interactionist approach to collective behavior was sociologist Orrin Klapp (1967, 1971, 1972, 1973, 1978). This theme

inspired his major work: four books on social movements, on collective behavior, on sociological models, and on information processing. The origi-
nality and coherence of Klapp's approach are hardly identified in recent
American overviews of collective behavior, for reasons that elude me.
Maybe the somewhat conservative undertone of some of his earliest and
latest works plays a role. It was only in an advanced stage of the development of this present book that I came to realize he had been onto a similar
track. But when I tried to trace and contact him, it turned out that he had
just died.

As I have said, he went back to two traditions: general systems theory
and symbolic interactionist theory (and its predecessors). Klapp (1972)
concurred with Norbert Wiener, that cybernetics could not only be applied
to machines and animals, but to man and society as well. Klapp (1973) also
concurred with Kenneth Boulding, who had identified various levels of complexity. (Similar schemes have repeatedly been revised since, but here it is
not the specific details but the general thrust of the argument that counts.)
Klapp (1973, pp. 289–291) distinguished nine levels, namely those of:

> (1) static structure; (2) simple dynamic system, like a clock; (3) cybernetic or
> self-adjusting system, like a thermostat; (4) self-maintaining open system, as
> in organisms which take in various forms of food and information; (5) ge-
> netic–societal system, as in the division of labor between cells in a plant to
> form a cell-society with "blueprinted" growth; (6) the animal system, charac-
> terized by mobility, enormous information intake, goal-seeking and self-
> awareness; (7) the human system, at which there is self-consciousness and
> symbolic language; (8) social systems; and (9) transcendental systems of
> which we have as yet little knowledge. Think of language, logic, mathematics
> (compare von Bertalanffly, 1968, pp. 28–29).

Klapp (1972) also concurred with Walter Buckley that general systems
theory could find useful applications in sociology. He claimed that within
society, feedback forms a complex adaptive system, not merely a homeostatic or equilibrium system (as was often claimed). It worked as an ongoing process or transaction, which continually evolved, kept and changed,
meanings and patterns of behavior (Buckley, 1967).

Klapp (1972) also noted that the use of systems theory and notions such
as feedback, information, and entropy made a new and different approach
to collective behavior possible. "It might be said, for example, that there is
a kind of equilibrium, sometimes disturbed by pendulum swings, in modern
society between the forces making for alienation and forces making for
'we' " (p. VII). Elsewhere, he spoke of safety valves and spillover effects,
whenever the social system could not cope with rising tensions. But mechanical analogies were too limiting, he added, and maybe biological metaphors (such as incubation and fermentation) could be of more help.

For a further elaboration of his alternative framework, Klapp (1972, 1973) harked back to typical American traditions such as the early psychoso- ciology of Charles Cooley and George Herbert Mead, whose theories of man and society were built around such notions as the emerging self and the "generalized other," and the role of symbolical communication and social construction therein. Think of the fur issue, and how changing notions of self and other repeatedly played a key role. Klapp (1972) quoted the afore- mentioned Blumer, according to whom interaction was a "formative and explorative" process in which participants "judge each other and guide their own acts by that judgment" (p. 146).

And Klapp (1972) concurred with systems-theorist James Miller who had said:

> Living systems at the group level and above maintain their cohesion by . . . memories; by messages signaling the interlocking relationships among their units; by common purposes and goals; by common rewards, payoffs, or grati- fications; or by common punishments, by boundary-maintaining processes for actions leading to dissolution of the system . . . Information flows over a channel or network are necessary to integrate a system, unless all compo- nents were pre-programmed by information stored in them at an earlier time. (p. 5)

It was along such lines, that Klapp tried to map various forms of collective behavior.

The key, Klapp said, was his (1972) 'feedback model' of collective iden- tity. But one might just as well think of individual identities, resulting from differential participation in collective identities with others. There was a kind of ongoing collective negotiation about those aspects of the collec- tive identity one accepted or rejected. There was some kind of ongoing transformation process, in which certain aspects of that identification came to wither away (increasing entropy or chaos), whereas others came to flourish (increasing negentropy or order). It was like a kind of psycho- social respiration, in which people alternately opened themselves up to, or shut themselves off from, alternative information. Just as happened in the fur case.

Klapp was not alone in trying to renovate collective behavior studies through a combination of general systems theory, symbolic interaction the- ory, and their predecessors. Our earlier chapter on crowds mentioned the "convergence" approach of Clark McPhail (1991), who reviewed and re- jected a range of earlier theories, to finally arrive at an alternative "social cybernetics" approach. Just like Klapp's (1972) attempts to develop an overly detailed model in cybernetic terms, however, McPhail's (1991) at- tempts, too, ultimately resulted in a morass of lines and symbols where the reader was soon unable to tell the forest from the trees.

Their major handicap was that they could not yet build on much of the "new wave" and wide range of new concepts on complexity and nonlinear change, which are discussed throughout this present book, because the emergence and consolidation of new patterns gradually came to be seen in different terms.

THE METAPRINCIPLE OF EMERGING PATTERNS

We have already looked at the general principles by which processes begin to run parallel and form synergy. In this chapter, we go a step further. We look at how relatively stable and coherent patterns emerge, and how this same metaprinciple plays a role in the emergence of opinion currents. In the next chapter, we take yet another step, and see how these patterns can ultimately "close"; how they can ultimately become self-organizing or "autopoietic" and relatively autonomous. This general principle in turn plays a role in the rise of social movements. Synergy may lead to emergence that may in turn lead to autopoiesis. They show how large collections of driven particles may evolve CAS involving nonlinear shifts.

Once again, these are metaprinciples of nature, which manifest themselves in life, as well as consciousness and social interaction. In their book, *The Frontiers of Complexity*, Peter Coveney and Roger Highfield introduced the subject in the following, lively way:

> When viewed in profound close-up, the universe is an overwhelming and unimaginable number of particles dancing to a melody of fundamental forces. All about us and within us, molecules and atoms collide, vibrate and spin. Gusts of nitrogen and oxygen molecules are drawn into our lungs with each breath we take. Lattices of atoms shake and jostle within the grains of sand between our toes. Armies of enzymes labor to turn chemicals into living energy for our cells.
>
> Yet we think of the universe as a single harmonious system or cosmos, as the Greeks called it. Now a new branch of science is attempting to demonstrate why the whole universe is greater than the sum of its many parts, and how all its components come together to produce overarching patterns. This effort to divine order in a chaotic cosmos is the new science of complexity. It is weaving remarkable connections between the many and varied efforts of researchers working at its frontiers, across an astonishingly wide range of disciplines. (p. 5)

This is exactly the drift of this present book, and thus the second part on the trinity of synergy, emergence, and self-organization that forms its central part. It deals with the question of how multiplicity may produce unity, how lower levels may evolve higher levels of interaction; so that wholly different layers of reality emerge, without being directly "reducible" to lower levels. Of course there is a certain inherent logic in all this. Yet it is not the mechanistic logic of determinism, but the ecological logic of probabilism. Something that seemed likely may finally not happen after all. Something that seemed unlikely may ultimately occur nevertheless. In this way, infinitely small causes may help bring about infinitely large effects.

This section surveys some of the implications of the metaprinciple of the emergence of patterns. It begins by taking a look at how this principle manifests itself in everyday natural processes, and then looks at how it also turns up in psychological and sociological processes. In those cases, one of the key dimensions is an ongoing negotiation between ourselves and our environment what or who we define as belonging to "us" or "them," to the "in-groups" and the "out-groups" (see also van Ginneken, 1998).

A Digression on Emerging Patterns in Nature

Emergence refers to the ways in which chaos and infinite complexity may evolve new levels of order and relative simplicity. In their book, *The Collapse of Chaos*, Jack Cohen and Ian Stewart (1994) put it this way:

> Emergence is the source of new simplicities, but since we understand the process of emergence rather poorly, that's not a terribly helpful observation. What it does is help make respectable the idea that a collection of interacting components can "spontaneously" develop collective properties that seem not to be implicit in any way in the individual pieces. Emergent simplicities "collapse chaos" ... (p. 232)

This metaprinciple can be seen at work, even at the level of dead matter; of solid, fluid, and volatile substances. But it is even more obvious at the level of living organisms; moreover, it is, in a way, the essence of life itself.

Let us go back to the level of small particles of solid matter, such as grains of sand. Under the influence of gravity and their own form, they "spontaneously" organize into coherent patterns. This is even clearer whenever they undergo the influence of wind or water. From the ripples along the water's edge on the beach, to the dunes further inland, one may note emerging systems and subsystems, which find their prolongation along the entire coastline, in the morass and moors beyond it, in the hills and mountains inland; or in the entire system of deltas and rivers, streams and brooks, embedded between them.

We also know this from the further "organization" of water in patterns. The mathematician Ian Stewart (1997) invited us to walk to the kitchen, and take a closer look: "Have you ever looked at how water flows from a tap? Really looked, I mean?" (p. 157). If you open the tap just a little bit, it may drip regularly: drip drip. If you open it just a little more, it may shift to a different pattern: drip drop or drip drip drop. It may become a regular little trickle or an irregular one. Now put a pan under it: ripples and rings will form. One may even go a bit further, and add some oil. Circles of infinitely different sizes will form on the surface. Put the pan on the stove, and make it come to a boil. Columns of bells will form between the bottom and the surface. So such fluids may continually form and reform emergent structures. Their global nature changes with the approximate circumstances, but the spatiotemporal details cannot be predicted with total precision.

Similar things hold for gases. It is not surprising that the processes of chaos and order were first problematized in meteorology. One famous example is the huge Red Spot, which has long been noted in the atmosphere of the planet Jupiter. The phenomenon has been reproduced in the laboratory, by enclosing gases or fluids between two glass cylinders, one enclosed in the other, and spinning at different speeds. Sometimes a local whirl may occur, which maintains itself for quite a while. If one changes the respective speeds, it may disappear again, but if one restores them, it may even reappear at the same place. Of course these principles are also familiar, from the vortexes forming in a sink or washtub emptying itself; or from twisters or tornado winds.

The whole weather system (just like public opinion) is a moving pattern of streams and substreams at many different levels; of water and air, of temperature and electricity. On one hand, it is extraordinarily complex. Even much better computers than we have today would still have trouble predicting the weather's precise evolution more than 1 week ahead. On the other hand, it is also extremely simple: Because it is made up of a combination of partial patterns, each one can easily be recognized and followed. During recent years, new insights into the principles of emergence have led to a better understanding of global superpatterns and weather trends. For instance, *El Niño* (Spanish for "the Christmas child"). For centuries, its manifestations had been noted along the coastline of the Latin American country of Peru; but only today do we understand that this on-and-off superpattern can modify entire seasons—from eastern Asia to western Europe. Something similar can be said of the cold water "pump" opposite Greenland, indirectly driving the warm water current brushing the western European coastlines. The greenhouse effect and minor temperature changes may shift or derail such superpatterns and thereby help provoke series of major natural disasters.

In his much-debated book *Gaia*, British author James Lovelock (1979) noted that the entire global climate and biosphere have become interrelated in many subtle ways, so that in many respects it has become one system, which somehow keeps some form of equilibrium or homeostasis. In his later book, *The Ages of Gaia*, Lovelock (1989) traced this idea back to German Romanticism and beyond. The suggestion that there somehow is a living "Mother Earth," which manages its own life, is obviously a step too far;

particularly if it leads to the false assumption that the earth will always find ways to deal with disruptions. But the contribution of this metaphor to the evolution of new "(w)holistic" insights has been considerable, and the scorn of reductionists too easy.

Meanwhile, it has become increasingly clear that the evolution of self-replicating molecules, such as RNA and DNA, and the evolution of life itself, did also form newly emerging patterns; that the development of unicellular to multicellular organisms, from microorganisms to mammals, formed a long chain of newly emerging patterns. The forms of plants, in turn, can often be foreseen in broad outline but not in precise detail, even in the seemingly perfect geometry of ferns and palms. We later return to the problem of *morphogenesis*, or the emergence of form. The most complicated mammal of all is man. His body has an astronomical number of cells, which grow into an intricate pattern, subsist, and even reproduce.

The human brain is the most complex adaptive system known on that scale. It is made up of billions of neurons in mutual interaction, and the potential number of patterns they may form is infinite. The neurons may convey signals with a speed of up to 100 meters per second. Neurons are made up of a nucleus, with a number of dendrites and synapses. The average neuron has 10,000 links to other neurons, often many different links with just one other neuron. The meeting points of neurons may bathe in some 50 different biochemical substances, which modulate transmission.

On the dissecting table of the pathologist, however, brains may look rather dull. They have been described as a wrinkled, half-deflated grey ball, which seems to have been fumbled into the skull with great haste; or as an organ with the form of a cauliflower and the substance of an avocado. But these are misleading images. Because it has also been said that if brains were so simply built that humans could understand them, humans would be so simple-minded that they could not understand them. The key to life and consciousness is the potential for the eternal exploration of new patterns, which makes the "frontiers of the possible" expand continuously, and in different directions. These types of evolution are open-ended.

Emergent Patterns in the Human Psyche

Contrary to what many experts and laymen maintained over recent decades, the human brain is not a complicated machine or computer; it is not just processing information according to simple logical rules: if A, then B. The human brain employs the principles of "parallel distributed processing" or even "fuzzy" logic. There are huge numbers of smaller entities (neurons, or clusters, or networks) doing approximately the same thing. Only for that reason are we able to alternately recognize different competing patterns in one and the same identical picture, to ponder its plausibility or use, and to change our opinion. Only for that reason are we able to think creatively, and to deal with ever new situations. (On this score, see McClelland and others, 1986). Otherwise we could never be won over to a different point of view in the first place, as happened in the fur case.

Every fleeting impression or vague memory is like an infinitely ramified thunderbolt, striking through thousands or millions of neurons, activating or deactivating some, and provoking minor adaptations. Every impression or memory forms a network, partly reinforces or dissolves a network, or rather, a network of networks. Even if no new impulses are fed to it, as in sleep or sensory deprivation, the brain will generate dreams or hallucinations. In these cases, it is the total pattern that counts, and not the sum of the parts. So it is just as important to understand the processes of emergence in a general sense, as well as to understand the details of all the elements involved. Perceiving, thinking, and remembering (and other overarching psychological processes) are fundamentally configurational. Even if we were able to specify all possible states for all possible brain cells, this would not necessarily teach us something about the emergence of patterns in the interaction between them.

Psychology has learned this the hard way; when it began, and also in recent decades (when most behaviorists suddenly "converted" to cognitivism). When psychology began, it first tried to distinguish as many functions and elements as possible and then put them back together again. Laboratory experiments investigated isolated aspects of thinking, feeling, and acting. It tried to identify general laws, and to abstract as much as possible from concrete everyday situations. In due course, however, it discovered that this only led to a very limited understanding. Because in reality, the processes were much more complex and interactive than the reductionist approach implied.

Perception psychology, for instance, initially started from the premise that people perceived separate elements, which they would then put back together again in their heads. But it turned out that this was not the case at all. By contrast, people perceived coherent patterns or Gestalts from the start. For example, we see two lines as belonging together, whenever they are similar or close together, or prolong each other, or make a whole. Over the years, many of such Gestalt principles have been identified, not only in the field of visual perception, but also in the field of auditory perception (think of melodies and music, in particular). But even with relation to smell, taste, and touch. These principles are "played off" against each other in ambiguous stimuli and perceptual illusions (to which we return in chap. 11). Magicians and tricksters exploit them to their advantage.

Similar patterns can be identified in cognition. It is not so very difficult to lead people onto the wrong path, as is illustrated by many riddles and mind traps; as the one of the car crash, in which the father perishes, but the son survives. The surgeon in the hospital says, "I cannot operate him, because he is my own son and my hand will tremble!" How can this parent be both dead and alive? The answer is of course that people do not follow logical rules in combination and deduction, but employ hidden assumptions as well. In this case, the hidden assumption is that the surgeon is a man. Crooks and swindlers are very good at exploiting such cognitive errors.

In this way, our views of the world are part of much broader belief systems—wide-ranging systems of assumptions about reality, which guide our perception and cognition, just as well as our emotions and actions. These systems are the accumulation of our socialization and education, but also of all formal and informal communication that take place thereafter, including all media exposure and conversation. It colors our intuition about people and issues, with appraisals and feelings. "Isolated thoughts" hardly exist; they are always part of wider networks and meaning-producing systems. And a few basic dimensions are often decisive.

At the same time, we are continually reviewing and revising these configurations or patterns. One example is the tendency to so-called "cognitive dissonance reduction," identified and researched by the social psychologist, Leon Festinger (1957). Something happens, for instance, which makes our various thoughts, feelings, and actions no longer in line with each other. Some adaptation may occur to restore coherence. An illustration: I have not given money to a beggar, although I usually sympathize with poor people; but, I add, he is probably a "good for nothing" anyway, and I cannot solve all the problems of the world on my own. (So I generate an additional element, to bring my thoughts in line with my actions.)

At the level of our actions themselves, there are coherent patterns as well—scripts and scenarios, tactics and strategies. The observation that perception and cognition, emotion and action, form coherent patterns and complex configurations has important implications. Because it once again points to the fact that the change of a minor detail may provoke a major shift in meaning. With the awkward combination of a German and English word, this is called a *Gestalt switch*. We see later that they do indeed play a role in many rapid, radical, and massive shifts in opinion and perception.

The repeated shocks or "mind quakes" with relation to fur are only one series of illustrations. Whether something is new or fascinating, subject to reproach or revenge, chilling or threatening, worthwhile or desirable, these are all value judgments that can easily be questioned. Under some conditions, furthermore, a reversal may well take place—as we see again in the next part of this book, on public mood shifts. But let us first take a further look at how mental configurations are intertwined with social ones. In this book, I willingly chose from the start not to separate psychology, sociology, and communication science. That would hide to what extent they should be closely intertwined; most of all in studying public opinion formation.

Emergent Patterns in Social Exchange

The existing literature often tends to separate these phenomena all too easily; the emergence of psychological patterns in the form of association networks and the emergence of sociological patterns in the form of communication networks. Yet these are two phenomena that are closely intertwined. It is important to note that exactly the same metaprinciples are at work here.

At the same time, I have certain misgivings about the widespread use of the word "networks" in this context. I find this usage awkward and slightly misguided, because the term *network* is not just an abstract concept, but has very concrete connotations. In my view, it implies too much solidity to include the fluid and volatile processes often involved; particularly if we primarily mean the many dozens of fleeting, informal, and coincidental contacts that we have with other people, with institutions and media, every day. The word "net" would be slightly better. But the term, "web," which Fritjof Capra (1977) proposed, and related terms such as "weaving," do better convey some of the temporality and fragility that is frequently involved. Only in the case of "objectified" social positions within a lasting, formal framework, is the term *network* (with its fixed lines and knots) really an appropriate metaphor.

But let us dwell for a moment on the question of how everyday communication really takes place. The alarm clock goes off, and turns the radio on. There is some interaction before, during, and after breakfast with family members or housemates. We thumb through the morning paper. There is some interaction with others during the morning rush hour. We meet colleagues at work, exchange greetings, read mail and e-mail, answer phone calls, go to a meeting, have lunch (same things during the afternoon). After work, colleagues sometimes share a quick drink together, go shopping on the way home, share dinner with family, look at TV evening news, walk the dog and wave to the neighbors, come home to read a book, and so forth. During all these behavioral sequences, we send and receive dozens of minor signals; all kinds of minor aspects of our view of the world and of our place therein are reconfirmed or revised, if ever so marginally.

The mental image that we have of an issue or public discussion (e.g., on the fur case) is continually tested against a range of information and sources. Will the neighbors still like us if we put on a fur coat? Structural contacts play a role, just as well as chance encounters, and combinations of both. Because we are part of many different networks at the same time—family and neighbors, friends and acquaintances, colleagues and shopkeepers, team-mates in sport, and co-members of associations; we partly choose those networks, and are partly chosen by them. The interaction with those networks, or networks of networks, helps to shape our thoughts, feelings, and behaviors, just as we contribute to shaping theirs. But the networks are emergent; they evolve all the time, so there is always a chance that one encounter more or less may trigger a major shift.

This configurational aspect of communication and persuasion networks also plays a role in the concept of *opinion leadership*, which Paul Lazarsfeld and others had first proposed in election studies. It noted that within every network, certain people are held to be better informed and more knowledgeable than others. This was supposed to lead to a "two-step flow" of information and persuasion; one step between media or organizations and opinion leaders, the next step between the opinion leaders and the wider public (Katz & Lazarsfeld, 1955). Celebrity endorsement is a related strategy (think of the role of female models and stars in the anti-fur campaigns).

Gradually, however, it turned out that this approach too was a simplification, because in real life, there is usually a multistep flow in persuasion attempts because most groups have more than one person exerting an "above average" influence; and also because people who are opinion leaders in one domain (e.g., politics), may not be in the next (car maintenance, gardening, cooking, sports, travel, etc.). Finally, there may be interference between the opinion leaders from various networks and domains in which people participate. Think of the wonderfully subtle moiré combination patterns that form when two geometrically regular patterns are superimposed, especially at an acute angle. Similar things hold true for psychosocial patterns; their mutual interference may create still other patterns, of still higher complexity.

Nonlinearity, emergence, and complexity manifest themselves in other ways, too; networks of networks may create surprise effects in their coincidental linking and unlinking. Within one and the same network of similar people, roughly similar information will make the rounds, which produces roughly similar effects. Within different networks of different people, however, dissimilar information will make the rounds, which produces dissimilar effects. This creates a paradox, which Mark Granovetter labeled "the strength of weak ties" (1973). According to this argument, some of the most fundamental changes and greatest reversals may occur, whenever there suddenly is some unexpected contact and information exchange between networks that had previously remained isolated from each other (see also Rogers, 1995). This is particularly noteworthy in the case of social unrest.

So everyday communication networks, too, have an emergent aspect and form new patterns. If some situation is very exceptional, emerging patterns (networks of networks) may quickly overpower established patterns. Research has shown, for instance, that the majority of the American public learned of the Kennedy assassination and the Challenger disaster within 30 minutes. Those who had heard it via radio or television began calling family members and friends by telephone. But they would also tell total strangers in the street, and burst into tears together. So networks should not be seen as a static concept, but as a dynamic concept. The river may suddenly overflow, and create new rivulets. The cables may suddenly become conducive, and carry signals. We return to such processes in chapter 8 (on "criticality") and chapter 10 (on "phase transitions").

Under normal circumstances, emergent patterns and established patterns will tend to prolong one another. Research into psychological crowds, social movements, and opinion currents shows that "mobilization patterns" will usually be based on preexisting contacts. Because apart from the deeper motivation to favor unconventional alternatives, people must also come in touch with the emerging process, and be in the position to join them. (In chap. 8, we return to the principle of *contiguity*, which plays a role here). But of course the positive or negative effects of such contacts will depend on one's current state of mind.

6

The Self-Organization of Social Movements

When smashing monuments, save the pedestals—they always come in handy.
—Stanislaw Lec, Polish author (Gross, 1987, p. 121)

A name that recurs frequently throughout this book is that of Greenpeace. Alongside Amnesty International, Doctors Without Borders and others, it is one of those international, "new social movements" that took root in the 1960s and 1970s. We begin this chapter with a description of the "case" of Greenpeace, its origins, and specificity. In the second section, we take a closer look at the growth of social movements in general, their emergence and shaping. In the third section, this growth will be related to the meta-principle of self-organization, which has been elaborated on in recent years. This will complete our basic scheme. We have already discussed the role of permanent mutation and feedback loops in complex adaptive systems. In this part, we have outlined synergy formation, pattern emergence, and self-organization.

CASE NUMBER SIX: GREENPEACE MAKES A WAVE

The next case concerns one of those new social movements that formed in the wake of the 1960s, playing a key role in several of the cases described later in this volume. In particular, we are interested more in the early rise of this social movement, not so much in its present form. At the very beginning, there were just a few isolated activists and various ad hoc groups, with different preoccupations. But these tended to coalesce, until the need for a more formal arrangement was recognized. Even today, the well-run organization is only the center of a much wider, informal movement, consisting of vastly larger numbers of sympathizers and outsiders. The question is how such movements evolve.

Greenpeace is the child of a marriage between two older strands of activism in North America: the ecological movement and the pacifist movement. By the late 1960s, the United States announced that it would hold underground tests for nuclear weapons on Amchitka, one of the farthest of the string of Aleutian islands opposite the coast of Alaska. The announcement provoked massive protests on the west coast of Canada, which was even closer to the testing area than the west coast of the United States itself. This whole west coast area seemed to be particularly prone to earthquakes. On the day of the first test, therefore, 10,000 demonstrators blocked the major border crossings between the two countries, holding banners imploring the authorities, "Don't make a wave" (Hunter, 1979).

One activist–journalist involved warned in the Vancouver *Sun*:

> Politicians, take note. There is a power out there in suburbia, so far harnessed only to charity drives, campaigns and PTA's [Parent–Teacher Associations] which, if ever properly brought to bear on the great problems of the day, will have an impact so great, the result of its being detonated . . . cannot be predicted. (Brown & May, 1991, p. 7)

It proved to be an accurate prophecy of things to come. When the United States announced another test for 1971, activists in the same Canadian port of Vancouver formed a "Don't make a wave" committee. This Green–peace, as it was later renamed, was to initiate a global eco–pacifist wave, unprecedented in history.

Among its early driving forces were two couples who had moved from the United States to Canada, because of the Vietnam intervention and the Cold War. The group rented a boat to sail to the test area, stage a protest, and generate media coverage. It received strong support from various groups in other cities, particularly in the San Francisco area. After further continuation of the tests in Alaska had been called off, other Greenpeace groups staged repeated intrusions into the Nevada test sites as well. Meanwhile, Vancouver had contacted former Canadian badminton champion and businessman, David McTaggart, in New Zealand, to stage similar protests with his yacht, Vega, against atmospheric nuclear tests that the French continued to hold on the Polynesian island of Mororoa in the Southern Pacific (see the case described in chap. 4). The first year the French rammed his boat; the second year they boarded it and maltreated him; after which he flew off to Paris to file a lawsuit and try to set up groups in London and elsewhere.

At the same time a young New Zealand psychologist, who had learned to "communicate" with orcas at the Vancouver Aquarium, had joined Greenpeace activists to set up Project Ahab for the protection of whales. They equipped boats to confront the Soviet and Japanese whaling fleets in the North Pacific, and later to confront the Soviet and Scandinavian whaling fleets in the North Atlantic. Gradually, Greenpeace extended its protests to the dumping of nuclear waste, and of toxic waste in general; and to the protection of dolphins, seals, sea turtles, and other endangered species.

For that purpose, it acquired and equipped the first permanent action ship, the Rainbow Warrior. It was named after an Indian legend that had inspired its first activists. When the end of the earth appeared near because of the devastation of the natural environment, the legend said, help would come from the skies:

> "The rainbow is a sign from Him who is in all things," said the old, wise one. "It is a sign of the union of all peoples like one big family. Go to the mountaintop, child of my flesh, and learn to be a Warrior of the Rainbow, for it is only by spreading love and joy to others, that hate in this world can be changed to understanding and kindness, and war and destruction shall end." (quoted in Brown & May, 1991, p. 12)

After the Rainbow Warrior, Greenpeace acquired and equipped a host of similar ships to patrol the oceans and prevent unnecessary damage to the environment.

Greenpeaces strategies and tactics in these cases derived from a form of moral protest that had been developed by the Quakers, a small Protestant denomination that had always been particularly influential within the pacifist movement. It was called "bearing witness" and meant that its activists would go to a spot where they felt something objectionable was going on, peacefully interfere with it (through sit ins or by chaining themselves to an object), and thereby draw public attention (and media attention), hoping to provoke an outrage. Greenpeace refined this formula by making the actions highly symbolic, visual, spectacular, and perfectly attuned to the pictorial news age.

At sea, they would cast themselves in the role of Davids confronting Goliaths; colorful hippies in rubber dinghies, against grey uniforms and striped suits lined up on colossal warships, floating factories, oil platforms, chemical plants, and so forth. For its actions on rivers and on land, it would recruit athletes; divers to plug underwater waste pipes, mountain climbers to occupy polluting chimney towers, and roll out huge banners with brief slogans, always under the watchful eye of the camera. Over the years, it focused on all landmarks with extra publicity value: the Statue of Liberty in New York, the Big Ben and Nelson's Column in London, the Little Mermaid in Copenhagen, the Atomium in Brussels, the Eiffel Tower in Paris, the Big Wheel in Vienna, the Opera House in Sydney, and others.

Their actions would usually provoke a scuffle, provide drama, and attract media coverage. Photo and film crews would relay their message. They kept it simple: well-chosen places and times; feasible demands and clear issues. Spokes(wo)men were carefully trained in photo ops and sound bites. Journalists were carefully selected and invited along. Greenpeace often proved to have much more media savvy than the much larger powers it confronted. At the same time, Greenpeace was repeatedly torn between the proponents of short-term direct action and of long-term solid organization and influence building (Knappe, 1993).

Hubris and charisma surrounded David McTaggart of Greenpeace, but also Paul Watkins, who founded the split-off group Sea Shepherd, Brian Davies, who founded IFAW, and others (see the previous case in chap. 5). Clashes between strong egos played a role in internal conflicts during the campaign against French testing and British dumping (see the previous Moruroa case in chap. 4, and the later Shell case in chap. 9). At the same time, Greenpeace and the broader environmental movement also had their martyrs in the Portuguese–Dutch photographer Fernando Pereira (killed in the French sabotage of the first Rainbow Warrior action ship), U.S. antinuclear activist Karen Silkwood, the Brazilian rainforest and land reform activist Chico Mendez, and others.

Meanwhile, Greenpeace continued to expand. Upon its fifth anniversary in 1976, global membership was estimated at only 10,000. Local, regional, and national groups developed, but at first there was little coordination. Greenpeace Canada had spread from Vancouver to other cities, but was heavily in debt. Greenpeace United States had spread from San Francisco to other cities but was rather fragmented. In the Pacific, groups had sprung up in New Zealand and Australia. In Europe, groups had sprung up in Great Britain and The Netherlands, and a much smaller one in France. After a major crisis, however, David McTaggart succeeded in federating all these independent groups into Greenpeace International. From then on, they all contributed between one quarter and one fifth of their revenue to a global headquarters, which was first located in Lewes (Sussex, England) and then in Amsterdam (The Netherlands).

From an action group and social movement, therefore, Greenpeace developed into a massive organization and environmental lobby. It participated in the campaign against sealing, already discussed. In 1995, it had two noteworthy campaigns against the Brent Spar dumping and the Moruroa tests, also discussed in this book. Upon its 25th anniversary in 1996, it had reached a total budget of some $120 million dollars, provided by close to three million supporters worldwide, which maintained a professional staff of 1,000 people and a dozen ships. Greenpeace claimed to have played a key role in promoting a long series of new bans and moratoria, conventions and treaties for conservation and against pollution, particularly in the oceans. "What makes Greenpeace unique is its ability to catalyze change," Thilo Bode, its new executive director, said on that occasion (1996). It is like Lorenz's butterfly; the tiny difference that provokes a huge shift.

Several elements we have already identified in previous chapters return here. Let us review just a few points. The emergence of the eco–pacifist movement was the result of the link-up of several long-term trends and newly emerging nuclei. The "crisis and war" generation, with its supposed emphasis on material values such as industry, competition, and technology, had been increasingly criticized by the postwar "Baby Boom" generation, which claimed "spiritual values" such as self-realization, cooperation, and naturalness. The former's alleged blindness to North–South inequality, and fixation on East–West confrontation, were challenged by Third World solidarity groups and by the antimilitarist movement.

Although the dire, late 1970's predictions of the Club of Rome (see chap. 11) did not come true, the 1980s and 1990s produced their own black scenarios around worldwide climate change; because of the hole in the ozone layer and the greenhouse effect, the shrinking of the rainforests, and the change in gulf streams, El Niño, and so forth. Greenpeace welded all these disparate elements together in a new meaningful configuration, a seemingly "single issue." Even elderly people joined younger activists in their quest.

The movement soon found its characteristic unique selling proposition—as marketers label it: the oceans. The oceans had long remained a grey and drab, unknown, and unattractive area beyond the distant horizon, where large corporations and powerful governments basically could do whatever they wanted. If on occasion there was some incident about the treatment of animals or the pollution of the environment, they and their representatives were the only eyewitnesses. In that way, they had a complete information monopoly and definition monopoly on what had happened or what did not happen. Greenpeace broke through this wall of silence by equipping ships for activists and journalists. The century old Quaker tactic of bearing witness by peaceful interference acquired a completely new meaning in the Canada of media guru Marshall McLuhan, and proved perfectly adapted to the television age. Greenpeace turned out to be a great "meme-breeder"; it provoked images that circulated around the globe and stirred immediate reactions.

It adroitly exploited the laws of present-day, emotional, live, and visual newsgathering; it provided compact and colorful and dramatic action, easy to register by cameras, with a simple storyline about Davids and Goliaths, about the good guys and the bad guys. It used well-known and newsworthy landmarks as backdrops; it recruited celebrities from the sports and entertainment worlds in heroic roles; it provoked outrages about animal suffering and environmental disasters. Greenpeace succeeded in becoming their prime advocate, in overtaking older movements active in these same fields and in forcing them to follow their lead.

There was a whole plethora of separate local activities, activists, and action groups that preceded Greenpeace. But a pattern of alliances (and rivalries) gradually crystallized around the international federation. Greenpeace became a "global brand name," instantly recognizable by all, worldwide. The organization had leaders and martyrs associated to it; the brand had images and slogans attached to it. A whole new social psychological configuration emerged; or "self-organized," as we see in the remainder of this chapter. Because in contrast to crowd gatherings and opinion currents, there is something more here: delineation, entity, and coherence. Let us see what this means.

THE PHENOMENON OF SOCIAL MOVEMENTS

The various cases of rapid, radical, and massive shifts in public opinion and perception described so far often involved emerging social movements. Think of the case study of the famine in Ethiopia, which was first ignored, and then hyped, when Biblical images were produced and pop stars came on the scene. It showed how the outline of a broad social movement emerged, but how the initiators decided not to give it a permanent, organizational form. The case studies on the nuclear tests in Moruroa and the baby seals in Canada also showed how the worldwide campaigns were supported by a broad coalition of groups, but how the social protests transcended these organizational forms. In the latter two cases, the new social movement Greenpeace played a major role.

There is a huge amount of literature on old and new social movements, and we also return to the subject in the later chapter on the public mood of outrage and protest (chap. 9). At this point, we take a closer look at two different families of approaches to social movements, each of which is focused on a different stage in development. On one hand, there is the family that looks at early social movements as a process; a process of emerging patterns of coordinated action. This approach is well in line with the previous chapter on opinion currents, and the symbolic interactionist view of the "natural history" of collective behavior. It is a differentiation process leading to the formation of a new social entity.

Some authors (such as Marx & McAdam, 1994) reminded us that the spontaneity and unconventionality of collective behavior must be seen as relative aspects, not as an absolute criterion, because such initiatives almost always take existing nuclei and mores as their point of departure. But on the other hand, there is a family of approaches that looks at full-fledged social movements as established structures; structures of formal groups that are more or less effective. This latter approach prevails in organization sociology. We return to this contrast in the last part of this section.

Social Movements as Emergent Self-Organization

So let us first look at the approach that sees social movements as the result of a process of emergent patterns of social action. Our description of the origins of Greenpeace provides ample illustration. The approach prevailed in early handbooks of collective behavior, such as those by Turner and Killian (1987), K. Lang and G. E. Lang (1961), and Smelser (1962). But it also informed later books that were specifically about social movements, such as those by Wilson (1973), Oberschall (1973), Genevie (1978), Lofland (1985), and others.

John Wilson (1973) defined social movements as "a conscious, collective, organized attempt to bring about or resist large-scale change in the social order by non-institutionalized means" (p. 8). This definition suits me well, although I would tend to replace the word "organized" with "coordinated," in order to not create confusion about the noninstitutionalized nature of the activity. We later return to that point. But it is true that this is a bit of a twilight zone, because both coordination and organization may cover a whole range of activities, from a completely informal ad hoc group to a legally established association with professionally run headquarters. But in both cases, this limited nucleus is usually transcended by a much broader fluid group of sympathizers.

The key to this approach is the early mobilization around some form of social unease. Wilson (1973) emphasized that they create an emergent "process of interaction that could not be predicted from antecedent conditions, properties of leadership, commitment and group structure" (p. 89). It is a qualitative transformation guided by a number of factors "such as the intensity of the deprivation, the presence of agitators and ideologies, the reactions of the authorities, the alternate responses available, and so on" (p. 90). So participation is not merely the result of predispositions "but entails the construction of a new identity in which the decision to commit oneself is negotiated through a series of encounters and interactions. Being willing, being able. Being encouraged, experimenting, and being labeled are all-important ingredients" (p. 90). So the possibilities for identification with a movement such as Greenpeace are of great importance.

In early systems-theoretical approaches, unease or a sense of "lack" are seen as an aspect of the dissolution of existing patterns, of emergent entropy. It is because psychosocial patterns cannot enforce conformity any more that some room is created for experimenting with alternative psychosocial patterns. One of those turns out to be more effective than others, and gains in power; for instance through positive feedback, amplification, and circular reaction; or through convergence, synergy, and resonance. Ultimately, emergent patterns may develop "operational closure" and self-organize into new collective units. The inner and the outer world becomes separated, and there will be self-reference to some kind of identity. It will also involve a shift in "locus of control" from the multitude to the new collective entity. From that moment on, the social movement will tend to survive on its own, to extend itself, and to gain more power and influence.

In the previous chapter on opinion currents, I referred to Orrin Klapp, who tried to develop a systems-theoretical approach to such phenomena throughout his oeuvre. In his book about social movements (Klapp, 1969), he noted, for instance: "If a social system is inadequate in feedback and symbolization, it cannot give individuals an adequate sense of meaning . . . Therefore, people easily feel outside and have to search for [alternative] roles and identities" (pp. XI, 14). He called this "groping," and compared it to a river seeking its bed through the landscape. This obviously held for the early environmental movement. In a collection of articles (Klapp, 1971), he had therefore said that it was important to look at emergent roles and developing structures—particularly within societies characterized by "formality, anonymity, mobility and change" (pp. 2–4).

His book on collective behavior (Klapp, 1972) discussed the role of meaning-seeking movements in transforming a public mood into a symbolic reality:

> The transformation occurs by negotiations in which activities, experiences, gestures, names, and concepts are put to people as proposals, selected and reinforced by feedback . . . The growth of the network and its communication events is the growth of the movement. Institutionalization of such a network transforms the old society or creates a new one . . . It is hard to trace them until they emerge as a structure (ideology, organized force, party, underworld system, etc.). (p. 362)

In his book about information processing (Klapp, 1978), he claimed that resonance and "good vibes" (p. 14) resulted in the closing of ranks. In his book about social symbols (Klapp, 1991), he showed that a true crusade offered a deep change "of self-conception and identity" through features such as "emotional revivalism, the feeling of a return home, a test by which to prove oneself, the break with normal life, reorientation, the heroic role, the purgative function of the image of evil, and the vision of the good" (p. 53).

So these are all emerging patterns which fuse in self-organizing new entities. The early rise of Greenpeace was just an example.

Role Differentiation and Self-Organization

Self-organizing early social movements see themselves confronted with a series of tasks, which are often intertwined with other forms of collective behavior. On one hand, they must build and maintain networks of social contacts. Social movements are longer lasting than psychological crowds, yet periodical get-togethers may play a major role in their lives; real mass meetings, too, because they offer a rare opportunity to experience the newly emerging identity "in the flesh," not only for the insiders, but often even for the outsiders as well. Social movements are more structured than mere opinion currents, on the other hand, as they will often try to project a well-defined image to the outside world about what is wrong, what should be done, who should do it, and in what way.

One of the central aspects is an emergent differentiation in roles. Psychosocial aspects are intertwined in roles; they imply an image or representation of ourselves and others, and also of the kind of behaviors that may be expected of both. Some roles are more important in the perspective of mental reorientation, other roles in that of social reorientation. Some roles are more important in a positive sense (to identify with), other roles more in a negative sense (to oppose). They are emerging fragments of structure, or structuring elements, in the psychosocial life in and around an early social movement.

With regard to the mental reorientation through altered cognitive associations, it is largely a question of splitting off and recombining (Keene, 1991). The reorientation brings to light certain negative aspects of our own behavior, which we tend to deny, minimize, or project onto others—outside (or opposed to) the social movement. The reorientation also brings to light certain positive aspects of our own behavior, which we tend to highlight, enlarge, and identify with the people inside (or at the head of) the social movement. The former process leads to rejection, blackening, and diabolization. The latter process leads to praise, white-washing and idealization—the looking for idols. Both processes are closely intertwined; they reinforce one another. Even though at the outset it may be easier to define what one is unconditionally against then what one is unconditionally for.

Rejection, blackening, and diabolization often involves ascribing "surplus evil," an excess of blindness and bad faith, to outsiders and opponents. They feature the "attribution error," whereby the negative elements are attributed to the "true nature" of the other, and the good elements are attributed to "chance circumstances." This implies that not too much should be expected from looking for compromise, because only full confrontation may bring results. Even if the undesirable state of affairs may have distant structural causes, one will seek to identify personal responsibilities. René Girard has shown that scape-goating is an essential part of group formation. Kurt Baschwitz has shown, in turn, how confusion over roles contributed to the witch hunts of the European age of transition, which had up to 500,000 victims (Baschwitz, 1951, 1981; Goode & Ben-Yehuda, 1994).

Praise, white-washing, and idealization, by contrast, often involves ascribing "surplus nobility" to insiders and sympathizers; an excess of nobility and lucidity. Here too, the attribution error is prominent. The good is attributed to the "true nature" of our idols, the possibly dubious to chance circumstances. It follows that their declared values and norms must be taken seriously, and that there is no need to back down a bit. Even if the change in the desired direction may be attributable to other factors, we rather ascribe it to the action of victims, martyrs, and heroes. *Victims, martyrs,* and *heroes* are people who were aware in different degrees of the risks they were taking to advance the good cause. The tendency to hero worship is a universal human trait. In ancient days, it primarily manifested itself in the fields of religion, nationality, and ideology. Today it extends to the domain of entertainment, media, and stars (with fan clubs).

As far as the social coordination in early social movements is concerned, there is a differentiation in the actual impact on decision making through communication networks. Some approaches employ an implicit hierarchy or pyramid scheme, with the highest leader or Messiah at the top, and the co-leaders or apostles around or below. Followed by the active minority or organizational nucleus of the movement, the passive minority or mere members of the movement, and the sympathizers or potential supporters outside the movement itself. This scheme was used from the start in Christendom and the Catholic Church, but more recently within socialist or communist parties. Beyond this primary force field, one may identify people who are neutral or indifferent. Then there is one or more layers of opponents. For example, a countermovement with opposite goals. (Think of the recent movements that try to portray hunters as the prime guardians of nature.) Finally, of course, there are official institutions and authorities, which may take action when they feel the established order and/or status quo is threatened.

There is a huge amount of literature on leadership, and James Mac-Gregor Burns's overview notes the existence of no less than 130 different definitions (1979, p. 2). With regard to emergent social movements and collective behavior, the discussion has often focused on the question of whether there is such a thing as "charisma," and of what it consists. One of the founders of sociology, Max Weber, noted that apart from bureaucratic and traditional authority, there seemed to be a third form; that is to say charismatic authority, whereby the followers attributed certain exceptional "gifts of grace" to the leader. A large number of supposed charismatic leaders of the 20th century have since been studied, but this produces a kind of "slanted sample" (see Willner, 1984). A large number of supposed charismatic traits have been identified, but their distillation does not completely convince me (see also Schiffer, 1973).

I feel a better key can be found in the works of Sigmund Freud (1921/ 1967), the founder of psychoanalysis. In his *Massenpsychologie*, he identified something like "hubris" as a central notion—although he did not give it that name; that is to say the typical (perceived) self-confidence of the typical leader, the apparent overconfidence of the leader, which locks in with the apparent underconfidence of the followers—even more so in a critical situation. This also helps to throw further light on the derailment of venerated leaders, whose hubris may fade into recklessness. Their reality-checking is undermined; therefore, they permit themselves excesses that may ultimately lead to exposure. Think of the obsessive philandering of Governor and then President Clinton, although it hardly matched that of Senator and then President Kennedy, and a range of other political leaders. Such processes of "ego-swelling" have been well analyzed by Manfred Kets de Vries (1989).

Of course, the key ingredients for charisma differ with social systems and the decisive forms of organization and communication therein. Door-to-door canvassing and dominating an organization demand different skills than giving television interviews and leading the polls. Today we have become even more aware that charisma should not so much be seen as the characteristic of a person, but rather as the characteristic of a relationship. Namely the relationship between the leader and the followers. That relationship is mediated by a variety of factors.

Within many early social movements there is only one typical leader, but often too he is only a *primus inter pares*—the first among equals. He takes on specific tasks and roles, and symbolically represents the wider group. But soon there are so many different tasks to be fulfilled that he gladly leaves other roles (such as actual organization building) to others. One set of key tasks is *agitprop*: agitation or the undermining of the established order; and propaganda or the preaching of a different order. Next to this avant-garde of pioneers, a broader, "active minority" can often be identified (Moscovici, 1976). This principle has been exploited by having claques at theatre premieres, but also by the religious order of the Jesuits, by the esoteric lodges of the Freemasons, or by the political parties of the Marxist–Leninists. Calculations from game and decision theory indicate that the number of a decided minority need only correspond approximately to the square root of the total number in an undecided group to be sure to carry the sway in the vast majority of cases (see Penrose, 1952).

The early social movement grows into an "adult" social movement, when the tasks of self-organization have been completed. That is to say that a clear identity has emerged to which one can refer, a clear distinction has been made between those inside and outside, often by having a formal membership with cards and dues. At that moment, a legal status will also be chosen; an official address, statutes, a program, an executive committee, terms, election procedures, membership criteria, an operational budget, periodic meetings, regular publications, and so on. At that point in time, the metaprinciples of pattern emergence and self-organization subside somewhat, and make room for more formal styles of division of labor.

Emerging Self-Organization and Established Organization

We have seen in the chapter on crowds how the psychological approach in terms of their irrationality was criticized in recent decades, and how the empirical research on gatherings resulted in a sociological emphasis on some kind of rationality. In the same way, we can note in this chapter on social movements that the psychological approach in terms of emergence was criticized in recent decades, and how the empirical research on movement organizations resulted in a sociological emphasis on (the potential for) "resource mobilization." This approach was primarily advocated by Zald and others (Zald & McCarthy, 1987).

They claimed the collective behavior approach of emerging social movements gave too much weight to dissatisfaction, because in most times and places, people would be dissatisfied with many different things. It seemed paradoxical, they said, that highly developed societies with considerable wealth had many more social movements than underdeveloped societies with widespread poverty. So it seemed much more interesting to look at the question from the standpoint of which initiatives were able to gather support, and how. Rather than the social movements themselves, it seemed to be the actual social movement organizations that mattered; and how social movement industries covered certain domains, or how all together formed the social movement sector. Because in a country such as the United States, it was not only underprivileged groups that tried to articulate matters of interest, but also middle-class groups that tried to articulate matters of ethics. They often formed professional organizations with a full-time staff, running recruitment and funding campaigns, with the help of modern technologies such as direct mail and TV ads. To a certain extent, there was cooperation between them, but there was competition too, because the citizen's dollar could only be spent once.

Just as in discussions about psychological crowds, I think the advocates of a more down-to-earth approach were only partly right. They were partly right in saying that the earlier, one-sided focus on emerging social movements had produced many interesting studies on premodern times and places, but resulted in few consistent comparisons, relevant laws, and general models relevant to present-day society. But they were partly wrong in their own one-sided focus on purely organizational aspects of the highly developed sociopolitical process in today's United States. This once again amounted to "throwing away the child with the bath-water," and underestimating the processes of emergence and autopoiesis that are characteristic for early social movements, even if they are harder to recognize.

I tend to go even further. Within true social movements, there usually is some kind of latent tension between the motives, feelings, and moods that originally gave rise to the emergent pattern; and the technobureaucratic organizations that have formed on that basis, which became relatively autonomous, and gradually took over. On an impulse, one decides to give money to a charity, only to find out that a large part is spent on feeding and refeeding your address to the direct mail machine of that same organization, and an ever-growing number of similar ones. The inherent logic is that the relationship will be stretched to the limit, until it finally breaks again.

Similarly, there is an inherent logic of the relationship between the many and the few, the elite and the masses, as social differentiation and the division of labor proceed. In early political sociology, this process was analyzed in theories about the "circulation of elites," formulated by Italians Gaetano Mosca and Vilfredo Pareto, in theories about bureaucratization and the "iron law of oligarchisation" by Max Weber and Robert Michels, and by others (see van Ginneken, 1992, pp. 90–95).

I want to add one further observation here, related to my experiences as a consultant. Organization sociology itself has discovered in recent years that many institutional problems are somehow related to the persisting latent tension between the explicit, formal "surface" organization and the implicit, informal "underground" organization. Deal and Kennedy's (1988) modern classic on *Corporate Cultures* noted: "A new employee isn't handed a booklet called 'The 50,000 Informal Rules You Need to Survive Here.' " Yet "we think that 90 percent of what goes on in an organization has nothing to do with formal events" (pp. 86, 98).

Many keys to what is going on need to be found in the informal organization, communication patterns, public moods, and in the "emotional economy." As Sigmund Freud and Freudians like Wilfred Bion have shown, people have a range of unconscious expectations in relation to organizations from which they derive a significant share of their social identity, such as defence against fear, uncertainty and dependence. In recent years, this approach has been further elaborated by de Board (1978), Miller and (most of all), the Dutch psychoanalyst and management consultant, Manfred Kets de Vries (Kets de Vries & Miller, 1987; Kets de Vries, 1989, 1995).

Within the framework of "microsociology," furthermore, a fascinating new approach focuses on the "emotional economy" that certain professions demand. A first study was that of Arlie Hochschild (1983) about stewardesses. Since then, there have been other studies of "typically female" professions such as nurse or social worker; and "typically male" professions such as debt collector, policeman, or fireman. The approach challenges the characteristic, modern-day myth of rationality, and means to

> position emotion as central to the process of organizing and as integral to participation in organizational life. Emotion, then, is not simply an adjunct to work; rather, it is the process through which members constitute their work environment by negotiating a shared reality. (Fineman, 1994, p. 36; see also Scheff, 1990)

Gareth Morgan (1986), in turn, has demonstrated in his book *Images of Organization*, that organization theory and management techniques to this very day remain prisoner of the metaphors that they had unwittingly adopted and that had continued to (mis)guide their thinking—up to the smallest details. Many corporations and other institutions still show traces of archaic organization forms such as the army (with its heavy emphasis on hierarchical authority), the bureaucracy (with its heavy emphasis on written rules), and the factory (with its extreme division of labor). These ways of doing things seem self-evident, but are not at all or at least not any more. Advanced and sophisticated organizations need to build an entirely different culture.

Rather than imposing rigid forms from the outside, innovative companies and divisions should tap the interior resources of employees; their motivation and intelligence, their application and knowledge. This is most obvious for departments at the beginning and at the end of the line, where creativity matters even more; that is to say, research and development on one hand, and advertising and marketing on the other; as well as forecasting and strategy, to which we will return in chapter 11. Personal initiative, responsibility, and self-correction should ideally lead to a learning and evolving whole, which is most in line with underlying, spontaneous patterns. The manager himself or herself turns from boss into coach and facilitator; someone who helps to build consensus, yet guides.

This has led to an approach with the aim of re-chaoticising organizations, liberating new energy and information streams, and promoting self-organization (see Stacey, 1993; Rowley & Roevens, 1996). This approach is of prime importance for understanding shifts in worker satisfaction and company morale, which often frustrate change. It is obvious that this fits in nicely with the rest of this present book, but it is too massive a subject to develop the argument here.

THE METAPRINCIPLE OF SELF-ORGANIZATION

We have seen how information may undergo continuous mutations in nature, and how some mutations may spread rapidly through positive feedback. We have seen how processes may gain strength through convergence, synergy, and resonance, and how new patterns may emerge. But in this chapter, we are taking a further and important step. Before, we have primarily focused on how such processes were driven "from below," by the interaction between multiple similar entities (Schwenk, 1976; Thompson, 1942). In this chapter, a major reversal is considered. Namely that by which an emergent pattern becomes relatively autonomous and embarks on a life of its own. When old "driven particles" or individuals fall away, the process will simply try to recruit others, so as to prolong its existence. This obviously holds for social movements, like Greenpeace.

It is a fascinating phenomenon. Arthur Koestler (1967/1989), who pondered it early on, called it the Janus effect. The German sociologist Niklas Luhmann (1984/1995) agreed that one could of course approach such patterns as emerging "from below" or constituted "from above." But he added that it was important to see that the complexity of systems of a lower level faded into the simplicity of systems of a higher level here; that there was a kind of disruption of a development, and a new start. This is exactly what happens in emergent social movements.

As we have already noted, primitive manifestations of this metaprinciple of self-organization can be found even in dead matter: in the realms of physics and chemistry, astronomy, and geology. But it is primarily the key to life itself and evolution, whether it began in a primeval soup or in wet clay. For decades, researchers have been looking for the precise ingredients of this arch event, linked or not to the evolution of RNA and DNA. But there is a good possibility that there has been no such arch event at all; that in reality, it was an ongoing series of small incremental steps on several parallel ladders of self-organization.

This section takes a closer look at the metaprinciple of self-organization, as it has been identified in recent decades. First we look at the self-organization of living organisms. Then we get to the question of whether it makes any sense to take another look at group formation in the animal world from a similar perspective. Finally we arrive at the question of whether it makes any sense to take another look at group formation in man from a similar perspective; and to what extent communication and social interaction contribute to the emergence of supraindividual entities that can take on a life of their own.

A Digression on the Self-Organization of Organisms

The problem of the formation of complex organisms presents itself both at the level of the evolution of species (phylogenesis) and at the level of the birth and growth of individuals (ontogenesis). How is it possible that life has been able to produce something as infinitely complex as the human being; a body with lungs and a heart, stomach and kidneys; a head with a mouth and a nose, ears and eyes—not to mention brains? The eyes alone are so subtle that creationists claim it is obviously impossible that they merely result from a blind process such as evolution. Yet this fails to incorporate the fact that evolution may happen in very small steps, which are each consolidated before the next step is made.

But even then, how is it possible that one egg cell and one seed cell develop into an embryo and a fetus, into a baby, and then into an adult? Cells that were similar at the outset develop into entirely different tissues, dependent on where they will end up; mucus or skin, hair or nails. How do they know? It we loose a minor piece of finger, how come a new piece of finger will grow there, and not a piece of toe? Is the detailed blueprint of the body somehow represented in each and every cell? Or is it that cells and chromosomes and genes get activated by a specific concurrence of circumstances; place and time, physical and chemical environment, electric and magnetic field, and so on and so forth? Or that some genes "turn on" other genes which in turn turn on still other genes—in an endless cascade of self-organization?

In the previous chapter we noted that information theory, cybernetics, and general systems theory, have long looked for answers to the question of how such processes develop. Gradually, attention shifted to "second order" cybernetics, where loops would link up and lock in, and lead to the formation of highly intricate and complex patterns that could maintain themselves and spread, or even reproduce and evolve. This gradually brought the focus on the overarching principle of "self-organization."

A very influential conceptualization was undertaken by biologists Humberto Maturana and Francisco Varela, most of all in their books *Autopoiesis and cognition—The realization of the living* (1980) and *The Tree of Knowledge* (1984). Yet it took some time for the significance of their contribution to be noted in Europe and America, where it was soon related to the new thinking about complexity and chaos. Maturana (1978) said:

> There is a class of systems that are realized, as unities, as networks of productions (and disintegrations) of components that: (a) recursively participate through their interactions in the realization of the network of productions (and disintegrations) of components that produce them; and (b) by realizing its boundaries, constitute this network of productions (and disintegrations) of components as a unity in the space they specify and in which they exist. (Maturana, 1978, p. 36)

They chose to call this special class of systems autopoietic or "self-producing" systems.

This quoted definition is somewhat cryptic, although there are good reasons for this precise formulation. In some key respects, self-producing systems are much more than mere emerging patterns. First of all, there is a clear distinction between the processes inside and outside the system. Second, the entirety of the processes inside is somehow linked to the "identity" of the system, that is to say, what it is or should be (respectively, what it was or could be). There is self-reference. Third, the system is operationally closed; it does not so much react to the outside world as to its own representations of this outside world. This representation is part of the inner world, which is operationally closed. An example: A chemotactic mollusc only reacts to (its own representation of) differences in the concentrations of certain substances in its environment, and not to other aspects of it.

The latter point is both very essential and rather controversial. Some authors had emphasized that dynamical systems were open, that there are exchanges with the environment. But Maturana and Varela (1980, 1984) stressed that the processes within the system have an entirely different logic and coherence than the processes outside. They even derived a series of major biological, psychological, sociological, and even philosophical consequences. Other authors concur, but maintain that the exchange simply gets a different character beyond the limits of the system (see Luhmann 1984/1995). The epistemological consequences of these views were spelled out in an important article by Maturana (1978), and discussed by Luhmann (1984/1995) in the last chapter of his key work on social systems.

The key importance of the notion of autopoiesis (and the related notions of self-reference, self-production, and self-reproduction) is that it moves beyond mere emergence and pattern formation. Luhmann (1984/1995) spoke of "reciprocal conditioning," which helps realize a "capacity for unity" (pp. 23–24). In a similar context, Leydesdorff (1997) referred to Herbert Simon's notion of "locking into resonances" and to Manfred Eigen's notion of "hypercycles." The complex pattern of interaction between components becomes self-regulating, self-differentiating, self-structuring, and relatively autonomous. So the parts give birth to a new whole that can survive on its own; whenever parts fall away, it may itself see that they are replaced.

The Self-Organization of Groups of Organisms

Of course, the impatient reader wants to know what the relevance of all this is for the study of collective behavior in a narrower sense; and for the study of psychology, sociology, and communication in a wider sense. This relevance lies in a deeper understanding of the nature and modalities of a coupling between the behaviors of individuals in a group: loose or tight, temporal or semipermanent. It looks as if the suggestion of even half-parallels between organisms and groups is absurd, and automatically implies a fallback to early 19th century organicism, or late 19th century social Darwinism, and therefore is way out of line. I think that this would be an overly hasty conclusion, and that it may still be useful to rethink and rediscuss some of these questions in the light of the current paradigm shift in fundamental natural philosophy.

There is an interesting school in present-day biology, for instance, that is reconsidering the supposed ways in which life evolved from unicellular to multicellular organisms, from microorganisms to macroorganisms, from simple to complex. If a number of unicellular organisms would cling together by chance, this would imply advantages as well as disadvantages; for example, together they would have a smaller outside surface than individually. On one hand, this would better protect them against disturbing outside influences, and even completely screen off those in the interior; on the other hand, the latter would have greater trouble feeding. If for some reason, though, the cluster would have a cavity inside, or even take on the form of a cylinder, the situation would be much better. Such things do not only hold for the exchanges with fluids and gases, but even for the exchange of sensory information with the environment. It is not surprising, then, that most higher animals share a cylindrical base plan. (These and similar questions are discussed in Volk's (1995) stimulating book *Metapatterns*.)

In many shrubs and bushes, for instance, bamboo roots and offshoots are connected under the ground—as Brouwer (1968) once noted in his mycelium model of formal and informal communication. So it is not immediately clear whether they should be considered many plants or one superorganism. Howard Bloom (1995) quoted the example of a familiar everyday object—the bath sponge. You may run it through a sieve into a bucket and it "breaks up into a muddy liquid that clouds the water ... a mob of self-sufficient cells." But "within a few hours, the water in your bucket grows clear, and sitting at the bottom is a complete, reconstituted sponge" (pp. 58–59). The micro-organism "self-organizes" into the structural form that best suits both their potential and limitations, and best enables their exchange with the environment. If it had been another plant or another animal, how big a difference would that have made?

The question is whether we should call such multiple cooperation projects social or biological? It could well be argued that in the first instance, they were social, later developed biological correlates, and even began to be reproduced in that way. Other biologists have suggested that certain organisms may well have originated from a larger organism enclosing a smaller organism, which performed useful functions. Their mutual division of labor might well have become more clear-cut and permanent in this way. Parasitism, symbiosis, and co-evolution are all forms of cooperation that are both social and biological in origin. We now know that co-habitation plays a major role within ecosystems, within food chains, and within other forms of dynamic equilibrium.

So the large numbers of individuals living together, who alternatively interact loosely or closely, periodically or permanently—are those phenomena of an absolutely different order, or only of a relatively different order? And in what way? Maybe the divide between biological and social self-organization is not as big as we have tended to make it. In both cases, small biological differences tend to be prolonged and enlarged in social differentiation, and groups tend to be welded together through some form of common activity and self-reference. Flemish scholar Arnold de Loof (1996) proposed to reinterpret biology as a kind of science of the communication of self-organizing systems. German scholar Niklas Luhmann (1984/1995) had already proposed to reinterpret sociology as a kind of science of self-organizing systems. So the new natural philosophy has apparently created new connections between disciplines that seemed to have drifted apart forever.

But there had been other initiatives to try to break out of the existing mold. The famous biologist and ant expert, Edward Wilson (1980), tried to demonstrate in his book, *Sociobiology*, that the behavioral repertoires of animals had a genetic basis and an evolutionary function. At the same time, these behavioral repertoires were often much more flexible than had been supposed. Alvin Toffler noted that, too.

In a recent study, ants were divided into two categories: One consisted of hard workers, the other of inactive or "lazy" ants. One might overhastily trace such traits to genetic predisposition. Yet the study found that if the system were shattered by separating the two groups from one another, each in turn developed its own subgroups of hard workers and idlers. A significant percentage of the "lazy" ants suddenly turned into hardworking Stakhanovites, or model labourers. (Prigogine & Stengers, 1984, p. XXIV)

Organization theorist Gareth Morgan (1986) also pointed to such examples of emergent self-organization and social cooperation:

Termites and bees engage in random behaviors that increase the variety of the systems to which they belong. If these random behaviors attract a critical level of support, they then often become incorporated in the ongoing organization of the system. For example, termites build elaborate arches and tunnels by making random deposits of earth, which, after they attain a certain size, become a focus of attention for other termites, and thereafter a focus of deliberate activity. Random piles of dirt thus become transformed into coherent structures. In these and numerous other living systems order and self-organization emerge from randomness, large fluctuations triggering instabilities and quantum jumps capable of transforming the whole system of activity. (p. 239)

In his book about artificial life, *Out of Control*, Kevin Kelly (1997), of the visionary computer magazine *Wired*, gave the example of the "moving" of a natural ants nest: "Large groups of ants head in one direction, with eggs, larva, pupae and all; other groups head in another direction; whereas still other groups run back and forth between the two camps. At a certain point, one approach gains the upper hand. A new site is 'chosen', and construction begins" (p. 12). Kelly uses these and other examples to highlight the cybernetic advantages and disadvantages of "swarm systems," with their emergent self-organization and parallel distributed processing.

The disadvantages are, Kelly (1997) says, that they are apparently nonoptimal (because they are redundant and inefficient); noncontrollable by one "authority"; nonpredictable; nonunderstandable; and nonimmediate. The latter means that they need to "slosh around" for some time before emergent patterns (at various hierarchical levels) settle down. But the advantages are, he says, that they are adaptable (to changing circumstances); may evolve to other levels (and other loci of adaptation); resilient; and boundless. But the most important thing is that they may generate novelty. Because the size of an effect need not be proportional to the size of a cause; there is an exponential number of ways to link up individuals; whereas variation and imperfection can be allowed.

Such forms of emergent self-organization on completely new levels cannot only be found in insects, but in higher animals as well. Think of the perfect "super-bird" V-shape, into which geese "self-organize" whenever they migrate. Part of that logic is in their organism, part in the situation, part in the way in which they fit together. Some mammals are more solitary, some more gregarious. Some cooperate only on occasion, some more or less continuously. Some form herds with only little role differentiation; some form hordes with much more role differentiation. Just before World War I, the British surgeon Wilfred Trotter spelled out what exactly it means to have a "herd" instinct. Soon after World War I, the Austrian psychoanalyst Sigmund Freud directly derived his notion of "super ego" from it and pronounced identification a central psychosocial process (van Ginneken, 1984, 1987).

So social animals and humans have a mental apparatus, a communication potential, and a behavioral repertoire to translate emergent self-organization into concrete forms of social cooperation. The mutual coupling may be loose and at a distance (in space or time), or heavily mediated by intermediary processes (e.g., through representations of the permanence and coherence of the group, or through "cultural conventions"). Or it may be tight and immediate, closely linked to sensory perception. There may even be an accelerated shift from one form of coupling to the next. We return to this phenomenon in chapter 10 about phase transitions.

The Self-Organization of Groups of People

Emergent self-organization is not only noteworthy in the psychological life of humans, where coincidences, associations, and connections help generate mental patterns, which may then take on a life of their own. It is also noteworthy in the sociological life of humans, where coincidences, associations, and connections, in turn, help generate communicative networks, which may also take on a life of their own—for instance, in early social movements. These psychosocial patterns refer back to each other and often it is hard to decide whatever was first—the chicken or the egg.

Over recent decades, therefore, we have gradually been forced to return to the key question, which was once formulated by the French pioneer of social science, Auguste Comte: How is it possible that the individual is both the cause of society, but also its effect? It was here that the ways of the early psychosocial scientists parted. Gabriel Tarde, for one, chose to emphasize the first part of the observation, and contributed to the founding of social psychology and psychosociology. Tarde inspired some major authors of the Chicago School and symbolic interactionism. Émile Durkheim, by contrast, chose to emphasize the second part of the observation, and thus laid the foundation for an "autonomous" sociology, which inspired structural functionalism (see van Ginneken, 1992a).

But it was at this point that things went wrong. Because the division of labor between disciplines and subdisciplines in Western thought separated questions that belonged intrinsically together. The Yin and Yang symbol from Eastern thought reminds us that it just depends on what one chooses to see as primary or secondary, as active or passive, as figure or background. European social thinkers and sociologists of the last generation, therefore, have all returned to Comte's dilemma, and have proposed different ways out of the maze.

Within French structuralism, our common language, carried by our common institutions, had long been declared the *trait d'union* between the psychological and the sociological; for instance, in the characteristically French neo-Freudianism of Jacques Lacan, or in the characteristically French neo-Marxism of Louis Althusser. Philosopher Michel Foucault, who called himself a "poststructuralist," reminded us that psychosocial practices are or-

ganized around discourses, that is to say "manners of speaking" (and thinking) about such things as health or illness, sexuality or deviance, normality
or abnormality, law or punishment, and even nature or culture. Such bear-
ers of collective subjectivity constructed our individual subjectivity, and
shaped our thoughts, feelings, and behaviors.

Within British sociology, Anthony Giddens (1984), in turn, developed his
"structuration" theory in *The Constitution of Society*, and other major works.
They too, tried to restore bidirectionality (and recursivity) in psychosocial
causation. Giddens (1984) said

> the basic domain of study of the social sciences, according to the theory of
> structuration, is neither the experience of the individual actor, nor the exis-
> tence of any form of societal totality, but social practices ordered across
> space and time. Human social activities, like some self-reproducing items in
> nature, are recursive. That is to say, they are not brought into being by social
> actors but continually recreated by them via the very means whereby they
> express themselves as actors. (p. 2)

So they are emergent patterns, continually readjusted. This is particularly
obvious in early social movements.

Within German sociology, in turn, Niklas Luhmann (1984/1995) developed his theory of communication networks in his magnum opus, *Social
Systems*. He proposed to approach social systems no longer as a sum or
whole of social actions, but as a sum or whole of social communications;
more specifically, "as systems whose basic elements consist of communications, vanishing events in time that, in producing the networks that produce them, constitute emergent orders of temporalized complexity" (Luhmann, 1995, p. XXIII). He also contested standard Western approaches of
the autonomous subject, and of social interaction as derived. He proposed instead to place recursive social communication networks in the
center of our frame of analysis.

Within Dutch sociology, Loet Leydesdorff (1993) tried to approach "science dynamics" along similar lines. He wrote:

> Once the various layers of communication are differentiated, the system can
> become self-organizing. As we saw in the paradigm-example, in a self-
> organizing system, control flip-flops: the contributors to the genesis and the
> maintenance of the system are no longer able to control the system's sub-
> stance, although this substance is logically a result of their interactions. The
> participants can only contribute to the communication, change it a bit, and re-
> produce it . . . The system may change gradually over time, but it is stabilized
> both in terms of what it regards as relevant variances, and in terms of rele-
> vant selections. (p. 335; also see Leydesdorff, 2001)

The sociologists in question do of course not fail to apply this type of thinking to their own domain; the evolution of knowledge, science, and "schools" of thought, the development of paradigms, networks, and "communities" of scholars. At the same time they recognize, that these new approaches in terms of emerging patterns, shifting levels, and self-organizing systems have much broader implications. The sociology of collective behavior has a longer tradition of considering these same questions within the framework of the study of early social movements; movements that arise, for instance, out of the common dissatisfaction of a limited number of individuals, but where communication and interaction patterns gradually stabilize through some kind of autopoiesis and the formation of a semi-permanent organization. Even if the individuals in question retire, the semi-permanent organization will still survive, and guarantee further recruitment and expansion; the example of Greenpeace is a good illustration of these processes.

Meanwhile the question remains: How can we further characterize, differentiate, and analyze these processes. One approach is to distinguish opinion currents by the "prevailing" mood expressed in it, because the "emotional coloring" of issues turns out to be a key aspect of the basic configuration. The next part of this book looks at these prevailing moods in greater detail.

III

SHIFTING PUBLIC MOODS

The heart has its reasons, which are quite unknown to the head.
—Blaise Pascal, French philosopher (Cohen & Cohen, 1993, p. 305)

Part II elaborated three metaprinciples of complex adaptive systems: synergy formation, emerging patterns, and self-organization. It is noteworthy that similar principles have already been pointed out, albeit unsystematically, in the literature about the twin disciplines of mass psychology and collective behavior sociology; and about the three phenomena of psychological crowds, opinion currents, and social movements. These are the foundations on which this book is built. We now develop further observations.

This part discusses three other themes relevant to thinking about complex adaptive systems: the theme of evolving contexts, the theme of critical thresholds, and the theme of possible attractors. They are a kind of *capita selecta* from complexity and chaos theory, applicable to rapid, radical, and massive shifts in public opinion and perception. Part III also discusses three typical modalities from the fields of mass psychology and collective behavior sociology, which can be related to shifting public moods. Yet the link between the complexity themes and the behavioral modalities is neither exclusive nor direct. All three complexity themes may be relevant to all three behavioral modalities. I have chosen to pair them because the modalities seemed to be the best illustrations for those themes.

So the question is how we can usefully distinguish different modalities within the realm of psychological crowds, social movements, and opinion currents; particularly the latter, because that is our main concern here. It is curious that many of the textbooks and overviews of mass psychology and collective behavior sociology, which we quote here, do often employ diverging subdivisions of the field—which often have something of an ad hoc character. Compare, for instance, the organization in parts and chapters of otherwise similar Anglo-American textbooks by K. Lang and G. E. Lang (1961), Smelser (1962), and Turner and Killian (1987); but also related texts and books before (R. E. Park, 1972; Blumer, 1969a) and after (Goode, 1992; Marx & McAdam, 1994; Miller, 1985). It turns out they use rather different grids.

I would plead for an organization on the basis of the notion of "emotional coloring," which I introduced at the end of the first chapter—of public opinion and issues. It is true that traditional mass psychology and collective behavior sociology tended to artificially separate unwelcome expressions, to "pathologize" them, and stick the label *irrational because emotional* on them. It is true that modern mass psychology and collective behavior sociology increasingly criticized this tendency from the 1960s on—and rightly so. But there is no reason why the discussion should remain stuck in the artificial, sterile, and misleading opposition between rationality and emotionality. I pointed out before that rational behavior often has an emotional, motivational side; whereas emotional behavior often has a rational, functional side.

So I rather agree with those scholars who have pleaded for a reconsideration of the emotional coloring of mass and collective behavior. Why? Orrin Klapp (1972) already wrote: "Because popular moods are the emotional weather favoring what collectivities are likely to do, we need to study such 'tides in the affairs of men'" (p. 361). John Lofland (1985), too, suggested that we distinguish various modalities of mass behavior according to the prevalent emerging emotion; most of all, the three emotions that are often identified as "primary"—namely joy, anger, and fear.

In line with what we have already said about this at the end of the section on public opinion (chap. 1), then, we may repeat that various emotions and moods activate various corresponding basic configurations and fundamental patterns. They may even be associated with the abstract notion of "basins of attraction or attractors"—further elaborated in chapter 9. Not only in a psychological sense, we might add, but also in a sociological sense. Joy and anger tend to generate different psychosocial patterns, with a different inherent logic. "Emotional coloring" was touched on every now and then in the traditional literature, but it was hardly ever developed systematically. By trying to link up with emotion theory, we might be able to come up with a better taxonomy.

Yet the problem is that even modern emotion theory has not developed completely coherent and elegant grids, and that various authors do in turn often use subdivisions of their own. There is near consensus about what the "primary" emotions are, but not about what secondary and tertiary emotions are. The organizational principles differ, and also have a cultural aspect. Sometimes the "opposite" of a prime emotion is given separate status, sometimes not. If joy is a primary emotion, for instance, why not sadness? If anger is a primary emotion, why not resignation? If fear is a primary emotion, why not fearlessness, courage, or hubris? And how about subtle but forceful secondary emotions such as jealousy, shame, and guilt?

I think we must resist the Cartesian tendency to try to impose completely "logical" classifications upon reality. The reason why it is so difficult to reduce emotions to one or two basic dimensions is precisely that they are not quantitatively different "things," but qualitatively different configurations. The dimension that may play a major role in one emotion may be completely absent in the next. Certain aspects are universal and innate, furthermore, whereas others are cultural and learned. The average Englishman does not have the same "emotional economy" as the average German or Italian, nor does their emotional vocabulary run entirely parallel. Yet one may identify a few basic dimensions, which can be found in each and every culture, and which may play a major role in shifting public moods.

I discuss three in this part, linked to the "primary" emotions mentioned before. First, the dimension of sadness and joy, with an emphasis on the latter; it is discussed in a chapter about the joyful interaction with "novelties," as in fashion and fads. Second, the dimension of courage and fear, with an emphasis on the latter; it is discussed in a chapter on risk perception and scares. Third, the dimension of resignation and anger, once again with an emphasis on the latter; it is discussed in a chapter on moral outrage and protest.

The development of each and every one of these public emotions has a certain inherent logic; it may lead to unification or division, to social integration or disintegration. Furthermore, each and every one of these moods tends to activate or deactivate certain mental and social circuits. They are qualitatively different configurations. In the emergence and dissolution of these patterns, or in the shift from one to the next, nonlinear shifts may manifest themselves.

7

The Evolving Context
of Fashion and Fads

Fashion, n. A despot whom the wise ridicule and obey.
—Ambrose Bierce, American journalist (1989)

This chapter begins with the case description of the "pog fad" originating in Hawaii, spread to mainland United States, and then to a range of other countries. Another recent example of a similar craze is the worldwide, "pocket monster" or Pokemon mania. Fads, crazes, and mania are similar to fashion, but more extreme in their rise and fall. They are often related to the joys of impressing and expressing oneself and others. But why is it that some fads catch on in some times and places, whereas they leave others completely indifferent? Among others, this is related to the metaprinciple of evolving contexts. Two events and phenomena never have exactly the same effects, because their context is never entirely the same. Sometimes they "resonate" with it, sometimes not.

CASE NUMBER SEVEN: POG-O-MANIA

A *fad* is behavior that is believed to be "(1) strikingly new, (2) nonessential, (3) short-lived, (4) engaging or important to people beyond the seeming intrinsic or 'common sense' worth of the activity, and (5) to quickly spread" (Marx & McAdam, 1994, p. 46). It often looks like a folly, a craze, a mania. Gadgets, games, toys, and premiums seem to be particularly suitable objects. Pog-o-mania was an example in point, but more recently Pokemania, too. The pog is something like a large and thin coin or chip, made of waxed cardboard or plastic, imprinted with various signs—for instance, comic strip characters. One could collect them, in order to get a complete series; or play with them, as with cards or marbles.

The item and game is derived from ancient Japanese examples, some 600 years old. They employed "menkos" or "little masks." Those were depictions of characters on flat chips of wood, clay, or ceramics. Japanese immigrants brought the game to the islands of Hawaii, which the United States had annexed after the Spanish-American war. Between World War I and World War II, a group of local milk producers began to imprint bottle caps with signs. During the 1950s, these were already used for collecting and games (Lewis, 1994). In 1991, one of the producers, Haleakala on the Northern island of Maui, introduced a new triple fruit drink called Passion, Orange and Guava. The caps imprinted POG were also used for child's play. On the main island of Hawaii, schoolteacher Blossom Galbiso remembered the menko game of her youth, and reintroduced it as "innocent fun" and a good alternative for all kinds of violent modern-day high-tech games (Shiroma & Kotero, 1995).

Tourists from the western United States brought the game back home to the mainland. Retired businessman Alan Ripinski bought the rights to the Pog name, set up a World Pog Federation, and organized championships in major theme parks such as Disneyland and Knott's Berry Farm. Tens of thousands of children participated. He expanded the craze into a business; various parties made hundreds of millions of dollars off production, licensing, and merchandising. There were Pog exchange fairs and exhibitions, magazines, and books. Fast food chains such as McDonalds™ and Burger King™, and soft drink producers such as Coke™ and Pepsi Cola™, explored various ways to join the fray. It soon became clear that the right to make and distribute such items could not be protected very well because the trade mark, Pogs™, could just as well be replaced by Trovs or Jots, and so forth. Many marketers launched their own variations of the game.

Drink and food giant, Pepsico, gave Pogs™ the name Tazo, added them as a premium to its Sabrita products in Mexico, and later also introduced them in Spain and Turkey. Others changed the name of Pogs™ into Hoppies, and introduced them in Israel. After some time, Pepsico also introduced the game in The Netherlands, under the name Flippos (just when others were at the point of introducing them under the Hoppy label). The name Flippo was derived from "flipping over," and selected from various alternatives through a series of tests. In 1992, Pepsico had become the co-owner of Smiths Potato Chips. Smith exploited a large chip-making plant in the province of North Holland, which had originally been set up in agreement with local potato farmers.

Let us take a somewhat closer look at how the craze played out in The Netherlands, just to give us a better sense of how these things work. Smiths had a marketing problem in The Netherlands. It controlled a large part of the Dutch potato chips market. But the Dutch were already the greatest potato, fries, and chips eaters in the world, so how could they expand any further? Research showed that potato chips were primarily eaten before and after dinner, by adults, in combination with drinks. So the goal had to be to have them eaten earlier in the day, by youngsters, as a meal substitute. For this purpose, Smiths developed funny chips and multipacks, which children could bring to school or the playground. That is, as a snack, instead of sandwiches, cakes, or candy bars.

Because Pepsico's Tazo campaigns had already had some success in other countries, it made the decision in 1994 to add Flippos as a premium to Smiths Potato Chips in The Netherlands. It made another deal with the Warner Brothers entertainment giant for the use of a series of well known comic strip characters—Bugs Bunny, Daffy Duck, Speedy Gonzales and others. The campaign started in March, 1995, with the introduction of a first series of one hundred Flippos. They were distributed door to door in neighborhoods with many young families. Others were brought into circulation via the major supermarket chain of the country, along with free color plates. Still others were distributed via the local edition of the Disney magazine, *Donald Duck*, along with "the rules of the game." A children's program on a major commercial TV channel demonstrated repeatedly how the game should be played. At the same time, a special telephone "hot line" was opened for further information.

It worked. The craze caught on in April. From May on, it was accompanied by a growing media hype and "moral panic" about real and supposed criminal incidents. They added spice to the story and recurring free publicity, however seemingly bad. It was reported that Flippos had been stolen from magazine wrappers at newsstands. It was also reported that some children had forced others to steal Flippos, and that some had robbed others of Flippos at knifepoint. It was reported that bags of chips had been opened in supermarkets in order to retrieve the Flippos, and that a shop window had been smashed in order to steal them. It was even reported that Smiths had been forced to fire employees over the stealing of Flippos. These repeated messages underscored the disproportionate value they had acquired, and stirred further media interest in the craze, as did the report that some TV "couch potatoes" had nearly choked on them, while inattentively emptying a bag of chips (DcLeeuw & Schmohl, 1996).

On one hand, there was widespread discussion about the question: What is it that Smiths fills its bags/pockets with? On May 31, the quality daily *NRC Handelsblad* (p. 3) reported that one primary school had a total ban on all Flippos; children could not be seen with them in classrooms or corridors, toilets, or playgrounds. This was justified by referring to the recurring unrest that they provoked; fighting or cheering over losing or winning. On the other hand, some educational authorities reassured teachers and parents. A well-known child psychologist wrote an article in a major quality newspaper, saying that it was just an innocuous pastime, which helped children train their "social skills" (Kohnstamm, 1995). An article in another major newspaper seemingly claimed the intellectual high ground by linking the fetish fever to classic texts such as Marx's, *The Origins of Private Property, the Flippo and the State*; as well as Freud's *Beyond the Flippo Principle*.

Meanwhile, Pepsico and Smiths were pleasantly surprised by the success of the craze, and could hardly keep up with the demand. At first, they planned the campaign to run until the end of the current school year, in June; but now they tried to prolong it with all means at their disposal, with new series and variations. Throughout the summer, autumn, winter, and then spring again—all through the entire next schoolyear.

The Flippo campaign even received the "Best of Europe" sales promotion trophy for 1996. Estimates of the total number circulated in The Netherlands published in 1997 ran from a quarter billion to over three-quarters of a billion—probably depending on whether one counted just Smiths' own Flippos or all kind of "fakes" (including the genuine American Pogs). Estimates for the rise of market share for Smith Potato Chips ranged from 15% to 40% at various points in time. At the beginning, no less than 95% of all Dutch children were said to have been affected by the craze.

Now what is so interesting about the Pogs craze in these various countries? First of all, the complete insignificance of the piece of cardboard in question, particularly in comparison to the electronic games that were advancing at the same time; even the cartoon characters were not nationally recognized. But a "surplus value" was somehow effectively superimposed because of some item's supposed "scarcity," and the apparent excitement that the game caused. It is noteworthy at the same time that the craze caught on in very different degrees in the various countries where a launch was attempted; depending on the timing of the launch, the marketing clout of the parties involved, but also previous crazes. In France, for instance, it hardly took off at all, although (or because) the country had witnessed an extraordinary "pins" craze a few years before. The pins craze, in turn, had hardly taken off in neighboring countries (van Ginneken, 1993b).

Although craze boosters do understandably boast of their achievements, we should keep in mind that these things are attempted all the time; just go to an average supermarket or gas station at any point in time, and you will see dozens of such campaigns that never attract very much attention. The Flippo craze in The Netherlands was apparently only a modest success in comparison to the original Pog craze in Hawaii. Lewis (1994) reported that a billion were circulated there, for a population 20 times smaller.

Like Pepsico and Smith, one may try to maximize one's chance at success by using an age-old concept, which has been well tested and incorporates key elements, such as collecting and playing. Yet it really depends on the broader context whether something new is able to attract and hold the attention of both the media and the public to provoke a real fascination and obsession. These complex configurations cannot easily be boiled down to mathematical models. But let us first take a look at some general considerations concerning fashion and fads.

THE PHENOMENON OF FASHION AND FADS

The first dimension of public moods we take a closer look at, then, is that of disphoria and euphoria, of mourning and joy. The emphasis is usually on the expression itself, and less on behavior that goes beyond it. One immediate cause for collective mourning may lie in loss; for instance, the loss of someone who was dear to us. It may be the death of a partner or close relative, a friend or acquaintance; but it may also be the death of a famous personality we did not know personally. A noteworthy case that occurred when I was developing this book, and on which I commented for various media, was the death of Lady Di. Until then, the British Royal family had apparently been unaware of the extent to which it had alienated itself from the feelings of "the ordinary (wo)man." It was completely taken by surprise by the wave of public sorrow that manifested itself throughout the country, and even throughout the world.

The death of admired members of a royal family, heads of state or government, leaders of parties and movements, and other public figures, often triggers a sudden change in public mood. The dying, the burial, or even the anniversary of a death, may invite the open expression of feelings that might otherwise remain hidden below the surface. In the case of political figures, this often takes the form of a political demonstration that not only demands respect for the deceased, but also a continuation of his or her work. Wherever and whenever there is no complete freedom of expression, this "cover" is often used to further political demands. China, for instance, has a long tradition in this domain, and these demonstrations have recurred time and again since the death of Mao.

This chapter, however, focuses on the opposite end of the spectrum: the collective expression of feelings of joy. This modality is found in all three categories of collective behavior: in psychological crowds, in social movements, and in opinion currents. Psychological crowds may suddenly burst into expressions of euphoria and joy that may be planned, spontaneous, or a mixture of both. A religious service may be joyful, for instance with "gospel singing" and "revivalism," Christian expressions of faith from the southern United States, with strong Black influences. A political meeting may be joyful if the candidate is inspiring and triumph seems near. A sports event may be joyful if the play is dramatic and the public is thrilled. A theatrical event may be joyful if the play is great and the audience is spellbound.

But the most noteworthy joyful happenings are musical concerts or dance events, where not only the mind but also the body can "join in." We have seen before that rhythm and melody provide a framework for synchronization and convergence. There seems to be some kind of fusion, or pleasurable deindividuation. It has also been called an "oceanic" feeling: a feeling of fusion with the group and the broader environment. Such meetings may have no purpose outside themselves. The goal is simply to enjoy oneself, and to enjoy the fact that others with whom one sympathizes, enjoy themselves. The massiveness of the event may further facilitate the collective experience and the expression of joy. Within the field of light classical music, the British "Last Night of the Proms" provides a noteworthy example, as well as overseas variations to this theme. Within the field of pop music, stadium concerts are an example, or other open air concerts. Woodstock is the best known example, but today many major cities have multicultural summer festivals that create a similar atmosphere.

Those physical mass meetings are often tied to a larger social movement. The fan following of a pop star often takes a form similar to a social movement. The word "fan" is an abbreviation of "fanatic" (he or she is a fanatical follower). Fan clubs (and sometimes even rival fan clubs) may form the small, half-organized nucleus of a broader movement, which supports and spreads the popularity of the star, and revels in his or her performances. Even if a fan club is formed by an agent or media company, it is still fueled by the enthusiasm of a few. The wider following, furthermore, is hardly limited or structured. The real or imaginary qualities of the star somehow compensate for the real or imaginary shortcomings of the fan. Think of our earlier observations on the functioning of charisma, in the subchapter on emerging social movements.

Often, such a fan movement is itself somehow a part of a broader opinion current. From time to time, attention is drawn to a new generation of pop stars, with a different style. It translates the life experience of (part of) a generation, and is marked by "life style" indicators—such as hairdo, clothing, and accessories; but also jargon, vocabulary, and talk. Examples of youth styles that have been identified over the last few decades are beat, pop, and rock, but also punk, disco, and house. Such styles are often generated by the media and the fashion industry, but their form and growth cannot be completely measured, predicted, and controlled. They are an "emergent" phenomenon.

According to the theory of "postmodernism," furthermore, such phenomena have lost their forceful nature. Within earlier, "modern" society, it is claimed, there was one overall framework of interpretative grids, which gave everyone and everything its proper place and evaluation—according to age, gender, class, and so forth. Within the current "postmodern" society, it is said, all kinds of new permutations and combinations have become possible—one "chooses" changing rules and perspectives, according to the moment of the day, one's mood, and so on. There is certainly some truth in this observation. But at the same time it does not preclude the manifestation of coherent opinion currents, around fashions and fads; in some respects, even more than before.

Fashion: The Joys of Expressing Oneself

Before we take a closer look at crazes such as "the pog," we first consider the related but milder phenomenon of fashion. *Fashion* is a social, artistic, or "appearance" code, which is broadly followed (within a certain social group and a certain period), but only temporarily. Key notions are self-presentation and change (Gaus, Van Hoe, Brackeleire, & Van der Voort, 1992). In the past, the sciences of man and society have usually only taken a marginal interest in these volatile phenomena. The classical German sociologist Georg Simmel, for instance, observed with respect to clothes fashion that only "Change itself does not change" (Marx & McAdam, 1994, p. 45). And the famous American anthropologist Edward Sapir said, "Fashion is custom in the guise of departure from custom" (Evans, 1969, p. 605). As with other forms of collective behavior, therefore, fashion is the domain of "conventions of unconventionality."

After the cultural revolution of the 1960s and 1970s, and the parallel disorganization of the "old" fashion system, interest in the subject grew somewhat in the course of the 1980s—for instance, in the United States. On one hand, new studies of fashion were published, such as Alison Lurie's (1981), *The Language of Clothes*, which approached fashion as a "language," with a vocabulary, grammar, and so forth. On the other hand, there was the first interdisciplinary conference about the psychology of fashion, organized by the Consumer Psychology section of the influential American Psychological Association (APA), by the Institute for Retail Marketing of New York University, and by Burlington Industries. It assembled 500 experts from different backgrounds in order to try and develop some common perspective (Solomon, 1985).

Fred Davis said that fashion in a narrower sense is about novelties and changing codes that somehow tickle the sensibilities of a culturally dominant audience—whether in a positive or in a negative sense. But "What some combination of clothes or a certain style emphasis 'means' will vary tremendously depending upon the identity of the wearer, the occasion, the place, the company, and even something as vague and transient as the wearer's and the viewer's moods" (Solomon, 1985, p. 17). He quoted the noted Italian semiologist, Umberto Eco, who spoke of "undercoding." When in the absence of reliable interpretative rules persons will on the basis of such hard-to-specify cues as gesture, inflection, pace, facial expression, context, and setting presume or infer, often times unwittingly, certain molar meanings in a text, score, performance, or other communication. (Solomon, 1985, p. 19)

So the "meaning" of elements of fashion and clothing depends on a specific context. A piece of black lace in the veil of a young widow at the funeral of her husband means something entirely different when reused for the decolleté neckline of a dress for a costumed ball 1 or 2 years later. That is the main point of this chapter. Fashions and fads are embedded in evolving contexts. The same elements do never mean exactly the same thing twice, neither to the individual, nor to the collective.

One may approach this "perpetual mobile" of change in fashion in various ways. The key is probably in ourselves, in the psychology of our "selves," and in the presentation of self in everyday life (also the title of a famous book by Ervin Goffman, 1959/1990). Because we know that people do not only judge us on our words and deeds, but also (more often, at an earlier moment, and at a greater distance) by our appearance and clothing. The first impression acts as a crucial keynote for later impressions. If we have the feeling that we present ourselves adequately, we feel good about it. If we have the feeling that we present ourselves inadequately, we feel bad about it. In the former case, we have the impression that others give us positive attention. In the latter case, by contrast, we get the feeling that others give us negative attention. So here we meet feedback loops again.

This attention and judgment may be completely imaginary; that is not the point. The sentiment itself colors our self-awareness, our self-confidence, our aura. If we have the feeling that our self-presentation is adequate, it heightens our self-confidence. If we have the feeling that our self-presentation is inadequate, it undermines our self-confidence. Part of this may be a self-fulfilling prophecy, that is again not the point. Furthermore, some people feel good when they are noticed; other people feel better when they are inconspicuous. But both tendencies are governed by the herd instinct that all gregarious animals have in common; they want to belong to one (part of a) group, and, even more importantly, not to another.

Timing is crucial. George Sproles tried to bring together approaches to throw further light on the sequential phases through which successive styles go. Namely, invention and introduction; fashion leadership; increasing social visibility; conformity; social saturation; and decline and obsolescence (Solomon, 1985). (James) Laver's Law had earlier formulated the phases through which adoption goes. He had noted that "objectively," the same clothes could well be "subjectively" experienced in entirely different ways. Whatever may have been seen as "shameless" 5 years before its time, may be seen as "daring" 1 year before its time, as "smart" just on time, "dowdy" 1 year after, and "hideous" 10 years after (Lurie, 1981, pp. 6–7).

Fads, Manias, Crazes: The Joy of New Impressions

Fashion cycles vary in speed; slow, medium and high. Classic fashion varies little and slowly: it remains more or less the same. We prefer classic fashion styles whenever an item is very expensive (jewelry) or rarely used (formal dress). Normal fashion varies somewhat; it emerges and disappears again. Most people renew their basic wardrobes every 3 to 5 years. Highly fashion-conscious people may do so every year, whereas people who are less fashion-conscious may do so every 7 years or so. Fads take us by surprise, but also fade very quickly. Often it is just one small detail that may be noteworthy for some time; think of piercing and tattoos.

The same holds for crazes like the one surrounding Pogs and Flippos. According to Marx and McAdam (1994):

> Implied in the popular definition of a fad is behavior that is believed to be (1) strikingly new, (2) nonessential, (3) short-lived, (4) engaging or important to people beyond the seeming intrinsic or "common sense" worth of the activity, and, (5) to quickly spread. (p. 46)

Various terms are used that do partly overlap: craze, folly, fad, mania; in foreign languages, furthermore, the denotations and connotations are often slightly different.

But they are something that commands attention, fascination, and obsession from the person, but also from the environment. So just as with fashion, there is a euphoric mood around some perceived novelty. In crazes, the emphasis is slightly less on making an impression on others, and slightly more on making an impression on oneself—but here too it is usually a combination of both. There are crazes that do not presuppose specific objects, such as "streaking" (running nude as a kind of provocation; a recurring campus sport). But there are also crazes that do presuppose specific objects, such as gadgets. In this case, the overwhelming motive is "wanna have"; you need to acquire the object if you want to join in (Deschamps & Nayak, 1995). In the framework of this book, I distinguish between crazes that concentrate on the object itself, the joys and regrets associated with it; and crazes that concentrate on the monetary value of an object. We return to market crazes and crashes in chapter 10. This chapter is mostly about craze objects, such as Pogs and Flippos.

The aforementioned textbooks on mass psychology and collective behavior often contain a few pages about crazes, but usually in a rather general sense. As far as I know, there are few monographs on the subject as such. One is *How to Create Your Own Fad and Make a Million Dol-*

lars by Ken Hakuta—the inventor of the Wacky Wallwalker. He says the name may play a great role, as well as the design, the activity, and the impression they make on others. The key aspect, I would say, is that it somehow has to strike the imagination of both the individual and the collective. Literature about sales promotion and premiums offer some insights in these domains, as do trade journals and fairs.

My earlier Dutch booklet (van Ginneken, 1993b) for a general audience on "Crazes and Crashes" has cases on the notorious Dutch "Tulipomania" of the Golden Age and the French "pins" case of a number of years ago, as well as the "sneakers" fad and the videogame obsession of youngsters; and even about crazes of "classical art" upon occasion. The notion of *craze* is used in a wide sense here. Charles Panati (1991) published an overview of American crazes for every decade of the last century; about books and music, dances, and broadcasting successes. The *Guinness Book of Records* with annual editions in many languages is an interesting source, but the picture remains fragmented and incomplete (see Bonifassi, 1993).

Fashion is most of all about clothing and has certain functional constraints, which limit possible variations and turnover speed. Fashionable details and fads are less limited in this sense. Real crazes are usually about media products and gadgets. Certain demographic categories, furthermore, may be more open to them because their lifestyles allow them more degrees of freedom; this is particularly true for young adults, adolescents, and children. Toys are very trendy; each year in January, manufacturers present the novelties that they hope will come to dominate next December's gift season.

Crazes may be spontaneous or "sponsored," but most fascinating are combinations of the two. They may, for instance, be based on marginal products or packaging. During my youth in the 1950s, when there were little money and material for toys, we used to collect empty cigarette packages. They were cut in two and made into some kind of playing cards. We also retrieved metallic milk caps, which were collected to be recycled. The money went to some noble cause. So Pogs and Flippos are not so new after all, even if marketers, the media, and the public have a notoriously short memory span.

Such crazes are based on a combination of various "attractive" elements. The first element is collecting. One may have variations and series of a certain item or package. Older and well-known examples are coins and stamps. The important thing is to "complete" a collection; rare items may acquire great emotional and monetary value. With cigar bands and sugar bags the emphasis is more on the items themselves, their exceptionality. With premiums such as chewing gum pictures of film stars or sports heroes, or plastic figurines, the idea to provoke a collector's craze is the prime reason to make them at all.

A second element in such crazes is the gambling aspect; one may win or lose. And a third element is the game involved. It should be agreeable, entertaining, exciting. The outcome should be uncertain, the stakes possibly high. Both the players and the spectators should be enthusiastic. Sometimes things go wrong with the lottery aspect, as when a major international soft drinks producer accidentally circulated too many caps with "winning numbers" in The Philippines, and then refused to pay up.

The point in all this is the following: There are crazes that are entirely sponsored by one producer, and subsequently copied by others. But only once in a while do these crazes really hit a nerve. Examples in the last few years were the Tamagotchi virtual pet and the Furby babbling dolls. They opened up an entirely new family tree of semielectronic craze products, which no doubt will generate more successes. There are also crazes that are largely spontaneous, such as worn-and-torn jeans. Often, it is some kind of combination of the two.

We are often tempted to consider it "logical" that some craze is a success. This is largely an illusion, because it is the result of a highly complex psychosocial process, which may on occasion take a rather unexpected turn. This can clearly be seen in recurring attempts to relaunch an older craze, such as yoyos. Sometimes it works, sometimes it does not. The reintroduction presupposes that it can make us (or a new generation) look at a familiar product with "other" eyes—make us rediscover aspects that we had already forgotten.

In a more fundamental sense, this is related to the "figure–ground" contrast, known from Gestalt psychology. The figure is whatever is highlighted, the background is easily overlooked. In my previous book, *Understanding Global News* (van Ginneken, 1998), I tried to demonstrate that it is rather arbitrary what is singled out as "true, real, and important" and what is not. In this book, we see this again. Whatever the media and the public consider noteworthy depends on the mental frames they bring to a new situation. So what is the metaprinciple behind all this?

THE METAPRINCIPLE OF EVOLVING CONTEXTS

Conventional thinking follows the naive empiricism of everyday life. We assume that most things are what they seem. Critical thinking, by contrast, notes that what we hold to be self-evident reality is largely framed by the ways in which observation and reporting are organized; for instance, the way in which we artificially separate "figure" and "ground," so that some aspects of the situation stand out, whereas others are overlooked.

A different approach tries to focus on the various ways in which figure and ground mutually define one another. Things are seen as embedded in a wider context, events in a longer evolution, meanings in a broader culture. This section is the first of several in which important aspects of emergent systems are further discussed, and related to public mood shifts. This particular section scrutinizes three interrelated themes: nested contexts, irreversible time, and experiential regimes.

Nested Contexts

Let us first return to our original point of departure, that of CASs. We tentatively defined them as large numbers of comparable entities, which behave in similar ways, in interaction with each other and with their environments; and in the process somehow generate both differentiation and cohesion. After that, we have considered continuous mutation and feedback loops, as well as the trinity synergy, emergence, and autopoiesis or self-organization. In this latter case, an entity may be formed on another, next level, which tends to become relatively autonomous; it results from the interaction between entities on a lower level, but cannot be reduced to it.

We have also seen that the autopoiesis notion of biologists Maturana and Varela (1984) stirred a discussion on whether such systems should be considered open or closed. One approach says both are true, but on different levels. Another nuance is that notions such as "unity" and "system" should not be considered absolute but relative because there are various degrees of unity and "systemness," of integration and wholeness. In later sections on critical thresholds and phase transitions, we will see, for instance, that such potentials may lie dormant until they are awakened by precise conditions, so that a shift from loose to tight coupling may occur, or vice versa.

It is also important to see that there often is an infinite nesting of systems within systems within systems; the link between levels being loose and probabilistic, rather than tight and deterministic. This holds true within the system. Within an organization and entities of a higher order, organizations and entities of a lower order can often be found as well. But it also holds outside a system. Beyond an organization and entities of one order, organizations and entities of another order may just as well be identified; and so on, *ad infinitum*. (Note that the notions of "higher" and "lower" are not self-evident; we will get back to this point.)

One conclusion is that each context is in fact layered, multiple, and hierarchical—a context of contexts. Only within the extremely simplified environment of a scientific laboratory can various situations be matched somewhat. But within "full reality" outside, the context of each situation is in fact unique. The simple fact that something happens again at another time or place already means that it is probably not the same. There may be similarities in the immediate conditions, but if one takes more distant conditions into account, the constellation is never entirely identical.

This observation inspired a 1994 article that Naomi Oreskes, Kenneth Belitz, and Kirstin Shrader Frechette contributed to the authoritative journal *Science*, about the validity of numerical models and computer simulations. They applied this primarily to their own field of the earth sciences, but the implications were much wider. Verification and validation could only provide certainty for closed systems, they said, but natural reality largely consists of open systems. In principle, therefore, a new concurrence of circumstances is always possible; therefore, a situation that was not foreseen, and could not have been foreseen either (Horgan, 1996, p. 202). This observation may appear trite, but is in fact fundamental.

Because such arguments do inevitably lead to contextualism and beyond that, to some kind of (w)holism. This means that one should not (only) try to understand phenomena by disassembling them into their smaller parts, but (also) by seeing them as part of larger wholes—somehow intertwined with their environment. It also means that in a broader sense, everything is connected with everything else, not only as a philosophical platitude, but also as a physical reality (Bohm, 1980).

An Excursion About Irreversible Time

One of the consequences of this whole new thinking about complexity is also a different approach to the nature of time. We have seen that we may approach reality as an interrelated stream, in which each situation is unique because it is nested in a unique constellation of contexts within contexts. We have also seen that we may view reality as increasingly intricate, even if growth in some respects is accompanied by dissolution in others. In a sense, it is precisely this subtle balance between negentropy and entropy that keeps reality as we know it "on the edge." The assumption that reality is simply ruled by "eternal laws" has had to be qualified and replaced by the idea that most of the time the eternal laws only define relationships within limited portions of time space.

Physicist Stephen Hawking (1988) calculated, for instance, that the rate of expansion of the universe is "just right" for the emergence of milky ways and solar systems. Had it been greater, such clusters would not have formed; had it been smaller, the universe would already have imploded again. Ecologist James Lovelock (1989), in turn, showed that the conditions on earth were just right for the emergence of a stable "climasphere" and therefore of life; had they been slightly different, we would not have been here to ponder them.

So within reality, there is a continuous emergence of new configurations of basic conditions—just as in a kaleidoscope that shows eternally shifting patterns. If there has been such an event as the Big Bang, Stephen Hawking (1988) said, then temperatures during the first few split seconds must have been so high (somewhere in the range of 16 million °C) that entirely different laws of nature applied. Only thereafter were the first particles formed, then atoms and molecules, which provided the main staple for physics as we know it. It was only over the first 10 billion years that the more than 100 elements were formed, which provided the main staple for chemistry.

Earth itself is estimated to be $4\frac{1}{2}$ billion years old. The first organic molecules probably formed within 300 to 400 million years. And the first bacterial life during another three to four hundred million years. That laid the foundations for evolution and biology (De Loof, 1996). The emergence of man and society provided the subject of psychology and social science. The rise of industry and technology over the last hundred years in turn affected the other levels again; the existing atmosphere and climates may be destabilized by the greenhouse effect and/or the hole in the ozone layer.

So over the years, reality has profoundly changed and so have the fundamental relations governing it. The question then becomes whether it makes sense to see time as a mere "fourth" dimension besides the three spatial dimensions. Because within Newtonian, mechanical, and much of scientific thinking, time is implicitly seen as reversible; whether the planets or a clock or a machine run forward or backward—that makes no difference. It is simply a mirror image. But within Prigoginian thinking (see Prigogine & Stengers, 1984), time is explicitly seen as irreversible. Whether a process of dissipation or emergence runs forward or backward makes all the difference in the world. Something that has happened there has happened forever.

According to the new thinking, then, the "arrow of time" is much more profoundly irreversible than is often assumed. Things happen in one direction. Of course there are partial processes that can be reversed, but the entire process of "becoming" (in which everything is related to everything else) cannot. Another question is whether the emergence of the universe, or evolution, betrays some unambiguous direction or not. Can clear-cut criteria be formulated, or is this just a gratuitous game? Do such criteria reveal some kind of overall order or hierarchy—even if one could identify other criteria that might reveal a different order, hierarchy, or none at all?

With regard to the history of the universe and evolution, such clear-cut criteria have indeed been identified; in a thermodynamic sense, for instance. Energy flow is different within "higher" forms of organization; from the Milky Way and the Sun to the climasphere and biosphere on earth; from lower life forms, such as plants, to higher life forms, such as mammals, and from lower organs to higher organs such as the brain (see Chaisson & Swenson, quoted by Goerner, in Robertson & Combs, 1995). In an organic sense, too, the quantity of DNA and the number of cell types per species have increased with evolution (Kauffman, 1991).

So reality does indeed seem to generate increasingly complex patterns in the organization of matter and energy, but even more so in information and the exchange of it. The prime driving forces, though, are chance and contingency; even though it is hard to imagine that intricate organs such as the human brain could ever result from such a "primitive" process.

The point is, however, that we tend to overlook one important element. First of all the chance of a suitable combination of elements may indeed be infinitely small, but the attempt is also repeated an infinite number of times. Second, there are processes at work that tend to consolidate each appropriate combination of elements, after which the process resumes for a third element, a fourth, and so forth. This is indeed what happens in the eternal two-step of variation and selection, variation and selection; as well as in the perpetual repetition of synergy formation, and pattern emergence and self-organization, at various different levels—physical, chemical, biological, and so forth.

Another question is whether we should see time as a homogenous dimension. Evolutionary biologist Stephen Gould (1992) elaborated the idea (previously hinted at by others) that evolution was not a gradual process during which the species changed very slowly, because if this were the case, then we should find fossils of all kinds of intermediary forms between species; but we do not. So according to him, evolution is, by contrast, rather a halting process. Long periods with slow change alternate with short periods of rapid change. This has been labeled the theory of *punctuated equilibrium*. Existing equilibria within and around species and "niches" are periodically disturbed. This may lead to radically different configurations; the (near) extinction of some old species, and the accelerated expansion of others.

Sociologist Niklas Luhmann (1984/1995) and others have pointed to the crucial importance of temporality and even volatility in this regard. If existing species did not die out, then new forms could not emerge. It is the disappearance of one that liberates the space, matter, and energy for the next. So not only is death the ultimate goal of life, but in a sense life is also the ultimate goal of death. The two are intertwined.

Just like we have seen earlier that the seeming solidity of things is an illusion, so is their persistence. Solidity and permanence are pervasive illusions because of the spatiotemporal scale in which we live and experience things. This is the scale of man himself; his corporal measures and life span. Our recurring perception of self-evident things is an artefact of the anthropomorphic perspective. If only you "zoom" in or out sufficiently, nothing is solid or permanent.

Regimes of Experience

What does all this have to do with ideas about man and society, psychology and sociology, or fashion and fads? They, too, are characterized by all kinds of "punctuated equilibria" at different levels, by spatiotemporal patterns that alternately change slowly and quickly. Typical mass phenomena and collective behavior usually accompany accelerated change, whereby old patterns loosen their grip, and new patterns fasten their hold. Such tides of ebb and flow can be noted all around us. But because of the rigid compartmentalization between the natural and the cultural sciences, between (sub)disciplines and (sub)schools of thought, the larger picture is often lost from sight.

Halfway through the 1990s, the Sociology Department at Amsterdam University took an interesting initiative to break through the pervasive lack of vision and interconnectedness that is built into the academic system. Following the example of William McNeill (1992) and David Christian (1991) elsewhere, Johan Goudsblom and Fred Spier (1996) organized an annual interdisciplinary lecture cycle about "Big History." Twice a week during one trimester, they invited scholars from a wide range of fields to come and speak about evolutionary processes and metapatterns. It began with the Big Bang and ended in the present. There were lectures on the beginning of the universe and the solar system, the earth and the continents, life and ecosystems, man and culture, civilizations and empires, the "world system" and industrialization, science and technology. It was a fascinating attempt to heal science from its first and foremost illness: fragmentation.

Throughout evolution, the Big History approach implies, there has been an endless succession, not only of nested spatial patterns, but also of nested temporal patterns, for instance in social history. French historian, Fernand Braudel, of the "Annales" school, distinguished three different time frames: the long-term time frame of geography and ecology; the conjunctural time frame of economics, society and politics; and the event time frame of individual people. Others have tried to organize social history around elementary techniques or production modes, growth areas and emerging civilizations, religions, states, and dynasties. Such epochs are invariably characterized by an alternation of evolution and revolution, as the noted Dutch anthropologist–sociologist Wim Wertheim (1971) pointed out. Dutch anthropologist Mart Bax (1987), and sociologist Abraham De Swaan (1985), later proposed to adopt the term *regime* as a blanket term. Johan Goudsblom proposed to reserve the term *social regime* for the whole of rules and procedures that people obey in their mutual relations. Fred Spier proposed to define a regime in its most general sense as "a more or less regular but ultimately unstable pattern that has a certain temporal permanence" (Goudsblom & Spier, 1996, p. 14).

One might say that spatiotemporal patterns emerge around technologies or organizations, and that the relative advances/advantages "play out" over generations in a succession of new combinations, permutations, and transformations. Until they reach the limits of growth, adaptability diminishes and rival systems take over.

It is particularly interesting to note how social and psychological changes are intertwined with "experiential regimes" (compare Goffman, 1986). German historical sociologist Norbert Elias claimed that the growing mutual dependence of people in western Europe over the past few centuries developed parallel to higher degrees of emotional control (Elias, 1978, 1982). The longer networks of interdependence demanded more fine-tuning, for instance, through the promotion of self-monitoring feelings of painfulness and shame. Noted French historians of mentalities have demonstrated that changing social practices of the last few centuries were intertwined with changing experiential regimes (also see: Peeters, 1978). The French sociologist Pierre Bourdieu proposed the term, *habitus* to indicate the habitual way in which people from different classes and professions (national and cultural groups, gender and age) experience life and behave (Accardo & Corcuff, 1986, pp. 69–85).

The notion of *generation* provides an important connection between temporal regimes and psychosocial patterns. The notion is not entirely uncontroversial, because one may very well maintain that in a strictly demographic sense, generations can hardly be identified. Babies are being born all the time, in more or less comparable numbers, with only slight variations; for instance, during periods of crisis and war, followed by a "baby boom" when the outlook gets better. One may speak of people born in the 1930s or 1940s, but that is a purely statistical criterion. At the same time, one may also insist that generations can indeed be identified in a psychosocial sense, even if that holds for only a part of the entire population and only for certain reference points.

Certain periods (such as the 1950s and 1960s) are characterized by more or less distinctive values and experiences. The key is primarily in the years during which members of a certain group become adolescents or young adults and mature. Those are years of accelerated change and formation, followed by a much longer period of decelerated change and consolidation. It concerns primarily the years between primary school and the completion of education—running into military service, and the start of a professional and family life. Those 10 to 15 years are crucial. For the Western generation that matured during the crisis and war years, for instance, work and money could never be taken for granted. Hard work, sparse living, and putting money aside was the rule—just like certain ideas about economic growth, social solidarity, and political freedom.

The generation that grew up after them, by contrast, took prosperity for granted and focused its attention on the "quality of life." Other defining events played a role for them: opposition to the Cold War, nuclear armament, and the war in Vietnam; solidarity with the third world and "liberation" movements, women's emancipation; but also pop music, the leisure culture as well as a "self-fulfillment" ideology. So in retrospect, it was not surprising that a generational clash would develop, further enhanced by the overburdening of the old education system and so forth. Fashion and fads fit into these very same patterns.

Since then, other generations and experiential regimes have come to the fore, albeit with a less clear-cut sense of identity and primarily defined by consumption patterns. But the important thing is that such spatiotemporal and psychosocial patterns emerge and dissolve all the time; which makes us experience the same realities in different ways, and respond to them in different terms. Something similar holds for a second dimension of public moods, to which we now turn: that of a sudden outburst of fear and panic.

8

Critical Thresholds
in Fear and Panic

Fear has many eyes and can see things underground.
—Miguel Cervantes, Spanish author
(J. M. Cohen & M. J. Cohen, 1993, p. 104)

Who does not remember the mad cow "madness," a food scare that made the greatly expanded beef markets collapse almost overnight in 1996? It is an illustration of collective fear and panic, which sometimes overwhelm us. Within our highly complex society, the perception of all kinds of vague risks has a highly capricious nature. The minute chance of a huge and strange disaster, for instance, stirs the imagination much more than the chance of a minor, everyday disaster. One important aspect is the metaprinciple of *critical thresholds*. The reputation of a product or brand, of an institution or person, may long remain more or less the same, but yet be gradually undermined or eroded. In that case, a minor incident may provoke a major shift.

CASE NUMBER EIGHT: THE MAD COW MADNESS

The following is an example of a rapid shift in the public perception of, and the public mood about, a product category. It is a typical example of a health scare (and a media hype) as they become increasingly common. A single news item may act as a trigger in a rapid, radical, and massive shift in public opinion. Suddenly, everybody turns away from the product. This may last days or weeks, months or years. But it is important to note, that much has preceded this outcome. The system will somehow have turned "critical"; trust in the sector and in the credibility of the authorities has already eroded—often through a fault of their own.

The attitudes of humans toward animal meat and meat eating have always been somewhat ambiguous—as Freud (1913/1971) already noted. On one hand, meat is considered an indispensable, strength providing, high-quality foodstuff by many. On the other hand, conservation is difficult, certain kinds of meat easily provoke repulsion, and some kinds are subject to the strictest of cultural taboos. Over the last few centuries, the growth of wealth and cities (primarily in the Western world) has led to an explosion of meat consumption (primarily beef). Farmland was widely shifted from labor-intensive agriculture to capital-intensive cattle raising. Later, animals came to be mass produced in a bioindustry. The new high densities of this mass production not only facilitated sanitary controls, but also provoked vulnerability to epidemics.

There may be as much human meat as beef meat walking around in today's world; there are less bovine animals, but most animals are heavier. In fact, the 1.3 billion bovine animals are mostly eaten by the 1.3 billion wealthy people. Only between $\frac{1}{4}$ and $\frac{1}{5}$ of the world population can afford to eat beef on a regular basis. Meanwhile, cattle occupies almost a quarter of the useful land surface of the earth. Cattle even eats a third of the world grain supplies. The average American already eats half a pound of ground beef per week, mostly in the form of hamburgers. Meanwhile, more than a billion people in the world cannot buy enough grains to fill their stomachs; they hardly ever eat meat, let alone beef (Rifkin, 1992).

After its capitalist revolution and the "enclosure" movement, Great Britain had been among the first western European countries to embark on beef production. The "roast" became a key element in its culinary and social life, as politicians of both major political parties were eager to point out. Conservative prime minister John Major wrote that the British people were especially sensitive on this score. And Roy Hattersley (deputy to Labor leader, Neil Kinnock), waxed nostalgic in *The Guardian* about popular audiences enthusiastically identifying with the song text, "The Roast Beef of Old England Made Us What We Are Today."

In spite of its strict quarantine laws, identifying "The Continent" as a major source of exogenous contamination, British cattle had long been infected with endogenous diseases. Sheep, for instance, often had *scrapie*, a mysterious affection of the brain and the nervous system. When they died, they were not thought fit for human consumption; but from 1981 on, they were used for animal consumption, and included in fodder. The reason was that, by including more such proteins in their diet, cows could be made to yield more milk. From 1986 on, these cows appeared to develop a new disease, *Bovine Spongiform Encephalopathy* (BSE), which ate "holes" in their brains and made the brains look like sponges. Their carcasses too, were kept in the food chain. A few years later, however, their consumption was forbidden for sheep and cows, and reserved for pigs and poultry instead.

Even at that time, foreign veterinarians criticized the handling of the epidemic as rather lax. Several countries had begun to issue "ID" papers for cows, in order to be able to trace such infections. If an epidemic broke out, furthermore, complete herds were eradicated as a matter of principle. There were severe inspections and sanctions. Nothing of the kind existed in Great Britain. Its conservative government was very much into deregulation at this point in time, and did not cease to emphasize that the European Community (EC) (and particularly Germany and France) were into overregulating.

Yet it did try to regulate information about the possible dangers of the epidemic, when there was a first limited media hype about them in 1990. Researchers in the service of the state apparatus got a speaking ban. This made journalists go to critics of the official policies. Microbiologist Richard Lacey suggested at an early stage that the disease might somehow affect humans (Pols, 1996). Already in 1992, BBC television aired a thriller about a farmer being infected, and the authorities trying to hush it up. By 1993, the epidemic reached crisis proportions, and 35,000 animals had to be killed in that year alone.

A disturbing coincidence was noted. Two farmers whose cattle had been infected with the animal disease, BSE, died from the human disease, Creutz-feld-Jakob Disease (CJD)—also an affection of the brain and nervous system. The disease was extremely rare; in 1995, only 55 people in the entire country of Great Britain died from it. That same year, British physician Philip Smith noted that three more farmers with BSE cattle died from CJD (Pols, 1996). Yet, veterinary authorities were still reluctant to sound the alarm, as it might trigger a "beef scare" and harm a major industry.

Creutzfeld-Jakob Disease had first been described around 1920, by a German neurologist and a psychiatrist of those names. After the crisis broke, magazines such as *Nature, The Lancet,* and *The British Medical Journal* devoted a growing number of articles and issues to its various aspects (Köhler, 1996). CJD was found to be related to a rare "cannibal disease" discovered in the late 1950s. It had raged among the Kuru tribe in the eastern part of Papua, New Guinea, but disappeared as soon as they gave up the habit of eating corpses. New research led to the discovery that such diseases might not be caused by bacteria or by viruses, but by enigmatic proteins named *prions.* They interfered with the functioning of neurons and therefore with motor coordination (hence the label, *mad cow*). The prions were thought to be species-specific, communicated by meat eating, and not inactivated by normal cooking procedures. After infection, it took some time before the disease manifested itself.

As the spring of 1996 approached, the British government finally sprung into action. On March 20, Health Minister Stephen Dorrell said that he was having experts look at a possible connection between BSE beef and the CJD death of some 10 people. The official position was that there was no cause for alarm yet, but that it would be better to be on the safe side (*NRC Handelsblad*, March 22, 1996, p. 1). Yet this casual approach could not prevent a full-blown media hype and a public scare, focusing on the "catastrophic potential" of the connection. A ban on recycling of infected meat was said to have been frequently broken. It was estimated that over the previous years, many hundreds of thousands of people had eaten beef that might have been infected. What if chances of developing the disease did not prove minimal but considerable? Later estimates in the authoritative *Nature* magazine concluded that the number of victims might (also because of the long incubation time) end up being in the range between 100 and 80,000 (Ford, 1996). Television channels all over Europe showed excerpts from veterinary instruction videos, displaying sheep and cows struggling to stay on their feet—and finally collapsing. This dramatic display was unique, graphic, and made a great impression. It was etched into people's minds.

Many domestic beef eaters went on an immediate consumer strike. Prices for ground beef collapsed. McDonalds canceled the sale of beefburgers in its 650 British outlets, and later replaced them with "completely safe" products; it had learned the hard way to be particularly alert to "meat rumors" (van Ginneken, 1993b, pp. 99). Many foreign countries banned British beef as well. (Beef products can be found in foodstuffs as diverse as soups and cheeses, cookies and chocolate, sweets and chewing gum, ice cream, etc.). Within a few days, more than 99% of the public had heard about the mad cow scare, and cattle markets saw their sales volume plummet by 98%.

Many cattle farmers and meat processors went bankrupt over the next few days and weeks, and some 9,000 people lost their jobs. The British Bureau of Statistics later estimated that the value of agricultural production went down with 5 to 10% for the next quarter, and that the entire gross domestic product thus grew .1 to .2% less than expected. Meanwhile, Prime Minister John Major blamed the "collective hysteria" of consumers and the media, encouraged by the opposition and by foreigners (Wittenberg, 1996). But the Chairman of the European Commission, Jacques Santer, blamed the mismanagement and "irresponsible behavior" of the British government instead (NRC *Handelsblad*, June 10).

The German-speaking European commissioner for agriculture, Franz Fischler, complained that he had not at all been consulted or informed, and the EC soon slapped a worldwide ban on British beef exports in order to protect consumer confidence in the meat industry of other European countries (NRC *Handelsblad*, June 4). British Secretary of state for agriculture, Douglas Hogg, contested these measures, and a wrangle developed which lasted several months (NRC *Handelsblad*, June 24). At first, some suggested that all 12 million British cows would have to be killed; *The Economist* estimated this would cost no less than 20 billion pounds (De Kam, 1996). Subsequently, it was proposed that only the 4 million least profitable older cows (that had stopped giving milk anyway) would be slaughtered; this would still cost 7 billion pounds. Then it was proposed that they would only be killed in shifts, as they reached that age. This way, the figures were brought down to 1 million cows and "only" two billion pounds. But it turned out that "destruction capacity" was too small anyway, and there was a scramble for compromise solutions.

Many in Britain felt that The Continent had overreacted to the crisis in order to further its own interests; whereas The Continent felt that Britain had been too lax all along. Frustration about the others "arrogance" once again ran high on both sides of The Channel, for instance in editorial comments. The *Daily Express* spoke of a "Mad Cow War," the *Daily Mail* of the "Great British Beef Battle," and *The Sun* of the "Cattle Battle" (*NRC Handelsblad*, May 24). The latter paper, owned by former Australian (now American) media tycoon, Rupert Murdoch, is not only the largest newspaper of the country (with a circulation of 4 million), but also the most unabashedly chauvinistic and xenophobic. It ran a poster of a proud British cow head against the Union Jack flag, and a list of 20 ways to "badger Germans." A member of parliament introduced a bill for a referendum on Europe, supported by a large part of the conservative Members of Parliament. According to a Gallup poll, 43% of the electorate would vote for a withdrawal from the EC at this point; $\frac{1}{6}$ more than a year before. But *The Economist* called such inflammatory policies, "Mad, bad and dangerous" (Wesseling, 1996).

Meanwhile, countries on the European continent had become wary of the British, too. Particularly when *Nature* revealed around the middle of June that Great Britain had boosted its exports of BSE-infected fodder to France and other countries, after domestic use had been restricted a number of years earlier (*NRC Handelsblad*, June 13, p. 5). France had also seen a rise in BSE cases, particularly in the northwest (and was to have one related CJD victim). Former French agriculture minister, Henri Nallet, said he felt outraged (NRC *Handelsblad*, June 13). Rightist politician, Philippe de Villiers, had earlier claimed in the weekly *Journal du Dimanche*, that EC experts themselves had also minimized the danger. Investigations by the center-left dailies *Le Monde* (June 14) and *Libération* (September 4 & October 10) confirmed this, and identified a French director-general of the EC agriculture department as one of the main culprits.

As the year progressed, the scare turned out to be, in some regard, both justified and unjustified. Justified, because there was growing evidence that prions could indeed "jump" species, and that BSE could indeed cause CJD. Unjustified, because the "plausible" cases of a connection between the two initially remained limited to a number of only 15 throughout Europe; a part of the world where people freely engage in all kinds of unhealthy eating, drinking, and smoking habits carrying much larger risks. New calculations proved, furthermore, that even without the new measures, BSE would die out naturally just after the turn of the century (Kitzinger & Reilly, 1997).

The upheaval did have major consequences, however. A few months after the crisis hit, it was estimated that within the EC (over the entire year), sales of cattle would fall by 2.3 million heads or no less than 11%, and prices would fall by 15%. It was unclear to what extent they would ever return to previous levels. British beef had lost market share, continental beef had gained some. Furthermore, consumer preferences shifted from beef to pork and poultry. But the pork industry was soon hit by swine fever, particularly in The Netherlands, which had long posed as "morally superior" with regard to cleanliness and hygiene. And the poultry industry continued to be plagued by high percentages of salmonella bacteria, which infected chicken meat and eggs alike, and continued to result in a high numbers of casualties (without, however, attracting much attention or triggering a health scare— so far).

Other consumers shifted emphasis from meat to fish, or to nonanimal and mere plant products. Vegetarianism became mainstream, and veggie burgers finally "broke through" in supermarkets. According to Ford (1996, p. 109) sales of the best-known vegetarian cookbook in Great Britain rose sixfold in the weeks after the crisis broke, and sale of other vegetarian cookbooks rose threefold. Information demand at the Vegetarian Society doubled, and at one point the society sent out some 200 packages per day. A spokesman for the Soil Association for Organic Agriculture said that the crisis had stirred more interest in their work than all campaigns of the previous 10 years. Shops selling biodynamic food products reported a sales rise of 40%.

So, as is often the case, there was a series of dozens of different circumstances, which all look perfectly logical in retrospect, but the exact configuration of which could hardly have been foreseen. Consumers had become gradually aware over previous decades that the idyllic image of quietly grazing cows in large green meadows did no longer hold true. On occasion, they had caught glimpses of a dark world beyond it: of boxed calves and hormone treatments, of incidents surrounding animal-unfriendly transports and large-scale slaughterhouses. Maybe a vague unease or even feelings of guilt played a role.

As far as mad cow disease was concerned, the veterinary authorities were soon facing a fatal dilemma and a "no win" situation. At first they sought to minimize the risks and to reassure the public. But this undermined their credibility and trust, which made the ultimate shift even more violent and uncontrollable. In a sense, therefore, the fear of a major image crisis became a self-fulfilling prophecy, because in this type of case, maintaining transparency and public support is of the utmost importance. Otherwise, tensions will build within the system that approach critical thresholds, and may be released by even the smallest trigger. But, of course, a further complication in this case was that it concerned a new affliction of a mysterious nature.

So the media hype and the public scare were facilitated by a range of factors. It was a new, invisible, form of contagion that proved hard to trace or demonstrate. It involved meat, which was easily mistrusted. Infection would attack the brain, considered the heart of personhood itself. The frequent reference to a "cannibal disease" did not make things better. The illness and dying were ugly, although it was noteworthy that the media and the public did not tend to focus on its details. The chance of incurring the illness was minimal, but it was always fatal. Almost everyone had unwittingly exposed himself over the previous years; it was not an informed choice that one could still make. The risk seemed primarily related to ground beef, to which certain vulnerable groups were proportionally more exposed: youngsters, the less wealthy, people in institutions.

It was not so much the real risk that stirred the imagination, but rather the catastrophic potential—the minute chance of a huge disaster (Gutteling, 1991, pp. 15, 31). And there was of course the search for a scapegoat. In England, critics reproached the conservative government that it had done too little too late; also because of its ideological stance on *laissez-faire*. But the conservative government reproached the Labor opposition of trying to exploit the situation electorally. Apart from that, there was of course the dimension of national pride and foreign criticism. The tug of war about responsibilities made finding solutions even more difficult. Once all these processes were under way, positive feedback loops further reinforced those same processes. This threw the entire perceptual system around beef off balance, and resulted in turbulence and chaos. Even if this stage did not last very long, it caused a considerable shift in certain long-term trends, such as those concerning meat consumption.

THE PHENOMENON OF FEAR AND PANIC

We have seen in previous chapters that processes within CAS may develop unevenly, and that stages of decelerated change may alternate with stages of accelerated change. One important metaprinciple in this context is that of *critical thresholds* between such stages. Invisible tensions may build within the system, which remain just below critical values. Relatively small changes in conditions, relatively small events, or combinations of both, may suddenly provoke a "crossing" of the critical threshold, and may thereby initiate an entirely different turn of events.

A dimension of shifting emotions where this is clearly notable is that of fear and panic—as in the case of the mad cow disease; it involves a possible endangering of one's physical well-being. People may encourage each other to take risks and challenges, which may ultimately lead to wounds, illness, or even death. They may embolden each other through mere physical presence, or active moral support. We have seen before (in the chapter on crowds), that mass assemblies of animals or people may have this effect. It is often no more than the feeling that "unity makes power."

The opposite of courage is fear and panic. Just as with other primary emotions, the literature on fear and panic often emphasizes only its most extreme expressions. Of course, this may be enlightening, as long as we keep in mind that it is a sliding scale—which also includes many milder emotional forms in between. Just as with other emotions and moods, fear and panic basically involve the activation of preprogrammed, fundamental circuits of thoughts, feelings, and behaviors—tuned to a particular type of situation. It strikes us, furthermore, that extreme panic may easily overrule conventional types of mental and social functioning. Therefore, such reactions have often been labeled *irrational*. But as we have seen before, this is a rather misleading notion. Because it very much depends on from *which* perspective its ratio is approached.

Phenomenology has thrown some light on the hidden logic of such seemingly hysterical responses in the behavioral repertoire of animals and men. This approach tells us that if we get the feeling that a conventional, mediated, moderate response is fundamentally inadequate to confront some overwhelming danger, then there are only three ways open to us: The first way is to just try anything, anything at all. There is a minor chance that such random, arbitrary behavior may lead to a way out—by mere luck.

The second way, by contrast, is to bet "all cards" on one possible way out—and one only. Although it may seem improbable that it will work, people try to force a solution. The third alternative, finally, is to become completely paralyzed and rigid, or even to faint. All this will immobilize us, as if we are dead. There is a faint chance that "the monster" will ultimately fail to notice us, or that our lack of resistance will limit the damage; not only physical damage, but also psychological damage, because at least we will not have to "live through" the ordeal. (Simply put, if you cannot eliminate the threat, then you can at least eliminate your experience of the threat.)

These three alternatives often manifest themselves in involuntary bodily reactions. But in less threatening situations, they have an obvious parallel in typical mental reactions. In the first case, there is complete disorientation, and a succession of far-fetched ideas. In the second case, there is some fixed idea, an obsession with only one solution to the problem. And in the third case, there is some kind of minimizing or even ignoring of the threat. Such reactions also played a role in the mad cow madness.

Panic After Disasters

These tendencies clearly manifest themselves in extreme cases of social panic and collective behavior after disasters. Whenever there is some acute overwhelming danger, and we have insufficient confidence in the effectiveness of an organized response, the usual social coordination disintegrates and "demoralization" occurs. This means that people will withdraw to some antisocial behavior; the ultraindividualist behavior of "everyone for himself." In a sense, this social panic is at once typical and atypical collective behavior because it is not an alternative form of social behavior that emerges, but a disintegration of social coordination. The basis for this lack of trust, though, has often been laid earlier and made the system vulnerable to collapse (Dynes & Tierney, 1994). Once the reversal gets underway in some, furthermore, it spreads rapidly to others—through self-reinforcing, positive feedback loops.

Let us once again consider how these phenomena manifest themselves in the three different categories of collective behavior: psychological crowds, social movements, and opinion currents. A well-known example is panic in a theatre. There are some whiffs of smoke from behind the stage. Someone shouts, "Fire!" Some people in the front row jump up and run to the exit doors. This unsettles others, who also jump up and begin to press toward the exit doors. A self-reinforcing process of fear-and-panic reactions is set in motion. The exits cannot accommodate the flux fast enough, the pushing and shoving escalates. Someone falls to the floor, other trample over him or her. Screams and curses add to the mayhem. Later it turns out that some people have been severely wounded or even killed.

People say that this was unnecessary, and could have been prevented if everyone had remained calm, and had evacuated the hall in an orderly manner; and therefore, the mass behavior was irrational. But that is a certain interpretation of the problem. The individuals who had been closest to the door had the best chance of survival by rushing out at once. The same held for the individuals who were next in line, and so on and so forth; so it was a sliding scale, with no clear structure. If someone with authority had shouted, "women and children first," this might have worked if there had been enough confidence. So the prevention of panic begins well before the actual panic may start; on one hand by making enough emergency exits (and seeing to it that they remain unblocked), and on the other hand by showing that one is prepared for the worst. In such cases, the fatal threshold may not be crossed, and there will be no all-out panic reaction.

This is reflected in social movements and social institutions that often have to deal with critical situations such as violence or disaster; in armed resistance groups, but also in the police and the army; in volunteer organizations, in the fire departments, and civil protection agencies. Social cohesion is increased with all possible means so that they can withstand a challenge. There is a conscious cultivation of a strong *esprit de corps* and mutual involvement, a strong hierarchy with visible insignias, clear procedures, and rules. Attempts are made to ban all ambivalence beforehand as to who is to give orders and who is to obey them. It is by building confidence that the organization will hold up, even under extremely difficult circumstances; that panic, demoralization and desintegration are prevented.

The same principles can be identified in opinion currents around disasters. People may barricade themselves in their houses, hoping to escape the worst. People may also jump into their cars, and try to flee the area quickly. The best scenario would be of course if they first turned on their radio or television sets to hear what the authorities have to say who often are in a better position to oversee the situation. But most important is that people have gained trust in these authorities beforehand; in their efficiency, concern, and credibility. If there are no doubts in that regard, the battle is already half won.

Disaster researchers have pointed out that it is rather surprising that there is so little panic after disasters in developed countries today because there is confidence in the effectiveness of the response. But even after disasters in underdeveloped countries, the social fabric often holds up rather well, and there is a lot of mutual assistance—rather than momentary disintegration. We have only limited room here to delve deeper into some aspects of fearful and panicky opinion currents. We successively take a closer look at panic after phoney disasters, at product risks, and at risk perception in general.

Panic After Phoney Disasters

It would be interesting to delve further into panics after disasters at this point, but maybe it is even more interesting to delve into some examples of panicky reactions after phoney disasters. Because it shows us even more emphatically how perceptions may play an almost autonomous role—separate from a thorough appraisal of the real threat. Broadcasting may play a particularly prominent role, because (in contrast to film and press) it may report "live." Also, the impression live broadcasting leaves is fleeting; one cannot immediately listen, look, or read back to verify whether one has fully grasped the "true" meaning and significance of the report. This has been demonstrated time and again by dramatized programs on radio and TV involving simulated or fictional disasters.

The classical example is, of course, the mass hysteria and panic that erupted in the northeastern United States during a "scary" Halloween night of late October, 1938. Once again, the precise context is crucial; if the context had been radically different, the reactions would most probably have been different as well. The country had survived the Depression, but more recently, a war threat had occurred on the distant horizon. Over the preceding 10 years, national radio networks had emerged, which had come to play an increasingly prominent role within the entire media spectrum with topical reporting and with entertainment. In this latter genre, there were radio plays and daytime serials; the so-called "soap operas" pitched to housewives, sponsored by producers of cleaning products. Producers and directors were increasingly looking for more spectacular formats, particularly during prime time.

Director Orson Welles, for one, had turned H. G. Wells's novel, *The War of the Worlds* (about an invasion of Martians) into a radio play. An estimated 32 million Americans tuned in (see Koch, 1970; Bulgatz, 1992). In order to make it sound more realistic, it was presented as a program of dance music, interrupted by extra news bulletins and eyewitness reports—purportedly from the area of the landing of the space ships. But many people missed the first few minutes, or did not listen very attentively, and therefore did not understand that these were not "factual" but fictional reports. A number of listeners panicked, phoned others to sound the alarm, and jumped into their cars to flee the area. Although the media and literature later exaggerated the scale of these reactions, it is true that a part of the audience panicked, if only for a while. A further study led to a famous book by the psychosociologist Hadley Cantril, published in 1941.

Although this "invasion from Mars" became the most noted case, similar incidents occurred after World War II; not only based on radio shows, but also around television plays; not only in North America, but also in western Europe. During the era of the Cold War, it turned out to be relatively easy to provoke a nuclear scare. In neutral Sweden, for instance, there was the example of panicky reactions to a fictional news bulletin about a radioactive leak at a nuclear plant, studied by communication scientist Karl Eric Rosengren and others (see Pugh, 1980). In England, there was considerable controversy about the question whether Peter Watkins' film *War Game* should be broadcast or not; a fictional but very realistic drama about the possible effects of a nuclear war. In all these cases, the makers seemed to overestimate the degree of attention with which the audience would follow disclaimers at the beginning or the end of the broadcast. But on occasion, the scare and hype suited their purpose rather well.

In The Netherlands, too, there were several such cases over the years. One of the latest incidents of this nature followed a television broadcast in 1997. It was part of a series, in which small groups of well-known, real-life politicians and former civil servants were asked to simulate crisis management in threatening situations. The very realistic games had been developed for training purposes by the Crisis Research Team of the Public Policy Department at Leyden University near the government seat in The Hague (see 't Hart & Rosenthal, 1990). One installment was purportedly about a radioactive cloud drifting into the country from the East because of a nuclear accident in nearby Germany.

Context was a major factor, once again. By coincidence, there had been a "real" training exercise to test coordination on both sides of the border only days before. It had turned out that mutual cooperation left much to be desired, and the local media had reported about the lack of mutual cooperation. So they had already "cued" the population that such things might happen. The crisis broadcast included highly believable news bulletins, with familiar anchormen, and with only marginal warnings that they were simulated. A number of people overlooked these warnings. Some elderly people and some foreign workers did not realize that the broadcast was only a simulation. Some called the police to inquire what they should do, or about the possible fate of family members; others tried to get away from the area. But at no point in time was there a real mass panic (*NRC Handelsblad*, 1998).

Product Risks and Risk Perceptions

Natural or industrial disasters may threaten the physical well-being and the physical security of large groups of people at the same time and place. But often the threat amounts to no more than a faint chance that something untoward may happen at a later time. That was also the case with the mad cow madness. The question is, of course, whether such a risk may be confidently estimated, by whom, and in what way. That is important because the risk of negative consequences may not be the same for everyone. The neighbors of a plant, for instance, run a different risk of being affected by problems at the plant than the owners of the plant. Furthermore there is a marked tendency for people to welcome the positive aspects of a public utility, but to reject the negative aspects. People agree that there should be certain plants (e.g., for energy generation and waste disposal), but "not in my backyard."

In recent years, there has been growing attention for the real or supposed risks attached to the use of certain industrial mass products (Covello, Menkes, & Mumpower, 1987). We read about negative consequences, which usually means "a small chance of negative consequences." There may be a news report, for instance, that scientific research has revealed that a certain type of product or packaging causes cancer. The problem is that the scientific report often involved all kind of difficult chemical names and complicated statistical jargon, which the public and many journalists cannot fully interpret and understand. Even many experts and policymakers may only have a vague idea of the possible implications. It often turns out later that the initial scare was extremely exaggerated; but by that time, turnover and profits of these products may already have taken a severe blow.

Today, the tendency toward such misperceptions is sometimes labeled *Zohnerism*, after a prize-winning research project by a 14-year-old American student, Nathan Zohner (reported in *The Skeptical Inquirer*, 1998). He approached 50 people with a petition against the chemical substance, dihydrogenmonoxide. Because it had been proven that (a) it plays a role in excessive sweating and vomiting; (b) it is the major component of acid rain; (c) it may cause severe burns in a gaseous state; (d) it may kill you if you inadvertently inhale it; (e) it contributes to erosion all around the world; (f) it diminished the effectiveness of car brakes; and (g) has been found in the tumors of terminal cancer patients. Of those approached, 43 (or 86%) signed the petition, whereas only 6 (or 12%) hesitated. Only one of them realized that in everyday life, the imputed substance is known under the name of *water*.

The example also illustrates why communication about dangerous substances fails so frequently. Until the present day, risk calculations and risk information are plagued and haunted by the "technicist illusion." Big problems do arise often out of a concurrence of minor circumstances. The precise configuration is much more than just the chance for Condition A, multiplied by the chance for Condition B, multiplied by the chance for Condition C, and so forth. And it is even more naive to think that lay people weigh things in these ways (Kok, 1992). Early decision theory supposed that people made purely rational calculations about the exact balance between the chance for positive outcomes versus the chance for negative outcomes before they made a choice; this is often not the case. Insofar as they do something of that nature, they do not use an objective appraisal, but a subjective one. As a matter of fact, the cognitive process involves so many possible sources of distortion that it may be almost impossible to map it in this way.

Citizens and consumers are guided by gross misperceptions of risks, which are often reinforced by journalists and media coverage. A good example is provided by average people's estimates of the chances they will fall victim to (a) traffic accidents with various means of transport; (b) violence at home and in the streets; or (c) terrorism. The perception of these risks, and media coverage of them, are highly distorted (van Ginneken, 1998; also see: Kitzinger & Reilly, 1997). But the same holds for many other domains.

Distortions and Shifts

The German sociologist Ulrich Beck (1986, 1998) pointed out that the present *Risk Society* is of an entirely different nature than other, earlier arrangements. British sociologist Giddens (1990) concurred. Because current scientific, technological, and commercial developments imply risks of an entirely new nature, and on an entirely different scale. The Mad Cow Disease, and the Chernobyl disaster (to which we return in chapter 11) are perfect illustrations of this trend.

As we have noted, industrial society was based on "to measure is to know, to know is to predict, to predict is to control." It was a world of seeming certainties and mastery, of clear-cut responsibilities and imputability. Within the current society, however, so many things have become so interdependent that it is increasingly difficult to make confident estimates of risks and probabilities. The so-called "millennium problem" was a case in point. That is to say the chance that computers running on standard programs might mistake the "00" in the year 2000 to indicate the year 1900, and thereby trigger a cascade of miscalculations resulting in major failures (van Ginneken, 2000, pp. 73–79). Yet in everyday life, we continually have to make snap judgments about vague risks and the possible validity of scientific proof. And if the public, the media, and policymakers have few failproof methods to do this, neither does the legal system or even insurers. They do not even have a consistent approach and calculation system, a precise language and standardized procedures to make confident predictions (more in Sprent, 1988, and Bernstein, 1996).

In estimating risks, the public uses heuristics or "rules of thumb"; simplified assessments that may not be entirely correct but are at least somewhat efficient. There turns out to be a huge divide between what traditional decision theory thinks people do and what empirical research shows they do (see Gutteling, 1991; Van der Pligt & Van Schie, 1991). A key role is played by how a problem is structured, and what references are implied. What is a normal risk, what is a great or small risk? Compared to what? For whom, and under what circumstances? Is it an immediate risk or a postponed risk? The lighting of a cigarette may produce immediate pleasure and tension reduction, for instance, and every single cigarette taken by itself has an insignificant impact; the risk seems to be very distant.

There is a considerable discrepancy between such heuristics and rules of thumb on one hand, and formal logic and probability calculation on the other hand. There are further distortions with very high, moderate, and very small chances. There are other distortions with chances for positive effects, negative effects, neither, or both. There are other distortions if things have gone well for some time and turn bad once, than if they have gone bad for some time, and turn well once. People have different estimates for what may happen to themselves or to others. Social psychologists (such as D. Kahneman, P. Slovic, and A. Tversky, 1982) have done a range of "lab experiments" on "gamblers fallacies" and other numerical illusions; but the complex reality out there is even more complicated than a simplified laboratory setup.

Cognitive "availability" is said to be a key overall factor. But that, too, turns out to be a complex composite of other subfactors. Sometimes, familiarity with a risk from everyday life breeds overperception, sometimes underperception. Sometimes unfamiliarity with a strange and distant risk breeds overperception or underperception. Sometimes invisible risks are experienced as more threatening, sometimes visible results are experienced as such. Obtrusive images, concrete events, personified results, lively representations, and spectacular possibilities may all contribute to higher impact, explicit perception, better retention, and reproduction.

Lowrance once distinguished ten risk dimensions: (1) voluntary or involuntary; (2) immediate or delayed effect; (3) alternatives available or not; (4) risks known with certainty or not at all; (5) exposure, essential or a luxury; (6) occupational or not; (7) common or dreaded hazard; (8) affects average or sensitive people; (9) used as intended or misused; and (10) reversible or irreversible consequences (quoted by Van der Pligt, 1992, p. 24). There may be multiple and complex combinations, as well as disproportional overperceptions and underperceptions of risks.

Let us limit ourselves to the seventh point. There is a perceptual enlargement of risks run by pregnant women, fetuses, babies, toddlers, children, youngsters, and adolescents, all "dependent" people. This may include the poor, the elderly, and the sick—particularly if they have been institutionalized in homes and hospitals. There is a perceptual diminution of risks run by young adult males, by contrast, because they are supposed to be robust and strong. Yet their student life, sports activities, military service, going out, and street behavior expose them to considerable risks. But few (except their mothers) seem to be inordinately worried about these. Surplus traffic risks are ascribed to the elderly and to women, yet the most deadly drivers are young males, who are further encouraged in this by macho images in advertising and popular culture.

Information campaigns, either through the media or directly aimed at the public, carry their own special problems concerning the perceived sources of the message, the nature of the message, the channels that are chosen, and the effect that is sought. Problems regarding sources may involve a lack of unanimity among authoritative sources, a lack of authority and credibility, and a loss of confidence. Problems around the nature of the message may result from a high degree of technicity or incomprehensibility, or from a lack of salience or liveliness. Problems around the choice of a channel may be related to audiovisual elements, the editorial environment, or the demographic reach. Problems around the effect may be related to the relation between cognition, affect, and behavior—as well as the permanence of the change (see Gutteling, 1991; Leiss, 1994).

However you look at it, products risks, the perception of product risks, communication about the perceptions of product risks, and crises in the communication about the perception of product risks, are all complex and configurational, dynamic and (potentially) unstable. Time and again, authorities and experts commit the mistake of underestimating this fundamental truth, as was done in the mad cow case; they often think that they have a good estimate of the risk, and that they can easily convey it. They underestimate the dilemmas and paradoxes of policymaking in these fields, and are often surprised by sudden crises and shifts. But what are the underlying metaprinciples of such sudden shifts?

THE METAPRINCIPLE OF CRITICAL THRESHOLDS

We have already noted that CAS do often evolve unevenly. Longer periods of decelerated change alternate with shorter periods of accelerated change, or even turbulence. During those long periods of decelerated change, systems are more or less in equilibrium, or able to correct disturbances through negative feedback. During periods of accelerated change, by contrast, disturbances are amplified by positive feedback, and the system is thrown far out of balance. It is important to note here that these two opposite tendencies are often separated by critical thresholds.

According to the dictionary, "critical" means in this case: "decisive" about the outcome of a process. If the threshold is not crossed, things will largely remain as they were. If the threshold is crossed, the course of events may take a radically different turn. Such critical thresholds may be related to the spatial distribution of a process, to the temporal evolution of a process, to the various parameters of the process, or to all at once. Within the older and newer thinking about critical thresholds, various notions play a role; from autocatalysts to critical mass and even self-organized criticality. This chapter reviews some of these notions, and discusses their possible relevance for the conceptualization of psychosocial processes in general, and rapid opinion shifts in particular.

An Excursion About Dominoes and Thresholds

As we have already noted, critical thresholds have two sides. As long as the threshold is not crossed, there will be no change, or at least no radical or nonlinear change. You may think about the "tolerance" of a system, its reserves, or a buffer. The system is able to absorb small cumulative changes—up to a point. But as soon as the critical threshold is crossed, there will indeed be change—a fundamental or nonlinear change. It is like the proverbial drop that makes the bucket overflow. The overflowing will not only involve the last drop; because the surface tension is broken, overflowing will involve a number of preceding drops as well. In other cases, stopping one drop may keep a dam or dike from breaking through, and the lowlands behind it from being inundated.

A well-known example of a system in a critical state, where the change of one small detail may trigger the change of many similar details, and thereby the state and nature of the system itself, is the domino game. Not the domino game in its original form, but in a subsequent variation, based on the fact that domino pieces happen to be narrow and rectangular. One may have them rest on their smallest side, facing in the same direction, close to each other, in long rows. If you flip over the first domino, this one may then flip over the second, which will flip over the third—and so on and so forth. One may even build elaborate patterns, in various colors. Championships are about the total number of pieces that one may tip over at once. The traveling of movement throughout the configuration is followed by cameras and a large audience. The result, if it is excellent, may be inscribed into the *Guinness Book of Records* (Bonifassi, 1993).

At first sight, it seems like a relatively simple situation. But on further inspection, a range of factors turn out to play a role. The system is built from a large number of more-or-less identical units. On one hand, the parameters of these entities themselves matter. Their stability or instability results from the proportion of height, breadth and depth, but also the flatness of their sides. On the other hand, the relationships between the entities do matter; their orientation and distance, for instance. One may also increase the "criticality" of the system by varying the nature of the underlying surface, or its angle. If the angle is made steeper (in the direction of the tumble), then the chance of them falling-over gets bigger, and vice versa. So it is important to see, that even within such a simple and familiar system, there is not one critical threshold but several. The same holds for comparable systems in nature, and also in man and society.

Another important element is the following: Within a simple unilinear set-up, the "failure" of one stone to fall over may stop the entire process. That is exactly the reason why attempts at breaking a record do usually not limit themselves to a unilinear setup, but include multiple lines and entire surfaces. If, by any chance, the process gets stuck in one direction, it may still proceed in another direction. In nature, both variations exist. If a stimulus traveling over one nerve path is interrupted, the related process comes to a halt. But in the brain (as well as many other organs and systems), such signals are often sent over various lines at once. So that a single failure will not stop the entire process.

Critical thresholds are not limited to the beginning of a process; they may also play a role halfway. And in a sense, the completion of a process may also be considered a threshold passed. Into many processes, some kind of "window" is built, where other processes link up. If one tries to start the process too early, little or nothing will happen. If one starts the process too late, little or nothing will happen. Only in between those two values, may an attempt to trigger a wider process be useful. In social and economic and technological processes, therefore, "just in time" acting during a "window of opportunity" is crucial.

Another complication in processes turning critical is the distinction between (distant) causes and precipitating factors or triggers—comparable to the trigger one pulls to fire a gun or cause an explosion. The precipitating factor or trigger of a process may be of an entirely different nature than the (distant) cause. For instance, in a quantitative sense: There may a dramatic disproportion between the first domino piece flipped over, and the millions of domino pieces spread out over the entire floor of the sporting facility, which may fall over as a result. But also in a qualitative sense, the trigger may belong to an entirely different domain than the cause (and even be an unrelated coincidence).

In chemistry, one speaks of a catalyst whenever a substance helps speed up or slow down a reaction, without being affected or altered itself. One speaks of autocatalysis whenever it is speeded up or slowed down by a substance that the reaction itself helps produce. This is another example of positive feedback, amplification, and circular reaction. Sometimes these processes grind to a halt when the "fuel" runs out. But sometimes they continue to spread because they will find new fuel. One speaks of hypercycles whenever processes develop coherence, spread, and continue to perpetuate themselves. Such processes can be identified in dead matter but most of all, in natural life, both at a microlevel and at a macrolevel (Goerner, 1995).

Furthermore such processes are not limited to nature, but can be found in culture as well, in man and society, as we have already seen, and will see again. In the case of the Mad Cow Disease, the system (the health perception of meat products) had already become critical. Only little was needed to cross the threshold and create a panic.

The Sandpile Model

In the course of the development of new ideas about complexity and chaos, some authors have suggested that some CASs may have a kind of inherent logic driving them to optimal complexity, to a kind of determined indeterminacy, to a combination of adaptation and vulnerability, to "the edge of chaos" (against the threshold, not over it). They are surfing against the top of the wave, so to say, where it is about to break into foam.

Some of the most pertinent observations on this subject come from granular physics; the physics of small, but visible, particles such as sand grains. This domain is so special because it is half–half. The particles do partly behave as a solid, partly as a fluid. This combination of permanence and changeability gives the domain its extraordinary paradigmatic strength, and makes it an interesting base model for the rest of reality. The most influential author in this field at the moment is Per Bak, a Danish physicist who (also) works in the United States. In 1987, along with two others, he published a first influential article about the so-called sandpile model (Bak, Tang, & Wiesenfeld, 1987).

The point of departure is relatively simple. Suppose you drop sandgrains at one particular spot, one after the other. A sandpile will form. It had been established before that structures will form within this sandpile. Not only is pressure within the sandpile unevenly spread, for instance between the lower center and the outer margins, but also some arches will form by chance, from the bottom up, comparable to those known in architecture, which can withstand the weight from above, and press themselves together. With each new sandgrain falling onto the heap, one of two things may happen. It may simply tumble down over a side and find a resting place, without displacing a disproportionate number of others; or it may unbalance such an arch, make it collapse, and cause a landslide.

Bak and his co-authors claimed that the sandpile, both on the surface and inside, both in partial structures and in its overall structure, continually organized and reorganized itself to the edge of criticality; that is to say, to a configuration where a new sandgrain might cause a landslide—or not. The problem was that the situation was so immensely complex that it was impossible to measure, predict, and control it. The only thing that could be said with some certainty was that the chance for a certain shift was in inverse proportion to its scope. There were many small shifts, and few big ones. This "law" that the chance for a certain type of event or phenomenon is inversely proportional to its size was already known in seismology. But similar observations had been made in other domains.

In 1997, Per Bak thereupon published the book, *How Nature Works*, which proclaimed this "self-organized criticality" to be a key principle of nature. It was one of the keys to the problematical relation between quantitative or gradual change on one hand, and qualitative or radical change on the other hand. Supposedly, it not only manifested itself in avalanches and earthquakes, but also in crucial episodes in the evolution of life (e.g., with the mass extinction of species such as the dinosaurs), and even in the functioning of consciousness. Within modern society, it could be noted in the curious phenomenon of traffic congestion (to which we will return in chapter 10).

The thesis is not uncontroversial. According to some colleagues, the processes in question cannot be consistently demonstrated, even in sand piles, let alone in other domains. But at the same time, the thesis is highly provocative and productive. In the 10 years between the article and the book, some two thousand papers about the notion of self-organized criticality appeared in scientific journals, more than about any comparable subject. And halfway through that period, it was even quoted in the best-seller, *Earth in the Balance*, as a model for the individual and collective development of man. This book had been written by a top politician, who had always been fascinated by a personal mix of high technological expectations and high environmental awareness, which squared rather well with the new ideas about chaos and complexity. His name was Al Gore, the Vice President during Bill Clinton's administration.

Contiguity and Critical Mass

Within the entire body of thought about triggers and thresholds, an important role is also assigned to the notion of critical mass. Within a CAS, we can think about a part or proportion that must be affected by change, before the process will begin to spread autonomously. In many instances, this does not seem to be related to the number of units that is affected, but to the proportion of relations between the units that is affected—and may spread the change. In some states and assemblies, these may concern the units "touching" or being adjacent to each other. The term *contiguity* is often used. In other states or assemblies, this may concern the units somehow "communicating" with each other. If the state of a critical proportion of such contacts changes, then the state of the whole will ultimately change as well.

The possible relevance of such phenomena for the sciences of man and society, had already been pointed out by American political scientist Thomas Schelling. He wrote:

> An atomic pile "goes critical" when a chain reaction of nuclear fission becomes self-sustaining; for an atomic pile, or an atomic bomb, there is some minimum amount of fissionable material that has to be compacted together to keep the reaction from petering out. . . . The principle of critical mass is so simple that it is no wonder that it shows up in epidemiology, fashion, survival and extinction of species, language systems, racial integration, jaywalking, panic behavior, and political movements. (quoted in Marwell & Oliver, p. 1)

In this context, one may think of the role of opinion leaders and active minorities in social movements, pointed out in chapter 6.

Schelling first noted these phenomena during the early 1960s, with the persistence of covert racial discrimination and the failure of racial integration in cities. If well-to-do Blacks began to hire or buy houses in an exclusively White neighborhood, nothing happened at first. Some kind of checkerboard emerged, where black and white squares would simply alternate. But if a certain proportion was reached, White moves to other neighborhoods accelerated. So there seemed to be some critical mass and "tipping point" (the integration tendency suddenly reverted into a segregation tendency; Casti, 1994). Similar patterns can today be found in certain neighborhoods in European cities, both in housing and in schools. Such processes can well be simulated on computers, with programmed entities, which behave in a certain way.

More recently, Latané and Nowak demonstrated that similar things hold for attitude change in general. On many issues, it is not true that the public changes opinion slowly and evenly, as is often implied; sometimes the change (and the "contagion" with a different point of view) is decelerated between different categories of citizens and accelerated within certain categories of citizens. Latané's earlier theory of "dynamic social impact" (1981) had already suggested that the pressure to change attitudes was proportional to the strength, immediacy, and number of individuals with opposing views, and in inverse proportion to those holding similar views.

Now Latané and Nowak (1994) added:

> Compared with the traditional view, these nonlinear, categorical models exhibit very different behavior. Instead of convergence, they lead to a complex dynamics of attitude change resulting in clustering and polarization of attitudes on the group level. Whichever opinion is initially in the minority will tend to decrease, but, most significantly, as people change their views, the minority opinion tends to locate in contiguous minds—resulting in spatially coherent clusters of opinion. (p. 243)

They illustrated this with a computer simulation of attitude change, within a quadrangle of $20 \times 20 = 400$ "contiguous" people. Ultimately, only "islands" remained, of people holding an opposing view. Together, they could just resist the pressure to conform, but isolated they could not.

Everett Rogers (1995) came to similar conclusions, both in his empirical research and in his theoretical reflections about the diffusion of innovations. Innovations were not evenly and gradually adopted by an entire public, he said, but conquered groups and networks one after the other. There were all kinds of circumstances that could delay or speed up such processes; for example, when the social resistance against a certain type of innovation was exceptionally great. He described the case of the progression of the utilization of the anticonception pill by Korean women. The introduction into each new group or network was slow, but once a certain proportional threshold was crossed and a certain "critical mass" reached, further adoption accelerated.

In this context, another special category was the diffusion of technical innovations with an interactive character, such as the telephone. It is clear that it makes little sense to buy a telephone, if few friends or relations have a telephone. But when a critical mass is reached, it becomes desirable to have one. If one is one of the very last to adopt it, life may become increasingly problematic. A fascinating variation is the first decelerated and then accelerated adoption of the fax machine. The principle of the fax had already been developed in both England and France around the middle of the 19th century, but it was subsequently superseded by the telephone. Its breakthrough only came after the mid-20th century, in East Asia; because the large number of characters in Chinese, Korean, and Japanese had delayed the introduction of the typewriter there, and had made written documents persist.

In North America and western Europe, the introduction of typed e-mail soon followed, which was clearly superior to faxing (because the receiver did not have to retype the message in order to be able to revise and forward it). Yet here, too, the fax remained successful, because many people (including myself) were reluctant to use the computer for this purpose, and because certain original documents had to be sent anyway. But even the first decelerated and then accelerated introduction of the Internet surprised many insiders. Even the very largest producers of hardware and software, IBM and Microsoft, had to change course at the eleventh hour—when they realized the Internet was to be more than just a fad.

So the notion of critical mass can help illuminate many psychological and social processes. A last domain in which it had already been introduced before was that of the growth of both capitalism and industrialism. In his famous study on *The Stages of Economic Growth*, Walt Rostow (1970) identified a clear threshold in the development process. It was not only related to capital accumulation and productivity increases, but also to social relations and psychological outlooks. As long as the threshold was not crossed, he said, the process developed only slowly; once it was crossed, it accelerated and reinforced itself. He employed a typical metaphor of those times: that of the airplane getting off the ground; once a certain speed had developed, it lifted itself into the air, and there was "takeoff."

The notion of thresholds, below which a change develops only slowly, and above which it facilitates itself, can thus be applied to many different domains. We have seen that it is particularly pertinent to an understanding of risks and scares. It involves the buildup of latent tension within a system, which may then suddenly come to a manifest release. Something similar can be seen in protest or outrage. There, too, some "trigger" may often lead to a "social explosion."

9

Possible Attractors in Outrage and Protest

Moral outrage is jealousy with a halo.
—H. G. Wells, British author (Bloom, 1995, p. 185)

We begin this chapter with a case study of the Brent Spar affair. Shell's plan to dump an obsolete oil platform into the deep sea provoked interference by the environmental organization, Greenpeace. The protests succeeded in mobilizing social resistance. It is an example of phenomena that have to do with collective expressions of outrage and hostility. We may also note them in moral panics, political scandals, economic boycotts, and other forms. It is hard to measure, predict, and control whether they will catch on, when and where. But once they cross a certain critical threshold, they seem to follow some kind of inherent logic; for example, polarization, escalation, and a conflict spiral of action and reaction—that proves extremely difficult to break out of. In this context, we look at the notion of "attractors": pathways and states to which the evolution of a system tends under certain precise conditions.

CASE NUMBER NINE: THE DUMPING OF SHELL

This case is about the emergence of public indignation, resulting in social protests and an economic boycott. It is interesting to reconstruct how the process of confrontation and the spiral of conflict progressed through successive stages. Various "points of no return" were passed along the way, and a new "basin" was entered on each occasion. This collection of basins embodied a kind of inherent logic, although some players obviously seemed to have a better "feel" for that than others. The history was as follows.

In the early 1970s, the newly formed Organization of Oil Producing and Exporting Countries (OPEC) succeeded in imposing a significant upward "adjustment" of world petroleum prices. The major importers, the United States and the European Union, suddenly realized how dependent they had become on foreign supplies; therefore, they accelerated the more costly drilling in their own backyards: the Gulf of Mexico and the North Sea. Over the next 20 years, some 400 oil rigs were installed in the North Sea alone: 205 in the British part, 105 in the Dutch, 71 in the Norwegian, 31 in the Danish, and 2 in the German part. From the early 1990s on, these installations gradually became obsolete again; they either had to be completely renovated or dismantled. Dismantling costs were estimated at an average of 10 million pounds (approximately 15 million dollars) apiece for the smaller ones, and double that or more for the larger ones. Total costs for the entire operation were thought to run into the billions of pounds.

One of the better known fields was the Brent field, and the first installation to be dismantled was the Brent "Spar." It was jointly owned by the American Exxon company and the Anglo-Dutch Shell company, but operated by Shell alone. The Brent Spar was basically a huge, immobile, storage buoy, where ships could come to load. It had lost a large part of its usefulness since pipelines had been laid. Its height was 140 meters, its largest width, 29 meters, and it weighed some 14,500 tons. It was basically a vertical version of a horizontal tanker. No one would nowadays seriously propose to deliberately dump a discarded oil tanker in the sea. But the Brent Spar was a different case. Or was it? That became the major bone of contention.

The problem was twofold. Upon its construction, little thought had been given to its inevitable dismantling. On its original voyage, furthermore, it had been seriously damaged. Therefore, de-construction might prove both costly and risky. At the same time, Shell had become the tenth largest company in the world, and the most profitable one. In 1994, it had announced record net profits of well over 4 billion pounds (approximately six billion dollars); over 1995, these were to be further topped. It was widely considered an excellent company, but it had one major flaw. It had always perpetuated its strong corporate culture through pure co-optation of like-minded people. This had gradually alienated it from the changing "spirit of the times."

It had remained a very "White Anglo-Saxon Protestant" or WASP company, with a somewhat colonial aura. It had repeatedly been subject to large-scale protest campaigns for its alleged cavalier attitude on Black rights and Third World issues. It had been considered the major breaker of the international embargo against minority governments in Rhodesia (Zimbabwe), South Africa and southwest Africa (Namibia), for instance. It remained a very "power-driven" company. It radiated an image of "we know best," and tended to wave away all outside criticism. This led to a string of controversies concerning alleged pollution, ranging from Curaçao in the Caribbean to Nigeria in west Africa (Moskowitz, 1980; Hendriks, 1987). The proposed "dumping" of the Brent Spar was to be another such controversy, and a major one at that.

Shell asked official permission to tow the Brent Spar to the Atlantic Ocean hundreds of miles away, and to dump it in the deep North Feni ridge. The relevant authorities of the conservative government of Great Britain were inclined to grant them permission to do so. By early February, 1995, Shell duly notified the governments of other countries around the North Sea. Shell claimed none of them voiced any objection within the regular 60 days, and not even after a further extension to 90 days. By early May, official permission was granted. Within a few days, however, the German government protested, soon followed by a string of others. What had happened? What had happened was that the Greenpeace environmental movement had launched a protest campaign, particularly in Germany and its neighbors.

We have already discussed the Greenpeace environmental movement, which originated in Canada but had spread its wings to the entire Western world. During the previous summer, Greenpeace had first got wind of the dumping plans. During the autumn, it had officially approached the relevant oil companies and governments, but to no avail. During the winter, therefore, it had secretly set aside a major war chest, begun to amass relevant means of transport and communication, and to investigate the logistics of possible actions. At that point in time, the Greenpeace organization was at a crossroads. Worldwide donations had decreased in previous years and paid staff had to be reduced. Membership had shifted from the North American continent and the Anglo-Saxon world to the western European continent and the Germanic world. The new international director was to be a German, and the international headquarters had been relocated to the neighboring Netherlands.

Over previous decades, environmentalism had become surprisingly popular in Germany. The huge forests that had always been thought to host some of the "soul" of the nation, and had been severely affected by acid rain. Many of the old industrial and urban areas had been heavily polluted. There was a taboo on radical politics of the extreme left and right, which favored the emergence of nontraditional issues. The "Green" party had long been torn between *sponti*, *fundi* and *realo* (spontaneist, fundamentalist, and realist factions), however, and been overshadowed by German reunification. But now, they had just staged a major comeback. With 7% of the national vote (and double that in certain regions), the Green party even tended to phase out the centrist "liberal" party altogether—the ally in reserve for the bigger parties. Thus the center-left social democratic party, the center-right Christian democratic party, and even the conservative Christian social party had gradually "greened," on a national, regional, as well as a local level. Citizens everywhere were confronted with new environmentalist regulations (such as limitations on cars and separation of waste). "So why should the most profitable multinational company in the world be let off the hook?" people tended to say.

In April 1995, Greenpeace issued a report claiming that there were no grounds for dumping. Simultaneously, it started a Europe-wide campaign culminating in the slogan, "The sea is no rubbish bin." The Brent Spar was the first of hundreds of such North Sea platforms to be dumped, Greenpeace said, and it would set a dangerous precedent if this were to pass unopposed. In various countries, Greenpeace was even to hire advertising agencies to help it "sell" its message in the best possible way. One agency, for instance, covered the top of the yellow and red Shell logo with thick and dripping black oil, and ran several such advertisements in major German papers such as the *Frankfurter Allgemeine Zeitung*, the *Frankfurter Rundschau*, and the *Handelsblatt*.

Shell soon responded that the Brent Spar was only an isolated case. It said that the Best Practical Environmental Option (BPEO) had in fact been selected after careful consultation with all major outside experts. De-construction was both expensive and risky, Shell said, and deep sea disposal was rather innocuous. Decomposition of the structure would take up to 4,000 years, so that possibly harmful substances would only be released very gradually and in minute quantities. There was very little sea life to speak of at that spot two kilometers below the surface, and the presence of an occasional wreck did more to promote biological diversity than a barren ocean floor.

On the last day of April, Greenpeace staged one of its trademark protests. Fourteen activists boarded the Brent Spar and occupied it. It took Shell well over 3 weeks to mobilize the maritime force needed to dislodge them again. Shell sent a huge floating crane that put a container aboard with security personnel, under the eyes of Scottish police. The activists were arrested, and transported to the Shetland islands by helicopter. Shell had obviously won this battle; but little did it realize that it could still lose the war. "Act one" had received relatively little media attention, but it had sent a warning signal. In this way, it influenced the policy agenda of the upcoming fourth ministerial meeting on the North Sea environment in Esbjerg, Denmark. Most representatives now pleaded against the dumping of oil platforms in general, and Great Britain became increasingly isolated.

Meanwhile, a Shell flotilla prepared for cutting the Brent Spar loose from its anchors and for taking it in tow. But Greenpeace had embarked a host of reporters on its action ship, Moby Dick, to witness the thwarting of that action "live." A skirmish developed, with small rubber boats being attacked by water cannons, and people falling overboard near the propeller of one of the main ships. Once again, Shell won; but once again, it also lost. The dramatic images of this "Act two" hit television screens all over Europe, and helped change the tide. Government ministers and majority parliamentarians in Germany and neighboring countries now openly joined the call for a boycott of Shell, which had earlier been launched by environmental organizations. Company headquarters in Hamburg received tens of thousands of agitated phone calls. Sales at 200 gas stations slumped, many were sprayed with aggressive graffiti such as "Shell go to hell"; some were even shot at or fire-bombed.

Within a week, Greenpeace had mobilized a helicopter and put two activists on the oil platform already in tow, and two more a few days later, for "Act three." It would be unthinkable to go ahead with the dumping with those people still on, but also hard to get them off again. At the summit of leaders of the G7 strongest industrial nations, German chancellor Helmut Kohl irritated British prime minister John Major by openly counseling him to back down. An opinion poll in the neighboring Netherlands showed that only 12% of the public supported Shell's stand, against an overwhelming 82% for Greenpeace's stand.

While John Major was still defending the decision in parliament, Shell UK and headquarters decided on a complete turnaround. It was the first time ever in Europe that an international consumer boycott had been successful on this scale. British newspaper headlines noted an "Anti-British mood in Germany" (*The Daily Telegraph*), "David's victory over Goliath" (*The Independent*), a "Historic victory" (*The Times*), a "Victory for the Planet" (*Daily Mirror*), a "U turn" (*The Sun*), and a "Shell-shocked Prime Minister" (*The Daily Mail*) (Hermans, 1996; Van Egmond, 1996). John Major felt highly embarrassed, and called the Shell directors "wimps." On top of that, newspapers proclaimed that the taxpayer would have to foot the bill—as current rules allowed compensation for de-construction. But Shell hastened to say that it would claim no such compensation. In Germany and neighboring countries, Shell bought another page in the papers, but this time with a solemn apology and a promise: "*Wir werden uns ändern*" (We will change).

Greenpeace had won a stunning victory, but there was a major backlash. The Brent Spar was towed to Norway, where its contents were inspected by independent experts before a further course of action could be decided. It turned out that Shell had slightly underestimated, but that Greenpeace had vastly overestimated, the amount of oil and sludge still on board. Greenpeace had made a major mistake, and was forced to admit it. This was then taken by some to mean that the entire campaign had been based on "a hoax." Earlier, others had already accused the organization of favoring emotionality over rationality, and of exploiting the tenets of mass psychology in ways "reminiscent of Joseph Goebbels" (the nazi propaganda minister), no less. Many in the media and some journalists came to reconsider their attitude toward the organization and its "staged dramas." And others claimed that "single issue" campaigners should never be allowed to "hijack" the democratic agenda.

Shell was left somewhat groggy, and it took some time before the board and the communication department had distanced themselves enough to draw some vital lessons from what had happened. Over the next few years, it undertook a thorough review and revision of its own code of conduct. With relation to human rights, Shell asked input from a range of independent organizations, such as Amnesty International; and with relation to the environment, Shell also asked input from a range of independent organizations. It approached independent "monitors," who would periodically report about the keeping of the code. These were steps that would have been unthinkable for Shell only a few years before.

Once again, one can make a series of additional observations on this case. It was a very complex concurrence of circumstances that made the case unfold as it did. With hindsight, it is always easy to reconstruct the "inherent logic." But along the way, it seems things may still take different directions. Yet with each crossing of a critical threshold, the confrontation and escalation processes embark on a new stretch of developmental trajectory—hereafter named a "basin of attraction."

We have also seen that new issues do more easily lend themselves to "preemptive strikes" on the definition front. It is important to recognize that the "definition of the situation" contained a number of arbitrary elements. It is true that the automotive culture leads to increasing pollution, but it is not clear who should be held responsible. It is true that the oceans are polluted by installations and ships, but it is not evident that the isolated case of the Brent Spar in itself would amount to a dramatic aggravation of pollution. It is true that Shell owned the platform, but so did Exxon. The oil companies that profited from the temporary boycott of Shell posed no less of a threat to the environment. But all this disappeared into the background.

Shell made a grave mistake by underestimating its opponent. By priding itself on a culture of "excellence," it had become insensitive to criticism, or blunted its capacity for self-criticism and gradually alienated itself from "the spirit of the times." Shell would never have dared propose to dump a normal, "horizontal" supertanker in the high seas, for instance, but it did propose to dump this special "vertical" supertanker. Was that fundamentally the same thing, or something completely different? Shell trusted that it would be able to impose its own "definition of the situation," as the one and only true expert. But that is not how it played out.

Greenpeace once again proved to be a highly adept issues manager; among other things, by not showing how well it had (financially and logistically) prepared for this symbolical struggle, and how many cards it still had up its sleeve at every stage of the game. The slogan, "the sea is no rubbish bin," cleverly linked two separate things. The ordinary citizens in the larger cities in Germany and The Netherlands became increasingly irritated for being forced to separate waste: glass in the glass container, paper in the paper container, chemicals in the chemicals container, and organic materials in a dirty, "green" bio-bin; while the most powerful and most profitable company in the world cut costs by simply dumping its waste overboard. Of course, that was a highly simplified way of presenting things, but it was also a highly effective one.

Other hidden factors on such occasions are always national differences. Germany had gradually become environmentally aware, but had meanwhile been forced to swallow increasing amounts of polluted air, polluted rain, and polluted surface water from its neighbors (particularly in the East). Germany was largely a landlocked country, with only a very small coastline and only a very small share of the North Sea—and therefore only a very small share of its oil and gas revenues. Great Britain, by contrast, was an island with an ingrained tendency to let polluted air be blown away by the winds, let polluted water be blown away by the currents, and to throw waste into the sea. Environmental awareness was more limited. Along with Norway, it had profited greatly from the North Sea oil boom and financed its deficits with the boom. More importantly, it is still in the habit of posing as the major source of Western civilization, heir to the greatest empire in world history, motor of the Industrial Revolution, and a victor in two world wars.

In media and popular culture, England still tends to depict even the great, strong, and reunited Germany as morally inferior, semibarbaric, as the embodiment of "the Huns." On this occasion, therefore, the German public was only too pleased to reverse the roles. Such latent undercurrents often play a major role whenever the correctness or incorrectness of a situation is judged, especially of a decision with international repercussions. Think of similar undercurrents during the mad cow crisis. Similar things play a role in crises involving the United States, France, or Scandinavia. They help shape "the blame game," once a critical threshold has been crossed.

THE PHENOMENON OF OUTRAGE AND PROTEST

We have seen that shifts in public mood are to some degree unpredictable. But we have also seen that the evolution of opinion or perception systems may follow an inherent logic. Once those systems have embarked upon a certain pathway, the next steps seem to be obvious. The situation is like a kind of "basin" within which the course of events will most probably unfold. This is clearest in the dimension of mood shifts, which we consider here—that of resignation versus rebellion, and in the case of social conflicts.

We have noted in chapter 4 on crowds that crowd and mass psychology as such derived from the systematic reflection on the noteworthy cases of crowd and mass rebellion. Within the sociology of collective behavior, too, social protest and collective violence have always received ample attention (Although this often involves extreme violence, and not the kind of peaceful protests that we discuss here). But once again, that often was a kind of one-sided and selective problematization. It may be just as surprising, for instance, that people continue to resign themselves to a situation that is flagrantly unjust in other people's eyes. They are indoctrinated, or feel intimidated, and accept the seemingly inevitable. The German-Dutch mass psychologist and communication scientist, Kurt Baschwitz (1938/1951), called this type of resignation in the face of terror "silent panic." Only when an individual or a group mounts a challenge, this example may be rapidly followed and the spell may be broken.

Frustration and aggression may suddenly transpire. Such a reversal may be triggered by a single example or a single event, or by a single image or a single word; it is the catalyst that marks the transition to a new "definition of the situation." At the same time, it is noteworthy that such expressions of outrage and hostility may seem to follow a certain inherent logic, once the die is cast. Whenever the first step has been taken, the first accusations have been spoken, the first clash has taken place, the first blood has flowed, and the first death has occurred, the process seems to become irreversible and move into a new stage. Within that new stage, the next steps seem to follow logically: the redefinition of the incriminated situation, and of the responsibilities; the redefinition of the victimized parties, and their mobilization. This happens through selective decontextualization and recontextualization (van Ginneken, 2001). Suddenly, all kind of things are forgotten, and other things remembered. So these redefinitions also imply a broadening and narrowing of fronts—a realignment. Whoever was an enemy may become a friend, and vice versa. The inherent logic is that of a new divergence of opinions: he who is not with me is against me. All those involved are surprised by the rapid shifts in the global power balance between respective alliances. The arrogance of (those in) power implies that this power will not be effectively challenged. But what first seemed to be a solid bloc may now turn out to be worm eaten, through silent desertions and loyalty shifts; what seemed to be only a highly vocal minority may grow in number and strength to pose a formidable challenge.

We have seen how this worked in the case of the Greenpeace protests against the planned dumping of the Brent Spar platform into the Atlantic Ocean. The national branches of the all-powerful Shell company in northwestern Europe at first seemed to be all united, and firmly supported by national governments. Only later did it turn out that confrontation and escalation triggered a psychosocial realignment, and this "united front" soon withered away.

Collective Expression of Hostility

Let us first take another look at the traditional research domain around indignation and protest, hostility and conflict; they all find their origin in some kind of unease or dissatisfaction. It is important to note that it is not only the "objective" deprivation that counts, but also the "subjective" deprivation; people may be exploited and repressed, but still not rebel, whereas other people may hardly be exploited and repressed (or no more than elsewhere or before), but still rebel. In his book, *Why Men Rebel*, Ted Gurr (1971) made a distinction between absolute deprivation and relative deprivation. A sense of relative deprivation arises when people experience a growing gap between what they feel entitled to (value expectations) and what they get (value capabilities).

Gurr said that value expectations and value capabilities may diverge in three characteristic ways. If value expectations remain the same, but value capabilities decrease, we speak of decremental deprivation. If value expectations rise, whereas value capabilities remain the same, we speak of aspirational deprivation. An interesting case is the "revolution of rising expectations." Whenever people are suddenly exposed to another and seemingly better "way of life" to which they also feel entitled, this may feed a sense of frustration and aggression against the people or system perceived to be in the way. The worldwide export of "First World" media materials (particularly film and television), for instance, has greatly contributed to the crisis of illiberal systems in the "Second" and "Third World" in the 1980s. But it also encouraged a push toward individual upward mobility through illegal migration.

Yet another case is when value expectations continue to rise, whereas value capabilities follow sometimes, but then peter off; expectations of growth are suddenly confronted with the reality of a shrinking economy. Think of the situation in several Pacific Rim countries after the Asian financial crisis of 1997, to which we return in chapter 10. This is called *progressive deprivation*, and may also create explosive situations (think of Indonesia). In his book, *When Men Revolt and Why* (1971), James Davies called this the "J curve." The line for value expectations is straight and continues to rise, whereas the line for value capabilities makes a slow turn downward—which looks like a letter "J" fallen over to the left. We encounter such processes in all three categories of collective or mass behavior.

Within a crowd, expressions of hostility may start in a variety of ways. It may be that the crowd has explicitly assembled to air grievances; it may also be that it has assembled for other reasons but suddenly turns vindictive; or combinations of the two. Those who actually turn to violence (assault and battery, plunder and arson) may be a tiny minority; think of the example of the Tahiti riots after the Moruroa nuclear test. Most of the time, there is a much larger group of peaceful demonstrators or even curious bystanders. But the problem is often that the intervention of the policy or army shifts the inherent logic of the events to a new "basin" of developments. The confrontation further dramatizes the situation, draws more curious bystanders, encourages the rebels, makes it harder to separate them, and thereby provokes a spiral of violence (rather than preventing it).

The riot may result from, or in, a broader social movement of protest and revolt. This often thrives on an emerging nuclei of primary organization, or new roles which existing organizations adopt (see, e.g., the works of Hobsbawm, 1969, 1959/1971; Rudé, 1964; and the Tillys, 1975). Testing the limits of the acceptable or permissible may play a role. Picket-line blockades or sit-in occupations, for instance, may alternately be seen as violent or nonviolent; it is a legal twilight zone. If the authorities choose to define these actions as intolerable, they force themselves to act with all means at their disposal. If they do not, by contrast, the actions may further drift to the manhandling or kidnapping of "trespassers" or staff. In both cases, the parties approach a "point of no return," beyond which a full-blown escalation will take off and follow its own course; then it is win or lose.

In some cases, this may destabilize an entire social order; for instance, when a broad opinion current turns against the regime or the system, which may lead to a complete revolution. Small and active minorities may play a decisive role, even if they are condoned by larger and passive majorities. Some authors (such as Crane Brinton, 1938, in his classic *Anatomy of Revolution*) tried to demonstrate that such a course of events often shows an inherent logic. Because once a certain threshold of violent confrontation has been crossed, the power play enters a new stage. Extremists try to "hijack" the revolt, and moderates are sidelined. It often takes time for them to recover, and to make up with the proponents of the "old regime." While the excesses deteriorate, the forces of compromise (or even restoration) regroup slowly, and prepare for the pendulum to swing back.

The paradox is the following: On one hand, many people may claim that a riot, a rebellion, or a revolution was "in the air"; but the time and place, trigger and form are highly unpredictable. Think of the collapse of the Soviet Union and the reunification of Germany. On the other hand, once a course of events begins to unfold, certain steps and a general direction seem to follow logically. These observations do not only apply to such highly dramatic and world historic turning points. But they do also apply to much milder phenomena in the various domains of opinion formation. Unfortunately we will have to limit ourselves to only three domains: those of moral panics, political scandals, and economic boycotts.

Moral Panic

The term *moral panic*, which has gained wide circulation in recent years, is slightly misleading because it has only a spurious relation with panic in a narrower sense, as we have discussed in the preceding chapter. Moral panic primarily refers to a wave of moral indignation that becomes visible every now and then, often fed by interested parties and media reports. We have seen in the chapter 3 section on media hypes how attention for issues may sometimes be amplified to the extreme, and how a critical reconsideration may be postponed.

The term *moral panic* was proposed in this sense by Stanley Cohen (1993), a South African exile to Great Britain who was surprised to note the level of indignation over a few skirmishes in a seaside resort between local adherents of two youth styles, the Mods and the Rockers. According to Cohen (1993), what happens is the following:

> A condition, episode, person or group of persons emerges to become defined as a threat to societal values and interests; its nature is presented in a stylized and stereotypical fashion by the mass media; the moral barricades are manned by editors, bishops, politicians and other right-thinking people; socially accredited experts pronounce their diagnoses and solutions; ways of coping are evolved or (more often) resorted to ... (p. 9)

Although a moral panic may be related to all kinds of true and imagined infringements on norms and values, a later study edited by Cohen and Young (1973) observed that three domains seem to be particularly conducive to moral panics: sex, drugs, and crime. What seems to be quick to tickle ordinary citizens is that some people want the fun but not the trouble. "If that attitude were to be accepted, where would we go?" The important thing is that the moral frontier between what is and what is not acceptable, is tested and reaffirmed time and again. It is a kind of ongoing collective negotiation process, in which all kind of groups try to claim stakes.

It is remarkable, for example, that the attitude toward sexuality in the Western world has shifted considerably and repeatedly over recent decades: from the hypocrisy of the 1950s to the permissiveness of the 1970s to the new "correctness" of the 1990s. The three Ps of perversity, pornography, and prostitution are defined and perceived differently. Intimidation, incest, and child abuse are brought out into the open and charges are brought. But on occasion this goes too far; fantasy, paranoia, and reality are not always kept separate. In 1996, boys of 6 and 7 years old were suspended from school, because they had kissed a girl in their class. In 1997, there were incidents in both France and The Netherlands where photographers and cameramen were arrested near beaches because they had been taking pictures of nude people on the beach—including children. These are typical expressions of a moral panic.

Some authors claim similar distortions in relation to drugs. Problems in relation to drugs form a sliding scale, which has arbitrarily been divided into clear-cut categories. Drugs that had become part of Western culture (such as tobacco and alcohol) and drugs promoted by pharmaceutical companies were hardly problematized until very recently. Exotic drugs that entered later onto the market (such as marijuana, hashish, and cocaine) were prohibited, the trade fell into criminal hands, and the situation became highly problematized. In The Netherlands and other countries and states, there is a legal distinction between soft drugs for home consumption and hard drugs for sale; in France and elsewhere, these drugs are considered the same. But

> according to the Surgeon General of the United States, in the United States the use of tobacco cigarettes is responsible for over 400,000 premature deaths, while alcohol use causes some 150,000 deaths; a crude extrapolation from hospitals and medical examiner's data yields premature acute deaths for illegal drugs (or the illegal use of prescription drugs) in the 20,000 or so territory. (Goode & Ben Yehuda, 1994, p. 44)

Crime, too, does sometimes draw much attention and reprobation. Tax evasion draws less indignation than social security fraud. White collar criminality generally draws less indignation than blue collar criminality—although there are exceptions to the rule. Theft abusing social position draws less reprobation than theft abusing physical strength. Violence between family members in the private realm draws less reprobation than violence between total strangers in the public realm. After some noteworthy incident, all kind of numbers are invoked to demonstrate that everything goes from bad to worse. We are never reminded that as new types of crime have risen, older types of crime have subsided (such as highway robbery).

In my previous book, *Understanding Global News* (van Ginneken, 1998), I showed that moral indignation about sex, drugs, and crime is often further amplified if there is (overtly or covertly) a cultural, ethnic, or racial side to it. It is to be expected that the share of various groups in various transgressions is not entirely identical. But these real differences are often enlarged beyond all proportion in media reports and public perception. Furthermore, there is ignorance and misunderstanding with regard to the factors leading to such contrasts; and blindness to the fact that, in other categories, times, and places, the emphasis is reversed. If traveling may contribute to a loss of social control, for instance, this may be demonstrated just as well with transgressions by overseas migrants in major Western cities, as by transgressions by Western tourists at major overseas destinations— for instance, in the sex trade and child abuse. Yet we tend to frame these particular categories in contrasting ways.

All moral panics have certain aspects in common. In a recent overview, Goode and Ben-Yehuda (1994) identified five:

> a heightened level of concern over the behavior of a certain group or category and the consequences. An increased level of hostility toward the group or category. Substantial or widespread agreement or consensus ... that the threat is real, serious and caused by the wrongdoing group members and their behavior. A sense on the part of many members of the society that a more sizeable number of individuals are engaged in the behavior in question than actually are. [This disproportionality is an important point and can often be established in different ways as well. For instance by comparison with similar situations elsewhere and before, which have received far less attention.] Moral panics are volatile; they erupt fairly suddenly ... and, nearly as suddenly, subside. (pp. 33–41)

Meanwhile there has been a range of studies about moral panics. But even for truly horrible crimes, one may often wonder why some get huge media coverage and public attention, whereas others are passed over in near silence. An American case that has drawn considerable attention was that of the Central Park Jogger; a beautiful, young, wealthy, and highly educated White woman who was attacked and gang-raped in New York at night (Didion, 1992). In those cases, there seems to be a deep resonance with archetypes.

Political Scandal

There are political and media scandals of all sorts and sizes. On occasion, they are related to questionable deeds of "ordinary people," or at least, people that would otherwise not be covered by the media. Such scandals often have a mythical dimension. By emphasizing stereotypical aspects of the main characters or the situation, they link up with cultural archetypes, perpetuate, or change these archetypes. On other occasions, media scandals are related to well-known people, such as sports stars or pop artists. Celebrities from the entertainment world thrive on their notoriety. It is part of the "deal" that they subject themselves to public controversy from time to time; this maintains public interest and fascination.

It is somewhat different for people who hold a high public office in the government, in corporations, or in private organizations such as a particular party, trade unions, churches, and so on. They depend to a certain degree on public acceptance. They have power, and they can abuse that power; that is why, within such bodies, there usually is some kind of separation of powers between the executive, the legislative, and the judicial branches. The media have been dubbed an independent "fourth" power, which must further fathom and test the actions of other power holders with the means at their disposal. They can do so by gathering information and making it public. Most important, in this respect, is "investigative" journalism, where neither time or money are spared to find out the truth and nothing but the truth, whenever abuse is suspected.

Within the present-day Western world, and even the world as a whole, "Watergate" has become the prime example of a fine case of investigative journalism. The *Washington Post* liberated its journalists Carl Bernstein and Bob Woodward from other work to find out who was behind a mysterious break-in into the offices of the Democratic Party in the Watergate Building. They found out that it was the reelection committee of the rival Republican Party, and therefore the White House of President Richard Nixon. Dustin Hoffman and Robert Redford played the main roles in a popular movie about this case, *All the President's Men*.

Since then, journalists often invoked the example of the Woodward–Bernstein pair, and with every new scandal, the suggestive suffix 'gate' was added. But it is often forgotten, that the "unmasking" of the most powerful man in the world had only been possible because of a very precise concurrence of circumstances. Alternative magazines had demonstrated long before how Nixon's campaign managers consistently used "dirty tricks," but the mainstream media had chosen to ignore this. High-level informers (such as the mysterious "Deep Throat") were only willing to talk because the political establishment was seriously divided over the Vietnam debacle. In later similar matters of flagrant power abuse (like the Iran–Contra scandal under Reagan and Bush Sr.) invoking "national security" proved sufficient to keep key aspects out of the public eye and to get a transparent cover-up accepted by the media.

So real investigative journalism is the exception rather than the rule. A really systematic investigation of a complicated affair involving power and secrecy may easily cost $100,000 or more. It is risky because for years it may disturb relations with political sources, large advertisers, or even considerable audiences. It results in an extremely complicated story, which is hard to follow or to summarize, even for insiders. So what is the point? Most scandals today, therefore, are "hit-and-run" cases. Interested parties play incriminating information into the hands of key journalists, who do some checking and then publish it. If it is particularly sensitive, it may first be carried by marginal publications or on the Internet before it is picked up by the mainstream media.

The media do increasingly copy each other, and do little thorough independent research of their own. Most scandals, furthermore, are semiprivate peccadillos artificially given a political twist. A string of investigations by an independent prosecutor into the private affairs of the Clintons came to nothing, after years and millions of dollars spent. But another infidelity and lie, leaked to the press, almost brought the president down in 1998. Such news soaps and media lynchings of public figures are increasingly common (van Ginneken, 2000).

James Lull and Stephen Hinerman (1997) edited a book on *Media Scandals*, which identified ten criteria:

> (1) social norms reflecting dominant morality must be transgressed . . . The transgressions must be performed by (2) specific persons who carry out (3) actions that reflect an exercise of their desires or interests . . . Further, individual persons must be (4) identified as perpetrators . . . shown to have acted (5) intentionally or recklessly and must be (6) held responsible . . . The actions and events must have (7) differential consequences for those involved. The revelations must be (8) widely circulated via communications media where they are (9) effectively narrativized into a story which (10) inspires widespread interest and discussion. (pp. 11–13)

Such a continuing story has new installments all the time. The story selectively refers to other previous scandals, and is compared in seriousness. Yet various groups may hold different views and interpretations. (Think about what we have said about issues in the section on public opinion.) Some public figures are more vulnerable than others. Effective crisis management may make them survive or lie low, until the storm blows over or another crisis diverts the public's attention. But the result of such efforts is always uncertain.

Media scandals "punish" office holders by tarnishing their reputation, and thereby making it hard or impossible for them to continue to function in the same role. If elected officials do not step down then their reelection will be in danger. But other domains have other ways of mobilizing public hostility. In the economic domain, the consumer boycott is one such way—as in the case of the Brent Spar.

Economic Boycott

The word, "boycott," refers back to the target of one of the first great boycotts of modern times; that of Captain Charles Boycott. He was supervisor on the Irish estate of a British count. Encouraged by the newly founded Land League, tenants refused all contact with the captain in 1880 and demanded a lowering of rent, because crop failures might lead to another famine (like the one that had claimed 1 million lives some time before). After that, the term boycott came to denote all such nonviolent forms of action, whereby the opposite party is ignored. This may be a particularly effective means of pressure, if the opposite party depends on the smooth progress of regular transactions—such as financial or economic ones. Citizens may boycott taxes; consumers may boycott services or products.

The consumer boycott reemerged as an effective form of pressure in the 1960s and 1970s. Western Europe and North America had boycotts of Outspan oranges from apartheid South Africa, and of Granny apples from military junta Chile. The export of fresh fruit from the moderate climate zones of the southern hemisphere to the northern hemisphere (where it would be scarce at this time of year) had only just taken off. Conservation methods were less sophisticated, and fruit was subject to deterioration. Yet the action was only a partial success. We earlier referred to the boycott of Beaujolais Nouveau wine after the French resumption of nuclear testing in the Pacific.

Today boycotts are increasingly directed against separate companies and the big brands of market leaders, such as Shell in the Brent Spar case. One may identify a whole series of conditions that determine whether a boycott may be successful. First of all, the critics must be able to lay a convincing link between the actions of the company and some kind of unwanted situation. Paradoxically, the largest and the best-known companies are the easiest targets. They are easily depicted as arrogant and greedy; also, they present a high profile. Points of sale may easily be turned into action targets; advertising slogans and logos can be paraphrased; particularly if the high-minded "mission statement" and "social responsibility" rhetoric of the company sounds hollow and empty.

Second, such an offensive usually only comes off the ground if it is supported by a broad coalition of prestigious people and groups—including mainstream ones. Celebrities may play a role (think of the aforementioned calls of models and movie stars to boycott fur). If, by contrast, the boycott is merely seen as the initiative of a radical splinter group, social support and the resultant impact will remain limited. But an important point is that action groups and their allies are easily seen as disinterested and therefore credible, whereas the company is seen as interested and therefore incredible. In an argument about "how bad" a situation really is, both the media and the public may therefore easily side with the accusers.

Third, such boycotts are often (temporarily) followed, if the boycotted product has many competitors, of comparable quality and price, and therefore highly interchangeable. It is really no great effort or pain to drink Italian wine rather than French wine for a few weeks or months, or to buy gasoline at BP rather than Shell stations. It is exactly because the difference is so small that consumers may easily decide to give off a "signal of displeasure" in order to force a company to change course on a particular issue. If the boycott is short and intense, even a minority of temporary brand switchers may be sufficient to make market share plummet, and give off a strong warning.

Shifts

It is important to see that in such cases the "problem definition" around a controversial issue is partly arbitrary and subject to sudden shifts. Murray Edelman (1988) eloquently demonstrated this in his book *Constructing the Political Spectacle*. What is a problem and what is a non-problem? What is a solvable problem that needs attention; and what is an unsolvable problem that may be ignored? What can be considered a possible solution and what cannot be considered a possible solution? To what domain does the problem belong: the moral, social, political, economic, or financial domain? Usually it belongs to several domains at the same time but is still assigned almost exclusively to one. Who can be held responsible to have caused or permitted the problem, who is imputable, who must suggest and effect a solution? These are all questionable categorizations, and there are dozens more.

This is most obvious when a completely new field of public concern emerges, such as the conservation of the environment. There is always a definition fight over what the true nature of the problems is, what the solutions are, how far they extend, and who is responsible. Whenever a new subissue comes up, the fight flares up again. An interesting case always emerges whenever it is said that something has no precedent but could become a precedent. It is of necessity a highly hypothetical problem area, which is hardly structured and relatively open. The party who takes the initiative to problematize something within that field has a decisive advantage. If the other parties do not see the danger and react appropriately, the matter is out of their hands. Through preemptive predefinition, certain courses of action are made legitimate and others illegitimate. Once this process is well under way, it becomes increasingly harder to break the emerging "frame," and make an alternative one stick.

The conflict between Shell and Greenpeace over the dumping of the Brent Spar was a case in point—unprecedented, but setting a precedent. It was a confrontation with a certain inherent logic, better exploited by Greenpeace than by Shell, particularly in the initial stages. But how can we understand such an "inherent logic," which seems to steer the course of events in a certain direction? How can we conceptualize such a curious combination of unpredictability in precise detail, but predictability in general outline? In order to develop these points, we need new insights into the evolution of CASs and new notions, such as abstract spaces and possible attractors.

THE METAPRINCIPLE OF POSSIBLE ATTRACTORS

The previous chapters have looked somewhat more closely at a number of aspects of rapid shifts in CASs. We have looked at nested contexts and irreversible time, which prove that every situation is unique. We have looked at decelerated and accelerated change, at critical mass, thresholds, and triggers. The drift of the argument is once again that it is not always easy to measure, predict, and control such processes. But, some ask, if it is often so difficult and certain, then why do we bother to do scientific research at all, or management for that matter? It makes sense even if it provides only a general understanding of such types of processes, which still enables us to act more responsibly. On occasion, we may be reasonably confident that we have an approximate idea of where certain processes are heading.

This section considers this problem more closely. It takes us into a domain of highly abstract reasoning. In the beginning this may look rather difficult to grasp, but after awhile, we get used to it. It is a type of reasoning that is familiar to mathematicians and natural scientists, sounds strange to scholars of man and society, and even stranger to laymen. Yet it may help to try to follow this reasoning for a while because it may lead to additional insights. In it, we try to trace the possible evolution of systems through abstract spaces and imaginary landscapes, identify possible "attractors" and take a brief look at so-called catastrophe theory.

An Excursion Into Abstract Space

We have discussed CASs (complex adaptive systems) and their possible evolution. In order to step up the level of reflection, we introduce a different form of representation of this evolution.

In it, the state of a CAS is represented in a simplified way, by a singular point in an abstract space. (This space is usually called a *phase space*, but I prefer not to use that term. On one hand, it is not absolutely necessary; on the other hand, it may create confusion with the terminology of the next chapter about phase transitions.) The singular point in the abstract space is defined by a combination of values on different axes or dimensions. They correspond to relevant variables. Because the states of the system are defined by various points, the evolution of a system through various states may be represented as a line or trajectory traced through such points; from one to next, and so on.

One may also make the system evolve through that space a number of times; ten, a hundred, a thousand, a zillion times. The trajectory need not be completely identical on each occasion; because of minuscule deviations and chance, one may imagine various possible evolutions under otherwise similar circumstances. Often these trajectories form bundles of lines because certain evolutions are more probable and frequent; but some may deviate because of less probable bifurcations somewhere along the way. We may also imagine these lines as running over a surface, which represents all possible developments. In theory, we may produce such abstract spaces with a huge number of variables and dimensions. But because we are most familiar with three-dimensional spaces, the exercise is most practical with no more than three of the most relevant variables.

A further simplification is to represent these abstract surfaces (for all possible evolutions of a system) as imaginary landscapes; and to represent the point (for the state of the system) as a drop of water finding its way through that landscape. Each location in the landscape once again represents a certain combination of precise values for relevant parameters. The evolution of the system may start on the highest point in the landscape; for instance, a hilltop. In the course of time, it follows its route downhill into a drainage basin. If we follow the evolution of the system a number of times, it may once again be that the drop of water will not always follow identical pathways, but may deviate on occasion. It may be that its progress is halted by an obstacle along the way. But most of the time, the evolution will culminate in a low point of the landscape; for instance, a valley.

Through this kind of representation, we may make explicit what the probable and improbable, the possible and impossible evolutions of a system are. From certain earlier points in the evolutionary process, the system will tend to certain later points. In this context, we speak of "basins of attraction" or "attractors." The best-known example is a simple pendulum; for example, an iron ball at the end of a string. If you move it up and down or back and forth, the pendulum will begin to swing. But for reasons of gravity, it will ultimately come to rest in one position—that closest to the ground. So it is called a "single point" attractor. But other systems may have other attractors. One particularly curious case is that of "strange attractors," related to deterministic chaos.

The question is whether one can describe and analyze the evolution of simple mechanic systems in this way, but also the evolution of complex living systems. If one takes a closer look at the evolution of ecosystems, for instance, it turns out they can often be well described in these terms; for instance, the relation between predator and prey populations. If the predator population grows too fast, the prey population will dwindle; this will make the predator population dwindle, and the prey population grow again. It is a kind of pendulum movement, which usually stays within a fixed margin, or even close to a persistent equilibrium.

This ecological equilibrium may, in turn, be upset and lead to the introduction of a new species, which also interacts with the predator and prey populations. Think of the introduction of European rabbits in Australia and New Zealand, the introduction of Asian rats in North America, or the introduction of African killer bees into South America. Often such animals brought new diseases as well, or were stopped by other diseases.

Psychosocial Attractors

In recent years, similar phenomena have also been noted in other disciplines; end states or provisional states to which a system tends from certain earlier conditions. It is like a fundamental pattern that gains the upper hand and persists. In neurology, for instance, it has been suggested to apply this perspective to qualitatively different Electroencephalogram (EEG) patterns that correspond to qualitatively different states of consciousness: waking, relaxation, daydreaming, dreamless sleep, and dream sleep. In psychophysiology, it has been suggested to assign a similar status to the emotions and moods that we discussed before. In clinical psychology, personality types, neurotic afflictions, and even family syndromes can be approached from this point of view. A first exploration of such themes can be found in a collection of papers edited by Robin Robertson and Allan Combs (1995), *Chaos Theory in Psychology and the Life Sciences*.

For our own consideration of rapid, radical, and massive shifts in public opinion and perception, the notion of "attitude" is particularly relevant. Richard Eiser (1994) explored this theme in his book about *Attitudes, Chaos and the Connectionist Mind*. A large part reviewed the origins and nature of the notion of attitude, the theme of connections, and of possible interactions. He also suggested to try and represent the possible evolution of attitude patterns in abstract spaces. One may think of representing the evolution simply along a straight line, or along a straight line with outside influences impinging upon it; but one may also think of a sloping surface within an abstract space, with cliffs and crevices for behavioral attractors.

Robin Vallacher and Andrzej Nowak (1994) in turn edited a book, *Dynamical Systems in Social Psychology*. It considers the evolution of social orientations in individuals, but also of possible interaction patterns between them. They also note that rapid shifts from one modality to a radically different one are quite possible. They even try to propose sophisticated mathematical models, to fathom the dynamics of such shifts. It would take us too far to discuss them in detail. But it is important to retain that the evolution of psychosocial systems may indeed suddenly shift from one inherent logic (succession of states, basins of attraction) to the next.

This also holds true for culture. A culture of pastoral nomads has an entirely different inherent logic than a culture of resident farmers. A culture of dry grains has an entirely different psychosocial logic than a culture of wet rice. For instance, the latter requires a much greater collective mobilization for the construction and upkeep of an irrigation system, and therefore different forms of social organization and even ideology. So a shift to another production system may have huge implications. In his book, *Explaining Culture*, Dan Sperber (1996) wrote:

> Cultural attractors emerge, wane, or move, some rapidly, others slowly, some suddenly, over historical time. Some of these changes have ordinary ecological causes; over-exploited ecological niches lose their economic attraction; rarely walked paths become overgrown; some practices tend to increase, and others to decrease, the size of the populations that might be attracted to them, and so on.
>
> Most historical changes in attractors, however, are to be explained in terms of interactions between ecological and psychological factors of attraction of a kind specific to cultural evolution. (p. 115)

Maybe at this point we should give a few examples of the role of possible attractors in the evolution of psychosocial systems. Let us consider a few examples from the field of competition and rivalry. Under some circumstances, they lead to an inherent logic of "centering"; under other circumstances they lead to a logic of polarization.

A well-known example is the problem of two ice-cream vendors, trying to cover a one kilometer stretch of beach on a hot summer's day. Sometimes one vendor will place himself at a quarter of the length, and the other at three quarters, so that they can both serve half of the stretch. But more often, we see that they both position themselves in the middle, try to cater to the entire population, and to outsell the competition. There seems to be an inherent logic that "drives" them to this attractor (more in Cohen & Stewart, 1994). We see similar processes at work in a two-party system like that of the United Kingdom or the United States. Rather than seeking a high profile to the left and to the right, both parties will primarily fight over the electoral center ground, because that is where victory is decided.

The opposite happens in polarization processes. In such cases, there will be an evacuation of the center ground (where an understanding and a compromise might be worked out), and an entrenchment in opposing camps. This was the case in the confrontation between Shell and Greenpeace about the dumping of the Brent Spar. Both parties let a "zero sum" game evolve; where the gains of one party would necessarily be the losses of the next (rather than a win–win situation). It generates the specific logic of manichaeanism, which precludes an armistice or a reconsideration; one sticks to his guns, despises the enemy, and ignores the other point of view. Only later, much later, may it become apparent that this can also be a self-defeating strategy, and that it may sometimes be better to keep the lines to the other party open, to talk to him, to maintain a dialogue.

Such processes also play a role in deviance and amplification, which we have discussed before, just like collective stereotypes and ethnic discrimination. Once certain prejudices have taken root, they seem to perpetuate and reinforce themselves. Something similar plays a role in conflict between countries and alliances. Once enemy images have taken root, they seem to perpetuate and reinforce themselves; a split takes place, on various levels. Unwelcome aspects of the self or unwelcome factions of one's own group tend to be associated with the other party from that moment on. One identifies even more strongly with welcome aspects of the self, or welcome factions of one's own group, and idealizes them. Ambivalent conflict matter, for example, about migrants and borders, is suddenly made clearcut, and reframed in terms of black and white. Every action of one party invites a (slightly stronger) reaction of the other party. The further escalation and conflict spiral are hard to stop.

One can see this same pattern return on other levels; for instance, in the age-old adage: The enemies of my enemies are my friends. It leads to the attractor of the checkerboard, where black and white squares alternate on maps. This tendency was clearly visible when the 1960s split of the communist bloc translated into the 1970s realignment of states. The Cambodia of the Khmer Rouge feared its stronger neighbor, Vietnam, and therefore aligned itself with China. Vietnam feared its stronger neighbor, China, and therefore aligned itself with the Soviet Union. China feared its stronger neighbor, the Soviet Union, and therefore aligned itself with a tiny state on its other flank—Albania. Other small states on this flank, like Yugoslavia and Romania, in turn, sought security guarantees from the still stronger Western alliance. All kinds of ideological reasons were developed and refined, but the inherent logic was simply one of power politics.

Catastrophes

The type of thinking that represents the evolution of a system as the trajectory of a point through abstract space (of which the dimensions correspond to the relevant variables) has also inspired other theoretical innovations. One of these is so-called catastrophe theory. A catastrophe—in this context—is not always a sudden negative event; it may just as well be a sudden positive event; the point is that it is a very specific concurrence of circumstances that leads to a radical shift.

The theory was originally developed by the French mathematician René Thom (1975), in the context of a further reflection on the problem of morphogenesis or the emergence of form (touched upon in our section on self-organization in chap. 6). Later, E. C. Zeeman tried to develop these onsets into a much more spectacular direction by applying them to capricious problems in entirely different disciplines, such as ethology, psychology, sociology, economics, and history. This led to a series of papers that were later collected in a volume on *Catastrophe Theory* (Zeeman, 1977). From the mid-1970s on, this new approach drew considerable attention. It led to special issues of scientific journals, but also to pages in general week-lies such as *Newsweek* (Jan. 19, 1976).

The theory invoked unusually curved surfaces in abstract space, to demonstrate how the evolution of systems could suddenly shift; therefore, it does not make much sense to approach these surfaces as imaginary landscapes. Some typical examples of such unusually curved surfaces were called the fold and the cusp, the swallowtail and the butterfly. Sometimes it boiled down to a situation where the same combination of exact values of two variables within this abstract space could correspond to two or more radically different values for a third variable. This implied that the system could take radically different forms under nearly identical circumstances, and that it could shift from one form to the next. It is like someone taking a walk in the mountains, over a plateau, and suddenly falling into a hidden crevice, hundreds of meters deep.

There have been several attempts to extend this type of reasoning to the sciences of man and society. One recent example is by Latané and Nowak (1994) about sudden attitude shifts in a book about psychosocial dynamics. They give examples of citizens heavily involved in a political process, who therefore tend to reject dissonant information longer than others, and then suddenly recognize it is true. Think of a liberal female supporter of the emancipatory policies of President Clinton, who long felt that the accusations of sexual transgressions were just part of a reactionary plot, until she suddenly recognized that they were indeed part of a protracted pattern of inappropriate behavior.

The authors postulate a space of three dimensions, where the favorability of attitude y is a combined function of two control factors: c_x is the positivity of information and c_z is the importance of the issue (to the person in question). They quoted Zeeman (1977) in this context:

> As the issue is such that more and more people become involved, for instance in the Dreyfuss [sic] affair or the Watergate affair we can investigate this as a slow drift of the points . . . [Ultimately] the uninvolved will hardly register any change of opinion, the slightly involved will change their minds smoothly, and the more involved will tend to suddenly switch opinions after some delay. (p. 629)

So for the latter group, the attitude change will take the form of a catastrophic shift.

Another problem to which Zeeman (1977) tried to apply this approach was derived from the well-known work of the German ethologist, Konrad Lorenz, about animal aggression. It was related to the inner conflict between reflexes of anger and fear, fight and flight, which competing dogs and other animals show under conditions of equal strength. Behavior may easily shift from one mode to the next. Others have proposed to apply a similar kind of reasoning to humans; for instance, to the shift from love to hate (after a messy divorce), or the shift from conformity to nonconformity (defiance after inappropriate pressure). In all these cases, one may try to devise abstract spaces to promote better insight into the inherent logic of behavioral developments, including "catastrophic" tipping points.

Zeeman (1977) also tried to apply this type of reasoning to collective behavior, as with unrest in institutions, or revolts in penitentiaries. One may continue in this same direction by applying it to revolutions and crises on a greater scale, like the implosion of social systems and complete civilizations (see Casti, 1994; also Tainter, 1988). The collapse of the Greek and Roman civilizations and the Maya and Inca civilizations, have been approached from this perspective. The collapse of the "old regime" in France, the French Revolution, the rise and fall of the Napoleonic empire, and the subsequent succession of monarchical regimes, revolutions, and republics can be approached from the point of view of attractors and catastrophes. The same holds for the Russian and Chinese revolutions.

One series of interesting reflections was related to the viability and nonviability of certain configurations of variables in huge, newly industrializing, semideveloped states such as Russia and China. They were used to throw further light on the dilemmas that the leaders of the communist bloc were confronting over the last few decades. Further technical development was unthinkable without a somewhat open society, which was unthinkable without a crisis of the system; the ultimate emergence of a reformer like Mikhail Gorbachev in the Kremlin, the fall of the Berlin Wall in 1989, and the implosion of the Soviet system can well be conceptualized in these terms. Similarly, one may also try to conceptualize a possible "breakout" of peace in the Middle East in such terms (see Casti, 1994).

Although these were very interesting mental experiments, however, their real use was increasingly questioned. The inventor of catastrophe theory, René Thom, said that the applications of Zeeman (1977) stretched its plausibility. The authoritative *Scientific American*, which had earlier published positive articles about the theory, now shifted to severe criticism. The same held for *Science* and *Nature* (Kolata, 1977; Zahler & Sussman, 1977). Many demonstrations had degenerated into mere mind games, opponents said, which had little to do with the clarification of shifts through mathematical and geometric models. Today, catastrophe theory is only invoked on a limited scale. At the same time, the general approach of the evolution of systems through abstract spaces, imaginary landscapes, and possible attractors, has retained some of its validity.

IV

CONCLUSIONS

I don't believe in an afterlife although I'm bringing a change of underwear.
— Woody Allen, American film director (Crawley, 1994, p. 130)

We have seen in the course of this book why certain standard types of reasoning from everyday life and from traditional science do not suffice to understand nonlinear shifts. All too often, we are mired in a somewhat reified approach to opinions and attitudes, as if they were a kind of brick, with an obvious permanence and fixed dimensions; and as if they aggregate like walls and buildings, through simple addition and accumulation. Similarly, our notions of change are often mired in a mechanicistic view; that is to say, with implicit reference to a simple type of interaction, as between the cogwheels in a clock or in a machine; direct and linear, with simple forces working in only one direction. But rapid, radical, and massive changes within a CAS should be conceptualized in entirely different terms—in terms of the emergence and dissolution of patterns, in terms of transformation and self-organization, and in terms of critical thresholds and evolving contexts.

This last part of the book once again consists of three chapters, and the first two chapters once again consist of three levels. They bring us to the final conclusion of our reasoning. At the most abstract level, this points to the metaprinciple of *uncertainty*. There turn out to be fundamental reasons, why certain phenomena and interactions are immeasurable, unpredictable, and uncontrollable. At the middle level, it brings us to the related idea of "forecasting." The policies of governments and corporations are based on looking ahead. Planning is based on forecasting, on predictions and extrapolations, from the past and the present. The problem is that there will always be events to disturb these expectations and to turn the course of history into radically different directions. We see in the final chapter that this also has consequences for our attempts at "issues management": the desire of major players in certain fields to influence the many ways in which public opinion and public perception are shaped.

CHAPTER

10

Phase Transitions
in Crazes and Crashes

Wealth is like sea-water; the more we drink, the thirstier we become; and the same is true of fame.
  —Arthur Schopenhauer, German philosopher (Gross, 1987, p. 86)

A "sound" banker, alas, is not one who sees danger and avoids it, but one who, when he is ruined, is ruined in a conventional and orthodox way along with his fellows, so that that no one can really blame him.
  —John Maynard Keynes, British economist (Gross, 1987, p. 109)

When I began developing this book, large parts of the world were confronted with a threatened slowdown in economic activity. This provoked a sudden shift in economic outlook, which subsequently spread to other countries and continents—like an oil slick. The previous part of this book discussed single mood shifts. This chapter is about a more complicated combination of euphoria and panic. But what remains noteworthy is that the financial system seems to be in an entirely different state, whenever it is relatively calm or highly agitated. Under certain conditions, it may slide from one state into an entirely different one, without this process being either completely foreseeable or controllable. In order to try and understand what is happening here, we take a look at a last metaprinciple of sudden change, that of so-called *phase transitions*. It is comparable to ice melting into a liquid, and to water evaporating into a gas, or vice versa.

CASE NUMBER TEN: THE ASIAN MELTDOWN

The next case is an illustration of the fact that various phenomena from mass psychology and collective behavior sociology are often intertwined. Also, there may be a sudden shift from interaction with a low intensity to interaction with a high intensity. The question is how we should conceive of such abrupt changes in modality. The Asian financial crisis of 1997 and 1998 is a case in point.

From the early 1990s on, there had been a rapid growth of investment. Within the Western nations, the Baby Boom generation began to age. There was concern about the sustainability of the social security system and pension funds. There was a widening search for new investment opportunities with good perspectives for long-term profitability. The collapse of communism and the triumph of capitalism led to supreme confidence in the golden future of a completely liberalized and globalized economy. In his book *False Dawn*, John Gray, an Oxford professor of political science, later compared the "rationalist hubris" of the market-utopians in this regard to the earlier misconceptions of the Marxist utopians (Pfaff, 1998c). And David Hale, a financial expert at Zürich Kemper research, reminded colleagues that "the market alone has a record of persistent miscalculation of risk and misallocation of resources" (Pfaff, 1998b).

New financial instruments, such as options and derivatives, further contributed to opaque financial constructions during these years. After the prestigious bank of Barings had collapsed, for instance, it turned out that the highest management in London had never fully fathomed how its junior representative, Nick Leeson, juggled with billions in Singapore. New developments in telecommunications, computers and automation made it possible to buy and sell faster, at greater distances in time and space. The most profitable opportunities seemed to present themselves in so-called "emerging markets." The "dragons" and "tigers" of east and southeast Asia became popular. There was talk of an "economic miracle" in the air, and of the inevitable approach of a 21st "Asian Century."

Investors returned enthusiastically from fact-finding missions to the region. In 1993, Barton Biggs of Morgan Stanley, for one, returned from a trip to Asia and declared himself totally convinced of the impending miracle: "tuned in, overfed and maximum bullish." According to the *Financial Times*, this "was a signal for a wave of liquidity" (Glassman, 1998, p. 8), that is to say more money pouring into the region. Figures later released by the Swiss-based Bank for International Settlements showed that lending surged. Around the mid-1990s, Thai debts amounted to 89% of gross national product (GNP), Malaysian debts amounted to 77%, and South Korea's debt amounted to 56%. There was difference of opinion as to whether this was "too much" or not; but some $100 billion turned into "bad loans" under the circumstances that developed.

Economist Paul Krugman was one of the very few who warned at an early stage that this rapid growth was unsustainable. He later said he was "intrigued that money managers could have changed their views of East Asia so quickly. Just a few months ago they extolled the virtues of the Asian miracle and now they denounce regional economies as inefficient and badly managed" (Fuller, 1997, p. 13). At that later point in time, a *Washington Post* editorial asked rhetorically, "What were the banks' research departments saying 6 months ago? Nor did the IMF, or rating agencies such as Moody's and Standard & Poor's, provide any warnings; all were issuing glowing report cards right up until the last" (*International Herald Tribune*, Jan. 7, 1998, p. 8).

The *New York Times* added:

The International Monetary Fund employs more than 1,000 PhD economists, many of whom constantly travel the globe looking for trouble in the making. They issued reports praising both Thailand and South Korea for "sound macro-economic management" only months before those countries were pleading for, and got, IMF bailouts. (Sanger, 1998a, p. 11)

Economics professor Jeffrey Sachs (director of the Harvard Institute for International Development) wryly observed: "You have to wonder just how much the IMF really knows about these countries" (Kuttner, 1998).

Nor did national governments see the storm brewing. This even held for the United States. A high official of the CIA later admitted that it was ill-equipped to analyze this type of economic crises, even if the crises might have considerable political and even military consequences. The highest White House adviser for the international economy, Daniel Tarullo, was puzzled in hindsight, that there had been no crisis meeting whatsoever (Sanger, 1998b), and the Secretary of the Treasury Robert Rubin said he was surprised that so few international creditors and investors proved to have the appropriate expertise and information to weigh the risks (Buddingh, 1998a).

Four months into crisis, the president maintained that there were just a few ripples on the surface. Former security adviser and "Realpolitiker," Henry Kissinger, concluded that no single government and hardly any economist had foreseen the crisis, understood its scope, or fathomed its tenacity. How was it possible that one of the greatest changes in the strategic climate of the late 20th century took the elites completely by surprise? In my opinion this was because the shift in public opinion and perception was first, highly psychological in nature; second, somewhat arbitrary in timing; and third, spread and deepened because of a specific set of circumstances.

Furthermore, the "coupling" of the behaviors of various actors within a slowly rising market and within a rapidly falling market is of a fundamentally different nature. It is reminiscent of a *phase transition*: a rapid shift in the fluidity or even volatility of a market.

The first domino to fall was Thailand. By mid-1997, almost half of its outstanding debts were short term ones, which would have to be paid off (or renegotiated) within a year. There were signals that this might prove difficult. Representatives of some large foreign banks exchanged faxes saying that five local commercial banks might prove unable to stay afloat. Local authorities reacted as they usually did whenever subjects stepped out of line; that is to say, they sent over a few police cars and raided the offices of the Japanese Nomura and the Anglo-Dutch Hoare-Govette ABN-AMRO. They confiscated files, and photographed employees—in order to find out who had spread these "malicious rumors." Rather than putting the doubts of the international financial community to rest, however, the local authorities further stirred them. Within a few hours, what had been left of foreign confidence had melted away, and the Thai currency went into a nosedive.

The bubble had burst, and suddenly people began to reevaluate the situation, and limit their stakes; also in other countries. Because of its greater riches in raw materials and its smaller population, neighboring Malaysia had a much stronger economy. But it had invested strongly in prestige projects such as monumental skyscrapers: the KL Tower in Kuala Lumpur, which was to surpass the Empire State Building in New York, and the Petronas Twin Towers, which were to surpass the World Trade Center. This had already raised some eyebrows on Wall Street. When the tide changed, furthermore, Islamic prime minister Mahathir had inconsiderately accused the Jewish financier, George Soros, of exacerbating the crisis (*IHT*, July 28, p. 11). It is true that he had earlier boasted of making 1 billion dollars in speculating against the British pound, but this time he denied being involved. (The accusations were thus seen to have an anti-Semitic undertone, which made matters even worse.)

South Korea was next in line. The bankruptcy of two major industrial groups, Hanbo Steel and Kia Motors, had raised doubts about the robustness of expansion, investment, and credits. By now, South Korea was the eleventh economy in the world; its foreign debt was high, but according to one commentator in the *International Herald Tribune*, Philip Bowring (1997), it was proportionally of the same level as that of the United States or Australia. He added that it was therefore dangerously misleading to speak of a "zombie economy," particularly because such exaggerations were "contagious." He said that bankers followed the sentiments of the crowd rather than applying consistent principles. Even the aforementioned George Soros denounced the stampede; when he expressed his confidence on one visit to Seoul, share prices climbed almost 3% back up again.

Where foreign investors had previously praised East Asian diligence and thrift, they now suddenly focused on "nepotism and opacity." Were these exclusively Asian traits, absent in other regions of the world? Did only local businessmen indulge in such behavior, or had foreign corporations always joined the fray? For instance, in Indonesia? After an aborted palace revolution in the mid 1960s, an estimated 500,000 leftist sympathizers had been killed. General Suharto took power, had himself elected and continuously reelected, and installed a spoils system for his family and friends. All this had been condoned by his Western allies, even though the CIA estimated that by the early 1990s, the "clan" had assembled a combined wealth of some 30 billion dollars; that was about the amount the IMF had to put up later to prevent complete bankruptcy. The rate of the currency and values tumbled. Within 1 or 2 years, half of the Indonesian population had fallen back into dire poverty (*IHT*, July 3, 1998, p. 12), and according to the regional director of Unicef, half of the children under age 3 became malnourished again (*IHT*, Oct. 14, 1998, p. 6).

Economic growth in the entire region came to a halt and even started to reverse itself. According to an article by the managing director of the authoritative magazine *Foreign Affairs*, Fareed Zakaria (1998), the value of the Indonesian economy shrank by 80%, the Thai economy by 50%, the South Korean economy by 45%, and the Malaysian economy by 25%. The International Labor Organization estimated that unemployment in the region would double during the course of the next year. I add that social security was almost nonexistent, and many savings had disappeared into thin air; thus, there was a rapid rise in social unrest. Government leaders were forced to step down, ethnic minorities became scapegoats, foreign workers were expelled, and tension between neighboring states rose.

Meanwhile, the generalized crisis of confidence began to affect developed nations as well. Japan depended for half of its exports on trade with the rest of Asia. It had earlier seen a "bubble burst," and was reluctant to take decisive stimulating measures. The three states (Washington, Oregon, & California) on the west coast of the United States also depended on Asia for $\frac{1}{2}$ to $\frac{2}{3}$ of their exports. California was one of the main "engines" of American technological growth. Developing nations elsewhere, however, were much worse off. There was a partial economic crisis in Russia and eastern Europe, and another partial crisis in Brazil and South America; in those regions, problems persisted for many years to come.

In the first instance, some $120 billion had been mobilized to douse the flames in the three worst hit countries. This did not prevent their currencies from collapsing, though, with all that implied. The funds came from the IMF and the World Bank—based in Washington. But both institutions got that money from governments, and thus from taxpayers, in contributing countries. At first the suggestion had been that the money had been used to help the poor populations of the receiving countries; but critics soon claimed that the exact opposite was in fact true.

The Republican chairman of the American Senate Commission for Banking Affairs expressed serious reservations over the demonstrated willingness to "save some very undisciplined investors" (Alvarez, 1998, p. 10). The vice-rector of the United Nations university in Tokyo, Ramesh Thakur (1998), called it a moral problem that those who had created the problem were saved, whereas the burden was shifted onto innocent bystanders (because the imposed austerity measures provoked a fallback for these innocent bystanders into extreme poverty). On top of that, foreign profiteers now bought up many local possessions for sale at "garage sale" prices. In this context, former American trade representative, Mickey Cantor, spoke of "a golden opportunity" (Khor, 1998). But others warned that this would inevitably provoke a backlash.

Still others claimed that ideological prejudice had played a role as well. *LA Times* commentator William Pfaff (1998a, 1998b) noted that deregulation always serves the most powerful players, that is to say those who dispose of sufficient means to be able to exploit the situation. He also said that the United States had always been opposed to the "development model" of countries like South Korea, because it had protectionist and voluntarist traits; but that did not mean they could not be effective and creditworthy, he added. The problems were of an entirely different nature than earlier ones in Latin America; imposing the same measures often led to opposite results. Others, too, called the IMF a "doctor with only one pill." It bled the patient until he got better—or simply died.

Even former national security adviser Henry Kissinger (1998) called it a strange paradox that the IMF restricted itself to a narrowly "economistic" policy because it imposed measures that led to social unrest and undermined the very political institutions that were necessary to carry out the favored policies. But this sudden awareness of the Western policy elite came rather late. The IMF director, Michel Camdessus, had first maintained that the crisis would be rather short-lived, and had later said that it was easy for outsiders to speak with hindsight. But later, he reluctantly admitted: "Yes, we have made mistakes" (*IHT*, Sept. 24, 1998, p. 13). The president of the World Bank, James Wolfensohn, was more forthright, and advocated openly admitting when and where they had "screwed up" (Ibidem).

The big question remained of course whether it was true that the real causes of the crisis were the result of the "nepotism and opacity" of the Asian countries in question, or whether these vices had suddenly been blown all out of proportion. The World Bank's foremost economist, Joseph Stiglitz, also a noted Stanford professor, admitted that monopolies caused inefficiencies, but denied the monopolies were at the root of the crisis. Otherwise those countries would never have been able to grow as well as they had over the previous 30 years. He said the crisis was, at least partly, due to a panic (Buddingh, 1998b).

Several economists from Boston, like Harvard's Jeffrey Sachs, and MIT's Lester Thurow, also claimed this (*IHT*, Jan. 6, 1998; Aug. 14, 1998). So the "great freeze" was partly to blame on a "rapid, radical and massive shift" in value perception among Western investors; and it was only partly related to objective shortcomings in the "real economy." As the crisis persisted, more experts conceded that mass psychology had been a major factor. In late 1997, the head of the Asian economic research department at J.P. Morgan's Bank, Bernhard Eschweiler, admitted that there had been a panic; in early 1998, he added that it had become a self-destructive, vicious circle (*IHT*, Jan. 7, 1998, p. 4), because the currency devaluations expanded the debt volume for local borrowers and further undermined capacity to pay.

Some experts maintained that the nature of the interventions had only made things worse. The aforementioned Harvard professor Jeffrey Sachs claimed that the IMF had indeed 'inflamed' the situation.

> The fund turned a dangerous situation into a calamitous situation, by very publicly and ostentatiously closing banks, raising interest rates, tightening credit, and signaling to anyone who didn't see it before that these economies would go into free fall'. It was like shouting "Fire, fire!" in a full theatre. (Blustein & Sugawara, 1998, p. 11)

The heart of the matter is that the gradual filling of a theatre is regulated by entirely different interaction processes than an emergency evacuation; the same holds for accounts and banks. Economic commentator Robert Samuelson (1998) noted in the *International Herald Tribune* that there was a chain reaction because something changed the perceptions of those involved. He, too, likened it to ice that suddenly melts, or water that suddenly vaporizes; this is a process which natural scientists call a *phase transition*. It implies a sudden, qualitative shift in the nature of the alignment of particles. We return to this notion in the third and final section of this chapter.

But let us first take a somewhat closer look at what is known about the alternation of crazes and crashes in financial markets in a more general sense.

THE PHENOMENON OF CRAZES AND CRASHES

Throughout the previous part of this book, I seized on various dimensions of public moods to demonstrate metaprinciples of rapid shifts. The preceding chapters discussed three "arch" dimensions, linked to so-called primary emotions: joy (rather than sadness), fear (rather than courage), and outrage (rather than resignation). The present chapter discusses another characteristic dimension: greed (rather than generosity); not so much related to the objects themselves as to their pecuniary value. The most noteworthy examples are economic *crazes*, or money manias, and economic *crashes*, or value implosions. They display certain similarities with fads and panics, but also certain contrasts; furthermore, the two are closely intertwined.

They have become a recurrent feature of our free market society, especially during recent, unruly episodes. They lend themselves to close scrutiny. We often have detailed information on exact trade volumes and price changes. Contrary to a widely held belief, however, financial economics is not an exact, objective science—which can reveal purely mechanical laws, however sophisticated. Because if surefire signals of impending crazes or crashes could ever be discovered, this knowledge itself would again change the behavior of those involved, and still other laws would emerge; so these are fundamentally unstable and paradoxical phenomena, with a highly subjective character and major psychosocial components.

So this section is largely devoted to the craving for profits and the fear of losses that have been most "problematized" in the past. But once again, this should not lead us to forget that there is occasionally typical "mass" or collective behavior in the other direction as well. In those cases, people "infect" each other with generosity. (Good examples are television marathons and solidarity campaigns after major disasters, and for good causes.) Some noteworthy cases date back to the early days of television, when there were still only two or three nationwide channels. But a more recent worldwide example was the many-sided, Band Aid campaign for Ethiopia in the mid-1980s, which we discussed in chapter 3 on media hypes.

Greedy Masses

Before we delve somewhat deeper into "crazes and crashes," let us take a brief glimpse at other examples of greedy masses: those who are entirely tuned into the acquisition of scarce or precious goods. We are familiar with such phenomena in all three previously identified categories of collective behavior: psychological crowds, social movements, and opinion currents.

Greedy crowds can sometimes be seen in a sale; whether it is a one-time event or a seasonally recurring one. If the sale begins at a day and time announced long in advance, and if there are only small batches or isolated specimens of desired articles at low prices to be found, the shop is often besieged in advance. The day before, people begin to line up; the night before, people save their place-in-the-line in sleeping bags. When the doors are finally opened, they rush to the floors in question, grab whatever they have in mind, and stuff their bags. It often escalates to pushing and shoving matches, to altercations, and even fistfights. At posh department stores, "fine" ladies and gentlemen can sometimes be seen battling it out.

One might label as greedy social movements those half-organized little worlds of amateur collectors who are less fascinated by the objects themselves than by their possible value. This often holds for stamps and coins, for bric-a-brac and antiques. It also expresses itself in the feverish atmosphere of some exchange markets and fairs. Auctioneers often simulate great interest and heavy competition in order to heighten emotion and drive up prices. Although once again, this often amounts to a kind of "conventionalized unconventional" behavior.

Greedy opinion currents manifest themselves in hoarding, for instance. There is a rumor circulating that some commodity is (or will soon become) scarce and that prices will go up; or even that extraordinary profits could be made in the black market on this commodity. In all cases, people flock to supermarkets or gas stations and buy larger stocks than they would otherwise, just in case, or even to be able to supply family and friends. The net result is that the articles in question are soon sold out. The sight of the empty shelves seems to confirm the rumor. After the stocks have been replenished, therefore, they may get re-depleted even faster. It is one of those "self-fulfilling prophecies," which we discussed in the chapter about feedback-loops; the fact that many people share such expectations contributes to making the expectations come true.

Speculative Bubbles and Bursts

In the case of financial speculation, as with the Asian crisis, similar principles apply. More than 150 years ago, Charles Mackay (1841/1980) published his overview of *Extraordinary Delusions and the Madness of Crowds*. The first 100 pages were entirely devoted to some famous examples of financial bubbles, and bursts. There was a chapter on the tulipmania of 1636 in Holland. Individual bulbs were sold at 3,000 to 5,500 guilders of those days (the equivalent of some $30,000 to $50,000 these days). A batch of forty bulbs was sold for 100,000 guilders (several million dollars today). Mackay's book also had chapters on other similar cases such as "the Mississippi scheme" and "the South Sea bubble." The latter made the famous Sir Isaac Newton lose part of his life savings, and made him observe that he could calculate the movements of the planets, but not the madness of people. The other 600 pages of Mackay's book discussed other examples of mass or collective behavior, hallucinations, and superstition.

Bernard Baruch, one of the most famous financiers of all times, described in his 1957 autobiography, *My Own Story*, how the reading of Mackay's first 100 pages saved him many millions of dollars because it made

him more aware of the role of mass psychology in the extraordinary rise
and fall of markets. During the 1920s, he did not get carried away by the
"Florida land boom," as so many others were. In the late summer of 1929,
Baruch began to wonder whether it was not high time to sell his stocks. He
consulted several experts, who advised against it. He decided to go ahead
anyway, and saved his fortune. Only a few weeks later, The Great Crash
took place, followed by the Depression; it took the stock market a quarter
century to recover to the previous level.

A few years later, Baruch wrote a new foreword to Mackay's classical
work. In it, he quoted a description of the mysterious alternation of coupling and uncoupling of behavior in masses that we have noted before:

> Have you ever noted in some wood, on a quiet sunny day, a cloud of flying
> midges—thousands of them—hovering, apparently motionless, in a sunbeam?
> . . . Yes? . . . Well, did you ever see the whole flight—each mite apparently pre-
> serving its distance from all others—suddenly move, say three feet, to one
> side or the other? . . . Great human mass movements are slower of inception
> but much more effective. (Baruch, 1962)

In 1992, Joseph Bulgatz published a sequel to Mackay's book, a kind of
second volume, entitled *Ponzi Schemes, Invaders From Mars and More Extraordinary Popular Delusions and the Madness of Crowds*. Once again, the
first 100 pages were devoted to financial bubbles and bursts. It had a chapter with new information about the aforementioned tulipmania in Holland, a
chapter on the aforementioned Florida land boom, and a chapter on the
Ponzi investment scandal—which dated back to Baruch's days. It also had a
chapter about the panic following the notorious early radio program about
an "Invasion From Mars," and other examples of mass and collective behavior, hallucinations, and superstitions.

But people, including savers and investors, are often pig-headed. New
generations and new social groups fall for the illusion that they have hit on
a way to become fabulously rich with little effort, with no risk that they
might instead become desperately poor. Around the early 1990s it became
obvious that capitalism had triumphed all around the "First World," that
communism was collapsing in the "Second World," and that the Third
World too seemed to have no choice but the market, the market and nothing but the market. In many semi- and underdeveloped countries, new
banks tried to lure little people to put their life savings into accounts. They
often offered exceptionally high interest rates, which they could only sus-
tain by paying off earlier clients with the money submitted by newer clients.

The logic and risks of such pyramid schemes are obvious, and have often been denounced. Yet time and again, people willing to gamble their future can always be found, spellbound by the lure of easy profits. In some

countries of the Second and Third World, such initiatives were even en-couraged by new, seemingly "reformist," politicians; until the flaws became suddenly apparent, there was a run on deposits, and the system collapsed. In postcommunist Albania, the poorest country of Europe, the crisis even provoked a revolution, a brief civil war, and an massive outflow of eco-nomic refugees to neighboring Italy.

But in developed nations, too, similar schemes turn up periodically. They employ the principle of the "chain letter," for instance. Everyone knows how this operates. You receive a letter, must make several copies, and pass them on to others. The number of letters in circulation should therefore rise expo-nentially. In the financial version, you must transfer money to the person at the top of the list of senders and may add your own name at the bottom. In principle you can expect to receive your stake back manifold, at some later stage. It is an old trick. Bulgatz (1992) described an episode during the De-pression, in which hundreds of thousands lost money.

The scheme exploits two cognitive illusions, or mental errors. The first is that naive people implicitly accept the contention that the chain will remain unbroken; that there will always be enough new people who obey the rules and faithfully transfer the money. But the number of credulous people in any given society is limited. Second, a critical analysis reveals that the early "happy few" may indeed make large profits, but that the sum total necessar-ily corresponds to the accumulated losses of many latecomers. Only with il-lusionist tricks (like enthusiasm raising parties with "champagne" toasts to ultimate success) can confidence be stretched and the "easy money" illu-sion be preserved—just long enough for the initiators to cash in. But ulti-mately, the bubble will surely burst.

Value Paper, Bears, and Bulls

At first sight, nothing seems as rock-solid as money. Increasingly, it even seems to have become the "objective" yardstick to measure the value of everything else. This makes us forget, however, that money is essentially a "confidence trick," based on people's beliefs. Once upon a time, all money was coin money, with the value of the coins more or less corresponding to the value of the precious metals contained therein. Of course, the value of those precious metals could be subject to rises and falls, for instance, when new trade routes or new mines were opened, or when new supplies became available. But most of the time, fluctuations were limited.

Gradually, however, the value of coin money was unlinked from the value of the precious metals therein, and instead linked to the creditworthi-ness and credibility of the sovereign or government who issued and guar-anteed them. A next step was the introduction of paper money. The printed paper was worth next to nothing, only the guarantee itself counted. Whenever a country or regime collapsed economically (as was the case with Germany after World War I), its money could rapidly lose its value. If a country retained the same amount of wealth but ran the money presses to produce more bills, this led to inflation and value loss. The exchange rates of one currency into the next were also related to the respective power and trade relations between nations. By anticipating and exploiting changes, speculators could make considerable profits.

Meanwhile, other types of value paper had come into existence as well. Letters of credit from banks, shares in the property of companies, and so forth. But the evaluation of the "value" of such companies and their perspectives were not only based on "objective" fundamentals but also on "subjective" appraisals. If everybody was confident, the share prices went up. If everybody lost confidence, the share prices went down. So there were zig-zag movements: minor, medium, major—all intertwined. Those movements seemed to be highly capricious, but market watchers tried to distinguish consistent patterns and to anticipate future trends.

In the case of a globally rising or "active" movement, people spoke of a "bull" market. In the case of a globally stagnant or "passive" movement, they spoke of a "bear" market. Bull markets and bear markets alternated, sometimes dramatically. This was particularly obvious in the United States, which became the leading economic and financial world power in the course of the 20th century. Periods of conservative government and free market euphoria were often followed by an economic fallback. The 1920 period of President Calvin Coolidge was characterized by unfettered optimism and expansion, but followed by the crash of 1929. The 1980 period of President Ronald Reagan was also characterized by unfettered optimism and expansion, but followed by the crash of 1987.

Now how does this come about? There have been many studies about 1929; the best known is the one by John Kenneth Galbraith (1955). There have been fewer studies about 1987; one of the better known is the one by David McClain (1990). Galbraith (1990) and Kindleberger (1989) are among those who have produced overviews that compared various crashes. At the outset, a rapid upward movement is often fed by noteworthy new possibilities to make investments and profits. This can be related to new products, new production techniques, new markets, or new infrastructures. It can also be related to the more general social and economic, political, and even military outlook.

Share prices rise, attract more investors and capital, continue to rise, and so forth. Gradually, the investment motive is overtaken by the speculation motive, and by the "easy money" illusion of dipping into the stream and floating upward with the movement—without any risk. This happens in a specific context, unique to the sociohistoric situation. But the more general context is usually that of a rapid influx of extra money, and the emergence of ever more complex and opaque financial constructions. The system reaches its limits, the turning point approaches. The chronic "manic" stadium may turn into an acute "panic" stage.

Often, there has been a gradual emergence of doubts on whether things could really go on like this forever. There were early warning signs that the tide might turn. Often the signs take some time to really sink in. After this, one or two incidents grab the attention, and set the "Gestalt switch" in motion; that is to say, the shift from one perceptual configuration to the next. It is important to understand that it is not only the "objective" significance of the news that is decisive, but rather the "subjective" salience. A household name company, for instance, which was long held to be a sure investment, suddenly collapses. This may have more of an impact than a $\frac{1}{4}$ point rise in interest rates, at least with a significant portion of the investing public, enough to provide a "critical mass" for change.

In stock markets, furthermore, the process is usually somewhat asymmetrical; the ascending line is flatter, the descending line is steeper. Really compact "manic" moods are usually limited to the sudden popularity of one particular stock. But really compact "panic" moods may affect complete national or international markets. So there is a kind of qualitative transition. In an ascending market, the coupling between the behavior of investors is often much looser and more indirect; they take time to decide and weigh alternatives. In a descending market, the coupling may become much tighter and more direct; there are instant reactions. The "here and now" comes to prevail, sensitivity to information increases to a hair-trigger response. Once a critical threshold has been crossed, positive feedback loops and circular reaction patterns take over. This is typical mass or collective behavior; everybody sells because everybody sells because everybody sells.

The nature of these latter psychosocial processes tends to be underestimated and misunderstood by financial experts, time and time again, at least according to William Sherden's (1998) new book, *The Fortune Sellers* (a pun on "fortune tellers"). It says, "Economic forecasters have routinely failed to foresee turning points in the economy: the coming of severe recessions, the start of recoveries, and periods of rapid increases or decreases in inflation" (p. 55). Sherden said that the stock market in particular was driven by an irrational herd instinct and mass psychology. It was a "psychological soup" (p. 77) of fear, greed, hope, superstition and a whole lot of other emotions and motives.

According to the Danish physicist Per Bak (1997), such situations, too, display a kind of self-organized criticality and unpredictable catastrophes:

Traditional economics does not describe much of what is actually going on in the real world. There are no stock market crashes, nor are there large fluctuations from day to day. Contingency plays no role in perfectly rational systems in which everything is predictable ... The obsession with the simple equilibrium picture probably stems from the fact that economists long ago believed that their field had to be as "scientific" as physics, meaning that everything had to be predictable. What irony! In physics detailed predictability has long ago been devalued and abandoned as a largely irrelevant concept. Economists were imitating a science whose nature they did not understand. (pp. 184–185)

The same can often be said of sociologists and psychologists, I would add.

Shifts and Gestalt Switches

The "chaos" economist, Brian Arthur (1990, 1993) and others did research about price formation and exchange rates for value papers, and how patterns emerged and suddenly shifted. In "lab" experiments with small groups of investors, it turned out that their interaction at first seemed to be guided by purely rational economic considerations, but that irrational psychological processes often took over after some time. They no longer acted on the basis of what they themselves thought the papers were worth, but what others thought the papers were worth, or what others thought still others thought the papers were worth. They were guided by their own subjective convictions about others' subjective convictions.

This also involves another human peculiarity. If one confronts people with a pattern that does not make sense, they will continue to look for a pattern that does make sense. Similarly, if one confronts people with an ambiguous stimulus that can be interpreted in two radically different ways, they will tend to: (a) prefer one interpretation over the other, and (b) have difficulty acknowledging that the second interpretation makes just as much sense. The shift from seeing bad omens to seeing good omens, for instance, can occur suddenly and arbitrarily. It one key player (like George Soros) shifts to a different interpretation of contradictory signs, furthermore, others may soon follow. So mood swings in the free markets of value papers are indeed subject to mass psychology and collective behavior sociology.

But it is important to remind ourselves that the coupling between the behaviors of investors is often much looser in rising market, and much tighter in a falling market. In order to understand what this implies, we must look at another metaprinciple from physics: namely, so-called "phase transitions."

THE METAPRINCIPLE OF PHASE TRANSITIONS

This section reviews one final metaprinciple that may help throw further light on the mystery of rapid, radical, and massive shifts in public opinion and perception; this is the metaprinciple of phases and phase transitions.

This metaprinciple, too, was originally conceptualized in physics, but gradually extended to other disciplines. In the framework of complexity and chaos theory, it acquired a wider meaning.

Attempts have been made, for instance, to apply it to a specific type of problems with human technology, such as the "congestion" of transportation, communications, and electronic systems. We will see that it may also help elucidate certain aspects of interaction in mass or collective behavior; for instance, in the case of crazes and crashes—as with the Asian crisis.

A Digression on Phases, Transitions, and Hypnons

The notion of *phase* and *transitions* (in this sense of the words) originally stem from thermodynamics. They refer to qualitatively different ground states of matter: such as solid, fluid, and gas (although other states or substates have been suggested). Here a phase means a homogenous state (chemically and physically uniform, that is to say, molecularly and atomically uniform). Matter in one phase can mechanically be separated from matter in another phase. The matter in question may be pure or a mixture of substances. Transitions between phases correspond to well-defined values for temperature and pressure.

In everyday life, we are most familiar with the phases and phase transitions of water. We are well acquainted with water (in an wider sense) in its solid phase of ice, its fluid phase of water (in a more restricted sense), and its gas state of steam. We are well acquainted with phase transitions in both directions. In one direction, we know that under normal pressure, ice will melt at zero °C, and evaporate at 100°C. The Celsius "centigrade" scale was devised by dividing the distance between those two major phase transitions into 100 equal parts. In the other direction, we know that under normal pressure, steam may condensate into liquid water, and water may freeze into solid ice.

The major ways in which patterns appear (i.e., the fundamental relations between form, structure, and movement) differ between these phases. Key patterns of ice may be crystals, key patterns of water may be waves, key patterns of steam may be clouds. Some scholars have even suggested to consider the crystal form a separate phase or subphase, and crystallization a separate (sub)phase transition.

In everyday life, we are somewhat familiar with the very subtle crystalline forms of snow, or the magnificent "flower" patterns that the steam of the tea kettle may paint onto a kitchen window in winter. The phase transitions present themselves as rather rapid transformations. Yet the moment and speed of the processes also depends on temperature and pressure. Additional factors (such as minor changes in composition, and/or catalysts) may also play a role. We all know "fondant" ice and half-melted snow as apparent half-forms, on which the fate of skating and skiing competitions may depend.

It is useful to point out here that this whole terminology of melting and evaporating, of condensating and solidifying, has in the past already been widely (but also very loosely) used within the sciences of man and society in general, within psychology and sociology, and in particular within mass psychology and collective behavior sociology. So there has long been some kind of intuition that something similar to phase transitions may indeed play a role in these phenomena. But few authors have paused to try and make the implications of these metaphors more explicit.

Meanwhile, the notions of phases and phase transitions have, in a general sense, spread to other disciplines in natural science as well. In the realm of electromagnetism, for instance, it has been proposed to consider resistance or conduciveness, too, as some kinds of different phases of the same material; and "becoming resistant or conducive" as phase transitions. (In this regard it is interesting to note the key role of conduciveness within Smelser's model of collective behavior, discussed in chap. 5 on opinion currents.)

Gradually, notions of phases and phase transitions have been introduced into general systems theory, particularly into theories about large collections of interacting particles with more or less similar behavior; or rather with more or less similar behavioral repertoires. In those cases, a kind of phase transition is related to the emergence of fundamentally different relations between those particles; and thereby, to the "waking" (or actualization) of qualitatively different aspects of their behavioral repertoires; from nonresponsive to each other, for instance, they may turn hyperresponsive. This may in turn lead to fundamentally different "alignments": organization patterns with respect to each other and the environment; that is to say, to so-called collective behavior.

This brings us back to key processes of CASs and shifting patterns, to the alternation of complexity and simplicity, of chaos and order. In this context, Prigogine and Stengers (1984) introduced the notion of "hypnons" (in their seminal book, *Order Out of Chaos*, mentioned in chap. 1). *Hypnons* or "sleepers" are particles (entities, individuals) that are—at that point in time—relatively indifferent to each other (or to the environment); or rather, they are in certain ways indifferent to certain aspects of each other (or of the environment). According to Prigogine and Stengers, this is often the case with systems that are more or less "in equilibrium." Qualitatively different aspects (and behavioral potentials) are "awakened," however, whenever the system slides into a "far from" equilibrium state; they become sensitive in different ways to other aspects of each other and/or of the environment.

The Congestion Phase and the Braess Paradox

One of the domains in which this type of reasoning has led to new insights over recent years is that of technology. In the realm of mechanics and clocks, machinery and cars, we are familiar with the principle of the coupling or "clutching" of cogs and wheels. When coupled, they transfer force and movement to each other; when uncoupled, they do not. By combining various wheel sizes, we may vary the power of the force and the speed of the movement. With a gearbox, we may choose various relations between power and speed. In each gear, the type of 'mediation' is slightly different.

CASs (in which large numbers of particles behave in similar ways, interact, and align themselves) may also display forms of coupling and uncoupling, which are somehow reminiscent of solid, fluid, and volatile states. In a solid state, particles seem to be entirely stuck in a certain position; there is no change or movement within the system. In a fluid state, they do move, but with a limited degree of freedom. In a volatile state, they move too, but with a greater degree of freedom. In phase transitions, they get stuck or unstuck, in lesser or greater degrees. The general conditions of such phase transitions can often be outlined, but the precise circumstances may not.

Such processes have been identified in transportation, communication, and electronics. Transportation routes, communication channels, and electronic circuitry are all characterized by a limited capacity, a limited number of "units" moving through a limited space: vehicles, messages, and bits. The system may be overtaxed, and the process may become blocked. It may be optimally taxed, when its capacity is used well, and processes run smoothly; and it may be undertaxed when processes do still run smoothly, but its capacity is underemployed. So one needs to promote the second alternative; the third alternative is acceptable on occasion, but the first is not.

One domain where this has become increasingly clear is that of traffic circulation. In many places outside city centers, simple intersections have been replaced by roundabouts over recent years. When you do not put traffic lights at crossroads, accidents may occur—particularly if it is unclear who has the right of way. When you do put in traffic lights, there may be fewer accidents, but it costs money and time. On roundabouts, with traffic already on them having precedence over traffic coming onto them, circulation and alternation may proceed much more smoothly; these circles are self-organizing and optimally flexible.

Sometimes the relation between capacity and traffic flow turns out to be paradoxical. German scholar Dietrich Braess first identified the paradox. In 1968, in order to try and alleviate congestion in the city of Stuttgart, municipal traffic authorities opened up a new connection between two thoroughfares. The unexpected result was that congestion became worse than before. The opposite happened in New York, in 1992. There, municipal authorities decided to reserve the busy 42nd Street for pedestrians on Earth Day (environmental day). Pessimists predicted that traffic would become totally stuck, but nothing of the kind happened, and circulation was even slightly better. A recent Dutch example was the addition of an extra carpool lane to the busy A1 motorway near Amsterdam, which produced more traffic jams than before. The paradox shows that the thin borderline between fluid and "stuck" traffic has "chaotic" aspects, and is extremely sensitive to precise circumstances.

These same themes were developed in a noteworthy article, published in the authoritative *Physical Review Letters* (Kerner & Rehborn, 1997). Over the previous 6 years, Boris Kerner of the Daimler-Benz research laboratory in Stuttgart, and traffic consultant Hubert Rehborn from Aachen, had proceeded to make precise observations on busy sections of the A5 and A44 motorways. After elaborate calculations, they concluded that traffic jamming is indeed comparable to phase transitions—as already described. Not one phase transition between two phases—moving and stuck—as had previously been supposed, but two phase transitions and a third phase, congestion, because this introduced a qualitatively different relation between (and elicited another behavioral repertoire from) cars and drivers. This was somehow comparable to water being solid, fluid, or volatile.

Other researchers had indicated earlier that some kind of instability arose whenever traffic circulation was at approximately 85% of its capacity (Browne, 1997). This would lead to the formation of slow lines, but it was not entirely predictable what the immediate consequences would be. It was quite possible that the compact lines kept a decent speed, and that circulation remained fluid for hours to come. But it was also possible that a relatively minor irregularity would halt the stream, and would provoke the initiation of a stop-and-go pattern that might persist for hours. The disruption could also "travel" upstream for many kilometers or even a dozen, so such phase transitions were not only characterized by critical thresholds but also chaotic aspects, and proved ultrasensitive to precise conditions (see also Bak, 1997).

Meanwhile, similar findings turned up in neighboring domains: such as robotics, telecom, and the Internet. Japanese researchers tried to program "automotive" robots in such a way as to not clog key trajectories, but adapt to each other's movements and thereby guarantee orderly traffic. British and American scholars in the telecommunications field have found that the addition of extra capacity may sometimes hinder rather than promote smooth connections. The clogging of the Internet sometimes displays similar characteristics (see also Kelly, 1997).

In all these cases, then, CASs may know qualitatively different states or phases, and the transitions between them may be hypersensitive to precise circumstances.

Back to Animal Behavior and Swarms

Plants and animals, too, may shift into entirely different states that can somehow be compared to phases. The locomotion of horses is an interesting behavioral example. They may walk footpace, trot, or gallop. The internal organization of those behaviors is qualitatively different. The transition is governed by speed, but also by other factors. In wild horses, the transition may be hard to predict. The same holds for other qualitatively different types of behavior.

Throughout this entire book, we have considered the question whether qualitatively different modes of psychosocial interaction exist, and how accelerated shifts occur. At this point, we may ask ourselves the question whether it makes any sense to compare these to phases and phase transitions. In order to find an answer, we may go back to the chapter on self-organization, and what we noted on different interaction modalities in animals; particularly on herds/hordes of walking/running animals, schools of swimming animals, and swarms of flying animals. It appears that the behavior and interaction of those animals may be governed by fundamentally different states.

First of all, we have seen in the chapter on collective moods that acute fear and extreme panic may provoke a kind of regression to ultraindividualist behavior. It may come to run parallel, reinforce itself, and make the habitual kinds of social coordination collapse (even if only in exceptional cases and for short periods of time). Second, one might say that under normal and balanced conditions, such animals may display a mixture of semi-individualistic and semisocial behavior. In these cases, individual sociality is controlled in a nonimmediate way, at a distance, because the behavior is highly mediated by all kinds of internal cognitive processes and circuits: social instincts, social learning, and even social representations. Third, we have noted that characteristic forms of crowd, mass, or collective behavior imply a kind of ultrasocial behavior. In the sense that there seems to be some kind of closer welding together of the collective in a "here-and-now" frame. In this context, terms like *de-individuation, mental unification,* and *group mind* have been employed.

This sounds rather abstract, so I interject another concrete example to illustrate this point. In his fascinating book, *Out of Control,* computer guru Kevin Kelly (1997) invoked his experiences as a lover of outdoor life, the environment, and nature:

> One fall I gutted a bee tree that a neighbor felled. I took a chain saw and ripped into this toppled old tupelo. The poor tree was cancerous with bee comb. The further I cut into the belly of the tree, the more bees I found. The insects filled a cavity as large as I was. It was a gray, cool autumn day and all the bees were home, now agitated by the surgery. I finally plunged my hand

into the mess of comb. Hot! Ninety-five degrees [Fahrenheit] at least. Over-crowded with 100,000 cold-blooded bees, the hive had become a warm-blooded organism. The heated honey ran like thin, warm blood. My gut felt like I had reached my hand into a dying animal. (p. 5)

Kelly (1997) further elaborated on the metaphor of one living organism consisting of many living organisms, welded together by a highly intense form of social interaction:

A hive about to swarm is a hive possessed. It becomes visibly agitated around the mouth of its entrance. The colony whines in a centerless loud drone that vibrates the neighborhood. It begins to spit out masses of bees, as if it were emptying not only its guts but its soul. A poltergeist-like storm of tiny wills materializes over the hive box. It grows to be a small dark cloud of purpose, opaque with life. Boosted by a tremendous buzzing racket, the ghost slowly rises into the sky . . . (p. 6)

This is a brilliant evocation, it sounds plausible, but what exactly is happening here? Individual bees may go about their business, discover flower fields, and communicate directions and distance through a "dance" upon their return. This is social behavior, heavily mediated by instinct, learning, and some kind of representations. But a beehive may also form a swarm, which moves around as if it is one body. Somehow the social behavior is much more tightly knit; sensory impressions (of each other and the environment) are almost instantaneously translated into motor movements, which amounts to a form of finely tuned social coordination.

I propose to approach those two different forms as fundamentally different modalities of psychosocial interaction; one modality of long and loose coupling of individual behaviors; another modality of short and tight coupling of individual behaviors. To a certain extent, they may be compared to phases, as outlined before (in the section on technology). The rapid and seemingly capricious shifts between the two may then be compared to phase transitions. Just like other phase transitions, they are governed by processes that we may globally understand, but cannot always precisely predict.

Mass and Collective Behavior as a Phase Transition

These same basic patterns can also be found in human behavior. Nature has equipped us with a behavioral repertoire and interaction patterns in more than one modality. One might distinguish a total of three basic forms: First, ultraindividualist and asocial (antisocial) behavior that may prevail in situations of acute fear and extreme panic; second, semiindividualist and semisocial behavior that prevails in most of everyday life; and third, somewhat "de-individuated" group—or collective behavior that comes to prevail in certain high-pressure mass exchanges.

In their most typical form, these are three clearly different modalities, separated by two transition thresholds, along one dimension (of aggregation). It is also a sliding scale, along which shifts may alternatingly appear in an accelerated or decelerated fashion. The same holds for the transitions between ice, water, and steam. One may globally appraise the conditions under which this takes place. But minute details (of place, time, and form) are hard to predict in a very precise manner.

These are situations where a critical threshold is passed. The prevailing modality somehow loses its propriety; for instance, the conventional everyday behavior, semi-individualist and semisocial, based on loose and distant forms of interaction. Under such circumstances, a rapid shift may take place. The process may rapidly shift to a radically different and less mediated modality. In situations of acute fear and extreme panic, there may be a shift away from social coordination, and toward ultraindividualism. In situations of a sudden outrage, there may be a shift away from individualist behavior, and toward improvised coordination. Both may draw interaction into a vortex of self-reinforcing trends, away from distant mediation, and toward immediacy. Such shifts have chaotic aspects; they may be globally understood, but cannot always be precisely predicted.

Such a view fares reasonably well with certain approaches that have previously been developed within the fields of mass psychology and particularly collective behavior sociology (within the latter tradition, see Turner & Killian, 1987; K. Lang & G. E. Lang, 1961; and Smelser, 1962). But also see newer overviews, such as the one by Goode (1992). Klapp's (1972, 1973) work evolved in a similar direction. In my view, newer overviews such as those by Marx & McAdam (1994), but most of all, Miller (1985) and McPhail (1991), justifiably warn that we must not exaggerate, and that the unconventional character of collective behavior must not be considered in absolute terms. Some behavioral directives loose their grip, whereas others remain in force.

But this should not lead us to deny, that typical mass or collective behavior does indeed exist, as some scholars do. It is true that collective behavior in its purest form is rather extreme and very exceptional. In the past, extreme forms have been unduly emphasized, and have been too easily identified with the milder and intermediate forms, which are much more common. In some respects, it can even be said that they are the constant undercurrents and countercurrents of the regular social process and also the wellsprings of social change and innovation. But a better understanding of the extreme forms may also throw some light on these milder and intermediate forms.

As a provisional conclusion of this whole argument, therefore, let me try to sum up in some ten points about what all this entails, and how we can indeed approach mass and collective behavior as some kind of phase transition. They are general observations on the emergence of alternative behavior and interaction patterns. They try to steer clear from a value judgment, and just approach these psychosocial phenomena as a different modality. The ten points are:

1. Typical mass and collective behavior patterns emerge whenever and wherever (and insofar as) the "habitual" responses in the relevant domain are being experienced as insufficient and inappropriate.
2. We disengage from the prevailing ways of thinking, feeling, and doing, and no longer support them effectively in social interaction, so that they loose their grip.
3. At the same time, we begin looking out (and open ourselves up) for alternate forms of cognition, emotion, and behavior, which are displayed and "proposed" by others.
4. One of these alternatives ultimately seems to be more appropriate, is adopted, and subsequently supported in social interaction, so that it gets some "grip."
5. Concrete, lively, and salient symbols (new words and images, events and people) play a key role. They facilitate and stabilize the process of "redefinition of the situation."
6. They also draw us into the vortex of a newly emerging psychosocial pattern. This is accompanied by excitement and a shift of attention in the direction of the immediate "here and now."
7. The fact that so many others seem to share our original disaffection and our current engagement legitimates the shift and eases our identification with the newly emerging collective.
8. Under the aroused and agitated circumstances of the shift, we tend to see (and evaluate) others not so much as separate individuals but as similar members of a diffuse group (of proponents and opponents).
9. This hampers critical evaluation of ourselves and individual others, and promotes transgressive acts as well as a diminished sense of imputability and responsibility.
10. Such processes tend to reinforce each other until some threshold is reached. At that point, the collective behavior is somehow transformed and incorporated into habitual behavior; or it volatilizes.

This holds for all three aforementioned categories of mass or collective behavior; that is to say, for physically assembled crowds, for intermittently assembled and intermittently dispersed social movements, and for physically dispersed opinion currents. It also holds for the "affectively colored" public moods, which we have examined before. And certainly for the "crazes and crashes," which were discussed in this chapter. There is a constant alternation of patterns. Old belief systems melt away and volatilize; new belief systems condensate and crystallize.

At the risk that the reader is tired of metaphors I would say that both our individual psyche and our social networks are some kind of boiling soup or brewing lake of volcanic lava—in constant movement. Some seemingly solid banks may suddenly give way, whereas new islands may suddenly emerge a little further. *Panta rhei*.

11

Prediction, Planning, and Fundamental Uncertainty

Prediction is very difficult, especially about the future.
—Niels Bohr, Danish physicist (Stewart, 1989/1997, p. 279)

Future. n[oun]. That period of time in which our affairs prosper, our friends are true and our happiness is assured.
—Ambrose Bierce, American journalist
(The Devil's Dictionary, 1989, p. 139)

This penultimate chapter tries to draw some general conclusions from what preceded. It begins with a "thick description" of a case, in which one human error, one second in duration, changed the course of history—because it led to the nuclear disaster of Chernobyl. This leads us to the phenomenon of forecasting and strategic planning. Many governments and other institutions make long-term commitments to future developments—also in the domains of public opinion and perception. The problem is that these expectations often turn out to be way off the mark, so that emerging threats and opportunities are seriously underestimated. In this context, we need a better understanding of the metaprinciple of all metaprinciples: that of fundamental uncertainty. The frameworks of complexity and chaos theory make clear why so many key processes cannot entirely be measured, predicted, and controlled. This fundamental uncertainty also demands a completely different management approach.

CASE NUMBER ELEVEN: THE CHERNOBYL FALLOUT

It is no exaggeration to claim that Chernobyl contributed to changing the course of world history in many different ways. The course of economic history because of the disaster in Chernobyl contributed to the freezing of further development of nuclear power in Europe for some 10 to 20 years; if not in eastern Europe, then certainly in western Europe. This in turn contributed to the further exploitation of other fossil fuels around the world, and gave a sudden boost to the timid quest for renewable energy, and so forth. The course of political history, too, was decisively affected by the event, because it further contributed to the awareness of the failure of the Soviet system, its inadaptation to the technological age, to it being given up even by its own leaders. Only 3 years later, the Berlin Wall fell; 5 years later, Germany was reunited. This in turn changed the course of military history because it ended the Cold War, and led to a redrawing of the strategic map of Eurasia. The incident might have happened a few years earlier, a few decades later, or not at all; in those cases, the course of both political and economic history might well have been rather different (Remnick, 1993).

More than 30 years before, in 1954, the Soviet Union had been the first country in the world to inaugurate a nuclear reactor for civilian purposes. The United States was quick to follow; that same year, successive chairmen of its Atomic Energy Commission praised the advantages of nuclear power: "Our children will enjoy electrical energy too cheap to meter," one said (Sherden, 1998, p. 170).

The dramatic oil price increases of 1973 and 1979 sharpened the general sense of an energy crisis and created new opportunities for nuclear expansion. But safety concerns helped drive prices up again, even though the costs of long-term waste disposal were often not explicitly taken into account, and implicitly shifted from the private to the public sector. One study by relevant U.S. authorities estimated that in 1995, it would cost between $230 and $350 billion to clear up the military nuclear mess at home.

One early serious accident occurred at Windscale (now Sellafield) in northwest England in 1957. The information was kept secret at the time, but it was later estimated to have leaked considerable amounts of radioactive Iodine-131 and radioactive Cesium-137 into the environment. One later serious accident occurred at Three Mile Island (near Harrisburg) in Pennsylvania. There was a partial meltdown, but radioactivity remained largely trapped within the containment building. The immediate cost of the event was estimated at several billion dollars. Also,

Worldwide output from pressurized water reactors fell by 15% because reactor managers felt they had to reduce power to "play safe," according to one British expert, and "in addition, costs rose because regulatory bodies piled on safety requirements . . . There is always a knock-on effect." (Hawkes, Lean, Leigh, McKie, Pringle, & Wilson, 1986, p. 222)

Japan and France, too, had several near misses over the years.

The Soviet Union had at least one serious early accident, but it was completely covered up, and sketchy details only emerged decades later. But the Chernobyl accident topped them all. It released no less than $\frac{1}{2}$ of its radioactive reactor core material into the environment. According to one Swiss expert, fallout during the first week "exceeded that from all previous atmospheric testing of nuclear weapons" over 40 years (C. Park, 1989, p. 76).

The plant at Chernobyl (Ukrainian for "Wormwood") was relatively new; the first reactor had been started up less than 10 years before, and all four reactors had been in operation for less than $2\frac{1}{2}$ years. Only a few months before the accident, the U.S. edition of the propaganda magazine *Soviet Life,* had still stated that the plant was completely safe. It had quoted the Ukrainian Minister of Power as boasting that "the odds of a meltdown are 1 in 10,000 years" (C. Park, 1989, p. 12). But after the accident, the head of the official Novosty news agency conceded that Soviet experts "had developed too much faith in nuclear power and had become negligent about its dangers" (Hawkes et al., 1986, p. 214).

Ironically, the worst nuclear accident resulted from a safety test. It began in the middle of the night on Friday, the 25th of April, 1986, just before the weekend (and its related lowering of demand). A succession of minor clumsy moves caused power to fall and then to rise slowly again. At exactly 1 hour, 23 minutes, and 40 seconds into the night, the operator put on the brakes and pushed the shutdown button, but the reactor reached "one hundred times full power" only 4 seconds later. The action blew the reactor's lid off, thereby releasing a burst of radioactive material into the environment.

The "cloud" contaminated the plant and its immediate surroundings, then drifted to the Ukrainian capital of Kiev (130 kilometers away). It continued its advance over the Byelorussian city of Gomel, to the Byelorussian capital of Minsk (1,250,000 inhabitants, 300 kilometers away) and then on to Poland. Yet, over the entire weekend, authorities treated the disaster as a purely local affair, severely underestimated the radioactive fallout, and belittled the incident. They simply sent in the ill-equipped fire brigade and rescue services. There was no immediate evacuation of the local population; and nearby districts were only reluctantly evacuated later, one after the other. The power and heat generated by the explosion, the height of the radioactive plumes, and the changing winds (and, therefore, the range of the fallout) were severely underestimated. For 3 full days, official sources kept completely quiet, and this time period might even have been longer if outside agencies had not picked up signals that something was terribly wrong.

Instruments in Stockholm first registered a marked rise in radiation levels on April 27. But because it was Sunday, there was no one present at the National Defense Research Institute, and therefore the alarm was only sounded on Monday morning, when staff returned to work. Other institutes confirmed the readings but no leakages were reported inside Sweden itself, nor in neighboring Scandinavian countries. Analysis revealed that the radioactive material had probably emerged directly from a reactor core. Winds had been blowing from the south and east, so the authorities hypothesized that the problem might be at a Leningrad nuclear plant in Russia, at Ignalina in Lithuania, or—a very remote possibility—at Chernobyl in the Ukraine. But in the latter case, it would have been a major explosion indeed, but Moscow had kept completely silent.

When pressed on Monday afternoon, the Kremlin at first flatly denied that anything had happened at all. On Monday evening, at last, there was a brief statement, admitting that an accident had occurred. But over the next few days, the Soviets continued to stall and play down the seriousness of the incident. As an official later admitted, because the key May 1st Labor Day was approaching, "it happened on the eve of a holiday . . . and we did not want to spoil the celebrations" (Park, 1989, p. 60). The Soviets also stalled any announcement because they did not want to play into the hands of Western "hawks" on the eve of the G-7 summit in Tokyo, which was to take place on May 4th. Only a day later, on day ten, did a senior Soviet official (Boris Yeltsin) make himself available for interviews. But he expressed himself in rather general terms. It was to take years before local and foreign journalists were able to piece together what had really happened and how (see Marples, 1988). At this point in time radioactivity was still pouring out of the reactor; an improvised "sarcophagus" was only completed on day twelve.

During all of this period, winds had been changing, thereby affecting more countries. There were intermittent rains, which accelerated fallout and created uneven, radioactive "hot spots" on the ground. Western European governments soon closed their borders to eastern European foodstuffs. The western European authorities advised their own population against eating certain fresh leafy vegetables, berries, mushrooms, and nuts. They also advised farmers to reign in the cattle, and against the consumption of milk and meat of cattle that had long remained outside in contaminated areas (such as cows, sheep, and reindeer). Yet, shipments of slightly contaminated products did later turn up in certain Third World countries such as Mexico.

Meanwhile the "body count" remained uncertain, and remained subject to controversy for years. The Soviet Union had first admitted to only two immediate casualties, then to over 30. In the West, there had been a lot of unsubstantiated rumors.

> There were reports from a ham radio operator about dead bodies being piled up in mass graves; the unfortunate UPI reporter who was informed by a Soviet citizen that there had been 2,000 deaths; accounts of two simultaneous meltdowns based on U.S. satellite information. (Marples, 1988, p. 125)

This was all wrong. But it proved true that evacuation had long been postponed, and remained incomplete. Thousands of "volunteers" had been sent into the area with little or no protective clothing or equipment, or even Geiger counters. Alternating brigades from elsewhere brought down the total doses of radiation to which each individual was exposed, but increased the total number of "volunteer cleaners" to no less than 800,000 people. How all this affected the health of people long remained unclear. Some research suggested that the sudden rise in physical complaints was largely caused by psychological stress (see Havenaar, 1996). Yet this was one disaster in which the number casualties might not fall, but rather rise with time.

An early report by experts of the International Atomic Energy Agency in Vienna, and some other international organizations claimed that both the radiation and the number of radiation victims had at first been lower than expected; but this claim changed from the early 1990s on. Environmental organizations such as Greenpeace claimed that there was rapid rise in thyroid cancer and other forms of cancer in children and adults; both among evacuees and volunteer cleaners, and that it might only reach its peak at the beginning of the 21st century. In 1994, the Kiev Ministry of Public Health even claimed that rather than 6,000, 125,000 people had died as a direct result of the Chernobyl disaster. Some 432,000 people received medical treatment, and a total of 3.7 million were said to have been affected in the Ukraine alone (according to news dispatches from all major agencies on the ninth anniversary of the event; also see: Glorieux, 1996).

The Byelorussian government estimated that the total clean-up would cost $235 billion dollars, more than 20 times the annual budget of this country of only ten million inhabitants at the time. The promised Western aid of several billion dollars to the region was mostly to go to making the remaining nuclear reactors safer. The Ukraine estimated that 7% of its territory was more or less contaminated; Byelorussia estimated that 30% of its (much smaller) territory was contaminated; and Russia that 1.6% of its (much larger) European territory was contaminated. The aftermath of the disaster, therefore, was to eat up a considerable percentage of the annual income of the people and governments of the three most contaminated "successor states" of the Soviet Union, and to act as another serious obstacle to their economic growth over decades to come.

A further question is how this "chance" accident affected the economic and political history of eastern Europe, western Europe and indeed the rest of the world. Chernobyl was one of the largest of the 18 nuclear plants with a total of 51 reactors in the Soviet Union, which together produced 10% to 15% of the country's nuclear energy. There was no question of completely giving up the plant or any other plants with the same RBMK design, even though it had proven unsafe. Furthermore, at the time there were no independent media or an independent public opinion in the country itself (or elsewhere in eastern Europe) to press for a policy review.

The same did not hold for western Europe, though, where significant groups had already voiced serious doubts about nuclear safety, which provoked further regulation and helped erode competitiveness with other sources of energy. Immediately after the disaster, there had been reports of hoarding of preserved food and antiradiation pills, but also of abortions and suicide attempts. Before Chernobyl, only a minority of public opinion had been opposed to nuclear energy; after Chernobyl this temporarily turned into a majority. If risks were so minimal, people asked, how come the small print in insurance policies from all major companies explicitly excluded nuclear accidents?

The industry line continued to be "It can't happen here" (the title of a video released by the relevant British authority, the CEGB at the time). But even mainstream politicians increasingly came to doubt this claim. Journalists from *The Observer* summed up their view: "The history of technology is littered with examples of new machines failing catastrophically ... The problem is that nuclear power poses dangers on an altogether larger scale" (Hawkes et al., p. 223). Even the *Times* conceded: "After Chernobyl, opponents of nuclear power can no longer be dismissed as green extremists or irrational nonscientists" (Park, 1989, p. 183). A U.K. parliamentary report had earlier concluded that "for most people radiation is inexplicable, unseeable, untouchable and almost mystically evil" (C. Park, 1989, p. 30). These archetypal fears were now revived once more, and came close to crippling the trillion dollar global industry.

A brief review, in Chris Park's (1989) excellent study on *Chernobyl—The Long Shadow* (see also Hawkes et al., 1986) shows that nuclear development was effectively frozen in almost all western European countries for many years. The only exception in western Europe was France. Proportionately, it was the most nuclearized country in the world, with 43 nuclear reactors at the time, producing 65% of its electricity, and with 20 more plants under construction. In France, the government, industry, and even a large part of the media have always been closely interconnected. During the entire Chernobyl episode, the authorities simply denied that there had been any significant fallout in the country at all. Only after citizen groups began to take their own samples and had them tested, and after Monaco reported increased radiation levels, it was reluctantly conceded that the east of France had indeed also been contaminated; radiation levels in the Alsace region, for instance, were up considerably.

On the day I wrote the first version of these lines in France, almost 11 years later, it was suddenly discovered that a family (and live game also) that had feasted on mushrooms collected from "hot spots" in the Vosges region displayed considerable increases in radiation levels. Ten years after Chernobyl, France was the only western European country still starting new construction of plants.

Even the U.S. nuclear industry, the largest in the world in absolute terms, was affected by the fallout from Chernobyl, both in the literal and in the figurative sense. It had 93 reactors producing 15% of all electricity, and 26 more reactors under construction. Chris Park (1989) reported:

> A survey by the national newspaper *USA Today*, soon after the accident, found that 58% of the people interviewed believe the kind of accident which happened at Chernobyl "can happen anywhere." A poll carried out for NBC News and the *Wall Street Journal* found 65% opposed the construction of more nuclear plants. Even stronger antinuclear views were uncovered by a *Washington Post*–ABC poll "which showed a record 78% of people [were] opposed to construction of more nuclear plants in the USA . . . That poll also found that 40% of people wanted existing plants phased out." (pp. 179–180)

The immediate results of the "Great Chernobyl scare" were mixed. On one hand, public opinion in many larger Western countries soon seemed to return to "normal" (Van der Pligt, 1992). On the other hand, relevant authorities still felt forced to "tighten the screws." Thus it became ever more difficult to build and run profitable plants in the developed countries of the First World. European producer Siemens, and American producer General Electric, gave up their plans for the development of a new generation of ordinary reactors; Westinghouse continued, whereas others began exploring different avenues. Much of the further expansion of the nuclear industry shifted to the developing countries of the Third World, where the public and the media would not form and express an independent opinion, so that companies and governments could more easily push through questionable projects. Yet Greenpeace predicted that nuclear energy would largely have been "phased out" in 20 years, and replaced by "clean" sources—although this may prove "wishful thinking" on its part.

There is a last, political (and ideological) dimension to the fallout from Chernobyl. At the time, Christian revivalists in the Soviet Union pointed to the Book of Revelations (8 Rev. 10:11) in the Old Testament, which had predicted that at one point in time, a great disaster would fall from the sky: a star by the name of Wormwood (in Ukrainian: *Chernobila*). It would poison the earth: "A third of the waters became wormwood and many men died from the water, because it was made bitter" (see also Havenaar, 1996; C. Park, 1989).

All over the world, there is a widespread belief that great disasters announce the end of great men and great empires. After the ultimate "sealing" of the reactor, Soviet premier, Mikhail Gorbachov, noted that

> The indisputable lesson of Chernobyl to us is that in conditions of the further development of the scientific and technical revolution, the questions of reliability and safety of equipment, the questions of discipline, order and organization assume priority importance. (C. Park, 1989, p. 165)

Chernobyl drove home the message (to the elite and to the masses), that the Eastern bloc would never match the technological level of the Western alliance, as long as it stuck to authoritarianism and irresponsibility.

Finally, this prepared the ground for the Kremlin belief in the Pentagon bluff that a strategic defense initiative or "Star Wars" shield would soon be able to neutralize Soviet nuclear missiles and thereby effectively disarm them. As Gorbachov later admitted, he felt he neither had the technology nor the money to match such a program. This made him give up the illusion that the Soviet empire or communism could still be saved. He gave up trying to contain the course of events that unfolded in Hungary, Czechoslovakia, and Poland. In 1989, the Berlin Wall fell; in 1991, Germany was reunited. "Wormwood" had contributed significantly to the end of the Cold War, which had dominated half a century of world politics (Remnick, 1993).

As is so often the case with such disasters, it was the result of a concurrence of circumstances. In theory, systems should be fail-safe; in practice, they are not. Every day, there are near misses—disasters that are closely averted, and often not even recognized as such. But every now and then, there is a hit. Events take a radically different turn. If one thing is predictable, therefore, it is that unpredictable things will always happen. We have to expect the unexpected. Because, as one bumper sticker says, "Shit happens!"

The perception of a disaster, and its impact on public opinion, also depend on a concurrence of circumstances. In this case, for instance, outside mistrust was further heightened by the fact that the accident had taken place in the "evil empire." The principle of synchronicity played a role as well. Disaster struck when the elites of the Soviet Union were already vacillating; thus the disaster became the catalyst that pushed awareness over a critical threshold. Developments that had been only vaguely related became intertwined and formed "super patterns." People and groups became sensitive to information that they had dismissed at first. Energy planners and issues managers in the West were taken by surprise. However hard they devised new "information campaigns," they completely lost control; at least for some time—until quiet returned.

THE PHENOMENON OF FORECASTING

In the course of this book, we have referred to a small number of large cases, and a larger number of smaller cases, of "rapid, radical and massive" shifts in public opinion and perception. Sometimes these events were the outcome of an extraordinary concurrence of circumstances, as in the Chernobyl case. It made old issues disappear from, and new issues appear on, the public agenda. It helped change the course of world history. Yet almost nobody had foreseen it, at least not in this particular form. Yet such major unforeseen events happen all the time, and transform the evolving landscape of future possibilities and impossibilities. If one thing is certain, therefore, it is that nothing is certain.

But people want certainty, and so do institutions. If there is no certainty, they will tend to produce it. Since the emergence of the modern natural sciences and the modern sciences of man and society, the emphasis on "measurement, prediction, and control" has consistently increased. According to one recent book, the forecasting business is a flourishing industry, with an estimated turnover of at least $200 billion per annum. After a documented analysis of the seven major forecasting domains, however, its author, William Sherden (1998) concluded that the forecasts that are commonly used as a basis for planning and strategy are only semireliable. They turn out to be reliable where linear developments can be simply extrapolated, and unreliable where nonlinear developments lead to sudden shifts.

This section is a further exploration of this problem, whereas the next section delves deeper into the deeper causes of this state of affairs. Predictions are always useful, except when you trust them to come true.

Technological Innovation and Forecasting

Fortune telling has been a key activity in all cultures and ages. Predicting the future has been labeled "the oldest profession but one." The situation changed somewhat, when the forecasting trade sought scientific underpinnings. It reportedly was the German sociologist Ossip Flechtheim who proposed the term *futurology*, in the wake of World War II. After the war, the Rand Corporation was founded as a "private think tank" in the United States, but came to earn much of its money by developing forecasts and strategic studies for the Air Force. Among others, this led to the 1960 study "On Thermonuclear War," about the chances for (and nature of) a World War III. It had been prepared by Herman Kahn, who said to have been the source of inspiration for the "mad scientist," Dr. Strangelove (played by Peter Sellers in Stanley Kubrick's movie of the same name).

A year later, Kahn set up shop for himself and founded the Hudson Institute in Croton-on-Hudson, New York, which developed "scenarios on the future" for military and civilian authorities, as well as multinational corporations. It soon was the biggest futurological think tank on the east coast, with 50 researchers and 100 consultants. In and around Washington DC, too, similar consultant firms of the so-called "beltway bandits" popped up everywhere. On the west coast, Olaf Helmer became co-founder of the Institute for the Future near Stanford, and was also involved with the Center for Futures Research at the University of Southern California. The forecasters founded a World Futures Society, which attracted many members (Loye, 1978). The discipline soon got a foothold in Europe as well.

During a corporate seminar in 1967, Herman Kahn revealed a list of 100 technical innovations likely to arise over the last $\frac{1}{3}$ of the 20th century. This list then appeared in a popular book, *The Year 2000*, which he published with Anthony Wiener (Kahn & Wiener, 1967). Examples of expected innovations were artificial moons, which would spread light during the night, weather control, and ocean mining. A generation later, Stephen Schnaars (1989) critically evaluated these items in his book, *Megamistakes: Forecasting and the Myth of Rapid Technological Change*. He said $\frac{1}{4}$ of the predictions were too vague to draw a conclusion, but at least $\frac{1}{2}$ were completely wrong. Only 10% proved more or less correct, and some 15% completely right. Since then, a few more items came closer to realization, but the score remains rather unimpressive.

More or less at the same time as the Hudson study, TRW Inc. asked top scientists to participate in a similar "probe of the future." According to Schnaars (1989, p. 10), the resulting predictions proved to be almost completely wrong. Around 1980, they had said, passengers would travel back and forth to the moon, where a permanent base would have been established, powered by a nuclear facility. During those same years, the professional magazine *Industrial Research* interviewed no less than 1,433 experts about the future, but with not much better results. According to Schnaars (1989, p. 23), other scenarios, published by specialized publications such as *Fortune, Business Week*, and the *Wall Street Journal*, also proved wrong. He even concluded that a clear pattern could be interpreted from those miscalculations.

They all assumed, for instance, that new inventions would automatically lead to large-scale and rather obvious applications, and that people would be willing to pay exorbitant prices for them. But the reality was much more complex. According to William Sherden (1998), some reasons why (successful) technological applications are so hard to predict are (a) Unworkable concepts, (b) unknown applications, (c) unproved value, (d) uncertain synergies (with other technologies), (e) creative destruction (of those other technologies), (f) lock-in of standards, and (g) chance events. Impending or current wars might lead to an acceleration of technological innovation somehow related to weapons systems, for example, whereas perceived or actual crises might lead to a deceleration of technological innovation some-how related to luxury products.

Many major breakthroughs in technological developments may have been vaguely sensed but not actually predicted, and their full implications were only slowly understood. According to Sherden (1998) this held for electricity and the light bulb, the telephone and wireless broadcasting, jet engines and radar. He quoted James Martin, who noted that:

> A reasonable forecaster in 1940 would not have predicted the computer; in 1945 he would not have predicted the laser; in 1955 he would not have pre-dicted ... synchronous communication satellites, in 1960 he would not have predicted holography or satellite antennas on rooftops; in 1965 he would not have predicted the hand-held calculator or the spread of microcomputers. (pp. 174, 178)

By contrast, reasonable forecasters did predict that we would today move around by rolling sidewalks and jet-propelled cars, by backpack helicopters or pervasive private planes. Plastic homes would be cleaned by feather-dusting robots. We would all eat dried food, treated with atomic radiation, and so on and so forth.

Throughout the last 50 years, experts were surprised time and again by unforeseen developments in the electronics industry. At the end of World War II, there were almost 1 billion bulky vacuum tubes in use (put end to end, they would circle the globe four times). When I was first writing this, the same capacity could be provided by less than 200 Pentium Pro chips fit-ting into a shoe box. During World War II, experts estimated that the world might need no more than four or five computers in all; this number was soon to be revised. Manufacturer Univac estimated in 1950 that no more than 1,000 would be in use by the end of the century, but by 1984 there were already 1,000,000. Around that time, many insiders still felt that home com-puters were unneeded. As late as the early 1990s, huge players such as IBM and Microsoft held that the Internet was of little consequence; so techno-logical forecasting is very complicated indeed—even with the help of com-puters.

The uses, profits (and joys) that customers can expect to derive from in-novations are always decisive. Steven Schnaars (1989) provided three prac-tical guidelines for a sober evaluation of product chances: First of all:

> Avoid technological wonder (p. 143). Secondly: Ask fundamental questions about the markets. Their size, the customers, the benefits of the product, its cost-effectiveness, the realized economies and adequate pricing. But also

whether the product fits into a wider trend or implies a radical break and goes against entrenched habits (pp. 144–145). Third, and most of all: Stress a down-to-earth analysis and eliminate harebrained schemes (p. 147).

Because that is what was wrong with the forecasts mentioned before, which proved way off the mark.

Economic Innovation and Forecasting

If it is so difficult to foresee technological developments, then how difficult is it to develop adequate approaches to strategic planning and management? The little booklet, "Developing Leadership for the 21st Century" (1996), observed that the old "controllosaurus" is becoming extinct, and that the CEO of tomorrow must be able to lead a team, be versatile, and be flexible. The military and technobureaucratic mentality must make room for people's own initiatives and self-organization, particularly within departments at the beginning and at the end of the line, such as research and development, and marketing and advertising. The organization must primarily be managed through a vision and a culture in which all employees can easily recognize themselves; but they must primarily be driven by their own motivation and insight. That is easier said than done.

Similar recommendations had earlier emerged from the worldwide bestseller *In Search of Excellence: Lessons From America's Best-Run Companies*, by Thomas Peters and Robert Waterman (1982). But within 5 years after its publication, $\frac{2}{3}$ of the exalted corporations proved to be excellent no more (Stacey, 1993). Had their recipes become outdated? Had they become complacent? Or was the whole eternal quest for miracle cures perhaps an illusion? Peter Allen (1994) later noted: "technological evolution is not about a single type of firm 'winning,' through its superior behavior, since, as we see, evolution is characterized more by increasing variety and complexity than the opposite" (p. 15). A study by Shell concluded that on average, companies' lifespans were found to be only half that of people, and that the famous Fortune 500 rankings of major corporations reveal spectacular rises and falls over the years.

After 10 years of research, Steven Schnaars concluded in an article: "There are almost no cases of companies that successfully predicted long-term trends and acted upon them" (see Sherden, 1998, p. 233). This may sound somewhat exaggerated, but his book gave scores of examples of companies that dominated in their respective fields, but proved unable to recognize key new trends and product developments, and were swept aside. So in his own book, Schnaars (1989) drew important conclusions about growth-markets: (a) Invention does not always lead to commercial success, (b) innovation comes from the outside, (c) ultimate uses and forms and customers are unforeseen, (d) growth will take longer than expected, and (e) timing is crucial.

Older reports from the Batelle Institute had said that it took twenty years on average for a technological breakthrough to lead to a successful industrial mass product (Schnaars, 1989, p. 138). But today in many sectors, these periods are considerably shorter. What happens is basically that ever new combinations and variations are tried out, and that only one survives.

John Ketteringham and P. Ranganath Nayak (1986) said that it was not so much products but rather markets that were invented in this way. Gary Hamel and C. K. Prahalad (1994) noted in *Competing for the Future* that far-sightedness about future markets could only be developed by relinquishing near-sightedness about present markets, products, and price-performance assumptions, and by being really focused on the customer and his needs; by being unprejudiced and curious, modest, and eclectic; as well as contrarian and creative.

In their book *Breakthroughs*, Ketteringham and Nayak (1986) of the consulting firm Arthur Little, said that there are major myths about successful innovations: Namely, that they result from ideas that no one had before, were realized by inventors, by "little people," that they needed considerable investments, a special environment, and were always reactions to unfulfilled needs. But reality is entirely different, they noted. An invention is a new configuration of elements, which develops in steps, through the involvement of many diverse parties. Its potential is hard to fathom, both for producers and consumers. It is a kind of Gestalt switch or "Aha" experience, which must be reached.

The economist Brian Arthur (1990), once explained in the *Scientific American* why market forecasters were so often wrong. He said that it was hard for them to concede that things could still move in many different directions. Minor random events could even prove decisive, because they could start a positive feedback loop, whereby small advantages might rapidly translate into complete market dominance. This already held for traditional branches such as mining and industry, but it held even more for ultramodern branches such as electronics and information. The original investment in product or "content" was sometimes considerable, but the cost of extra copies could be almost negligible, and extra turnover might thus help profits explode. We should therefore "portray the economy not as simple but as complex, not as deterministic, predictable and mechanistic but as process-dependent, organic and always evolving" (Arthur, 1990, p. 85).

Illustrations of this observation can be found in computers, peripherals, and programming (as well as in the media). One example was the user-friendly home computer that had originally been developed (but not immediately mass-produced) by Xerox, which was improved by Apple Macintosh and even threatened IBM. Game maker Atari in turn doubled its turnover every year between 1977 and 1982, but soon lost out to the more sophisticated products of Nintendo. From 1984 on, Hewlett-Packard attacked the printer market; after 10 years, this product had a $10 billion dollar turnover. Sony introduced CD-Rom players in 1985 and sold 10 million in 7 years, and then another 10 million in 7 months (Moore, 1995). Microsoft bought the DOS computer system for $50,000, and sold it to IBM and its clones. After that, the introduction of the Windows computer system by Microsoft soon made its owner, Bill Gates, the richest man in the world. But it was largely based on the principles that Xerox and Apple Macintosh had pioneered long before. So it really is like a horse race, with new candidates pulling up and others falling behind all the time.

Thus, developments in what is today called the Information and Communication Technology (ICT) business can be capricious and hard to predict; fortunes can be created and destroyed over periods of years or even months. This has turned classical thinking on its head regarding the spread of innovations. According to the aforementioned ideas of Everett Rogers (1995), the innovator must conquer the five customer categories of innovators and early adopters, the early and late majority, and finally the laggards—one after the other. But according to *Inside the Tornado: Marketing Strategies From Silicon Valley's Cutting Edge* by Geoffrey Moore (1995), this demands a repeated flip-flop in strategy, at exactly the right moments: "That is, the very behaviors that make a company successful at the outset of the mainstream market cause failure inside the tornado [immediately thereafter] and must be abandoned" (p. 10). Other authors, too, emphasize the vital importance of a correct appreciation of "windows of opportunity" and acting "just in time" in today's business environment.

Rather than "eternal recipes," the rapid changeability of the market must be the continuous focus of management's attention—and therefore a radically different way of developing and implementing policies must be used. The relevant force field is always complex and dynamic; it also demands a thorough appreciation of societal trends and opinion currents.

Social Innovation and Forecasting

Technological and economic developments are interwoven with social trends. The invention of the steam engine and of the combustion motor, for instance, long seemed to be an unequivocal blessing. Factories and electrical plants, heating and air-conditioning, cars and ships brought products, comfort and mobility; first for a small group, then for the majority of the population in Western countries. After decolonization had been more or less completed in the 1960s, the road seemed to be wide open to a further spreading of the immense benefits of the Industrial Revolution. So the aforementioned "futurologist" Herman Kahn predicted, that the year 2000 would mark the beginning of a long period of stability and growth throughout the world (Kahn & Wiener, 1967).

But with the help of very similar methods of forecasting, others reached conclusions that were diametrically opposed. One could, of course, extrapolate rising numbers on production and consumption in this way, these others said. But one could also extrapolate rising numbers on raw materials and waste in this way. If all continents were to reach the same spending levels as North America and western Europe, they said, stocks would soon become depleted and the environment would soon be overburdened.

There would not be enough resources and food for a growing population. In 1967, William and Paul Paddock published their study on *Famine*; in 1968, Paul Ehrlich published his study on *The Population Bomb*. The alarmist mood caught on and spread. During 1968, a group of concerned scientists and policymakers met in the Italian capital and formed the Club of Rome. Money to support its activities initially came from a foundation with Fiat funds, and later from a foundation with Volkswagen funds.

Through a board member, contact was made with Jay Forrester and the famed Massachusetts Institute of Technology in Cambridge, Massachusetts, which had just begun to make the first computer models of future world developments. A team was formed under the leadership of Dennis Meadows. The results of the first study came out in 1970, and were later supplemented and published as *The Limits to Growth*. In various editions and languages, no less than nine million copies were sold. The major conclusion was that if current developments were allowed to continue, the beginning of the new millennium would be characterized by rising shortages and pollution. These trends would reach their peak around the mid-21st century, and ultimately lead to a complete breakdown of civilized society. The plausibility of this scenario seemed to receive a further boost by the founding of the Organization of Petroleum Exporting Countries (OPEC), which initiated major oil price hikes in the 1970s and provoked a worldwide shock wave.

With hindsight, it is easy to criticize these doom scenarios. Estimates for stocks, for instance, had been limited to known reserves exploited at current prices; whereas new reserves could be developed at higher prices, and even substitutes found. The authors had not dealt with the continued weakness and division of the Third World; or with the continued strength and power of the First World and its multinational corporations, which soon began to spread supplies and build strategic reserves to contain prices; nor had they included the effects of their own publications on environmental awareness and conservation policies. So the reports of the Club of Rome are a good illustration of a "self-defeating prophecy." As is so often the case, the predictions contributed to their own failure (because human social behavior is not a completely "blind" process).

Dealing With Unpredictability

Every now and then, there is an expert or a fortune teller who claims to have predicted this or that uncertain event with certainty. But usually, there are various problems with such claims. First of all, one must check how these predictions were exactly formulated, and whether or not they included time, place, and details. Second, one must check whether that prediction was made public, and in the presence of independent observers—preferably skeptics, who were well equipped to see through ambiguities. Third, one must check whether there were no other signs pointing in that direction. Finally one must check whether the expert or fortune teller made more such predictions, and whether there was more than a chance probability that he or she scored a hit (think of the old practice of putting 10 different predictions in sealed envelopes in 10 different places, or even entrusting them to 10 different notaries, and then to have only the correct one discovered after the fact).

If all kinds of people make all kinds of predictions all of the time, one is bound to come true every now and then, but this hardly proves extraordinary powers. So among the thousands of fortune tellers making predictions for the New Year, a few will always be right ("A government leader will be shot"; "A disaster will strike the country"). According to critics of the "expert" prediction business, such as Schnaars (1989) and Sherden (1998), only very lame forecasts come true—most of the time. With respect to economists, for instance, Sherden (1998) concluded, after scrutinizing the evidence:

> They cannot predict turning points, their skill is as good as guessing, there are no individuals/schools/ideologies doing consistently better, increased sophistication provides no improvement, etcetera. And he quoted Nobel Prize winner Paul Samuelson, who said, "I don't believe we're converging on ever improving forecast accuracy. It's almost as if there's a Heisenberg . . . [Uncertainty] principle." (p. 68)

That is exactly the point of this book. We take a closer look at it in the next section of this chapter.

Over the years, then, there have been all kind of attempts to improve forecasting methods in different fields. Once upon a time, there was just "trend analysis" (when tendencies clearly visible in statistics and graphs were just extrapolated to the future). Then came "scenario analysis," which usually identifies three possibilities (even today); namely, everything will go on as before, things may get slightly better, or things may get slightly worse. Then there is the "Delphi method," which submits a range of questions to a range of experts; the answers are ordered into various categories, then resubmitted for comment and suggestions. This procedure may be repeated a number of times. One may ultimately try to distill a consensus, or majority and minority views, or a range of patterns, accompanied or not with numbers and percentages (for probability). The latest twist is to have experts bet significant amounts of their own private money on possible outcomes; within this entire framework, this method produces the best results.

But there is a fundamental problem with all these approaches, whether they are applied by experts or lay people, because the future is always predicted on the basis of the past and the present. A generation's "memory span" may play a role. If there has been a major war or crisis less than 20 or 40 years ago, then this possibility is still taken into account; but after that, it fades from people's perspective. The "spirit of the times" may play a role, or "situational bias." It is in the terms of the present that one tries to grasp the future. This is nowhere more clear than in science fiction, however imaginative, because it usually turns out to bear identifiable traces of the specific time in which it was created. The same even holds for many "scientific" forecasts, because it is extremely hard to make a Gestalt switch, or a cognitive "jump" into an entirely different reality. Or, as creativity gurus say: Learning new assumptions and reflexes is difficult, unlearning old assumptions and reflexes is even harder.

The heart of the matter is the fact that the future does not exist—not yet; nor is it entirely predefined. But instinctively, we always tend to see the future as a simple extrapolation of the present and the past. This may do in 9 cases out of 10, but the ultimate tenth case may be nonlinear and profoundly alter the name of the game. As long as systems are more or less in equilibrium, changes are often proportional and linear, and easy to predict. But as soon as systems slide far out of equilibrium, minute details may provoke dramatic shifts, and prediction is largely in vain. Furthermore, dynamic developments interact in complex ways. This means that fundamental aspects of the future cannot and will not be foreseen, whatever "model builders" claim.

We may continue to do things "as if," except that we will be taken by surprise every now and then; so we must take things from there and muddle through. But it might be better to give up our mechanicistic illusions of "measurement, prediction and control," to accept uncertainty as a key fact of life, and to incorporate it into our strategic thoughts and actions; because at the level of metaprinciples, it has become increasingly clear, *why* the future will always continue to surprise us.

THE METAPRINCIPLE OF FUNDAMENTAL UNCERTAINTY

In the course of the last 10 chapters, we have seen how a series of metaprinciples may contribute to sudden shifts, and how we can try to conceptualize nonlinear change in different terms. Nine times out of ten, the paradigm of Newton's apple seems to be relatively adequate to help us understand what is going on; but every once in awhile, we really need the paradigm of Lorenz's butterfly instead. Infinitely small details may become decisive in the dissolution of an existing pattern, and the emergence of a new one (Tennekes, 1990). It is very important, then, to recognize that for that reason, the future may often turn out radically different from what we imagine today, rather than to trust that everything will always be "under control."

From the early 20th century on, the metaprinciple of *fundamental uncertainty* began to assert itself in physics: in Albert Einstein's relativity theory, for instance, although he himself did not recognize the ultimate consequences; or in Werner Heisenberg and others' quantum theory, which said that precise measurement and prediction were unattainable at the electron level—for fundamental reasons. The latter gave this observation a wider significance by proclaiming "the uncertainty principle." Many scientists long remained reluctant to accept its implications, but many philosophers soon went along, because, they said, total control was an illusion.

Ironically, it was the gradual spread and refinement of the computer itself that ultimately put "incomputability" on the map (Broer, Van de Craats, & Verhulst, 1995). It turned out that the outcome of many complex adaptive processes could not be foreseen. In this section, we take a closer look at the subprinciples of immeasurability, unpredictability, and uncontrollability. They have suddenly been recognized to be all around, not only in the natural sciences, but also in the sciences of man and society (Van Dijkum & De Tombe, 1992). Rapid, radical, and massive shifts in public opinion and perception, too, are sometimes immeasurable, unpredictable, and uncontrollable for similar, fundamental reasons.

Infinite Detail, Fractals, and Immeasurability

In everyday life, as well as in scientific research, we often implicitly assume that it is relatively easy to decide "whatever is the case," and what the exact proportions of the units and forces "at play" are in a particular situation. But this is far from being always the case. Often, for instance, the precision of a measurement may be related to the precision of the instrument employed. A more precise instrument would have produced a more precise measurement, with many more decimals. In many cases, one could go on forever, refining it; even in such a seemingly unimportant case as measuring the length, width, and height of a brick (but this is even more problematic with "natural" forms).

Mathematicians illustrated this with the so-called "coastline" problem (Davies, 1989, pp. 57–58; Gleick, 1987, pp. 91–92; Stewart, 1997, pp. 203–204). If we want to measure the length of the coastline of an island, such as England (plus Scotland and Wales), then we also choose a scale at which we mean to do this. If we use a minimal measuring unit of one hundred kilometers, then we may end up finding a total length for the coastline of 3,800 kilometers. But if we use a minimal measuring unit half as big of say, 50 kilometers, then we will note that the length of the same coastline has suddenly grown to some 6,000 kilometers. If we use a minimal measuring unit that is even smaller (a kilometer, a meter, a millimeter), then the coastline continues to "grow." So how long is the coastline of England? It depends! The same holds for many other measures of natural phenomena, which we employ unthinkingly. Because much of reality is "infinitely frayed."

The French mathematician Benoît Mandelbrot discovered, in turn, that the edges and fringes of many natural objects have very special characteristics. Traditional geometry is almost completely irrelevant in rendering these forms.

> One reason lies in its inability to describe the shape of a cloud, a mountain, a coastline, or a tree. Clouds are not spheres, mountains are not cones, coastlines are not circles, and bark is not smooth, nor does lightning travel in a straight line . . . Nature exhibits not simply a higher degree but an altogether different level of complexity. The number of different scales of length of natural patterns is for all practical purposes infinite. (quoted by Eiser, 1994, p. 175)

Mandelbrot therefore proposed a radically different geometry, with a radically different set of basic forms. He labeled these "fractals" after the Latin word *frangere* (breaking). *Fractals* are forms that display the same basic pattern at an infinite number of levels. Think of a branch that branches into two branches, which further branches into four branches, and so on. Whether one enlarges such a pattern 10 times, 1,000 times or 1 zillion times, one may sometimes see the same pattern recur time and again. This produces an infinitely complex figure, but it can result from applying a set of relatively simple rules, over and over (Lauwerier, 1992). According to Mandelbrot, many natural phenomena follow this fractal principle, on many different levels, although of course not really infinitely; it holds for coastlines and mountains, as well as for streams or thunderbolts. "Living" nature follows this same principle even more frequently for generating complex forms, such as ferns or cauliflowers, lungs or brains.

There is good reason to reconsider mental and social forms and patterns in the light of such observations about infinite details and fractals. When he had just come to work for IBM, for instance, Mandelbrot discovered that many, free-market, price-formation patterns followed fractal principles; for instance, cotton prices, which had long been registered in the United States, and in great detail. The price charts formed zig-zag patterns. If one "zoomed in" on them, they revealed even finer zig-zag patterns; and so on. Many charts and tables are the result of rounding off, which hides finer details. Yet such infinitely small details may well become decisive in dynamic interactions with other "frayed" variables.

In a sense, economists even have an advantage here, because market prices and trade volumes are traced and registered in such great detail in many domains, and have acquired the status of "hard facts" and "objective data." Psychologists and sociologists are at a disadvantage, by contrast, because similarly subtle shifts in meaning attribution may not be traced and registered as massively, permanently, and in great detail; yet it is clear that similar principles apply there. The evolution of opinions and attitudes held by individuals or groups, for instance, may well follow fractallike, infinitely detailed, zig-zag patterns.

In popularity polls for politicians, or electoral preference for parties, this is clearly visible—although in a much cruder form. The inevitable imperfections of "measurement techniques," furthermore, often translate into inevitable imperfections in predicted outcomes; particularly whenever there is a face-off of two parties or coalitions of comparable strength, and 51% against 49% may be decisive—as is often the case. (In such electoral confrontations, also, complex patterns may display a tendency to evolve into subtle levels of self-organized criticality which we discussed in chap. 8). So that until the very last moment, it remains unclear "which way the cookie will crumble."

Unstable Equilibrium, Bifurcations, and Unpredictability

So many natural phenomena are 'frayed'; their exact dimensions may be hard to give; it depends with what level of detail we are satisfied. But if there are such infinitely small differences, then there also is an infinitely big chance that two natural objects, forces, or processes are not entirely the same size; and an infinitely big chance that they cannot remain in equilibrium for a prolonged period. If inertia or resistance do not play a role, then one phenomenon will sooner or later prove bigger or stronger than the other, even if only slightly so. So perfect equilibrium is rather rare; potential disequilibrium is rather ubiquitous. Note that this is even the case in "straightforward" confrontations, which do not yet involve exponential factors.

Because we usually do not know the smallest details of the phenomena in question, the outcome of confrontations or interactions may always surprise us; it can go one way or the other (very often, it is hard to say). Many developments are thus characterized by so-called *bifurcations*, which introduce a further element of unpredictability. Even more so, when there is a succession of bifurcations one after the other, it is even harder to foresee the outcome. On some occasions, these bifurcations come increasingly close to each other; in these cases, we speak of a "bifurcation cascade." This is particularly the case when a system slides into a "far from equilibrium" state, into turbulence and/or chaos; because under these conditions, infinitely small details may define the patterns that ultimately emerge.

If a confrontation between two apparently equal forces may have an unpredictable outcome, this holds even more for a confrontation between three apparently equal forces. This is well illustrated by the so-called "three magnets" experiment in physics. In it, one places three magnets of equal strength at an equal distance from each other, at the angles of an equilateral triangle, and assigns each one a primary color—red, blue, and yellow. At a well-defined height above them, one releases a pendulum, for instance, a white iron ball on the end of a string. It will move back and forth, but ultimately come to rest over one of the three attractor points. One may try to map how various original points of release translate into various outcomes.

Right under the original position of the ball, for instance, one may paint a dot in the color of the magnet above which the ball ultimately comes to rest. The next time, the outcome must be exactly the same because the force field remains the same. But if one repeats this a thousand times, a curious pattern emerges. Immediately around the magnets, there will be a monolithic area in the same color; this is to be expected. But between these areas, surprisingly, considerable intermediary zones are far from well-defined. They form an extremely detailed fractal pattern, reminiscent of the many-colored, "Turkish" comb patterns that one could find on the special paper used for the inside of old book covers (that is to say, infinitely frayed and closely intertwined). In practice, therefore, it is completely impossible to predict where the ball will go when released. If the outcome of a confrontation between three comparable electromagnetic forces is so unpredictable, then how capricious may it be for a confrontation between three comparable psychosocial forces?

But let us return from this complex, three-way confrontation to a simpler, two-way confrontation. We are all familiar with simple, two-way equilibria from popular psychology (e.g., the perception of ambiguous stimuli; i.e., stimuli that can be perceived in two radically different and mutually incompatible ways). Simple examples are line-drawings of cubes or stairs, which one can equally well interpret as "seen from above" or "seen from below." A slightly more complex example is that of the vase shape, formed by two opposite faces. Still more complex examples are famous comical drawings such as "my wife and my mother-in-law," or "the hunter and the rabbit." Usually one recognizes one possible interpretation right away, and has trouble making the Gestalt switch to recognizing the other as well, or going back and forth. Our expectations or "mind-sets" play a key role. Think of the series A, B, and C; and the series 12, 13, and 14. The characters in the middle may have almost the same shape, but are automatically interpreted in contrasting ways—because our expectations (mind-sets) differ.

This does not only hold for perception, but for thinking as well. We do not think logically, but psychologically; that is to say, we use simple heuristics or rules-of-thumb—simplified ways to reach rapid conclusions. In doing this, we often make mistakes. This is demonstrated by riddles and brain twisters, employed in society games such as "Mind Trap," but also by magicians and crooks. Our thinking thrives on simplifications and generalizations, and also on stereotypes and discriminations. We constantly refer to our background (age, gender) and experience (education, culture) to reduce complex patterns to simple ones.

Different groups do this in different ways, by definition, and often in opposite ways. Think of the audience perceptions of the classic 1960's and 1970's comedy, "All in the Family." The main character, Archie Bunker, made derogatory remarks all the time; the idea was that viewers would laugh because it was such nonsense. But research showed that many viewers identified with him, by contrast, mocking "politically correct" views about women, youngsters, and minorities. So liberals and conservatives "read" the same texts and images in completely opposite ways. Also think of the ways in which major racial confrontations in the United States are interpreted differently by Whites and Blacks: the Rodney King affair, the Los Angeles riots, the O.J. Simpson case.

Or think of the opposite ways in which president Bill Clinton's affair with intern, Monica Lewinsky, was read by liberal Democrats or conservative Republicans, which stirred an unexpected electoral backlash in the late 1998 congressional re-elections. The course, power, and speed of such processes of reaction formation (around a person or institution, a brand or an issue) are characteristically hard to predict. Many details play a role. Fairly recently, a DNA test proved beyond a doubt that the admired president Thomas Jefferson, had indeed had children out of wedlock with his Black mistress. It reinforced the popular belief that many high-placed politicians may on occasion be adulterous without necessarily being bad leaders.

The finding, at exactly this point in time, created one of those unpredictable coincidences that may have considerable consequences. In this context, one may refer to the principle of "synchronicity." Paul Davies (1989) said:

> One can envisage constellations of events in spacetime, associated in some meaningful way, yet without causal association. These events may or may not be spacelike separated, but their conjunction or association might not be attributable to causal action. They would form patterns or groupings in spacetime representing a form of order that would not follow from the ordinary laws of physics. (p. 163)

One may attribute a role to synchronicity in physical or chemical processes, but also in biological or psychological processes. The famous physicist Wolfgang Pauli, and psychologist Carl Gustav Jung, even tried to assign synchronicity some kind of paranormal or supernatural role (Van Meij-gaard, 1998). But one may very well accept the principle without making that final step.

Chance, Contingency, and Uncontrollability

There is a third level of certainty and uncertainty, namely that of free will and choice, but also of management and control. It has been suggested that human free will is a function of bifurcations, and always balances on the edge of two equal opportunities. Physicist Freeman Dyson, surmised:

> I think our consciousness is not a passive epiphenomenon carried along by the chemical events in our brains, but is an active agent forcing the molecular complexes to make choices between one quantum state and another.

And physicist James Crutchfield said:

> Innate creativity may have an underlying chaotic process that selectively am-plifies small fluctuations and molds them into macroscopic coherent mental states that are experienced as thoughts. In some cases, the thoughts may be decisions, or what are perceived to be the exercise of will. (quoted by Davies, 1989, p. 190)

This may not only hold for the mental level, but also for the social one. Certain isolated acts of certain isolated individuals may give a radically different twist to a course of events (also see Turner, 1997). Think of the Chernobyl case.

This also brings us back to the role of individual action in history, and to "what if" questions. Would the historical process indeed have taken a different turn if certain major leaders had not come to power (such as Alexander and Caesar, Cromwell or Napoleon, Bismarck or Lenin; to limit ourselves to some noteworthy leaders of major European empires)? Would the historical process indeed have taken a different turn, if these leaders had made slightly different decisions at major junctions? The outbreak of various major wars, for instance, was not only triggered by huge forces but also by minor incidents. Furthermore, at least one of the major leaders or countries or alliances severely miscalculated their ultimate outcome. Would there have been a nuclear war, if key players had misjudged the "missile crisis" around Cuba (and Turkey) in October, 1962? Sherden (1998) gave various examples of decisive battles, which gave history another turn because either weather conditions changed abruptly or weather predictions proved wrong.

More peaceful illustrations of unpredictability and uncontrollability come from social geography. As soon as the "attractiveness" of a certain place in a certain domain slightly begins to outshine that of the next, everyone may begin to flock to it. A different urbanization or industrialization pattern may take over and become relatively autonomous (e.g., see Prigogine & Stengers, 1984; and Arthur, 1988). A mere concurrence of circumstances made a handful of early electronics producers converge on what is now Silicon Valley: the climate, the proximity of some first-rate universities, of some major transport junctions, and so on. Today, it has more than 1,000 of those firms. The conurbation has surpassed nearby San Francisco as the 11th urban economy of the United States, and has surpassed New York in the value of its exports (*IHT*, 1998). Elsewhere in the country and in the world, urban planners confidently proclaim every now and then that they will build Silicon Valleys of their own; but that does not happen.

Of all the miscalculations of planners and managers, however, the most fascinating are those where an initiative results in the exact opposite of what was intended. It happens all the time. In his fascinating book, *Management of the Absurd*, psychologist Richard Farson (1996) pointed out that policymakers ask outside consultants for "quick and clean" solutions to "dirty and stubborn" problems. Whatever does not fit onto one overhead sheet cannot be taken into serious consideration because it produces too much confusion in too many people. This also explains why there is a merry-go-round of management fashions, in which one panacea is often replaced by its exact opposite: expansion versus downsizing, diversification versus core business, and so on. Farson, by contrast, emphasizes that every deal is both good and bad, leadership is essentially the management of dilemmas, and tolerating ambiguities is a fundamental quality.

The chapters scan all kinds of domains for which this is true. Farson (1996) counseled, "Once you find a management technique that works, give it up" (p. 35). Other chapter titles are "Effective Managers Are Not in Control"; "The More We Communicate, the Less We Communicate"; "Listening is More Difficult Than Talking"; "Big Changes Are Easier to Make Than Small Ones"; "Planning is an Ineffective Way to Bring About Change"; "Every Great Strength is a Great Weakness"; "The More Experienced the Managers, the More They Trust Simple Intuition"; "To Be a Professional, One Must Be an Amateur"; "Lost Causes Are the Only Ones Worth Fighting For"; and last but not least, "My Advice is, Don't Take My Advice." Similar observations can be found in Senge's (1990) book on the (non) learning organization, and in the book by Dauphinais, Price, and Pederson (1996) on paradoxes. Farson (1996) illustrated his own book with a great number of examples of self-defeating strategies, for instance, in the environmental domain:

In Pakistan, for instance, applying the technology of irrigation and fertilization to land that does not drain adequately has had such adverse effects that more land is going out of cultivation than is being brought under cultivation. Closer to home, we have come to see that air-conditioning pollutes the air, widening highways increases congestion not only on the highway but in the cities and towns that it connects; pesticides and preservatives endanger our health. With every application of technology a counterforce develops that is the exact opposite of what we intended. (p. 45)

A generation earlier, the social philosopher Ivan Illich tried to document in some controversial books that clinics and hospitals are bad for our health, and that schools and universities are bad for our intellect. (I tend to agree from my own experience).

So it is very important to recognize that certain developments follow their own course, and may not as easily be corrected as we think. Many phenomena are fundamentally immeasurable, unpredictable, and uncontrollable; therefore, we will always be taken by surprise. Because the course of events may always take a different turn from what we expected (e.g., through capricious reaction formation). This does not only hold for natural phenomena, but also for psychosocial phenomena. It is a fundamental principle of dynamic evolution within CASs. Public opinion and the public perception of people and institutions, products and issues, are only a special case. Sooner or later, there will always be major developments, which come by complete surprise; therefore the question is whether something like completely confident "issues management" is a realistic proposition.

12

Epilogue:
Issues Management?

The illusion of knowing what's going to happen is worse than not knowing.
  —James Utterback, American professor (Sherden, 1998, p. 191)

So let us briefly recapitulate the central argument of our book at this point. We have repeatedly observed that our engrained thinking about the world time and again tends toward reification: a kind of conventional "thingishness" is continually ascribed to it, implying unequivocality, permanence, substance, extension, and so forth. The interaction between phenomena, furthermore, is usually understood in mechanicist terms; implying regularity and proportionality of effects. Such assumptions often lead scientists and managers to put a too much trust in the "measurability, predictability, and controllability" of processes.

In recent years, however, the natural sciences have (re)discovered radically different views. Many phenomena are reinterpreted in terms of CASs, driven particle ensembles, and so forth. Large numbers of similar entities and relationships constantly form and reform dynamic configurations, which are eternally evolving. This may imply rapid shifts between levels; between what is visible or invisible, manifest or latent, realized or potential. On one hand, the details mutate all the time. On the other hand, many of these minute changes have little effect on the whole, a few have some effect, and an even smaller number has a considerable effect; for example, through positive feedback, amplification, or circular reaction. The result is that seemingly capricious and disproportional reactions may occur (radical shifts).

"Emergence" manifests itself at three different levels: First, at the level of synergy; processes running parallel may come to manifest themselves in convergence, synchronization, and resonance. This undermines resistance to change, and boosts power. Second, at the level of pattern formation, such as association networks or communication networks; only one new interconnection between such networks, for instance, may provoke a decisive reconfiguration. Third, some kind of self-organization may appear: self-reference, self-production, self-reproduction. This may bring a shift in "locus of control." New processes result from previous processes, but cannot be reduced to them.

To these basic principles, one may add a few others. The principle that entities, relations, and processes are usually nested in others. Phenomena must be seen in their contexts, situations must be placed in a wider evolutionary perspective, etcetera. This also draws renewed attention to the fact that time is irreversible, that two situations are almost never completely identical, and that we must be careful not to put too much trust in "timeless" laws. Processes may slow down or gear up, reversals may occur whenever critical thresholds or critical mass are reached, and even catastrophes may be provoked. Though seemingly capricious, these processes are not completely arbitrary. Many well-defined CASs tend to evolve in certain probable directions; of so-called attractors. A final observation is that all this may lead to a qualitatively different state, to a phase transition.

Such metaprinciples turn out to apply rather well to a range of enigmatic phenomena previously studied within the disciplines of mass psychology and collective behavior sociology. The principle of *ubiquitous mutation*, for instance, can well be illustrated in the realm of informal communication and conversation, hearsay and rumor. The principle of *positive feedback* can well be illustrated in the realm of formal communication and media hypes. The threefold *emergence processes* of synergy, pattern formation, and self-organization can well be illustrated in the three traditional domains of crowds, opinion currents, and social movements. After that, we further delved into public moods and shifts. In the success or failure of fashions and fads, for instance, the principle of evolving contexts seems to play a key role. In the triggering of fear and panic, in turn, the principle of critical thresholds seems to play a predominant role. And in the expression of outrage and hostility, the principle of *possible attractors* is somehow manifest.

In the last part, finally, we observed that in composite public mood shifts, such as crazes and crashes, the principle phase transitions may deepen our insight. In the preceding chapter, this brought us back to the initial observation that measurement, prediction, and control can often be useful, but sometimes not. Whenever we try to anticipate the outcome of technological, economic, and social developments, we must acknowledge that these are fraught with fundamental uncertainties. Therefore flexibility and alertness are prime requirements, as well as an open mind. The latter seems relatively easy, but is extremely difficult, because our personal history and everyday interaction with like-minded people within large institutions continually indoctrinate us with the seemingly obvious and self-evident "truths" of the past and present, and make us forget the unprecedented nature of the future.

So we have seen that opinions and attitudes, perceptions and images, may shift much more rapidly, radically, and massively than we generally supposed. This has probably always been the case, but is certainly true for a so-called mass society, mass media society, and media society (see Giner, 1976, for a history of these notions). Mass and media societies can be approached in different ways.

One might well claim that we derive our beliefs ever less from our own "direct" everyday experience, and that we increasingly derive them from all kinds of obviously "mediated" information (particularly education, science and the media). Furthermore, this information can circulate quicker and be evoked in ever more lively ways than before. This holds particularly true for the multimedia revolution currently under way, in which connections and transformations, data and video images seem to melt into one huge global information maelstrom. The incipient revolution of "virtual reality" seems to be only one final step.

One may just as well claim that this increasing volatility is counterbalanced by new stabilizing processes, such as all kinds of new ties between the individual and the collective; for example, on the intermediary level of the wholly new world of voluntary associations, which has sprung up over the last 100 years or so; lately, even on the international level of nongovernmental organizations and new social movements such as Greenpeace, Doctors Without Borders, Amnesty International, etcetera. So it would be simplistic just to decry uprooting; the individual is also rerooted back into society in many new and unprecedented ways.

It is true that governments, corporations, and other social actors have to learn to deal with an increasingly complex world in which it is not only important what they objectively are and do, but also how they are subjectively experienced and seen (Boorstin, 1961/1980). Perceptions and images emerge, which play a growing role in determining their effectiveness. It is not surprising that those involved try to shape these by using the means at their disposal: power, money, demagoguery; not only their own image, but the perception of all issues in which they somehow have a stake.

They have gradually become aware that they are not simply dealing with "the public" or only one audience, but with many publics or partial audiences for whom entirely different issues are of importance. Take the example of a company. A first public is that of the shareholders and the stockmarket, the banks and the financial world. The second public is that of the competitors, trade organizations, and the economic world. The third public is that of the employees, the unions, and the social world. The fourth public is that of possible future employees, schools, and the educational world. The fifth public is that of the clients, distribution chains, and consumers in general. The sixth public is that of civil servants, relevant departments, and the authorities in general. The seventh public is that of politicians, parties, and the electoral world. The eighth public is that of news reporters, media people, and opinion leaders in general. The ninth public is that of action groups, societal organizations, and associational life in general. The tenth public is that of plant neighbors, coinhabitants of quarters and towns. And there are more. One-sided corporate communication strategies (e.g., too overtly privileging the first over the other nine) are often at the root of major tensions. Effective communication strategies know how to juggle publics and issues (I say that somewhat cynically).

In all these domains, issues do constantly come and go, which may facilitate or burden key contacts. So senior communications managers have an obvious interest in following the changes in this many-faceted forcefield as closely as they can (Van Riemsdijk, 1994). There are various ways to do this. One must follow the media; both the specialized and the general ones. This may be further structured by an ongoing formal content analysis of relevant news and an ongoing discourse analysis of the arguments currently popular. One must follow survey results of opinion and attitude research. This may be further enhanced by qualitative probing through in-depth interviews and focus groups. And finally, senior policy makers must establish and explore informal personal contacts with a wide range of concerned people from different backgrounds. Management, marketing and communication, by "walking around," may provide important insights and signals, provided one knows how to "appreciate" them. Always beware of the proverbial ivory tower.

Once issues have crystallized, form and content may become hard to influence decisively. For that reason, interested parties try to intervene as early as they can—to be proactive rather than reactive. This is particularly true for the grey area between public relations and public affairs. For instance, new technologies do constantly emerge on distant horizons, which may give rise to controversies and to new regulations. Lobbies and pressure groups try to weigh in on these debates as soon as they can in order to influence the language and imagery in which the debates will be framed and put on the public agenda. They "scan" the environment and "monitor" relevant discussions. In recent years, multinational corporations and other bodies have created the position of "issues manager" (one who must try to track and steer the interaction between the organization itself and a broader society) (Renfro, 1993; Schoonman, 1995; van Ginneken, 2001).

This is a logical step, except when it is based on excessive confidence in one's capacity to measure, predict, and control opinions and perceptions. Rather than making things manageable, it contributes to making them unmanageable on decisive occasions; for example, when decision makers fail to fathom the uniqueness of each crisis, and simply follow the book. The elaborate case descriptions in this book have illustrated time and again how extremely powerful institutions overplayed their hand, and had themselves completely taken by surprise in public mood shifts. Even the usual scenarios with contingency planning may fail. Most of the time they work, but every now and then they blow up in the faces of zealous techno-bureaucrats (Schwietert & Ten Berge, 1996).

So how can we deal with this? By constantly realizing ourselves that reality is much less solid and stable than it seems; by acknowledging that under the quiet surface, there may be deeper forces at work, which prepare the ground for a mind quake; by recognizing that long periods of manageable change will sooner or later cede to short episodes of violent turbulence. Whoever does not count this in, will inevitably be swept away—when the time comes. It is like one of those cool mountain rivulets, in which one is quietly paddling on a bright summer's day. Dark clouds appear on the horizon, the weather may have already changed several miles upstream, and torrential rains may have begun falling from the skies. In a flash, a wall of water may come rushing down the ravine, crushing everything and everyone in its way. Local signs and guides warn that this may happen, but some visitors will always be taken by surprise. The climate of opinion may change just as well, the mood on an issue may suddenly shift.

So the first aspect of issues to which one must always remain alert, is what I prefer to call the *psychodynamism*; the taken-for-granted empirical reality hides further or deeper layers, which are not easily observable at that point in time. One must always find ways to question what seems to be obvious, see the other side of the coin, the dark side of the moon, the black holes. Any opinion or attitude, any perception or image, has a shadow or dark side that may suddenly flip up, because they are all paradoxical; both white and black, one thing and its opposite. This may well be illustrated by two opposed examples from marketing. Heineken first introduced its no (or low) alcohol Buckler beer in the home market it easily dominates, The Netherlands. It was very successful, until a stand-up comedian ridiculed it as a non-beer for wimps on a widely viewed New Year's eve TV show. Ultimately, it had to be taken off the home market, but remains one of the market leaders everywhere else in the world.

The opposite example is that of Unilever, which launched an extra-strong 'Power' ingredient for its Omo and Persil brands throughout Western Europe. But when its competitor, Procter & Gamble, distributed pictures showing that these two brands of detergents ate holes in clothes, and when consumer organizations and research institutes confirmed that it was a bit overactive, they felt forced first to reformulate and then to recall the products. Both examples show that the image of "light" and "strong" products is always vulnerable, because these images can easily be reframed as "too light" or "too strong." One may acknowledge that possibility, but it is no certainty; it may happen, but it does not need to; it not only depends on the product itself, but also on the wider context. Sometimes the Gestalt switch does not come from the inside, but from the outside.

A second aspect to which one must always remain alert is what I prefer to call the sociodynamism. There may be all kinds of reasons why a perception shift begins and spreads through a population. We have seen in chapter 2 and chapter 3 that juicy stories about well-known institutions reproduce much more easily than others, particularly if they resonate with deeper fears or resentments. The public feels it is interesting conversation material; the media feel it is sensational news material. Attention is refocused, circulation accelerates, and the story may begin to be the top news item. This may well be illustrated by a third example from marketing.

Successful German carmaker Daimler Benz decided to introduce an entirely new model: the A-class or Baby Benz. The initial reception by test drivers, car magazines, the media, and the public was highly enthusiastic, until one "Baby" tipped over in Scandinavia, on the occasion of a highly unusual "Elk" test, typically designed for extreme winter conditions. The feat was registered and reproduced in front of cameras, and the pictures traveled all over the world. Had it been another, less prestigious brand, this might not have caused such a row. But is was a Mercedes, the perceived embodiment of German solidity (and maybe also ascribed arrogance), so everybody felt it was hilarious. Only much later did it turn out that many comparable models from other manufacturers could not easily survive the Elk test either (Schmid, 1998). Discretely, the car makers adopted the same changes in design.

These examples once again concern some of the most powerful and successful corporations in the world, with decades of experience in crisis and communication's management. What is noteworthy is that, according to later accounts, they did not see what hit them, nor could they find ways to parry it. The combined loss for all three corporations (Heineken, Unilever, and Daimler-Benz) ran into billions. These were rapid, radical, and massive shifts in public opinion and perception, which took them completely by surprise. Our understanding of such phenomena is profoundly inadequate, we need to conceptualize them in entirely different terms; this book is only a first and imperfect stab at the problem. But it may have demonstrated that the sciences of man and society may indeed learn much from the natural sciences, which they have always attempted to emulate—for better and for worse. But this time the lesson is not that everything may ultimately be brought under control, but on the contrary, that the only certainty is uncertainty.

Organization and communication experts may have to give up the illusion that they can always "steer" the course of events. They must acknowledge that there are many autonomous forces at work that may escape their mastery; effective action recognizes that profound truth, rather than ignoring it. It is not boxing or wrestling, but judo or jujitsu; not rowing but canoeing; not speedboat racing but sailing. One does not directly try to dominate one's opponent or the elements, but intuitively tries to sense their power and direction, in order to exploit them for one's own purposes. The most successful communicators we have met in this book were surfers. Surfers on the waves of public opinion.

References

Accardo, A., & Corcuff, P. (1986). *La sociologie de Bourdieu*. [The sociology of Bourdieu]. Bordeaux: Le Mascaret.

Allen, P. M. (1994). Evolutionary complex systems. In L. Leydesdorff & P. van de Besselaar (Eds.), *Evolutionary economics and chaos theory: New directions in technology studies* (pp. 1–7). London: Pinter.

Allport, G. W., & Postman, L. (1947). *The psychology of rumor*. New York: Holt.

Alvarez, L. (1998, Jan. 13). Opposition to IMF loans in Asia mounting in US Congress. *International Herald Tribune*, p. 10. (From New York Times).

Anonymous. (1995). Arrest of Leeson—Sale of Barings to ING. *Keesing's Record of World Events, 41*(3), 40470–40471. (Also see pp. 40422, 40868).

Anonymous. (1995). Brent Spar sea dumping controversy. *Keesing's Record of World Events, 41*(6), 40627.

Anonymous. (1995, Sept. 12). Frans virus moest Greenpeace stoppen [French virus was halt Greenpeace]. *NRC Handelsblad*, p. 1.

Anonymous. (1996). *Twenty five years as a catalyst for change*. Amsterdam: Greenpeace. (Brochure).

Anonymous. (1996). *Developing leadership for the 21st century*. London: The Economist Intelligence Unit (with Korn Ferry).

Anonymous. (1998, Jan./Febr.). Oh, the dangers of dihydrogen monoxide. *Skeptical Inquirer, 22*(1), 5.

Arthur, B. (1988). Urban systems and historical path dependence. In J. H. Ausubel & R. Herman (Eds.), *Cities and their vital systems: Infrastructure past, present and future* (pp. 85–97). Washington, DC: National Academy Press.

Arthur, B. (1990, February). Positive feedbacks in the economy. *Scientific American*, 80–85.

Arthur, B. (1993, February). Pandora's marketplace. *New Scientist* [Suppl.], 6–8.

Bak, P. (1997). *How nature works*. Oxford: Oxford University Press.

Bak, P., & Chen, K. (1991, January). Self-organized criticality. *Scientific American*, 26–33.

Bak, P., Tang, C., & Wiesenfeld, K. (1987). Self-organized criticality. *Physical Review Letters, 59*, 381.

Barasch, M. I. (1983). *The little black book of atomic war.* New York: Dell.

Barrows, S. (1981). *Distorting mirrors: Visions of the crowd in late-nineteenth century France.* New Haven, CT: Yale University Press.

Baruch, B. (1957). *My own story.* New York: Holt.

Baruch, B. (1962). Foreword. In C. Mackay, *Extraordinary delusions and the madness of crowds* (p. XIII). New York: Noonday.

Baschwitz, K. (1951). *Denkend mens en menigte* [Rational man and the crowd]. Den Haag: Leopold. (Original work published 1938)

Baschwitz, K. (1981). *Heksen en heksenprocessen* [Witches and witch trials]. Amsterdam: Arbeiderspers. (Original work published 1963)

Bateson, G. (1984). *Mind and nature: A necessary unity.* London: Wildwood.

Bax, M. (1987). Religious regimes and state formation. *Anthropological Quarterly, 60*(1), 1–11.

Beck, U. (1986/1996). *Risk society—Towards a new modernity.* London: Sage.

Benthall, J. (1993). *Disasters, relief and the media.* London: Tauris.

Berger, P., & Luckmann, T. (1981). *The social construction of reality: A treatise in the sociology of knowledge.* Harmondsworth, England: Penguin.

Berk, R. A. (1974). *Collective behavior.* Dubuque, IA: Brown.

Bernstein, P. L. (1996). *Against the Gods—The remarkable story of risk.* New York: Wiley.

Bierce, A. (1989). *The enlarged devil's dictionary.* London: Penguin.

Bloom, H. (1995). *The Lucifer principle: A scientific expedition into the forces of history.* New York: Atlantic Monthly Press.

Blumer, H. (1969a). Collective behavior. In A. M. Lee (Ed.), *Principles of sociology* (pp. 65–122). New York: Barnes & Noble. (Original work published 1939)

Blustein, P., & Sugawara, S. (1998, Jan. 7). IMF's remedy for Asia—Whose fault if it fails? *International Herald Tribune,* p. 11. (From Washington Post).

Boef, C. (1984). *Van massapsychologie tot collectief gedrag: De ontwikkeling van een paradigma* [From mass psychology to collective behavior—The development of a paradigm]. Unpublished doctoral dissertation, Leiden University, Netherlands.

Bohm, D. (1980). *Wholeness and the implicate order.* London: Routledge.

Bonifassi, C. (Ed. Dir.). (1993). *Le livre Guiness des records* [The Guiness record book]. Paris: Ed. TF-1.

Boorstin, D. (1980). *The image: A guide to pseudo-events in America.* New York: Atheneum. (Original work published 1961)

Boot, W. (1985, March/April). Ethiopia: Feasting on famine. *Columbia Journalism Review,* 47–48.

Bosso, C. J. (1989). Setting the agenda—Mass media and the discovery of famine in Ethiopia. In M. Margolis & G. A. Mauser (Eds.), *Manipulating public opinion.* Pacific Grove, CA: Brooks/Cole.

Bowring, P. (1997, Dec. 17). South Korea isn't bankrupt, and outsiders had a role. *International Herald Tribune.*

Brinton, C. (1938). *The anatomy of revolution.* New York: Norton.

Broer, H., Van de Craats, J., & Verhulst, F. (1995). *Het einde van de voorspelbaarheid?: Chaostheorie, ideeën en toepassingen* [The end of predictability—Chaso theory, ideas and applications]. Bloemendaal/Utrecht, The Netherlands: Aramith/Epsilon.

Brouwer, M. J. (1968). *Stereotypen als folklore* [Stereotypes as folklore]. Vinkeveen, NL: Fringilla.

Brown, M., & May, J. (1991). *The Greenpeace story: The world's most dynamic environmental pressure group.* London: Dorling Kindersley.

Browne, M. W. (1997, Nov. 26). When is a traffic jam like an ice cube? *International Herald Tribune.* (From New York Times).

Brunvand, J. H. (1981). *The vanishing hitchhiker: Urban American legends and their meanings.* New York: Norton.

Brunvand, J. H. (1986). *The Mexican pet: More "new" urban legends and some old favorites*. New York: Norton.

Buckley, W. (1967). *Sociology and modern systems theory*. Englewood Cliffs, NJ: Prentice-Hall.

Buddingh, H. (1998a, April 15). Azië-crisis ontketent veel zelf-onderzoek [Asia crisis triggers much introspection]. *NRC Handelsblad*.

Buddingh, H. (1998b, June 27). Waarom al die kritiek op de Aziatische tijgers? [Why all this criticism of the Asian tigers? Interview with Joseph Stiglitz]. *NRC Handelsblad*, p. 18.

Bulgatz, J. (1992). *Ponzi schemes, invaders from Mars and more extraordinary popular delusions and the madness of crowds*. New York: Harmony.

Bulmer, M., Bales, K., & Sklar, K. K. (Eds.). (1991). *The social survey in historical perspective 1880–1940*. Cambridge, England: Cambridge University Press.

Burger, P. (1992). *De wraak van de kangeroe: Sagen uit het moderne leven* [The revenge of the kangaroo—Sagas from modern life]. Amsterdam: Prometheus.

Burger, P. (1995). *De gebraden baby: Sagen en geruchten uit het moderne leven* [The baked baby—Sagas and rumors from modern life]. Amsterdam: Prometheus.

Burger, P. (1996). *De gestolen grootmoeder: Sagen uit het moderne leven* [The stolen grandmother—Sagas from modern life]. Amsterdam: Ooievaar.

Burger, P. (1997). Organ snatchers. *The Skeptic, 11*(2), 6–11.

Burns, J. M. (1979). *Leadership*. New York: Harper Torch.

Campion-Vincent, V., & Renard, J.-B. (1992). *Légendes urbaines: Rumeurs d'aujourd'hui* [Urban legends—Present-day rumors]. Paris: Payot.

Campion-Vincent, V. (1997a). *La légende des vols d'organes* [The legend of organ thefts]. Paris: Les belles lettres.

Campion-Vincent, V. (1997b). Organ theft narratives. *Western Folklore, 56*, 1–37.

Cannon, W. B. (1933). *The wisdom of the body*. New York: Norton.

Cantril, H. (1940). *The invasion from Mars*. Princeton, NJ: Princeton University Press.

Cantril, H. (1941). *The psychology of social movements*. New York: Wiley.

Caplan, A. L. (1978). *The sociobiology debate*. New York: Harper & Row.

Capra, F. (1975). *The tao of physics*. Boulder, CO: Shambala.

Capra, F. (1997). *The web of life: A new synthesis of mind and matter*. London: Flamingo.

Cartwright, D., & Zander, A. (1959). *Group dynamics—Research and theory*. London: Tavistock.

Casti, J. (1994). *Complexification: Explaining a paradoxical world through the science of surprise*. London: Abacus.

Childs, H. L. (1965). *Public opinion: Nature, formation and role*. Princeton, NJ: Van Nostrand.

Christian, D. (1991). The case for 'Big History'. *Journal of World History, 2*(2), 223–238.

Cohen, J., & Stewart, I. (1994). *The collapse of chaos: Discovering simplicity in a complex world*. New York: Penguin.

Cohen, J. M., & Cohen, M. J. (1993). *Dictionary of quotations* (Rev. ed.). London: Penguin.

Cohen, S. (1993). *Folk devils and moral panics—The creation of the mods and rockers*. Oxford: Blackwell. (Orig. 1972).

Cohen, S., & Young, J. (Eds.). (1973). *The manufacture of news: Social problems, deviance and the mass media*. London: Constable.

Converse, J. M. (1987). *Survey research in the US: Roots and emergence 1890–1960*. Berkeley, CA: University of California Press.

Cooper-Busch, B. (1985). *The war against the seals: A history of North American seal fishery*. Montreal, Canada: Queen's University Press.

Cornelius, R. R. (1996). *The science of emotion*. Upper Saddle River, NJ: Prentice Hall.

Covello, V. T., Menkes, J., & Mumpower, J. (1987). *Risk evaluation and management*. New York: Plenum.

Coveney, P., & Highfield, R. (1995). *Frontiers of complexity—The search for order in a chaotic world*. New York: Columbine.

Crawley, T. (Ed.). (1994). *Dictionary of film quotations*. Ware, England: Wordsworth.

Crowley, D., & Mitchell, D. (Eds.). (1994). *Communication theory today*. London: Polity.

Dauphinais, B., Price, C., & Pederson, P. (1996). *The paradox principles*. New York: Times Mirror.

Davies, J. C. (Ed.). (1971). *When men revolt and why*. New York: Free Press.

Davies, P. (1989). *The cosmic blueprint: Order and complexity at the edge of chaos*. London: Penguin.

Dawkins, R. (1976). *The selfish gene*. Oxford: Oxford University Press.

Dawkins, R. (1986). *The blind watchmaker*. London: Longman.

Deal, T., & Kennedy, A. (1988). *Corporate cultures: The rites and rituals of corporate life*. London: Penguin.

De Board, R. (1978). *The psychoanalysis of organizations*. London: Tavistock.

De Boer, C., & Catsburg, I. (1988). The impact of nuclear accidents on attitudes toward nuclear energy. *Public Opinion Quarterly, 52*, 254–261.

De Kam, F. (1996, April 2). Gekke koehandel [Mad cow trade]. *NRC Handelsblad*, p. 17.

De Leeuw, S., & Schmohl, I. (1996). *Jeugd flipt op flippo's* [Youngsters like pogs]. Master's thesis, Communication Science Department, Amsterdam University.

De Loof, A. (1996). *Wat is leven?: De onstoffelijke dimensie* [What is life?–The immaterial dimension]. Leuven: Garant.

De Mause, L. (1982). *Foundations of psychohistory*. New York: Creative Roots.

Denselow, R. (1989). *When the music is over: The story of political pop*. London: Faber & Faber.

Deschamps, J.-P., & Nayak, P. R. (1995). *Product juggernauts: How companies mobilize to generate a stream of market winners*. Boston, MA: Harvard Business School Press.

De Swaan, A. (1985). *Het medisch regime* [The medical regime]. Amsterdam: Meulenhoff.

De Vries, N. K., & Van der Pligt, J. (Eds.). (1991). *Cognitieve sociale psychologie* [Cognitive social psychology]. Meppel, NL: Boom.

Didion, J. (1992). *After Henry*. New York: Random House.

Diener, E. (1976). Effects of prior destructive behavior, anonymity and group presence on deindividuation and aggression. *Journal of Personality and Social Psychology, 33*(5), 497–507.

Diener, E. (1979). Deindividuation, self-awareness and disinhibition. *Journal of Personality and Social Psychology, 37*(7), 1160–1171.

Diener, E. (1980). Deindividuation—The absence of self-awareness and self-regulation in group members. In P. B. Paulus (Ed.), *Psychology of group influence*. Hillsdale, NJ: Lawrence Erlbaum Associates.

Dipboye, R. L. (1977). Alternative approaches to deindividuation. *Psychological Bulletin, 84*(6), 1057–1075.

Dorfman, A., & Mattelart, A. (1975). *How to read Donald Duck: Imperialist ideology in the Disney comic*. New York: International General.

Downs, A. (1987). Issue attention cycles. In R. H. Turner & L. M. Killian (Eds.), *Collective behavior* (pp. 170–185). Englewood Cliffs, NJ: Prentice Hall.

Dynes, R. R., & Tierney, K. J. (1994). *Disasters, collective behavior and social organization*. Newark, DE: University of Delaware Press.

Edelman, M. (1988). *Constructing the political spectacle*. Chicago: University of Chicago Press.

Ehrlich, P. (1968). *The population bomb*. New York: Ballantine.

Eiser, R. (1994). *Attitudes, chaos and the connectionist mind*. Oxford: Blackwell.

Elias, N. (1978). *The history of manners—The civilizing process* (Vol. 1). New York: Pantheon.

Elias, N. (1982). *Power and civility—The civilizing process* (Vol. 2). New York: Pantheon.

Elliot, M. (1993). *Walt Disney: Hollywood's dark prince*. New York: Carol.

Evans, R. (Ed.). (1969). *Readings in collective behavior*. Chicago: Rand McNally.

Eve, R. A., Horsfall, S., & Lee, M. A. (1997). *Chaos, complexity and sociology: Myths, models and theories*. Thousand Oaks, CA: Sage.

Faber, H. (1980). *The book of laws*. London: Sphere.

Fair, J. E. (1992). Are we really the world?: Coverage of U.S. food aid in Africa, 1980–1989. In B. Hawk (Ed.), *Africa's media image* (pp. 110–120). New York: Praeger.

Farson, R. (1996). *Management of the absurd: Paradoxes in leadership.* New York: Touchstone.

Festinger, L. (1957). *A theory of cognitive dissonance.* Stanford, CA: Stanford University Press.

Festinger, L., Pepitone, A., & Newcomb, T. (1952). Some consequences of deindividuation in a group. *Journal of Abnormal and Social Psychology, 47,* 382–389.

Fineman, S. (1994). *Emotions in organizations.* London: Sage.

Fischer, A. (1991). *Emotion scripts.* Unpublished doctoral dissertation, Leiden University.

Ford, B. J. (1996). *BSE: The facts. Mad cow disease and its risk to mankind.* London: Corgi.

Fraser, C., & Gaskell (Eds.). (1990). *The social psychological study of widespread beliefs.* Oxford: Clarendon.

Freud, S. (1967). *Massenpsychologie und Ich-analyse* [Group psychology and the analysis of the ego]. Frankfurt, Germany: Fischer. (Original work published 1921)

Freud, S. (1913/1971). *Totem und Tabu* [Totem and Taboo]. Frankfurt, Germany: Fischer.

Fuller, T. (1997, Dec. 22). Time to look East again? *International Herald Tribune,* p. 13.

Galbraith, J. K. (1955). *The great crash.* Boston: Houghton Mifflin.

Galbraith, J. K. (1990). *A short history of financial euphoria: Financial genius is before the fall.* Knoxville, TN: Whittle Direct.

Gaus, H., Van Hoe, J., Brackeleire, M., & Van der Voort, P. (1992). *Mensen en mode: De relatie tussen kleding en konjunktuur* [People and fashion—The relationship between clothing and economic climate]. Leuven: Garant.

Geldof, B. (with Vallelly, P.). (1986). *Is that it?* Harmondsworth, England: Penguin.

Genevie, L. (Ed.). (1978). *Collective behavior and social movements.* Itasca, IL: Peacock.

Geursen, G. (1993). *Tijdens de verkoop gaat de verbouwing gewoon door: Over de nieuwe, chaotische orde in ons denken* [Sales continue during reconstruction—About the new, chaotic order in our thought]. Houten, NL: Stenfert Kroese.

Geursen, G. (1994). *Virtuele tomaten en conceptuele pindakaas: Hoe interactiviteit, zelforganisatie en bewustzijnsverruiming de marketing op zijn kop zetten* [Virtual tomatoes and conceptual peanut butter—How interactivity, self organization and growing awareness put marketing on its head]. Deventer: Kluwer.

Giacalone, R. A., & Rosenfeld, P. (Eds.). (1991). *Applied impression management: How image-making affects managerial decisions.* Newbury Park, CA: Sage.

Giddens, A. (1984). *The constitution of society.* London: Polity.

Giddens, A. (1990). *The consequences of modernity.* Cambridge, England: Polity.

Giner, S. (1976). *Mass society.* London: Martin Robertson.

Glassman, J. K. (1998, Jan. 14). Bailout of Asia is likely to fail, and perhaps it should. *International Herald Tribune,* p. 8. (From Washington Post).

Gleick, J. (1987). *Chaos: Making a new science.* New York: Viking.

Glorieux, E. (1996). *Chernobyl: Het jaar tien* [Chernobyl—The year 10]. Berchem, Belgium: Epo.

Goerner, S. (1995). Chaos, evolution and deep ecology. In R. Robertson & A. Combs (Eds.), *Chaos theory in psychology and the life sciences* (pp. 17–38). Mahwah, NJ: Lawrence Erlbaum Associates.

Goffman, E. (1964). *Stigma—Notes on the management of spoiled identity.* Englewood Cliffs, NJ: Prentice Hall.

Goffman, E. (1986). *Frame analysis: An essay in the organization of experience.* Boston: Northeastern University Press.

Goffman, E. (1990). *The presentation of self in everyday life.* London: Penguin. (Original work published 1956)

Goode, E. (1992). *Collective behavior.* New York: Harcourt Brace Jovanovich.

Goode, E., & Ben-Yehuda, N. (1994). *Moral panics: The social construction of deviance.* Oxford: Blackwell.

Goudsblom, J., & Spier, F. (1996). *Geschiedenis in het groot: Syllabus* [Big history—Readings] (2 vols.). Amsterdam: Amsterdam University Sociology Department.

Goudsmit, A. (1998). *Towards a negative understanding of psychotherapy*. Unpublished doctoral dissertation, Groningen University.

Gould, S. (1992). *Ever since Darwin*. New York: Norton.

Granovetter, M. S. (1973). The strength of weak ties. *American Journal of Sociology, 78*, 1360–1380.

Graumann, C. F., & Moscovici, S. (Eds.). (1986). *Changing conceptions of crowd mind and behavior*. New York: Springer.

Gross, J. (1987). *Aphorisms*. Oxford: Oxford University Press.

Grzimek, B. (Ed.). (1984). *Animal life*. New York/London: Van Nostrand.

Gurr, T. R. (1971). *Why men rebel*. Princeton, NJ: Princeton University Press.

Gutteling, J. (1991). *Contouren van risicovoorlichting* [Contours of risk information]. Unpublished doctoral dissertation, Twente University, Enschede, The Netherlands.

Hamel, G., & Prahalad, C. K. (1994). *Competing for the future: Breakthrough strategies for seizing control of your industry*. Boston: Harvard Business School Press.

Harré, R. (Ed.). (1986). *The social construction of emotions*. Oxford: Blackwell.

Harrison, P., & Palmer, R. (1986). *News out of Africa: Biafra to Band Aid*. London: Hilary Stripman.

Hatfield, E., Cacioppo, J., & Rapson, R. L. (1994). *Emotional contagion*. Cambridge, England: Cambridge University Press.

Hattersley, R. (1996, April 3). Brit moet wennen aan Brussel [The British have to get accustomed to Brussels]. *De Volkskrant*, April 3. [Translated from *The Guardian*].

Havenaar, J. M. (1996). *After Chernobyl: Psychological factors affecting health after a nuclear disaster*. Unpublished doctoral dissertation, Utrecht University.

Hawkes, N., Lean, G., Leigh, D., McKie, R., Pringle, P., & Wilson, A. (1986). *The worst accident in the world: Chernobyl, the end of the nuclear dream*. London: Heineman/Pan.

Hawking, S. (1988). *A brief history of time*. New York: Bantam.

Hendriks, F. (Ed.). (1987). *Shell*. Amsterdam: Somo.

Hermans, R. (1996). *Opinie-dynamica en de Brent Spar case* [Opinion dynamics and the Brent Spar case]. Master's thesis, Communication Science Department, Amsterdam University.

Hersovici, A. (1985). *Second nature: The animal-rights controversy*. Toronto/Montreal: CBC/Les Entreprises Radio Canada.

Hertsgaard, M. (1985, August 27). Strictly from hunger. *The Village Voice*, pp. 38–39.

Hobsbawm, E. (1969). *Bandits*. London: Weidenfeld & Nicholson.

Hobsbawm, E. (1971). *Primitive rebels: Studies in archaic forms of social movements*. Manchester, England: Machester University Press. (Original work published 1959)

Hochschild, A. (1983). *The managed heart—Commercialization of human feeling*. Berkeley: University of California Press.

Horgan, J. (1995, June). From complexity to perplexity. *Scientific American*, 74–79.

Horgan, J. (1996). *The end of science: Facing the limits of knowledge in the twilight of the scientific age*. London: Abacus.

Hunter, R. (1979). *The Greenpeace chronicle*. London: Picador/Pan.

Illich, I. (1970/1981). *Ontscholing van de maatschappij*. Bussum, The Netherlands: Wereldvenster. (Or. Deschooling society).

Illich, I. (1975/1978). *Grenzen aan de geneeskunde*. Bussum, The Netherlands: Wereldvenster. (Or. Medical nemesis—The expropriation of health).

Kahn, H., & Wiener, A. J. (1967). *The year 2000*. New York: MacMillan.

Kahnemann, D., Slovic, P., & Tversky, A. (Eds.). (1982). *Judgment under uncertainty—Heuristics and biases*. New York: Cambridge University Press.

Kapferer, J.-N. (1990). *Rumors: Uses, interpretations and images*. New Brunswick, NJ: Transaction.

Katz, E., & Lazarsfeld, P. (1955). *Personal influence*. Glencoe: Free Press.

Kauffman, S. A. (1991, August). Antichaos and adaptation. *Scientific American*, 64–70.

Keene, S. (1991). *Faces of the enemy: Reflections of the hostile imagination.* San Francisco: Harper Collins.

Kelly, K. (1997). *Out of control: The new biology of machines, social systems and the economic world.* Reading, MA: Addison-Wesley.

Kerner, B., & Rehborn, H. (1997). Experimental properties of phase transitions in traffic flow. *Physical Review Letters, 79*(20), 4030–4033.

Kets de Vries, M. (1989). *Prisoners of leadership: Overcoming counterproductive styles of management.* New York: Wiley.

Kets de Vries, M. (1995). *Life and death in the executive fast lane: Essays on irrational organizations and their leaders.* San Francisco: Jossey-Bass.

Kets de Vries, M., & Miller, D. (1987). *Unstable at the top.* New York: New American Library.

Ketteringham, J. M., & Nayak, P. R. (1986). *Breakthroughs.* New York: Rawson.

Khor, M. (1998, Jan. 15). Are Asian partners to be helped, or rivals to be hurt? *International Herald Tribune.*

Kiel, D. L., & Elliott, E. (Eds.). (1996). *Chaos theory in the social sciences: Foundations and applications.* Ann Arbor: University of Michigan Press.

Kindleburger, C. P. (1989). *Manias, panics and crashes: A history of financial crises.* New York: Basic.

Kissinger, H. (1998, Oct. 5). The IMF's remedies are doing more harm than good. *International Herald Tribune.* (From Los Angeles Times).

Kitzinger, J., & Reilly, J. (1997). The rise and fall of risk reporting. *European Journal of Communication, 12*(3), 320–346.

Klapp, O. E. (1969). *Collective search for identity.* New York: Holt, Rinehart & Winston.

Klapp, O. E. (1971). *Social types: Process, structure and ethos.* San Diego: Aegis.

Klapp, O. E. (1972). *Currents of unrest: An introduction to collective behavior.* New York: Holt, Rinehart & Winston.

Klapp, O. E. (1973). *Models of social order: An introduction to sociological theory.* Palo Alto, CA: National Press Books.

Klapp, O. E. (1978). *Opening and closing: Strategies of information adaptation in society.* Cambridge, England: Cambridge University Press.

Klapp, O. E. (1991). *Inflation of symbols: Loss of values in American culture.* New Brunswick: Transaction.

Knappe, B. (1993). *Das geheimnis von Greenpeace* [The secret of Greenpeace]. Vienna, Austria: Orac.

Koch, H. (1970). *The panic broadcast.* New York: Avon/Hearst.

Koenig, F. (1985). *Rumor in the marketplace: The social psychology of commercial hearsay.* Dover, MA: Auburn House.

Koestler, A. (1989). *The ghost in the machine.* London: Arkana. (Original work published 1967)

Köhler, W. (1996, April 4). WHO wil verbod op alle dierlijke resten in veevoer [World Health Organization demands ban on all animal material in fodder). *NRC Handelsblad,* pp. 1, 5.

Kohnstamm, R. (1995, May 20). Flippo's van verbondenheid [Pogs of union]. *NRC Handelsblad,* p. 9.

Kok, G. (1992). *Gezondheids-voorlichting* [Health information]. Muiderberg: Coutinho.

Kolata, G. (1977, April 15). Catastrophe theory—The emperor has no clothes. *Science.* (Also see June 17 and August 26).

Kuhn, T. (1962). *The structure of scientific revolutions.* Chicago: University of Chicago Press.

Kuttner, R. (1998, Jan. 6). Dr. IMF prescribes recession for some patients. *International Herald Tribune.* (From Washington Post).

Lang, K., & Lang, G. E. (1961). *Collective dynamics.* New York: Crowell.

Lasswell, H. D. (1948). The structure and function of communication in society. In L. Bryson (Ed.), *The communication of ideas.* New York: Harper & Brothers.

Latané, B. (1981). The psychology of social impact. *American Psychologist, 36,* 343–356.

Latané, B., & Nowak, A. (1994). Attitudes as catastrophes. In R. R. Vallacher & A. Nowak (Eds.), *Dynamical systems in social psychology*. San Diego: Academic Press.

Lauwerier, H. (1992). *Fractals: Meetkundige figuren in eindeloze herhaling* [Fractals—Geometric figures in endless repetition]. Bloemendaal, NL: Aramith.

Lavigne, D. M. (1991, July). A blizzard of lies. *BBC Wildlife*, pp. 445–447.

Le Bon, G. (1966). *The crowd: A study of the popular mind*. New York: Viking. (Original work published 1895)

Lee, A. M. (Ed.). (1969). *Principles of sociology*. New York: Barnes & Noble.

Leiss, W. (1994). Risk communication and public knowledge. In D. Crowley & D. Mitchell (Eds.), *Communication theory today*. Cambridge, England: Polity.

Lewin, R. (1992). *Complexity*. New York: MacMillan.

Lewis, T. (1994). *The milkcap guide*. Kansas City: Andrews & McMeel.

Leydesdorff, L. (1993). Is society a self-organizing system? *Journal of Social and Evolutionary Systems, 16*(3), 331–349.

Leydesdorff, L. (1997). The non-linear dynamics of sociological reflections. *International Sociology, 12*(1), 25–45.

Leydesdorff, L. (2001). *A sociological theory of communication—The self-organization of the knowledge-based society*. Parkland, FL: Universal Publishers.

Lindberg, O. F. (1988). Report from the government of the seal hunt. Photocopy, unpublished manuscript, 35 pages.

Lindzey, G., & Aronson, E. (Eds.). (1954). *Handbook of social psychology*. Cambridge, MA: Addison Wesley. 1st ed., 2 vols. (2nd. ed., 4 vols. 1969).

Lister-Kaye, J. (1979). *Seal cull—The grey seal controversy*. Harmondsworth, England: Penguin.

Lippmann, W. (1947). *Public opinion*. New York: MacMillan.

Lofland, J. (1985). *Protest: Studies of collective behavior and social movements*. New Brunswick, NJ: Transaction.

Lovelock, J. (1979). *Gaia*. Oxford: Oxford University Press.

Lovelock, J. (1989). *The ages of Gaia: A biography of our living world*. Oxford: Oxford University Press.

Loye, D. (1978). *The knowable future*. New York: Wiley.

Luccioni, X. (1986). *L'affaire Greenpeace—Une guerre des médias* [The Greenpeace affair—A media war]. Paris: Payot.

Luhmann, N. (1995). *Social systems*. Stanford: Stanford University Press. (Original work published 1984)

Lull, J., & Hinerman, S. (Eds.). (1997). *Media scandals: Morality and desire in the popular marketplace*. London: Polity.

Lurie, A. (1981). *The language of clothes*. New York: Random House.

Lynch, A. (1996). *Thought contagion: How belief spreads through society (The new science of memes)*. New York: Basic.

Mackay, C. (1980). *Extraordinary delusions and the madness of crowds*. New York: Harmony. (Original work published 1841)

Major, J. (1996, June 19). Verbod Brits rundvlees is irrationeel [Ban on British beef is irrational]. *NRC Handelsblad*, p. 7.

Marples, D. R. (1988). *The social impact of the Chernobyl disaster*. London: MacMillan.

Marwell, G., & Oliver, P. (1993). *The critical mass in collective action: A micro-social theory*. Cambridge, England: Cambridge University Press.

Marx, G. T., & McAdam, D. (1994). *Collective behavior and social movements: Process and structure*. Englewood Cliffs, NJ: Prentice-Hall.

Maturana, H. R. (1978). Biology of language: The epistemology of reality. In G. A. Miller & E. Lenneberg (Eds.), *Psychology and biology of language and thought* (pp. 27–63). New York: Academic Press.

Maturana, H. R., & Varela, F. J. (1980). *Autopoiesis and cognition—The realization of the living* Boston: Reidel.

Maturana, H. R., & Varela, F. J. (1984). *The tree of knowledge: The biological roots of human understanding.* Boston: Shambala.

Mayo, E. (1933). *The human problems of an industrial civilization.* New York: MacMillan.

McClain, D. (1990). *Apocalypse on Wall street.* Homewood, IL: Dow Jones/Irwin.

McClelland, J. S. (1989). *The crowd and the mob: From Plato to Canetti.* London: Unwin Hyman.

McDougall, W. (1920). *The group mind.* New York: Putnam.

McNeill, W. H. (1992). *The global condition.* Princeton: Princeton University Press.

McPhail, C. (1991). *The myth of the madding crowd.* New York: De Gruyter.

McQuail, D., & Windahl, S. (1993). *Communication models* (2nd ed.). London: Longman.

Meadows, D., & Behrens, W. (1970). *The limits to growth.* New York: Universe.

Merton, R. K. (1948). The self-fulfilling prophecy. *Antioch Review, 8,* 193–210.

Milgram, S., & Toch, H. (1969). Collective behavior. In G. Lindzey & E. Aronson (Eds.), *Handbook of social psychology* (Vol. 4, pp. 507–605). Reading, MA: Addison-Wesley.

Miller, D. L. (1985). *Introduction to collective behavior.* Prospect Heights, IL: Waveland.

Molière. (1673). *Le Malade imaginaire* [The imaginary invalid].

Moore, G. A. (1995). *Inside the tornado: Marketing strategies from Silicon Valley's cutting edge.* New York: Harper Collins.

Morgan, G. (1986). *Images of organization.* Thousand Oaks, CA: Sage.

Morin, E. (1969). *La rumeur d'Orléans* [The rumor of Orleans]. Paris: Seuil.

Moscovici, S. (1976). *Social influence and social change.* London: Academic Press.

Moscovici, S. (1985). *The age of the crowd: A historical treatise on mass psychology.* Cambridge: Cambridge University Press.

Moskowitz, M. (Ed.). (1987). *The global marketplace: Most influential companies outside America.* New York: MacMillan.

Moskowitz, M., Katz, M., & Levering, R. (Eds.). (1980). *Everybody's business: The irreverent guide to corporate America.* San Francisco: Harper & Row.

Mucchi-Faina, A. (1983). *L'abbraccio della folla: Cento anni di psicologia collettiva* [The crowd—A hundred years of collective psychology]. Bologna, Italy: Mulino.

Noelle-Neumann, E. (1984). *The spiral of silence: Public opnion, our social skin.* Chicago: University of Chicago Press.

Noelle-Neumann, E. (1994). The influence of the spiral of silence on media effects research. In C. Hamelink & O. J. Linné (Eds.), *Mass communication research* (pp. 97–120). Norwood, NJ: Ablex.

Nye, R. (1975). *The origins of crowd psychology: Gustave Le Bon and the crisis of mass democracy in the Third Republic.* London: Sage.

Oatley, K., & Jenkins, J. M. (1996). *Understanding emotions.* Oxford: Blackwell.

Oberschall, A. (1973). *Social conflict and social movements.* Englewood Cliffs, NJ: Prentice Hall.

Olson, M. (1965). *The logic of collective action—Public goods and the theory of groups.* Cambridge, MA: Harvard University Press.

O'Sullivan, T., Hartley, J., Saunders, D., & Fiske, J. (1989). *Key concepts in communication.* London: Routledge.

Paddock, W., & Paddock, P. (1967). *Famine 1975!* Boston: Little, Brown.

Panati, C. (1991). *Fads, follies and manias: The origins of our most cherished obsessions.* New York: Harper Perennial.

Park, C. (1989). *Chernobyl: The long shadow.* London: Routledge.

Park, R. E. (1972). *The crowd and the public.* Chicago: University of Chicago Press.

Park, R. E., & Burgess, E. W. (1970). *Introduction to the science of sociology.* Chicago: University of Chicago Press. (Original work published 1922)

Parmentier, C. (1996). *Het dier en zijn mensenrechten* [The animal and its human rights]. Kapellen, Belgium: Pelckmans.

REFERENCES

2

Paulos, J. A. (1993). *A mathematician reads the newspaper*. New York: Basic.

Peeters, H. F. M. (1978). *Historische gedragswetenschap* [Historical science of behavior]. Amsterdam: Boom.

Penrose, L. S. (1952). *On the objective study of crowd behavior*. London: Lewis.

Perry, J. B., & Pugh, M. D. (Eds.). (1978). *Collective behavior: Response to social stress*. St. Paul, MN: West.

Peters, T. J., & Waterman, R. H. (1982). *In search of excellence: Lessons' from America's best-run companies*. New York: Harper & Row.

Pfaff, W. (1998a, Jan. 3–4). New Year's resolution—rethink the deregulation fad. *International Herald Tribune*. (From Los Angeles Times).

Pfaff, W. (1998b, Jan. 12). American remedies won't work in the Asian crisis. *International Herald Tribune*, p. 8. (From Los Angeles Times).

Pfaff, W. (1998c, July 14). What happens when market forces get out of control. *International Herald Tribune*. (From Los Angeles Times).

Philo, G. (1993). From Buerk to Band Aid: The media and the 1984 Ethiopian famine. In J. Elridge (Ed.), *Getting the message* (pp. 104–125). London: Routledge.

Pols, B. (1996, March 28). Slapeloze nachten na overlijden van boeren [Sleepless nights after death of farmers]. *NRC Handelsblad*, p. 19.

Portnoy, E. (1978). *Broodje aap: De folklore van de post-industriële samenleving* [Monkey sandwich—Folklore of the post-industrial society]. Amsterdam: De Harmonie.

Prentice-Dunn, S., & Rogers, R. W. (1980). Effects of deindividuating situational cues and aggressive models on subjective deindividuation and aggression. *Journal of Personality and Social Psychology, 39*(1), 104–113.

Prentice-Dunn, S., & Rogers, R. W. (1982). Effects of public and private self-awareness on deindividuation and aggression. *Journal of Personality and Social Psychology, 43*(3), 303–313.

Price, V. (1992). *Public opinion*. Newbury Park, CA: Sage.

Prigogine, I., & Stengers, I. (1984). *Order out of chaos: Man's new dialogue with nature*. Toronto: Bantam.

Pugh, M. D. (Ed.). (1980). *Collective behavior: A source book*. St. Paul, MN: West.

Reicher, S. (1982). The determination of collective behavior. In H. Tajfel (Ed.), *Social identity and intergroup relations* (pp. 41–83). Cambridge, England: Cambridge University Press.

Reicher, S. (1984). Social influence in the crowd. *British Journal of Social Psychology, 23*, 341–350.

Reiwald, P. (1946). *Vom Geist der Massen: Handbuch der Massenpsychologie* [About the spirit of the crowd—Manual of mass psychology]. Zürich, Switzerland: Pan.

Remnick, D. (1993). *Lenin's tomb: The last days of the Soviet empire*. New York: Random House.

Renfro, W. L. (1993). *Issues management in strategic planning*. Westport, CT: Quorum.

Rifkin, J. (1992). *Beyond beef: The rise and fall of the cattle culture*. New York: Penguin.

Robertson, R., & Combs, A. (Eds.). (1995). *Chaos theory in psychology and the life sciences*. Mahwah, NJ: Lawrence Erlbaum Associates.

Rogers, E. (1995). *Diffusion of innovations* (4th rev. ed.). New York: Free Press.

Rose, J. D. (1982). *Outbreaks: The sociology of collective behavior*. New York: Free Press/MacMillan.

Rosenthal, R. (1976). *Experimenter effects in behavioral research*. New York: Irvington. (Enlarged ed.).

Rosenthal, R., & Jacobson, L. (1968). *Pygmalion in the classroom—teacher expectation and pupil's intellectual development*. New York: Holt, Rinehart & Winston.

Rosnow, R., & Fine, G. A. (1976). *Rumor and gossip: The social psychology of hearsay*. New York: Elsevier.

Rostow, W. (1970). *Les étapes de la croissance économique* [The stages of economic growth]. Paris: Seuil.

Rowley, R. M., & Roevens, J. J. (1996). *Organize with chaos*. Antwerp, Belgium: Universitas.

Rudé, G. (1964). *The crowd in history*. New York: Wiley.

Ruse, M. (1979). *Sociobiology: Sense or nonsense?* Dordrecht: Reidel.

Rushdie, S. (1990). *Haroun and the sea of stories.* London: Granta.

Rushkoff, D. (1996). *Media virus: Hidden agendas in popular culture.* New York: Ballantine.

Sahakian, W. S. (1982). *History and systems of social psychology.* Washington: Hemisphere.

Samuelson, R. (1998, Jan. 8). Small changes, then unexpected upheaval. *International Herald Tribune.*

Sandelands, L., & St. Clair, L. (1993). Toward an empirical concept of the group. *Journal for the Theory of Social Behavior, 23*(4), 423–458.

Sanger, D. (1998a, Jan. 5). In the 'Sit Room', generals make room for economists. *International Herald Tribune*, p. 11. (From New York Times).

Sanger, D. (1998b, July 7). A year old, Asian crisis just keeps deepening. *International Herald Tribune.* (From New York Times).

Scheff, T. J. (1990). *Miscrosociology: Discourse, emotion and social structure.* Chicago: University of Chicago Press.

Schiffer, I. (1973). *Charisma: A psychoanalytic look at mass society.* New York: Free Press/MacMillan.

Schmid, J. (1998, March 7–8). Spin control—Opel and VW in a flip flap. *International Herald Tribune*, p. 1, 4.

Schnaars, S. P. (1989). *Megamistakes: Forecasting and the myth of rapid technological change.* New York: Free Press.

Schoonman, E. (1991). *Issues management: Omgaan met de publieke opinie.* Deventer, Netherlands: Kluwer.

Schoonman, E. (1995). *Issues management: Anticiperen op de publieke opinie.* Alphen aan de Rijn, Netherlands: Samsom.

Schwenk, T. (1976). *Sensitive chaos: The creation of flowing forms in water and air.* New York: Schocken.

Schwietert, C., & Ten Berge, D. (1996). *Imago-beschadiging en imago-herstel* [Image damage and image recovery]. Den Haag: BZZTôH.

Senge, P. M. (1990). *The fifth discipline: The learning organization.* New York: Doubleday.

Shannon, C., & Weaver, W. (1949). *The mathematical theory of communication.* Urbana: University of Illinois Press.

Sherden, W. A. (1998). *The fortune sellers: The big business of selling and buying predictions.* New York: Wiley.

Shibutani, T. (1966). *Improvised news: A sociological study of rumor.* Indianapolis: Bobbs Merrill.

Shiroma, R., & Kotero, G. A. (1995). Blossom Galbiso. *Collector Caps, 1*(6), 13–19.

Simon, H. (1973). The organization of complex systems. In H. H. Pattee (Ed.), *Hierarchy theory: The challenge of complex systems* (pp. 1–27). New York: Braziller.

Smelser, N. J. (1962). *Theory of collective behavior.* London: Routledge & Kegan Paul.

Solomon, M. R. (Ed.). (1985). *The psychology of fashion.* Lexington, MA: Lexington/Heath.

Sperber, D. (1996). *Explaining culture: A naturalistic approach.* Oxford: Blackwell.

Spier, F. (1996). *The structure of big history: From the Big Bang until today.* Amsterdam: Amsterdam University Press.

Sprent, P. (1988). *Taking risks—The science of uncertainty.* London: Penguin.

Stacey, R. (1993). *Managing chaos: Dynamic business strategies in an unpredictable world.* London: Kogan Page.

Stewart, I. (1997). *Does God play dice?: The new mathematics of chaos.* London: Penguin. (Original work published 1989)

Tainter, J. A. (1988). *The collapse of complex societies.* Cambridge, England: Cambridge University Press.

Tajfel, H. (1978). *Differentiation between groups—Studies in the social psychology of intergroup relations.* London: Academic Press.

Tarde, G. (1897). *L'opposition universelle* [Universal opposition]. Paris: Alcan.

Tarde, G. (1903). *The laws of imitation*. New York: Henry Holt.

Ten Berge, D. (1989). *The first 24 hours*. Oxford: Blackwell.

Tennekes, H. (Ed.). (1990). *De vlinder van Lorenz - De verrassende dynamica van de chaos* [Lorenz's butterfly—The surprising dynamics of chaos]. Bloemendaal: Aramith.

Thakur, R. (1998, Aug. 13). How East Asians are finding fault with the IMF. *International Herald Tribune.*

't Hart, P., & Rosenthal, U. (1990). *Kritieke momenten: Studies over beslissen in moeilijke omstandigheden* [Critical moments—Studies about decisions in difficult circumstances]. Arnhem: Gouda Quint.

Thom, R. (1975). *Structural stability and morphogenesis*. New York: Addison-Wesley.

Thompson, D. W. (1942). *On growth and form*. Cambridge: Cambridge University Press. (Original work published 1917)

Tilly, C., Tilly, L., & Tilly, R. (1975). *The rebellious century*. Cambridge, MA: Harvard University Press.

Toscani, O. (1995). *La pub est une charogne qui nous sourit* [Advertising is a smiling bitch]. Paris: Hoëbeke.

Turner, F. (1997). Chaos and social science. In R. A. Eve, S. Horsfall, & M. E. Lee (Eds.), *Chaos, complexity and sociology*. Thousand Oaks, CA: Sage.

Turner, R. H., & Killian, L. M. (1972). *Collective behavior* (2nd ed.). Englewood Cliffs, NJ: Prentice-Hall.

Vallacher, R. R., & Nowak, A. (Eds.). (1994). *Dynamical systems in social psychology*. San Diego, CA: Academic Press.

Van der Pligt, J. (1992). *Nuclear energy and the public*. Oxford: Blackwell.

Van der Pligt, J., & Van Schie, E. C. M. (Eds.). (1991). Beslissings- en beoordelingsprocessen [Decision and evaluation processes]. In N. K. De Vries & J. Van der Pligt (Eds.), *Cognitieve sociale psychologie* [Cognitive social psychology]. Amsterdam: Boom.

Van der Wurff, R. (1997). *International climate change politics: Interests and perceptions*. Unpublished doctoral dissertation, Amsterdam University.

Van Dijkum, C., & de Tombe, D. (Eds.). (1992). *Gamma chaos: Onzekerheid en orde in de menswetenschappen* [Gamma chaos—Uncertainty and order in the human sciences]. Bloemendaal: Aramith.

Van Dooren, R. (1994). *Messengers from the promised land: An interactive theory of political charisma*. Leiden, The Netherlands: DSWO Press.

Van Egmond, F. (1996). *Brent Spar: Communication analysis*. Master's thesis, Psychology and Communication Science Department, Amsterdam University.

Van Ginneken, J. (1984). The killing of the father: The backgrounds of Freud's Group Psychology. *Political Psychology, 5*(3), 391–414.

Van Ginneken, J. (1987, September). Trotter, the herd instinct and the transformation of British liberalism. Paper presented at the 6th Annual Scientific Meeting of the European Cheiron Society for the History of the Behavioral and Social Sciences. University of Sussex, Brighton, England.

Van Ginneken, J. (1992a). *Crowds, psychology and politics*. New York: Cambridge University Press.

Van Ginneken, J. (1993a). *De uitvinding van het publiek: De opkomst van het opinie- en marktonderzoek in Nederland* [The invention of the public—The emergence of opinion and marketing research in The Netherlands]. Amsterdam: Cramwinckel.

Van Ginneken, J. (1993b). *Rages en crashes: Over de onvoorspelbaarheid van de economie* [Crazes and crashes—About the unpredictability of economic behavior]. Bloemendaal: Aramith.

Van Ginneken, J. (1995). The social construction of the collective subject. In S. Jager (Ed.), *Psychologie im soziokulturellen Wandel* [Psychology in sociocultural transformation]. Frankfurt, Germany: Europaïscher Verlag der Wissenschaften.

Van Ginneken, J. (1996/1997). Het publiek. In J. Jansz & P. Van Drunen (Eds.), *Met zachte hand* [With a gentle hand]. Utrecht: Elsevier/De Tijdstroom.

Van Ginneken, J. (1998). *Understanding global news: A critical introduction.* London: Sage.

Van Ginneken, J. (2000). *Verborgen verleiders* [Hidden persuaders]. Amsterdam: Boom.

Van Ginneken, J. (2001). *Schokgolf—Omgaan met opinie-dynamiek* [Shock wave—Dealing with opinion dynamics]. Amsterdam: Boom.

Van Ginneken, J. (2002–3, in press). Social orientations. In J. Jansz & P. van Drunen (Eds.), *The social history of psychology.* Cambridge: Blackwell.

Van Meijgaard, A. H. C. (1998). *Wolfgang Pauli and his interaction with Carl Gustav Jung.* Enschede, The Netherlands: Twente University (doctoral dissertation).

Van Niekerk, J. (1993). *De Benetton case: Analyse van een spraakmakende reclame-methode* [The Benetton case—Analysis of a controversial advertising method]. Master's thesis, Communication Science Department, Amsterdam University.

Van Riemsdijk, M. J. (1994). *Actie of dialoog?: Over de betrekkingen tussen maatschappij en onderneming* [Action or dialogues—About the relations between corporations and society]. Delft: Eburon.

Van Schravendijk, H. (1995). *Produktgeruchten: Lariekoek en achterklap bij de consument* [Product rumors—Nonsense and gossip among consumers]. Utrecht: F & G.

Van Vught, F. (1979). *Sociale planning: Oorsprong en ontwikkeling van het Amerikaanse planningsdenken* [Social planning—Origin and development of American thought on planning]. Assen: Van Gorcum.

Vasterman, P. (1995). Media hypes: Een theoretisch kader [Media hypes—A theoretical framework]. *Massacommunicatie, 3,* 159–176.

Vasterman, P. (Ed.). (1997). *Media hypes: Reader.* Utrecht: Journalism School.

Volk, T. (1995). *Metapatterns: Across space, time and mind.* New York: Columbia University Press.

Von Bertalanffy, L. (1968). *General system theory: Foundation, development, applications.* New York: Braziller.

Vreeken, R. (1995, May 31). Geinige fiches. *De volkskrant.*

Vuijst, F., & Ziv, I. (1987). Consuming hunger. [Two part TV documentary, unpublished transcript]. New York: PBS.

Waldrop, M. (1992). *Complexity: The emerging science at the edge of order and chaos.* London: Penguin.

Wertheim, W. F. (1971). *Evolutie en revolutie* [Evolution and revolution]. Amsterdam: Van Gennep.

Wesseling, H. L. (1996, June 6). Mad cows and Englishmen. *NRC Handelsblad,* p. 9.

Wiedemann, E. (1983, April 4). Die Robben-Schlacht [The slaughter of seals]. *Der Spiegel.*

Wiener, N. (1986). *Cybernetics.* Cambridge, MA: MIT Press.

Willner, A. R. (1984). *The spellbinders: Charismatic political leadership.* New Haven, CT: Yale University Press.

Wilson, E. (1980). *Sociobiology.* Cambridge, MA: Harvard University Press.

Wilson, J. (1973). *Introduction to social movements.* New York: Basic.

Wittenberg, D. (1996, March 28). Britten stellen vernietiging veestapel uit [British postpone the destruction of their cattle]. *NRC Handelsblad,* p. 22.

Wright, S. (1978). *Crowds and riots: A study in social organization.* Beverley Hills, CA: Sage.

Zahler, R., & Sussman, H. (1977, Oct. 27). Claims and accomplishments of applied catastrophe theory. *Nature.* (Also see Dec. 1 and 29).

Zakaria, F. (1998, July 17). An open global economy needs growth in East Asia. *International Herald Tribune.* (From New York Times).

Zald, M. N., & McCarthy, J. D. (Eds.). (1987). *Social movements in an organizational society: Collected essays.* New Brunswick: Transaction.

Zeeman, E. C. (1977). *Catastrophe theory: Selected papers.* London: Addison-Wesley.

Zimbardo, P. (1969). The human choice: Individuation, reason and order, versus deindividuation, impulse and chaos. In *Nebraska symposium on Motivation* (Vol. 17, pp. 237–307). Lincoln: University of Nebraska Press.

Author Index

289

Subject Index

About the Author

Jaap van Ginneken is an Associate Professor for the Department of Communication Science at the University of Amsterdam in The Netherlands, but simultaneously an independent psychologist and consultant based near Nice in France.

Dr. van Ginneken has long worked as a roving reporter and foreign correspondent, and continues to do frequent work in the field of science communication. Over the years, he has published a dozen books in Dutch about applied, social, economic, political, media psychology, and persuasion. He is a regular contributor to newspapers and broadcasters, and in recent years has co-developed formats for several series of television programs on popular science.

Dr. van Ginneken's more specific expertise, however, is in the field of public opinion, mass psychology, and collective behavior sociology. His belated doctoral dissertation on *Crowds, Psychology and Politics* was marked 'with distinction', and was subsequently published by Cambridge University Press in 1992. His book *Understanding Global News* was translated for Sage in 1998. This current Erlbaum publication, *Collective Behavior and Public Opinion* received rave reviews from early readers, as being very original and stimulating.